INDUSTRIALIZATION IN AN OPEN ECONOMY: NIGERIA 1945-1966

INDUSTRIALIZATION IN AN OPEN ECONOMY: NIGERIA 1945-1966

PETER KILBY
Wesleyan University

CAMBRIDGE
AT THE UNIVERSITY PRESS
1969

CAMBRIDGE UNIVERSITY PRESS
Cambridge, New York, Melbourne, Madrid, Cape Town, Singapore, São Paulo, Delhi

Cambridge University Press
The Edinburgh Building, Cambridge CB2 8RU, UK

Published in the United States of America by Cambridge University Press, New York

www.cambridge.org
Information on this title: www.cambridge.org/9780521071567

First published 1969
This digitally printed version 2008

A catalogue record for this publication is available from the British Library

Library of Congress Catalogue Card Number: 69–11149

ISBN 978-0-521-07156-7 hardback
ISBN 978-0-521-08401-7 paperback

TO *MARIANNE*

CONTENTS

LISTS OF TABLES AND FIGURES

Tables

Table

Figures

ACKNOWLEDGEMENTS

The work on which this study is based began in 1959 when I first went to Nigeria under a Fulbright research grant to study labour productivity. From 1960 to 1962 I served with the U.S. Agency of International Development; during this period I was primarily concerned with the problems of indigenous enterprise. From 1962 to 1965, while at St Antony's College, Oxford, I was generously supported by a Foreign Area Fellowship. To all these sponsors I express my gratitude.

Much of the information in this book was collected by personal interviews over the period 1959–65, more than four hundred in all. While it is impossible to thank everyone who has given of his time and knowledge, I would like to acknowledge those upon whom I placed particularly heavy demands. In the United Africa Company and its subsidiaries I am especially indebted to C. E. Abebe, Dr Edward Hallett, F. J. Harlow, F. S. Haywood, J. Hunt and F. J. Pedler. Extensive data, including written histories of the activities of their company, were kindly supplied by W. H. L. Gordon, W. T. G. Gates, A. C. Pace and G. W. E. Tait of John Holt & Company. Detailed information on the cement industry was generously given to the writer by J. D. Milne of Associated Portland Cement Manufacturers, J. A. Mackintosh and Leslie Hewitt of the Tunnel Portland Cement Company, and the General Manager of Nemco Ltd. My knowledge of the Nigerian textile industry owes much to Paul Barnes of English Sewing Cotton, Alan Smith and R. F. Miles of Kaduna Textiles Ltd, and E. Hallett of the United Africa Company. For the history and operations of the Nigerian Tobacco Company I am indebted to J. H. Maslen, Anthony Jellings, Adrian Howard, G. C. Hargrove and I. H. M. Mason.

Other individuals who provided valuable information on more than one occasion are David Buchman of Chase Manhattan Bank, S. H. Hughes of the Commonwealth Development Corporation, Christopher Leventis of A. G. Leventis Ltd, A. E. Peel of British Oil & Cake Mills, and Michael Aidin of the Sierra Leone Development Corporation. I owe a particularly large debt to D. L. Payne of D. L. Payne Ltd and G. G. Asnanee of K. Chelleram Ltd, not only for the many hours they spent in discussion with me, but for educating me to the central importance of market strategy in explaining investment behaviour.

Of the many Nigerian businessmen who were kind enough to submit to lengthy interview, I would like to single out the following: J. O. Odoeme, E. A. Idowu, John Okwesa, T. A. Oni, Joseph Asaboro, J. A. Odutola, J. Ade Tuyo, S. O. Gbadamosi, John Edokpolo, D. N. Oji,

Sir Mobolaji Bank Anthony, S. I. Fawehinmi and C. T. Onyekwulo. Among the Levantine businessmen who kindly gave me their time, I would like to thank Charles Gazal, George Calil, John Abdalla, G. M. Rokas, E. S. Mandrides and Saul Raccah.

Turning from the commercial sector, I received much help in assembling data from the following individuals: John Adler of the World Bank, R. A. Clarke of the Federal Ministry of Finance, Ken Masters of the Department of Statistics, Robert Ward of Arthur D. Little Inc., Norman Schmidt of the I.L.O., J. W. Gailler of the Federal Ministry of Education, Richard Sharpe of the E.W.A. advisory group to the National Manpower Board, Paul J. Bennett of the U.S. Embassy, D. A. Borrie of the Nigerian Employers Consultative Association, Elizabeth Orr of the Tropical Products Institute, James S. Raj of the Nigerian Industrial Development Bank and Petter Schimmin of the Eastern Nigeria Development Corporation. I would also like to record my thanks to the following organizations upon which I relied time and time again for information and expert opinion: Federal Ministry of Labour, Federal Loans Board, Federal Institute of Industrial Research, United Africa Company and Arthur D. Little, Inc.

The final version of this study has gained much from the criticisms of earlier chapter drafts by a large number of individuals. However I would like to single out for special thanks Werner Baer, William J. Barber, A. O. Hirschman, W. R. Hughes, E. F. Jackson, Bruce F. Johnston, Stanley Lebergott, William Mudd, Hla Myint, Richard Sharpe, Paul Streeten and Robert J. Willis.

Part of chapter 5 appeared in the May 1967 issue of *Food Research Institute Studies*; the material in chapter 9 was published in substantially its present form in the July 1967 issue of the *Journal of Developing Areas*. I am grateful to the editors of these journals for permission to use this material.

PETER KILBY

Middletown, Connecticut

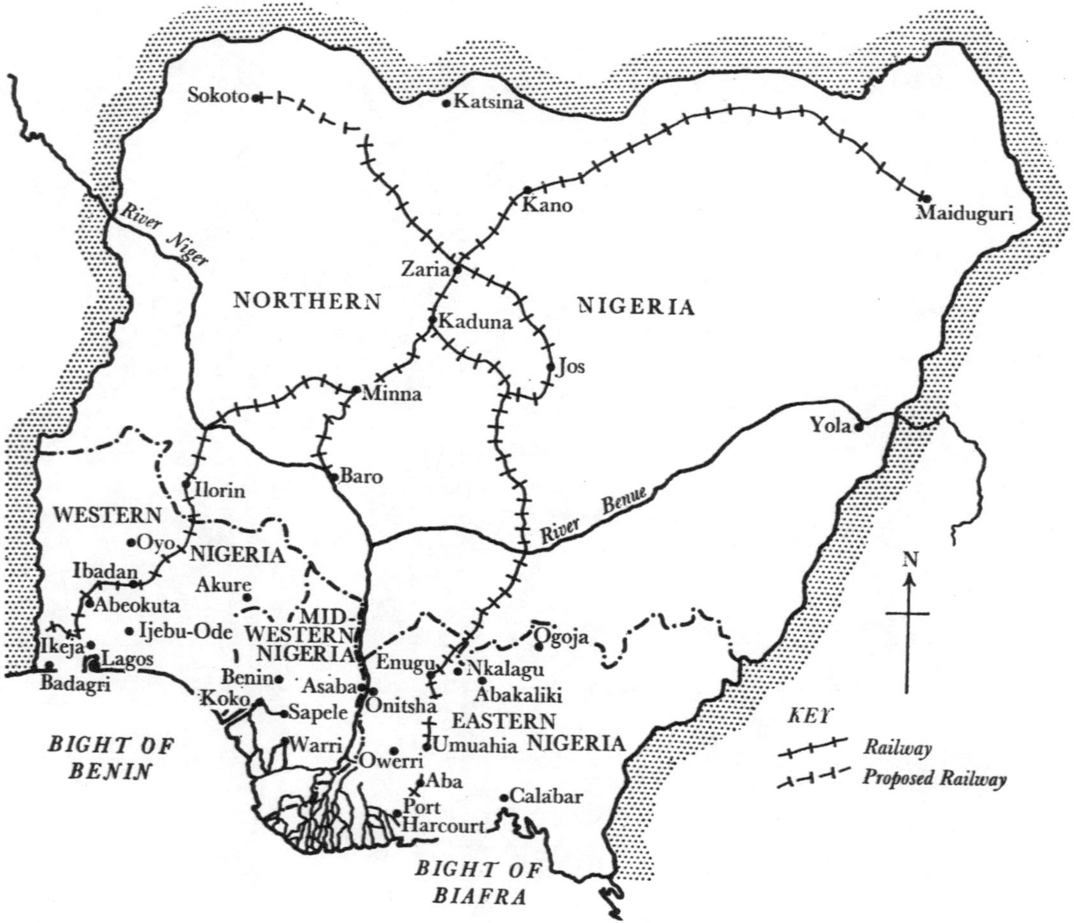

Nigeria 1966

INTRODUCTION

This study is an analysis of the process of industrialization in Nigeria over the period 1945–66. Within the framework of a fairly comprehensive historical treatment of the subject, certain aspects of the industrialization process are selected for intensive exploration. In several areas, on the basis both of the Nigerian findings and corroborative evidence from other countries, alternative interpretations of the observed phenomena are offered in lieu of the propositions of conventional development theory.

The book is divided into six parts. The first two chapters provide a brief sketch of the overall structure of the Nigerian economy and an analysis of the market environment in which nascent industrial development has taken place. Parts 2 and 3 treat industries based upon import replacement and domestic raw materials respectively. There is a break after Part 3 where the focus shifts from industrial production to a scrutiny of domestic factor inputs, with particular attention given to the institutions which determine the quality of the human resources – labour, management and entrepreneurship. The concluding chapter, part summary and part speculative, attempts to isolate the key problems of the industrialization process and to suggest an optimum development strategy.

The characterization of Nigeria in the title of this study as an open economy summarizes a number of important features of the socio-economic environment during the period under consideration. By following a conservative monetary policy and avoiding foreign exchange restrictions, Nigeria has remained open to international trade to an unusual degree. Beyond the immediate gains from international specialization (exports constitute nearly a fifth of national product), relatively free trade has meant that Nigeria's internal price structure has been fairly closely related to world prices[1] – bringing efficiency in domestic resource allocation and the avoidance of high rates of inflation. Free entry to foreign capital, foreign entrepreneurship and foreign technical skills has been of central importance to industrial development. So too has the absence of extensive state intervention contributed to an open, market-orientated economy. A similar openness and mobility based on achievement has obtained in the modernized segments of Nigerian society. Whether in politics, commerce, administration or the professions, all careers have been open to talent with few

[1] Nigeria's *ad valorem* import duty level has ranged between 20 and 30 %, as compared to implicit tariff levels of 200 % and over for most Latin American and Asian countries.

impediments to upward progress. Taken together these various forms of openness and free mobility, which differentiate Nigeria from many other underdeveloped countries, have exerted a profound influence on the course of economic development in the two decades following World War II.

Every empirical investigation of any rigour that covers a wide field must, perforce, be selective. Hence it is apposite that the investigator declare the values, prejudices and predispositions which have influenced him in the choice of areas to be examined and in questions posed. In the present case, the viewpoint which has influenced the selection of subjects and animated the analysis may be described as a concern with organization and technical efficiency.

The process of economic growth can be broken down into three components: (*a*) factors determining the volume of resources available for expanding the economy's productive capacity, (*b*) the allocation of these investment resources among possible uses, and (*c*) the efficiency with which the factors of production are combined in the given lines of production. By and large economists have concentrated on (*a*) and (*b*), giving only passing attention to questions of non-allocative efficiency. However, changes in the latter affect average productivity while variation in the investment-GNP ratio and shifts in resource allocation involve only incremental changes at the margin of production.[1] If organizational slack and technical inefficiency are both substantial and capable of manipulation, then it is likely that attention paid to this area will yield far greater returns in accelerating economic growth than further intensification of effort to increase aggregate investment or improve resource allocation. Accordingly, the problem of moving from actual performance to a point closer to the existing production possibility frontier, as determined by current levels of technology and capital accumulation, is given particular emphasis throughout this study.[2]

Although economic development is part of an interdependent process of social change, disciplinary competence and the sheer quality of economic facts to be analysed have combined to limit the present study

[1] Consider a simple example. Assume that industrial output is 100, that the capital-output ratio is 2, and that net investment is zero. An expenditure of 5 on additional capital equipment will raise output by $2\frac{1}{2}$; if the same expenditure on industrial engineering services and supervisory training only raises average productivity by 3 % (and the evidence is that the improvement is much greater) it represents a superior use of resources. While the potential for such gains is exhausted at some point, it is a limitation that most underdeveloped countries need not concern themselves with for some time.

[2] The formulation presented here was first developed by the writer in 'Organization and Productivity in Backward Economies', *Quarterly Journal of Economics*, May 1962. Harvey Leibestein has attempted to extend and elaborate this notion in 'Allocative Efficiency versus "X-Efficiency",' *American Economic Review*, June 1966.

to purely economic phenomena.[1] Beyond general sociological considerations, the most important exogenous factor impinging upon economic outcomes is their political and administrative context. Fortunately an excellent synthesis of the political sociology of Nigerian economic policy and governmental administration has recently been made by Father James O'Connell.[2] The motivation and quality of political leadership, the nature of the colonial inheritance, the operation of the civil service, and all the non-economic considerations affecting economic decision-making in the public sector – traditionalistic attitudes, communal loyalties, regionalism, corruption – are expertly analysed in Professor O'Connell's essay reprinted as appendix D.

A few remarks are in order on the subject of Nigerian political history. Formally annexed as a colony in 1900, it was granted internal self-government in 1951, at which time Nigerians took up all but a few of the ministerial portfolios. Complete independence was obtained in October 1960. In January 1966 parliamentary government was ended by a military coup; a second coup followed in July, accompanied by the tragic killings of several thousand Ibos in the northern region. In mid-1967 civil war erupted. At the time of writing, Nigeria's future as a politically unified country is still unclear. Although the study does not extend beyond 1966, any examination of development sequences by its very nature involves analysis of past performance in terms of its implications for the future. Thus the study contains many policy prescriptions which are founded on the premise that the basic geographic and institutional facts of the past will hold for the future.

For all but the last three years of the period being reviewed Nigeria was divided into three regions and the federal territory of Lagos. Each of the regions was composed of one dominant tribe (Yoruba in the west, Ibo in the east, Hausa in the north), constituting about 65 % of the region's population, with a number of smaller tribes making up the balance. Political parties were tribally based so that the regional governments were controlled by the dominant tribe, with the opposition party in each region representing the minority tribes. Each of these minority parties was allied to the dominant party in one of the two other regions. In 1963 a new region, Mid-Western Nigeria, was created

[1] The best historical and political treatment of twentieth-century Nigeria is James S. Coleman, *Nigeria: Background to Nationalism*, Los Angeles 1958; for the pre-colonial period see Michael Crowder, *A Short History of Nigeria*, 2nd ed., New York 1966. Major economic works on Nigeria covering the period 1920 to 1950 are Margery Perham, ed., *The Economics of a Tropical Dependency*, 2 vols., London, 1948; and P. T. Bauer, *West African Trade*, Cambridge, 1954. A work which complements the present study is G. K. Helleiner *Peasant Agriculture, Government and Economic Growth in Nigeria*, Homewood, Ill. 1966.

[2] J. O'Connell, 'The Political Class and Economic Growth', *Nigerian Journal of Economic and Social Studies*, vol. 8, March 1966, pp. 129–40.

out of the eastern provinces of Western Nigeria. Unless otherwise indicated, for purposes of continuity the new region will be treated as part of Western Nigeria. Until the end of 1964 the Federal Government was controlled by an alliance of the Hausa and Ibo-based parties. After the elections of December of that year the Northern Peoples' Congress held a majority of seats in the Federal Parliament.

Lastly, the population census of 1952–3 (compounded at 2 % per annum)[1] has been selected as the source for demographic data in preference to the more recent but politically embattled census of 1963. The difference between these two censuses is considerable: applying a 2 % growth figure to the 1952–3 total, Nigeria's population in 1963 was 37·1m. as compared to the officially reported count in that year of 55·6m. The choice between the two is clearly a momentous one; however, it is the opinion of most observers, including the writer, that the earlier count was the more reliable of the two.[2]

[1] This is the rate traditionally employed by the Federal Office of Statistics and is consonant with the sample survey findings in the mid-1950s of a 50 % infant (under 5 years) mortality rate.

[2] The 1952–3 census was carried out under tranquil conditions and was supervised by European administrative officers who judged their margin of error to be in the neighbourhood of 5 %. The censuses of 1962 (nullified) and 1963 were carried out under conditions of considerable political tension, where the pressure to inflate figures for purposes of parliamentary representation and control of the federal government was very great. The 1962 census was nullified for just this reason, and yet the 1963 results were virtually the same. The 1963 enumeration was carried out by Nigerians, a number of whom, including the chief census officer, resigned in protest against irregularities. Two major political parties and the Eastern Nigeria Government did not accept the census. Finally, on the basis of *per capita* consumption of such items as textiles, salt, cigarettes and beer (the total consumption of which is known) the 55·6m. would rank Nigeria far below any other country in Africa, many of whom have considerably lower reported *per capita* incomes.

A recent estimate by I. I. U. Eke based upon voter registration and the 1952 age structure of the population, places the 1963 figure at 41·3m. 'Population of Nigeria: 1952–1965', *Nigerian Journal of Economic and Social Studies*, vol. 8, July 1966, pp. 289–310.

Part 1

CHAPTER I

GROWTH OF THE NIGERIAN ECONOMY 1900–1966

In 1900 when the British Government took over from the Royal Niger Company the jurisdiction and administration of the Niger basin, the 373,250 square miles that would in 1914 be called Nigeria, comprised thousands of largely self-sufficient communities engaged in the traditional production of food, clothing and utensils. Exports in 1900 were £1·7m., of which palm oil and palm kernels (purchased by European traders operating in the coastal 'oil rivers') constituted about 90 %.

With the establishment of law and order by the colonial administration, the development of a communications network and the presence of intermediary European traders, the Nigerian economy underwent a process of integration both internally and with the world economy. New export crops were introduced – groundnuts, cotton, rubber, cocoa – and cassiterite (tin ore) and coal deposits were uncovered and exploited. While the colonial government gradually built up social and economic infrastructure, Christian missionaries shouldered the burden of primary and secondary education. This process of integration and 'economy formation' is most graphically seen in the growth of exports, Nigeria's leading sector.

Nigeria's rapid export expansion represents a classic instance of Hla Myint's 'vent for surplus'.[1] Owing to the fact that subsistence production did not fully employ all potential labour time and productive land, these surplus or under-employed resources were committed to the new export crops with no corresponding diminution of domestic production. Thus, unlike the conventional case where the factors of production are fully employed, imported consumer goods were gained at no cost save at the sacrifice of leisure. On the other hand, expanded production was achived without significantly altering traditional agricultural technology: productivity of employed resources remained more or less constant. But improved technology was embodied in the new crops and motor and rail transport; and greater specialization as between food and export crops occurred in the agricultural sector. Indeed, if we define the technology inhering in capital and intermediate goods as embodied technology and all other types of productivity-influencing factors as disembodied technology, we are likely to find that the former

[1] Hla Myint, 'The Classical Theory of International Trade and the Underdeveloped Countries', *Economic Journal*, June 1958, pp. 317–37.

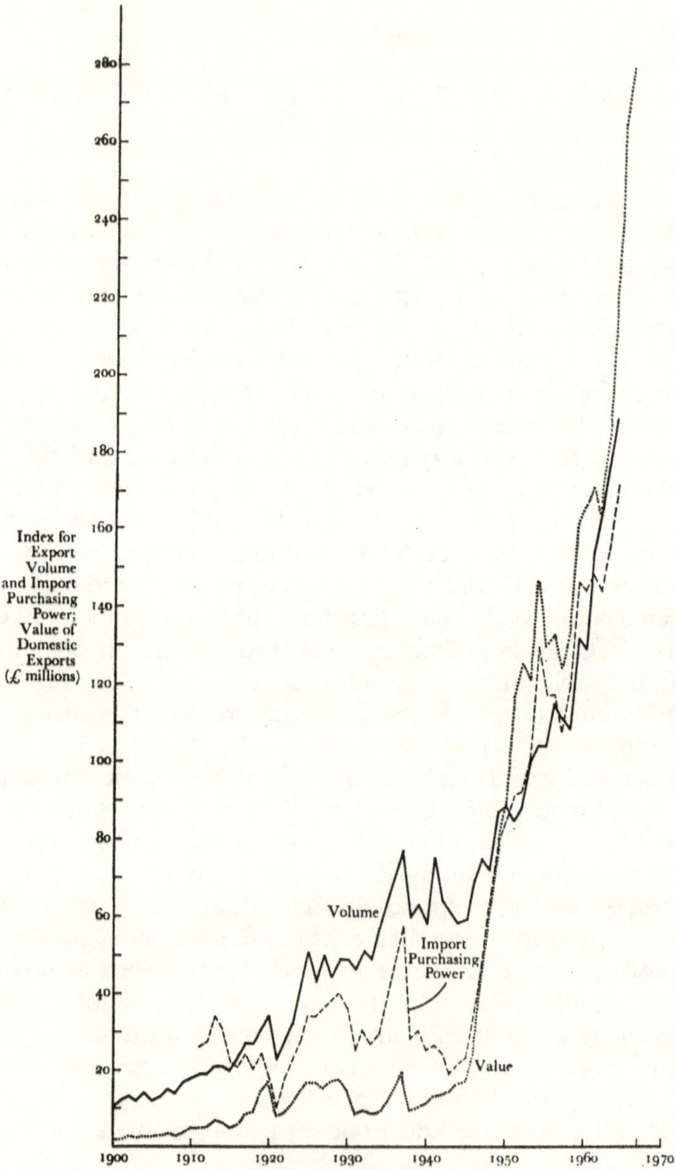

Fig. 1. Nigerian exports, 1900–1966.

Note: Import purchasing power (the income terms of trade) is computed by dividing an index of export value by an index of import prices.

sources: G. K. Helleiner, *Peasant Agriculture*, tables IV–A–1,–2,–6; International Monetary Fund, *International Financial Statistics 1966/7*, p. 187.

has played a leading role in the modernization of the Nigerian economy while the latter has constituted the major brake to more rapid progress.

Table 1. *Selected economic indicators, 1913–1966*

	1913	1937	1946	1954	1966
Imports (£000)	6,332	14,625	19,824	114,069	256,265
Currency in circulation (£000)	1,934	7,986	16,657	51,753	91,622
Demand deposits (£000)	—	3,808	9,401	25,098	56,012
Cement consumption (tons, 000)	6	51	96	368	1,137
Electricity generated (kwh, 000)	...	15	96	179	1,208
Railway freight (ton-miles, m.)	253	408	429	909	1,215
New vehicles registered	...	2,781	2,467	9,895	27,705[a]
School enrolment (000)					
Primary	36	239	619	1,673	2,912[a]
Secondary	1	4	10	28	220
Federal Govt. expenditures (£000)	2,916	7,376	14,052	60,668	214,301
Exports (£000)	6,779	19,242	23,738	146,242	277,742

[a] 1965.

SOURCE: Helleiner, *Peasant Agriculture*, Statistical Appendix; Federal Office of Statistics, *Economic Indicators*, January 1967.

The growth in export proceeds entrained a more or less proportionate growth in other sectors of the economy, as shown in table 1. With the exception of transport and construction, which have grown with the volume of exports, by far the greatest part of the economic expansion that has taken place during the twentieth century has occurred since the tremendous improvement in export prices and the terms of trade which dates from 1946. Official national income estimates are available for the years 1950–64. On the basis of these figures, growth in domestic product, adjusting for inflation, has averaged 4·3 % per annum. Population growth is estimated at 2 to 2·5 %, which means that *per capita* income has been growing at about 2 %.

Table 2 below presents comparative data on the rate of growth of domestic product, gross investment and export receipts. The proportion of national output invested in the maintenance and expansion of productive capacity, shown in the third column, has followed an upward trend since 1950. Yet changes in the investment ratio appear to have had little influence on the economy's growth rate; stated another way, the incremental capital-output ratio has varied from as low as 1 : 1 to as high as 5: —1.[1] On the other hand, movement in export earnings,

[1] For a comprehensive treatment of investment and growth in a national income accounting framework, see Ojetunji Aboyade, *Foundations of an African Economy: A Study of Investment and Growth in Nigeria*, New York 1966, chapters 1, 3, 4. Aboyade's pioneering work has been updated and extended in an excellent paper by Peter B. Clark, 'The General Characteristics of the Nigerian Economy and Its Economic Statistics', mimeograph, A.I.D., March 1967.

at least for the years 1950–6, does show a certain degree of correlation with changes in national output.

Table 2. *Gross domestic product, investment and export earnings*

	Growth of GDP (1957 prices) (%)	Growth of exports (curr. prices) (%)	GFI/GDP (curr. prices) (%)	GFI/GDP (1957 prices) (%)	PGFI/GFI (curr. prices) (%)
1950	...	11·2	5·9	6·9%	...
1951	7·7	31·8	7·1	9·1	...
1952	7·0	7·3	8·8	9·7	...
1953	2·3	−3·4	9·3	10·7	...
1954	7·5	21·0	10·8	12·9	39·0
1955	2·7	−11·6	12·8	14·7	47·6
1956	−2·4	1·9	14·3	15·4	44·6
1957	4·2	−6·1	10·6	10·6	43·7
1958	−1·1	6·9	12·0	11·5	41·5
1959	4·3	20·9	12·9	12·8	50·5
1960	4·6	3·2	13·1	12·1	42·6
1961	3·3	2·7	13·7	13·0	39·8
1962	5·8	−3·6	13·1	12·0	40·3
1963	4·6	12·7	14·4	12·8	35·8
1964	6·3	14·0	...	...	...

GFI = Gross Fixed Investment.
PGFI = Public Gross Fixed Investment.
1957 prices = valued at 1957 prices.
curr. prices = valued at current prices.

SOURCES: Federal Office of Statistics, *Annual Abstract of Statistics, 1964* and *Economic Indicators*, January 1967.

Nigeria's performance well illustrates that aggregate investment does not cause economic growth, nor can it even be correlated in developing economies with advances in real output, given that non-market-directed public investment represents a significant share in total investment. As Cairncross and others have pointed out, the greater part of aggregate investment in any economy consists of items which tend to follow rather than cause a rise in income. The capital requirements of the growth-initiating sectors are typically very small; it is investment in housing, public buildings, transport and power made in response to demand generated by the original increase in income that is responsible for the overall magnitude of aggregate investment. This is especially true for underdeveloped, predominantly agricultural economies. Since 1950 Nigeria's peasant agricultural sector has accounted for approximately half of the growth in real output while its share in total investment has averaged only 12 %.[1] Moreover, annual movements in

[1] Computed from Aboyade, *op. cit.* pp. 142–3, and Federal Office of Statistics, *Estimates of Capital Formation*, mimeograph, for the years 1956–63.

agricultural output are affected far more by changes in cultivation practice (e.g. the use of improved seed varieties), in export prices and in the weather, than by a change in the amount of fixed investment.

The fourth column of table 2 shows that real capital formation has grown at a slower rate than the investment-GDP ratio. This is attributable to a sharp rise in construction costs relative to the general price level; between 1950 and 1963 the former rose by 285 % while the latter increased by only 36 %.[1] The largest single component of this cost inflation can be traced to the shift from direct construction by the Ministry of Public Works of road and other public projects to contract tendering to Nigerian and, for the larger projects, expatriate construction firms. In addition to serious problems of qualitative standards with regard to many of the Nigerian contractors, the system has been regularly employed to extract a sizeable contractor 'kick-back' payable to the treasury of the ruling political party and the politician responsible for the contract award.[2]

Table 3. *Sectoral output as a share of gross domestic product*

(at 1957 prices)

	1950 (%)	1954 (%)	1957 (%)	1958 (%)	1961 (%)	1964 (%)
Agriculture	56·0	55·0	52·7	60·2	56·6	53·6
Livestock	8·7	6·4	6·3	5·8	6·3	5·6
Fishing	1·4	1·2	1·5	1·7	1·5	1·8
Forest products	1·4	1·4	1·6	1·2	1·3	0·9
Mining and oil	1·1	0·9	1·0	0·8	1·4	2·8
Manufacturing and utilities	0·6	0·9	1·4	2·8	3·9	4·7
Transport and communications	4·5	6·1	8·5	3·5	4·6	4·7
Building and civil engineering	3·0	4·3	4·7	2·5	2·7	3·2
Crafts	2·3	1·9	1·9	2·3	2·0	2·4
Government	2·2	2·0	3·4	3·2	3·6	3·5
Other services	18·8	19·9	17·0	16·1	16·1	16·8
	100·0	100·0	100·0	100·0	100·0	100·0
GDP (£m.)	689	872	910	900	1,014	1,232

SOURCE: Federal Office of Statistics, *Economic Indicators*, January 1967, p. 48.

[1] Computed from Clark, *op. cit.* table 3. For a detailed discussion of changes in construction costs see Aboyade, *op. cit.* pp. 121–7.

[2] Similar practices with regard to the purchase of capital equipment for state-operated industrial enterprises are discussed in chapter 4. The writer became aware of the 'kick-back' phenomenon shortly after his arrival in the country, when he and his wife were living in a newly constructed public housing estate in Ibadan. One night during a rainstorm all windward-facing houses (one-third of the total) had their roofs blown off, accompanied by partial collapse of the walls. It was later revealed that the contractors, who had substituted more sand for cement and reinforcing rods, were compelled to refund 40 % of contract proceeds to the regional political party.

The sectoral composition of Nigeria's domestic product is seen in table 3; growth rates for real output and changes in price levels are presented in table 4. In table 3 figures are given for 1957 and 1958 to indicate the different estimating procedures in the two periods 1950–7 and 1958–64.[1] Specifically it is evident that the estimates are inconsistent with respect to agriculture, manufacturing, transportation and crafts. Given this discontinuity and other anomalies noted hereafter, all statements about growth in GDP and changes in the economy's structure are necessarily tentative.

Table 4. *Sectoral growth: real output and price level*
(% price change in parenthesis)

	1950–4 %	1955–9 %	1960–4 %
Agriculture	24·3	6·9	20·1
	(20·3)	(−2·2)	(−3·6)
Livestock	−7·3	3·9	13·0
	(38·6)	(18·8)	(19·0)
Fishing	6·2	45·6	48·0
	(10·6)	(23·3)	(30·9)
Forest products	30·9	−2·2	−21·2
	(16·2)	(15·7)	(42·1)
Mining and oil	6.6	−26·7	411·9
	(87·6)	(9·6)	(−9·5)
Manufacturing and public utilities	202·6	351·7	61·8
	(6·2)	(4·7)	(−3·7)
Communications and transportation	70·9	−43·5	42·0
	(14·2)	(20·9)	(6·2)
Building and civil engineering	86·2	−16·2	17·4
	(85·6)	(23·9)	(51·6)
Crafts	2·5	24·4	46.6
	(0·0)	(−10·3)	(−9·6)
Government	17·3	55·1	22·0
	(26·3)	(19·8)	(16·6)
Other	33·4	−·2	23·8
	(7·5)	(4·0)	(11·0)
GDP	26·6	4·8	25·6
	(19·4)	(4·1)	(5·6)

SOURCE: Clark, 'The General Characteristic of the Nigerian Economy,' tables 3 and 7; Federal Office of Statistics, *Economic Indicators*, January 1967, pp. 48, 50.

[1] The estimating procedures used by Jackson and Okigbo in compiling the 1950–7 series are ably evaluated by I. I. U. Eke who places their margin of error in excess of 30 %. After nearly a decade the Federal Office of Statistics has still to make known its estimating procedures. See I. I. U. Eke, 'The Nigerian National Accounts – A Critical Appraisal', *Nigerian Journal of Economic and Social Studies*, vol. 8, November 1966, pp. 333–60.

The most significant fact to emerge from table 3 is that no major structural transformation has occurred over the 15-year period. In 1964 agriculture, livestock and fishing still account for more than 60 % of total product.[1] Although the growth in agriculture has been slightly slower than the other sectors taken as a whole, food production has more than kept up with population growth, as evidenced by falling prices. The two sectors experiencing the highest growth rates are mining and oil and manufacturing and utilities. Since 1958, with the beginning of the petroleum industry, mining and oil has been Nigeria's fastest growing sector and is likely to continue as such well into the 1970s. Given the very small size of the manufacturing and utilities sector in 1950, an average annual growth rate in excess of 30 % has failed to raise its share in total product to the 5 % mark.

The relationship between sectoral growth in output and attendant price change is seen in table 4. One might expect to see one of two broad patterns here: either all prices moving up together at approximately the same rate, or the fastest growing sectors exhibiting a higher rate of inflation as a consequence of encountering greater bottlenecks. Neither of these expectations is borne out. The highest rate of inflation is found in the building and civil engineering sector, as we noted earlier. Price changes in mining and oil and forest products are related to export prices. The very slight inflation up to 1959 and deflation thereafter shown for the manufacturing and utilities sector are difficult to reconcile with available evidence; the latter suggests that there has been a moderate but steady inflation throughout the period.[2]

The most important intersectoral price relationship is agriculture's terms of trade with the rest of the economy. From 1950 to 1957 agriculture's terms of trade remained more or less stable; from 1958 onwards agricultural prices declined relative to non-agricultural prices.[3] Although the national income accounts probably exaggerate the extent

[1] With regard to the apparent downward trend in the relative size of the agricultural sector between 1961 and 1964, given that its share remained constant at 56 % for the five years 1959–63, the drop in 1964 could be due to random rather than trend influences.

[2] The writer knows of only one product for which the price has fallen, cement. The price of electricity rose twice between 1950 and 1956, thereafter remaining constant. The ex-factory price of cigarettes and beer has risen continuously at two-to-three-year intervals; in the case of the latter the 1950–64 rise was 98 %. The price of textiles rose sharply in 1964; between 1955 and 1964 the price of bar soap rose by 45 %. More generally, there has been a steady increase in industrial prices owing to increasing tariffs on imported raw materials, the imposition of excise taxes and rising wage costs. As shown in appendix A, basic wages trebled between 1950 and 1964.

[3] The following price indices (1957 = 100) are implicit in the national accounts.

	1950	1952	1954	1956	1958	1960	1962	1964
Agriculture	75	76	90	98	95	84	100	81
Non-agriculture	74	80	87	102	98	106	116	119

of the adverse movement (in 1964 the agricultural – non-agricultural rate of exchange was 69 % of the 1957 parity), producer price data for primary exports and urban retail food price indices confirm the direction of this movement.[1] The continued advance of agricultural output in spite of declining terms of trade since 1957 has been a critical ingredient in the growth of the other sectors of the economy. Increased supply in the face of declining relative prices is to be explained in terms of productivity gains via improved purchased inputs (e.g. new plant varieties, disease control, fertilizer), a growing rural road network and the availability of surplus cultivable land.[2] If producer prices had been set closer to world prices, which would have also raised food prices as farmers shifted to export production, the agricultural sector would no doubt have grown faster than it did.

Until the 1960s the performance of Nigeria's leading sector has depended almost entirely upon agriculture. Recent trends in total export earnings and changes in composition are shown in table 5.

Table 5. *Exports of principal products*

(£m.)

	Average 1950–4	Average 1955–9	Average 1960–2	1963	1964	1965	1966
Cocoa	28·6	28·2	34·9	32·4	40·1	42·7	28·3
Groundnut produce	22·0	29·1	34·7	36·6	34·3	37·8	40·8
Raw cotton	5·5	7·6	7·7	9·5	6·1	3·3	3·3
Palm produce	34·6	34·4	32·9	30·2	31·7	40·1	33·4
Rubber	4·1	7·6	12·2	11·8	11·0	11·0	10·6
Tin, tin ore and columbite	9·2	7·6	8·0	9·6	13·8	16·1	16·1
Timber, logs and sawn	3·6	4·8	6·5	6·7	8·0	6·4	5·8
Crude petroleum	...	...	10·7	20·2	32·1	68·1	92·0
All exports	119·5	135·9	166·6	184·7	210·4	263·3	277·7

SOURCES: Federal Office of Statistics, *Annual Abstract of Statistics, 1964*, and *Economic Indicators*, January 1967.

After stagnating during the years 1959–62, primary exports pushed ahead during 1963–5, only to fall in 1966 with political disruption. In 1964 crude petroleum joined palm produce, cocoa and groundnut

[1] For the downward trend in producer prices see Helleiner, *Peasant Agriculture*, Statistical Appendix, table II; and Central Bank of Nigeria, *Annual Report and Statement of Accounts for the Year ended December 31 1965*, p. 17; The Federal Office of Statistics publishes in mimeograph form a retail food price index for fourteen urban areas which has moved as follows over the period 1961–6: (1953 = 100) 137, 150, 125, 121, 122, 168. The jump in 1966 reflects the partial disruption of normal transport and distribution channels accompanying the post-coup period of political instability.

[2] For a discussion of long-run changes in input productivity in agriculture and its causes, see Carl Eicher, 'The Dynamics of Long-term Agricultural Development in Nigeria', mimeograph paper read at the annual meeting of the American Farm Economic Association, August 1967; and Helleiner, *op. cit.* chapters 3 and 4.

produce as a major export. In 1965 traditional exports were up again, but oil had more than doubled, with the result that export earnings enjoyed their largest jump in history – £53m. over the preceding year. And the projections for oil production indicate continued rapid expansion before levelling off in the early 1970s. There can be little doubt that petroleum oil extraction, far from being an enclave industry, will be Nigeria's most dynamic sector over the next decade.[1] In 1965 the oil industry provided direct employment to 17,178 Nigerians who received wages and salaries of £3·6m., it generated £15·8m tax revenue for the Federal Government,[2] it paid £2m. in harbour dues to the Ports Authority, and earned (after allowing for its own requirements) a net addition to foreign exchange of £30·2m. While employment is expected to level out at about 23,000 all the other contributions to the economy are expected to grow many fold. In addition, oil production promises significant growth-inducing linkages to other sectors of the economy.

A full appreciation of the extent to which the oil industry will unbind the Nigerian economy from the growth-attenuating and structurally distorting restraints, typically the lot of developing economies, can be gained from a glance at Nigeria's balance-of-payments situation. Since the start of the first five-year development plan in 1955 (and the end of the abnormally high export prices of the Korean War period), Nigeria's merchandise imports have surpassed her exports every year until 1966, reaching a cumulative balance-of-payments deficit on current account of £621m. by the end of that year.[3] This deficit has been financed by the drawing down of accumulated reserves, private foreign investment, receipt of grant foreign aid, and external borrowing (£227m. as of April 1965). In response to increasing balance-of-payments pressure as a result of the growing burden of debt servicing and the continuation of aggregate investments at a higher level than domestic savings, tariffs have been progressively raised to curtail imports and to increase public saving.

[1] The factual data for the following discussion of the oil industry are drawn from a comprehensive survey by Wilson Schmidt and Scott Pearson, 'Nigerial Petroleum: An Empirical Look at the Enclave Thesis', forthcoming.

Exploration for oil was first begun in 1937 by a partnership of Royal Dutch Shell and British Petroleum. Discontinued with the war in 1939, the search for oil resumed in 1947 with the first significant discoveries occurring in the mid-1950s. Shell–B.P. began exporting in 1958, the same year that the Mobil Oil Company began its explorations. By 1966, in addition to Shell-BP and Mobil, three other American, one French and one Italian oil exploration companies were operating in Nigeria.

[2] Total tax revenues include rentals, royalties, custom and stamp duties and corporate and personal income taxes of the oil companies and associated Nigerian and expatriate employees.

[3] Although exports exceeded imports in 1966, payments abroad for debt servicing, profit remittances, shipping services, etc., resulted in a net deficit of £58m. International Monetary Fund, *Balance of Payments Yearbook*, vols. 10 and 19.

The tendency to increase tariffs in response to balance-of-payments and revenue considerations, which has become particularly marked since the August 1964 increases, has, in addition to the traditionally recognized inflationary impact, two powerful adverse effects on the economy's growth. First, such tariffs provide excessive protection to import-substitution industries with resultant high costs and truncated development of the emerging industrial sector; at the same time, because such tariffs bear no proportion to the value-added of the manufacturing activity that they implicitly protect, a distorted industrial structure is likely to result. Second, increased tariffs on consumer goods turn the intersectoral terms-of-trade against agriculture (urban wage rates are adjusted upward with rises in the cost-of-living while domestic food prices are not): this tends to discourage agricultural production and to promote the exodus to the cities, further adding to unemployment, political instability and the need for further public investment in urban amenities.

It is precisely these two binding constraints of inadequate domestic saving and deficient foreign exchange earnings from which the oil industry can free Nigeria. Total Federal and Regional Government recurrent revenue in 1965–6, exclusive of oil revenues, was about £172m.[1] Revenues to the Government deriving from oil extraction are variously projected to reach £75m. to £115m. by 1970. Similarly, net additions to foreign exchange by 1970 and after are unlikely to be less than £100m., more than the combined trade deficit of the two worst years Nigeria has had. Thus with ample domestic savings and foreign exchange insured by the oil industry Nigeria will be uniquely free to pursue an optimal tax policy for both intra- and inter-sectoral growth.

In addition to its potential for releasing the Nigerian economy from its growth constraints, the oil industry promises important industrial linkages. In November 1965 the £10m. Alesa–Eleme refinery came on stream near Port Harcourt, replacing imports of petroleum products valued at £18m. Natural gas, a joint product with most Nigerian crude oil, appears likely to generate a whole range of industries: electric power (one station already established), a large-scale liquefied natural gas export industry, polyethylene plastic, caustic soda, salt finishing, carbon black and nitrogenous fertilizers.

THE INDUSTRIAL SECTOR

As indicated earlier, the industrial sector has grown very rapidly since 1950. In that year value-added in manufacturing establishments employing ten or more was £2·7m; by 1964 net output had grown

[1] Federal Office of Statistics, *Economic Indicators*, January 1967, pp. 39–42.

more than 25-fold to £68·6m.[1] Industrial production in smaller scale establishments is extensive, but its exact magnitude is unknown.[2]

For any underdeveloped country it is very difficult to describe accurately the character of 'the industrial sector' and to specify its outer boundary, and Nigeria is no exception. Representative points on a continuous spectrum would include highly capital-intensive European or government-owned enterprises, medium-scale processing and assembly enterprises of a more labour-intensive character but still employing advanced technical processes, small-scale yet capital-intensive producers, skilled artisanate industries utilizing mainly hand tools, marginally employed semi-skilled producers making crude consumer goods, and lastly commercial processing in the household.

Industrial production in Nigeria thus exhibits wide diversity in terms of the degree of specialization and division of labour, technology, factor proportions, the quality of raw material input and product finish, the character of markets being served, and entrepreneurial organization. This diversity is typically recognized in a polar form, as giving rise to a modern industrial sector and a semi-traditional industrial sector. For some purposes (e.g. wage determination) the positing of a simple dualism is a convenient simplification which does not undermine the validity of the conclusions reached. In other cases, however, especially regarding the development of indigenous enterprise and small scale industry and the effect of various policies thereupon, the existence of a continuous gradation is of central importance.

Beginning with rural cottage industry, the only information on this subject comes from the 1965 rural economic survey. On the basis of a sample survey of 199 rural villages, the Federal Office of Statistics estimated that 900,000 households are engaged in manufacturing activities.[3] The major areas of production are food processing, textiles, palm oil extraction, clothing, mats and metal products.

Although far from complete, data on the extent and nature of small

[1] (E. F. Jackson and) P. N. C. Okigbo, *Nigerian National Accounts 1950–7*, Federal Ministry of Economic Development, Enugu 1962, p. 78, and Federal Office of Statistics, *Economic Indicators*, January 1967, p. 13. On the basis of the implicit sectoral price index in the national accounts, about 38 % of this rise is attributable to inflation. Figures for both years represent valuation at market prices and exclude utilities.

[2] For the most part small scale industrial activities are included under 'Crafts' or not counted. In this sense the very small manufacturing sector revealed in the national accounts is quite misleading. Still, on the basis of this restrictive categorization, Nigeria has the largest industrial sector of any black African country. Relative to its GDP, however, Nigeria's manufacturing sector is smaller than those of the Congo (13 %), Kenya (10 %) and Uganda (7 %). The other African countries fall into the same 4 – 6 % category as Nigeria. United Nations, *Yearbook of National Accounts Statistics, 1966*, New York 1967, International tables, no. 3.

[3] Federal Office of Statistics, *Productive Activities of Households*, mimeograph, 1966, p. 4.

scale urban industries are considerably better. Surveys have been carried out in fourteen towns in the east, Lagos, Ibadan, and five towns in the north.[1] These surveys reveal a high degree of uniformity between geographic areas. Table 6 summarizes the results of the eastern region

Table 6. *Small industry in fourteen Eastern Nigerian towns, 1961*

	Industry	No. of firms	Total employment	Firms by no. workers (%) 1	2–5	6–9	10+
1.	Tailoring	3,450	7,288	49	47	3	1
2.	Carpentry	2,773	7,173	30	63	5	2
3.	Shoe-making (L)	118	401	25	57	14	4
4.	Shoe-making (R)	180	428	37	58	5	—
5.	Shoe repair	390	616	59	41	—	—
6.	Motor repair	396	2,968	2	41	30	27
7.	Welding/battery charging	221	848	25	56	13	6
8.	Blacksmithing	369	763	42	55	2	1
9.	Tinsmithing	491	1,029	43	54	3	—
10.	Printing	146	938	12	59	16	13
11.	Baking	221	1,341	—	77	8	15
12.	Mattress-making	266	488	43	57	—	—
13.	Radio repair	236	906	18	61	14	7
14.	Photography (i)	157	424	23	73	3	1
15.	Corn milling	65	131	29	69	2	—
16.	Goldsmithing (i)	267	516	50	48	2	—
17–25.	Minor industries (i)	768	1,485	59	38	1	2
26–35.	Miscellaneous industries	198	932	11	67	12	10
	Total	10,728	28,721	38	54	5	3

(L) stands for leather and (R) for tyre-sandals; (i) stands for incomplete, but estimated to represent more than half of the total number of firms in operation. Minor industries include dry cleaning, typewriter and sewing machine repair, weaving, manufacture of musical instruments, vulcanizing, sign painting, clock repair, bicycle repair and traditional wood carving. Miscellaneous industries include the manufacture of nails, singlets, wooden bus bodies, raffia products, wrought iron furniture, brushes and the sewing together of plastic shopping bags, bottling of soft drinks, silver working and rice milling.

SOURCE: Kilby, *The Development of Small Industry*, p. 6.

survey. Of the 10,728 firms, 60 % were housed in raffia sheds, corrugated metal huts or market stalls. Only 9 % possessed a power-driven machine, while 58 % used nothing other than simple hand tools. Over a third of the concerns are one-man operations, and in the larger firms more than half of the labour force consist of apprentices. As compared

[1] Peter Kilby, *The Development of Small Industry in Eastern Nigeria*, U.S. Agency for International Development, Lagos 1962, tables I–VI; Federal Office of Statistics, 'Lagos Pilot Survey of Small Scale Industry', mimeograph, Lagos 1966; Archibald Callaway, 'Crafts and Industries in Ibadan', a mimeographed paper prepared for the Seminar on Ibadan in the Changing Nigerian Scene, Institute of African Studies, University of Ibadan, February 1964; and Kilby, 'Nigerian Industry in the Northern Region, A Preliminary Report', U.S. Agency for International Development, Lagos 1961.

to an average size firm of 2·7 persons in the east, the Lagos average (1965) was 5·1 persons per establishment; 10 % of the Lagos establishments engaged ten or more workers, although only in half the cases were there ten or more *paid* employees.[1] The Office of Statistics estimated that there are about 9,700 small industry concerns in the greater Lagos area. Callaway enumerated 4,770 craft and industrial establishments in Ibadan (1963) and reported patterns nearly identical to those found in the east as regards the size of firm, proportion of unpaid labour, housing and the nature of capital equipment.[2] The writer's enumeration in the five largest towns of the north (1961), although incomplete, revealed small industry activity to be of the same character but far more limited than in the south.[3]

There are a number of features of urban small scale industry that should be noted. First, such enterprise is not evenly spread geographically, but tends to be highly concentrated in the new commercial and administrative cities where there is considerable wage employment; there is comparatively little small industry in the large traditional towns of the northern and western regions. This clustering occurs because the products of small industry are consumer goods and it is only where there is a concentration of consumer purchasing power that these essentially satellite activities can be supported on any scale. Second, at least three different types of producers can be identified in the small industry sector: unskilled producers of crude consumer goods whose number is closely related to the volume of urban immigration, the skilled artisan producers of simple but better quality products (e.g. cabinet-making, leather shoes, goldsmithing, motor vehicle repair), and relatively complex modern small-scale industry (e.g. baking, soft drink bottling, singlet manufacture). Third, total employment in urban small-scale industry would seem to be in the neighbourhood of 100,000, which is less than in rural cottage industry but greater than the number employed in establishments of ten or more.

Turning to the latter, the most recent information on firms employing ten and over is provided by the industrial survey of 1964. A total of 686 establishments with a labour force of some 76,000 returned completed questionnaires. Employment, gross output and value-added by industry groupings are given in table 7. It should be noted that more than half of value-added for the sumptuary products, beer and cigarettes, consists of indirect taxes; with the possible exception of miscellaneous chemical products, such taxation is relatively slight for all other industries.

Since only the summary of results has been reported for 1964, for

[1] 'Lagos Pilot Survey', p. 3. [2] Callaway, *op. cit.* [3] Kilby, 'Nigerian Industry'.

a more detailed picture of this sector we must turn to the 1963 survey.[1] Of the 649 establishments returning information in that year, 59 % employed 10 to 49 workers, 33 % employed 50 to 299, and 8 % employed 300 or more. Perhaps more interesting than their size distribution is the pattern of ownership. Of the paid-up share capital of 321 limited companies, 68 % was of foreign origin. Of the remainder,

Table 7. *Employment and output of firms employing ten or more, 1964*

	Number employed	Gross output (£000)	Value-added (£000)
Flour milling	518	4,489	1,176
Bakery products	2,013	2,136	721
Cigarettes	2,553	14,465	10,132
Beer brewing	2,860	13,207	8,943
Soft drinks	1,140	1,355	786
Manufacture of textiles[a]	7,637	7,690	3,955
Footwear	1,324	1,635	650
Saw milling	8,233	5,535	3,916
Furniture and fixtures	3,516	3,428	1,388
Printing	5,753	3,163	1,844
Rubber products	6,894	10,790	4,800
Vegetable oil milling[b]	3,866	20,459	5,355
Miscellaneous chemical products[c]	3,158	11,276	5,312
Cement	2,349	6,840	3,506
Metal products[d]	4,943	10,638	3,769
Motor vehicle and bicycle assembly	1,701	8,222	1,200
Motor vehicle repairs	7,722	29,764	6,522
Other[e]	9,716	23,708	4,656
Total	75,896	178,800	68,631

[a] Includes cotton ginning.
[b] Groundnuts and partial coverage of large-scale palm oil extraction.
[c] Soap, cosmetics and pharmaceutics.
[d] Metal doors and windows, aluminium-ware, brassware, enamelware, cans, steel drums and tanks, corrugated roofing sheets and other metal products.
[e] Meat products, dairy products, fruit canning, confectionery, soft drinks, wearing apparel, made-up textiles, other wood products, paper products, tanning, travel goods, industrial chemicals, paints, bricks and tiles, pottery and glass, concrete products, basic metals, electrical equipment and boat building.

SOURCE: Federal Office of Statistics, *Economic Indicators*, January 1967, p. 13.

22 % was Nigerian public and 10 % Nigerian private. Those industries in which private Nigerian firms are prominent include bread baking, sawmilling, rubber crêping, furniture, printing and wearing apparel. Investment by Nigerian public authorities is both in participation with foreign investors and in wholly government-owned projects.

[1] Federal Office of Statistics, *Industrial Survey of Nigeria 1963*, Lagos 1966, pp. 1–49.

It is not surprising that foreign enterprise plays a leading role in Nigeria's industrial sector. Foreign private investment, particularly British investment, has long been an important feature of many sectors of the former colonial economy. Table 8 summarizes the results of the most recent survey of foreign investment. The stock of foreign capital in

Table 8. *Total foreign investment, 1964*

(£m.)

	Paid-up capital and reserves	External debt	Total	Fixed assets
Mining and oil	43·2	85·5	128·7	146·2
Manufacturing and processing	28·4	30·3	58·5	63·5
Agriculture and Forestry	3·9	1·5	5·4	5·9
Transportation	2·1	1·4	3·5	3·0
Construction	5·2	7·1	12·3	8·2
Trading and services	40·5	60·5	101·0	47·5
Other	2·5	9·3	11·8	5·9
Total	125·6	195·6	321·2	280·2

Net flow of foreign investment[a]

	1961	1962	1963	1964
Mining and oil	6·9	7·5	12·5	35·3
Manufacturing and processing	5·9	20·5	11·0	9·2
Agriculture and forestry	−1·1	−0·2	0·5	0·5
Transportation	0·3	0·2	0·2	0·9
Construction	0·7	4·6	2·4	1·4
Trading and services	14·6	−15·4	11·6	4·5
Other	—	0·5	−0·2	10·6
Total	27·3	17·7	37·9	62·4

[a] Additions to paid-up capital, reserves and debt.

SOURCE: Central Bank of Nigeria, *Economic and Financial Review*, vol. 4, June 1966, p. 6.

mining and oil overtook that of the distributive sector in 1964; the flow of new investment is primarily to oil and manufacturing. Other shifts in the composition of investment have been a withdrawal from plantation ventures, a proportionately reduced investment flow into water and road transport, and increased activity in large-scale construction projects. Regarding the financing of foreign companies, the large proportion of borrowed funds to total capital employed is worthy of note; the reasons for such a high degree of debt financing will be discussed in chapter 4.

The distribution of foreign investment by country of origin in 1964 was as shown at top of page 22:[1]

[1] Central Bank of Nigeria, *op. cit.* p. 5, and A. N. Hakam for industrial investment from his 'The Motivation to Invest and the Locational Pattern of Foreign Private Industrial Investments in Nigeria', *Nigerian Journal of Economic and Social Studies*, vol. 8, March 1966, p. 65.

	Total (%)	Industrial (%)
England	56·5	63·6
France	23·6	1·8
Holland		4·6
Germany		1·5
Italy		3·3
U.S.	12·1	9·4
Lebanon	7·8	6·6
Other		9·2

As a former British colony it is not surprising that the English control over half of aggregate foreign investment; that an even greater preponderance should hold for the comparatively new industrial sector is not quite so obvious. An explanation for this latter fact will be given in chapter 3.

THE ROLE OF GOVERNMENT

As has been the pattern in virtually every underdeveloped country since World War II, the Federal and Regional Governments have taken an active role in promoting economic development in general and industrialization in particular. Nigeria's first development plan was launched in 1946.[1] Since 1955, in addition to the federal plan, each region has had its own plan. Until 1962 plans were primarily collections of infrastructure investments and government sponsored development schemes; the document for the 1962–8 period included macroeconomic projections, sectoral targets, resource and foreign exchange requirements, and policy implications.

Still, once allowance is made for the increased sophistication of the presentation and the broader coverage, the latest plan does not look terribly different from its forerunners. Separate plans were again written by each of the governments in the Federation, and they still consisted, in the main, of lists of projects which it would be desirable to have.[2]

How much detailed attention was devoted to planning on the project level is difficulty to establish. In some areas, notably the plans of the Ports Authority, the Electricity Corporation, the Niger Dam, and various transport facilities, careful forecasts were apparently made and costs and benefits evaluated, although this work would have been undertaken regardless of the existence of a national plan. In the majority of others, limitations of data or time apparently prevented much analysis. Most of the projects listed in the four plans have therefore not been evaluated any more carefully than those which appeared in earlier planning documents; the manner in which

[1] For an excellent review of Nigeria's planning experience, see Helleiner, *op. cit.* chapter 14.
[2] *Ibid.* p. 335.

the sums listed under many broader heads were intended to be spent remained unspecified. Broad priorities there were, but detailed micro-level studies were scarce and, in some instances, badly needed. This being so, it is difficult to take the aggregates in the plan very seriously.

The progress of the Nigerian economy during the years since the National Development Plan was prepared has probably not been affected very much by the existence of the plan itself.[1]

The lack of impact of the 1962–8 and earlier plans can be traced to overspending on administration, underspending on directly productive projects for lack of executive capacity, and investing in prestige projects not included in the plan. Moreover, the 1962–8 plan overestimated the availability of foreign aid and underestimated imports. While economic planning as such has had little effect upon the course of events, government policies and public investment have been of critical importance in determining both the path and the speed of economic development.

Measures taken by public authorities to promote industrialization are of two kinds, direct and indirect. Indirect measures include the provision of social infrastructure, guarantees to private investors against uncompensated nationalization, and freedom for foreigners regarding the sale of their assets and repatriation of profits. The direct measures may be grouped into three categories: fiscal incentives, support activities, and direct public investment in manufacturing.

The fiscal incentives extended by the Federal Government for the purpose of promoting industrial investment include tariff protection, import duty relief, accelerated depreciation allowances and pioneer income tax holidays. Both tariff protection (in addition to the pre-existing tariff) and import duty relief on material imported for use in manufacturing are obtained by direct application to the Federal Government and each case is decided by the Ministers-in-Council on the advice of the Ministries of Commerce and Industry and Finance.[2] Accelerated depreciation of 40 % for plant and equipment and 20 % for buildings may be claimed by all investors in the year in which the expenditure is made in addition to normal capital amortization of 10 % or more based on the expected life of the asset. Thus an investor is usually able to write off 50 % of his fixed investment in the first year;[3] however total depreciation allowances may not exceed 100 %

[1] *Ibid.* pp. 339–40.

[2] Industrial Development (Import Duty Relief) Ordinance 1957.

[3] Income Tax (Amendment) Ordinance 1958, superseding a similar ordinance of 1943. Obsolescence allowances are given when equipment is scrapped before full depreciation. Where the taxable income does not absorb the full capital allowance, the unabsorbed balance may be carried forward against future taxable profits; the same treatment is afforded unabsorbed losses.

of the asset's cost, as is sometimes permitted in a number of developed countries. Pioneer income tax relief provides a tax holiday of five years to those companies which obtain a pioneer certificate – where the investment is less than £100,000 the relief period is shortened on a graduated basis.[1] Losses and full depreciation allowances may be carried forward and deducted from taxable income as from the sixth year of profitable operation.

Support activities undertaken by public agencies cover a wide field. Direct support includes (*a*) the provision of debenture and equity capital by the regional Development Corporations, the Federal Loans Board and the Nigerian Industrial Development Bank,[2] (*b*) the construction of industrial estates, (*c*) compulsory patronage by public bodies of approved domestic manufacturers, and (*d*) various technical assistance schemes for development of indigenous manufacturing enterprise. Indirect support of the industrialization effort is provided by the government-sponsored system of technical education and the activities of the Federal Institute of Industrial Research. All of these activities will be scrutinized during the course of this study.

Lastly, agencies of the Federal and Regional Governments have undertaken direct industrial investments. Major projects of this type, where public authorities have provided 90 % or more of the capital, include a fruit cannery, four cement mills, two large sack factories, a paper mill, two breweries, an integrated textile mill, two soft drink bottling plants, a ceramics factory, a mint, a glass factory and four oil-seed crushing plants. Total investment in these projects is in excess of £35m. For reasons discussed in chapter 3, none of these investments have proved profitable – at least as of 1966.

Public investments outside the industrial sector, other than of a social overhead character, include a five-ship merchant marine, an international airline, three olympic-sized sport stadia, four television broadcasting stations and five luxury hotels. Only the merchant marine has operated at a profit.

Beyond the necessary symbols for nation building, such loss-making investments contribute nothing to economic growth and yet are made at considerable cost. First and most obviously, there is the value of the resources squandered and the burden of recurring subsidies which

[1] Industrial Development (Income Tax Relief) Ordinance 1958, superseding the Aid to Pioneer Industries Act 1952.

[2] The NIDB, opened in 1964, was an outgrowth of the Investment Company of Nigeria established in 1959 by the U.K. Commonwealth Development Finance Company. In addition to a majority holding by the Federal Government, CDFC, the International Finance Corporation and private international banks also hold shares in the NIDB. The Commonwealth Development Corporation (formerly the Colonial Development Corporation) also operates investment companies in the northern and eastern regions in partnership with the respective regional Development Corporations.

unliquidated losing enterprises entail. Second, because virtually all public revenue is raised by indirect taxes which have adverse substitution effects, favouring leisure over work, unnecessary taxation tends to reduce production. Third, the restraint in consumer spending implied by higher taxation limits the market for developing home industries. Fourth, and most important, high taxes and slow growth – sacrifice out of proportion to gain – are a politically explosive mixture.[1]

Having sketched the basic outlines of the Nigerian economy and the setting of the industrial sector therein, we are now in a position to embark upon our analysis of the process by which the manufacturing sector has come into being and from which it has taken its particular form. This process consists of the interaction between the economic environment and entrepreneurial behaviour. In chapter 2 the essential characteristics of the market, transportation and import taxation are considered as the key features of the economic environment. In chapter 3 these environmental features are combined with a hypothesis about entrepreneurial behaviour to provide an explanation for the timing and nature of import-replacing industrialization in Nigeria.

[1] This last point has been forcefully put by Wolfgang Stolper, a former Nigerian planner: 'To insist on high taxation – on austerity – in order to transfer resources which might have been consumed to projects that lose money and slow down the rate of growth is irresponsible and politically explosive. . . . The projects requiring subsidies require more taxes. The sacrifices required are thus to go backward, since losses mean that as the end result of your development you come out with less resources than you started with. . . . The large programs that look so impressive on paper can only be achieved by including projects that will not pay off either in terms of growth or in terms of satisfactions. In fact larger programs are likely to achieve less growth than smaller ones, and this causes political troubles when larger sacrifices are needed for smaller gains. . . . The austerity imposed has been not to achieve growth but to hide mistakes: for pet projects of politicians, for show, for jets or factories. These are juju or playthings. It is no wonder there have been revolts.' W. F. Stolper, 'Politics and Economic Development', *Revistia di Politica Economica*, Rome, June 1963, pp. 12, 22.

CHAPTER 2

THE MARKET

Sufficient demand for manufactured goods is clearly the first requisite for the establishment of manufacturing. The size of her market has been Nigeria's prime asset in her effort to industrialize. Despite a low *per capita* income of about £30, her population of some 40m. (30m. in 1950), a relatively even distribution of income and a well developed system of transportation have given Nigeria Africa's second largest market, surpassed only by South Africa.[1]

Three separate markets have provided opportunities for Nigeria's industrial development: the home market for consumer goods, the home market for intermediate and capital goods, and the export processing market. External markets for manufactured goods have not developed and are not deemed obtainable for the forseeable future (*a*) because of high production costs in terms of the world market, and (*b*) in the case of an African common market because of widely manifest political rivalry, administrative hurdles, product specification difficulties and, not least of all, because Nigeria would stand to lose more by way of allocation of industry than she could gain by an enlarged market in any regional grouping with her far smaller neighbours.[2]

In this chapter we shall focus on three aspects of the market environment which are most critical for the development of industry. Section I deals with the contemporary pattern of demand. Section II treats the historic role of transportation in widening and deepening the Nigerian market and its implication in terms of natural protection for domestic manufacturing. Section III considers import tariffs as they affect the size of the market and provide incentives for local investment; tariffs are also discussed with reference to their impact on the industrial cost structure and the possibility of sustained industrialization based on vertical linkages.

[1] Statistical Office of the United Nations, *Yearbook of National Accounts, 1966*, New York 1967.

[2] In the same month Nigeria agreed in principle at an ECA conference in Monrovia that there should be but one integrated iron and steel industry for all West Africa, government authorities announced that Nigeria was to build two such plants on her own. See *West Africa* (London), 16 November, 1963 and 23 May 1964. See also G. K. Helleiner, 'Nigeria and the African Common Market', *Nigerian Journal of Economic and Social Studies*, vol. 4, November 1962.

I

In 1963 Nigerian consumers purchased an estimated £955m. worth of goods and services.[1] On the basis of the 1957 composition of consumer expenditures, almost 70 % went to food, slightly less than 10 % to clothes, and 10 % to other consumer goods.[2] An additional £177m. in 1963 was spent on maintaining and enlarging productive capacity; of this amount, outlays on hard goods – vehicles, building materials, fixtures, plant, equipment – would account for about two-thirds. Thus Nigeria's aggregated demand for goods of all kinds (including food) in 1963 would appear to have been of the order of £1,100m.

THE IMPORT MARKET

While the processing of domestically produced food provides important long term industrial opportunities, the largest immediate potential for manufacturing is the 20 to 25 % of aggregate expenditures which goes to imports. Table 9 shows the growth in imports, their changing composition and average tariff levels.

Table 9. *The composition of import demand*

	Per cent of all imports				Average tariff			
By SITC Group	1954	1958	1962	1964	1954	1958	1962	1964
Food	11	11	12	8	6	4	22	16
Drink and tobacco	4	3	2	1	120	120	160	182
Mineral fuels	5	5	7	8	42	41	83	75
Chemicals	4	5	6	7	18	16	16	17
Manufactured goods	48	40	36	35	17	24	31	34
Machinery and transport	18	24	24	30	4	5	11	13
Misc. manufactured articles	8	9	11	9	22	24	27	32
Other[a]	3	3	4	2	...	...	...	...
	100	100	100	100	19	21	30	30
Value of imports in £m.	114	166	203	254				

By use	1950	1955	1960[b]	1965
Consumer goods	60	59	57(61)	45
Intermediate goods	10	10	11(17)	24
Capital goods	30	31	32(22)	31
	100	100	100	100

[a] Crude materials, animal and vegetable oils, miscellaneous transactions.

[b] Figures in parenthesis for 1960 are those given by the Central Bank as are the 1965 figures. The 1950–60 percentages were estimated by O. Aboyade.

SOURCE: Federal Office of Statistics, *Digest of Statistics* and *Trade Reports*, various years. Helleiner, *Peasant Agriculture*, table IV-A-17, and Central Bank of Nigeria, *Annual Report, etc., 1965*, p. 24.

[1] Gross domestic product + net imports – gross investment. All national income figures from Federal Office of Statistics, *Economic Indicators*, March 1966.

[2] (Jackson and) Okigbo, *Nigerian Accounts 1950–7*.

The absolute size and rate of growth of Nigerian imports is the obvious first point to note – the scope for import substitution would appear very great. Indeed the changing composition of imports is partially a reflection of the beginning of such import-replacing industry. The shares of food, drink and tobacco, and manufactured products have declined with the establishment of local production. On the other hand, minerals and fuels, chemicals and machinery and transport have enlarged their share under the pressure of development programmes and the import requirements of new industry. This same pattern is seen when imports are classified as consumer, intermediate and capital goods. The share of consumer goods imports has fallen while the aggregate share of capital and intermediate goods has risen. This distribution of imports is mirrored in Nigeria's industrial production, two-thirds of which in 1963 were consumer goods.[1]

With regard to tariff levels, the most striking fact is their comparative modesty. Low tariffs, as well as free convertibility and the general absence of quotas, derive from Nigeria's good fortune of never having experienced a prolonged balance-of-payments crisis. This in turn reflects the comparatively late date at which Nigeria has departed from her comparative advantage and the still low ratio of domestic industrial production to foreign trade. Until 1958, with the exception of a few protective tariffs, the aim of import taxation was to raise public revenue; since that time, as foreign exchange reserves have fallen, tariffs have been used increasingly to check the imbalance of external payments. If tariff data were available for 1965 and 1966, average import duties collected would almost certainly exceed 50 %.

Returning to the changing distribution of imports revealed in table 9, it is necessary to qualify a straightforward concept of import substitution to the extent that the changing composition of imports is a result of the establishment of import replacing industries. It is now recognized that import substitution leads to a shift toward less processed goods and factor services which are inputs into the import-substitute industry, and that home production may even result in a net addition to total payments abroad. Because the industrial surveys do not distinguish imported input purchases and do not show profits, it is impossible to determine whether Nigeria's import substitution has resulted

[1] Clark, 'The General Characteristics of the Nigerian Economy', p. 69. Given the inherent arbitrariness of distributing commodities between use categories, the consumer-intermediate-capital goods classification should not be taken too seriously. The three distributions made for imports by Aboyade, the Central Bank and Clark are all substantially different, agreeing only that the share of consumer goods is declining. On the other hand, according to Clark's grouping of domestic industrial products for the three years 1957, 1962 and 1963 the share of consumption goods is falling here as well; the implied increase in the domestic saving ratio is not confirmed by national income data.

in a savings or augmentation of the foreign exchange requirement per unit of consumption. On the basis of the specific evidence presented in chapter 4 and upon the general importance of (*a*) foreign investment – approximately two-thirds of the total, (*b*) foreign managers and technicians – accounting for 30 % of total labour cost,[1] and (*c*) substantial import requirements of capital equipment and intermediate inputs, one is inclined to estimate that import substitution has resulted in a slight increase in imports per unit of consumption. Net import substitution will be achieved as foreign factors are replaced by Nigerian personnel and capital and as the level of technical efficiency rises.

Table 10. *Commodity imports: major items*

(£000, c.i.f.)

	1946	1954	1958	1962	1964
Food					
Flour	94	1,736	2,117	2,965	170
Stockfish	97	5,659	7,480	7,221	6,248
Salt	512	1,409	1,797	2,012	2,075
Sugar	124	2,108	3,353	3,228	3,048
Milk	58	554	1,079	2,280	2,982
Beer	165	2,265	3,319	2,826	787
Clothing					
Cotton piece goods	5,921	16,488	16,295	18,655	21,952
Rayon piece goods	751	10,423	10,790	3,840	3,506
Ready-made clothing	...	2,238	3,782	5,496	...
Footwear	161	1,923	2,715	2,837	2,501
Consumer durables					
Cycles	247	1,713	1,390	954	784
Cars	202	2,114	4,446	6,326	8,216
Household utensils	...	3,487	3,343	2,531	1,695
Capital goods					
Trucks	405	3,027	6,761	3,274	8,747
Electrical machinery	...	3,075	5,935	10,814	12,842
Railway equipment	...	1,785	4,687	823	763
Corrugated iron sheets	71	3,557	2,472	2,041	1,096
Constructional steel	...	2,952	6,412	7,416	17,822
Cement	475	3,065	4,101	2,363	1,193
Bags and sacks	731	1,610	2,192	4,007	3,720
Other					
Tyres and tubes	...	1,631	2,455	3,008	1,601
Paper and board	...	999	2,083	4,145	6,091
Petroleum oils	...	5,118	8,394	13,379	18,573

SOURCE: *Digest of Statistics* and *Nigerian Trade Journal*, various years.

Table 10 focuses more sharply on specific import substitution possibilities. Once again the extremely rapid growth of the economy and

[1] Federal Office of Statistics, *Industrial Survey of 1963*, table 6.

the market it afforded following World War II is evident. By 1954 most of the product markets were already of sufficient size to support two or more plants. However it is not until 1962 and 1964 that the presence of local industry can be detected – in flour, beer, household utensils, cement, corrugated iron sheets and tyres and tubes. Moreover substantial production was initiated in sugar, milk, textiles and footwear, the import replacement effects of which were swamped by growth in demand. In all of these industries, save sugar and flour milling, from two to eight firms have been established, and in most cases there is room for more.

In addition to its absolute size, the growth of the market has been a powerful incentive for potential investors. The total import market grew fourteen-fold over the period 1946–65, averaging 13 % per annum during the 1950s and 5 % during the first half of the 1960s. The prospective acceleration in oil export earnings promises a new spurt in import growth to match that of the Korean war period.

INCOME ELASTICITY OF DEMAND

We now move from aggregate demand to individual consumer behaviour. By examining household budget studies it is possible to obtain an idea of how demand patterns, and hence investment opportunities, are likely to change with rising income. In addition to six urban consumer surveys carried out by the Federal Office of Statistics, there is a breakdown of consumer expenditure in the national accounts.

Table 11. *Consumer household expenditure patterns*

(%)

	National average	Urban average[a]	Lagos 0–150*s*.	Lagos 350–550*s*.	Lagos 950–1,150*s*.	Lagos 1,350–1,550*s*.
Housing	1·5	8·8	20·5	11·6	12·3	17·0
Food	69·9	46·9	46·4	41·4	42·5	26·3
Drink	1·9	7·7	5·8	9·3	8·1	6·5
Tobacco and kola	2·2	4·1	4·5	2·9	1·9	0·4
Fuel and light	1·5	3·5	2·9	3·3	3·6	2·6
Transport	2·6	4·8	7·3	6·3	7·0	16·4
Clothing	9·5	11·1	7·4	10·7	8·8	10·9
Other goods	6·0	6·7	3·4	6·8	7·7	8·8
Other services	4·7	6·4	1·8	7·7	8·1	11·1
	100·0	100·0	100·0	100·0	100·0	100·0

[a] The average household expenditure pattern from the first five surveys in the income range from 100*s*. to 500*s*. per month. The 1959 Lagos survey, shown separately, covered upper income households as well.

SOURCES: (Jackson and) Okigbo, *Nigerian National Accounts 1950–57*, pp. 104–7; Federal Office of Statistics, *Urban Consumer Surveys in Nigeria* (Lagos 1959 and 1963) Lagos 1953–4, Enugu 1954–5, Ibadan 1955, Kaduna and Zaria 1955–6, Lagos 1959.

The first point to note is the difference in housing and food between the national (predominantly rural) and the urban expenditure pattern. The very low proportion of income devoted to housing for the national average is explained by the virtual absence of rent and the extremely simple nature of the rural mud dwelling. The high percentage of the farmers' modest income which goes towards food (and home-processed food at that) would seem to indicate that apart from textiles and clothing a smaller portion of his income is available to purchase manufactured goods; and yet the share of income spent on 'other goods' (consumer durables, toilet articles, pharmaceutics, books) is not significantly lower than that of his city cousin. If the 1959 Lagos survey may be taken as a guide[1] the urban demand for food is surprisingly income-elastic up to the 1,150*s*. level whereafter it manifests the expected Engleian pattern; as income rises there is a shift from carbohydrates to proteins, from cassava to bread, from palm oil to margarine, from domestic to imported foods – generally a shift from a lesser to a higher degree of industrial processing. As household income goes up there is more than a proportionate increase in outlays for clothing, consumer durables, cycles and cars (under Transport), toilet articles, pharmaceutics, books and stationery. Thus any growth in *per capita* income is likely to have very favourable repercussions on the market for consumer goods.

REGIONAL DISTRIBUTION

As in many other countries the geographic distribution of demand for manufactured goods is uneven. In addition to the usual urban concentration, there is a north-south inequality arising from differences in purchasing power, in the coverage of the distribution network, and in intensity of desire for modern consumer goods.

Regional differences in purchasing power will approximate differences in regional *per capita* income; unfortunately no regional estimates have been attempted since the World Bank mission's 1953 up-dating of the 1950–1 estimates of Prest and Stewart.[2] Indices of urbanization and road density give a rough idea of the relative efficiency of distribution arrangements. It is seen from the figures below that the predominantly rural northern region has both a lower *per capita* income (although the gap is thought to have narrowed in recent years) and a more thinly spread transport network.

[1] Rents are very much higher in Lagos than in other towns in Nigeria. The previously cited household budget studies revealed that 16 % of the low income group's expenditures goes towards accommodation as compared to 10 % for Enugu and Ibadan and 13 % for Kaduna.

[2] A. R. Prest and I. G. Stewart, *The National Income of Nigeria, 1950–51*, Colonial Office, H.M.S.O., London 1953. Jackson and Okigbo did not attempt regional estimates.

	Income per head (1953) (£)	Population per sq. mile (1963)	% Population in towns[a] (1953)	Miles of road per sq. mile (1963)
West	34	162	29	0·24
East	21	298	6	0·49
North	17	73	3	0·07

[a] Towns of 20,000 or more.

SOURCES: Federal Office of Statistics, *Annual Abstract of Statistics, 1964*; International Bank for Reconstruction and Development, *The Economic Development of Nigeria*, Federal Government Printer, Lagos 1954, p. 398.

The third factor, differences in the intensity of desire for modern consumer goods, results from the conservative influence of religion and the socio-political system of Northern Nigeria. Islam, the semi-feudalistic emirates and the exclusion of western (missionary) education on religious grounds, combined with a later and less intensive contact with the western world, have meant that in the north the whole process of modernization – changes in the way of living, values and skills, as well as in directly material terms – has lagged behind that of the east and west.

This demand pattern, reinforced by such supply considerations as skilled labour availability, proximity to a seaport, industrial water supplies, better transport facilities and nearness of suppliers, has led to a concentration of industry in the southern half of the country. The regional distribution of foreign and governmental industrial enterprise in 1964 was reported by A. N. Hakam as follows:[1]

	No. of firms (%)	Capital (%)	Employment (%)
Lagos	30·2	20·5	22·0
West	32·1	24·8	26·5
East	16·4	31·1	23·1
North	21·4	23·6	28·4

Although the north accounts for more than half of the country's population and geographic area, less than a quarter of large and medium scale industry as measured by number of firms or capital employed was located there. The factors which have brought about investment in the north include the natural protection of distance, differentiated markets (e.g. non-alcoholic perfumes, ceremonial brass holloware, cotton blankets),[2] financial incentives provided by the regional government, and political pressures on firms supplying northern markets from

[1] Hakam, 'The Motivation to Invest and the Locational Pattern of Foreign Private Industrial Investment in Nigeria', *Nigerian Journal of Economic and Social Studies*, vol. 8, March 1966, p. 64.

[2] This point is drawn from Hakam, *loc. cit.* p. 56.

southern factories (e.g. the Nigerian Tobacco Company, Nigerian Breweries). At a more general level, potential regionalization of the Nigerian market has played an important role in the location of light industry.

As might be expected, there is considerable concentration of industry in a few large towns: Lagos and the adjacent Ikeja-Mushin area contain 33 % of industrial investment as recorded by Hakam, and Port Harcourt and Aba in the east and Kaduna and Kano in the north account for another 37 %.[1]

MARKET SEGMENTATION

There is one final aspect of the market, alluded to briefly in chapter 1, which is worthy of note. For a great many products there is not a single demand, but a number of demands for varying qualities of the item at different prices. Such 'product differentiation' is to be found in the markets of developed countries but the range in quality and price is comparatively narrow, the difference in price seldom exceeding, say, 100 %. In underdeveloped countries this range is very much greater. To give a few examples, an arm-chair made in a small-scale Nigerian workshop sold in 1964 for £2 while the same model chair – but constructed from seasoned wood, squarely joined and perfectly flush on the floor – sold for over £6 from any one of the country's major furniture manufacturers. In the case of sandals there is a wide range of possibilities starting with the tyre-sandal at 2*s*. 6*d*. (cut from discarded automobile tyres with a plastic thong tacked on) and going up to the 55*s*. English 'cross sandal'. The soap market is supplied by black wood-ash soap from cottage producers, cold process caustic soda soap from modern small scale Nigerian firms at a price about 80 % above that of black soap, and finally hot process emulsion soap from large scale expatriate-run factories at double the price of the cold process soap. Even in the case of so seemingly homogeneous a product as bread, four distinct submarkets were identified.[2]

This phenomenon of market segmentation flows from the low level of *per capita* income. With severely limited purchasing power, the community's poorer members will often choose inexpensive low-quality products such as tyre-sandals or household utensils beaten out of scrap by the tinker in preference to the higher quality, more durable, dearer alternative. As incomes rise and consumer time preferences for present over future goods diminish, the value placed on durability and quality increases and the market share of inferior goods falls.

[1] Hakam, *loc. cit.* p. 64.

[2] Peter Kilby, *African Enterprise: The Nigerian Bread Industry*, Hoover Institution, Stanford 1965, pp. 42–3.

The practical consequences of market segmentation for industrialization are two. First, in the majority of cases the cheaper, lower quality products are manufactured by the indigenous small industry sector. Although possessing far less financial resources or technical skill than their larger, more mechanized competitors, the small-scale operator enjoys substantially lower costs in terms of wage rates, overheads, distribution and sometimes even materials cost. From the view point of indigenous entrepreneurship, under certain circumstances this segmentation of the market may provide a natural shelter within which Nigerian entrepreneurs can learn skills, gain experience and accumulate capital before going into the 'primary' market to compete on equal terms with the expatriate firms.[1] In so far as the emergence of a significant class of local industrialists is essential for any enduring industrialization, the existence of such market segmentation can make an important contribution to the development process. The issues involved, as well as the facts of the matter, will be treated at some length in chapter 10.

The second practical consequence of market segmentation is its implications about the size of the market for large scale projects. Traditionally imports are used as the measure of the size of the market; however they often fail to indicate the full range of potential demand. Local ex-factory prices significantly lower than the previously ruling landed import price (c.i.f. +tariff) will often disclose a larger market than was supposed. It is estimated by the cement manufacturers that the largest component in the expansion of their market has occurred as a result of a shift from traditional construction materials to cement in house-building brought about by a lower delivered price in the inland regions. The demand for tyres and tubes on the basis of imports was judged large enough to support but one plant; it was later discovered that a large number of *used* tyres were being imported and that when these were excluded from the market by a prohibitive tariff, a second plant of equal size became viable.

The possibilities for expansion of the primary market owing to the existence of submarkets, unconnected with population growth or *per capita* income rises, can be significant in rendering marginal industries viable and contributing to economies of scale in other industries. It also implies that as large-scale industry gets well established and begins to bring costs down some of the sheltered markets of the small-scale sector are likely to be eroded.

[1] Demand for the standardized, mass-produced factory item usually, but not always, constitutes the primary market. A notable exception is furniture. In the case of footwear, small scale artisan production dominated the market until the advent in 1957 of the inexpensive plastic sandal.

II

Transportation affects the size of the market in two ways. First, and most obvious, some system for the carriage of goods must exist before a particular physical area can be brought into the market: manufactured goods must be carried to the consumer and his produce in exchange evacuated. Thus the *availability* of transport may be said to fix the geographic size or 'width' of the market. Secondly, the *cost* of transport will influence the volume of exchange or the 'depth' of the market: if transport costs fall not only does the consumer receive a greater income for his produce, but the price of manufactured goods offered to him is reduced by an equal measure.[1] Conversely, if transport cost increases, the gain from trade is reduced and the volume of exchange will be restricted. Just how important the transport factor can be in determining the gains from trade is seen by comparing the rate of exchange of groundnuts, the principal export crop for the north, for imported cement and salt, first at the port and then in two northern towns.[2]

Point of exchange	One ton of groundnuts is equal in cost to	
	Salt (tons)	Cement (tons)
Lagos	2·0	4·8
Sokoto	0·9	1·7
Maiduguri	0·7	1·2

Equally transport costs are often the key factor in determining the viability of processing industries whose low-value bulky by-products must be carried to a widely dispersed local market. And finally the cost of sea and land carriage influences the social cost of import substitution (i.e. the amount of protection required) as well as the pattern of internal industrial location.

DEVELOPMENT OF THE TRANSPORTATION SYSTEM

During the nineteenth century the only means for conveying goods, beyond human porterage, was by water transport along the Niger and its tributaries. This suited well enough the needs of the existing palm-oil trade which was centred in the Niger delta. Hence it was more

[1] In a literal sense the distinction between availability and cost is a false one, as some form of transport is almost always available. It was reported by Armsby-Gore in 1926 (Cmd. 2744) that freight could be moved by human porterage for 2*s*. 6*d*. per ton-mile. Fifteen years earlier Lord Lugard had put the figure at 5*s*. However, for all practical purposes (i.e. volume capability, economic cost) the distinction is a useful one.

[2] U.A.C., *Statistical and Economic Review*, no. 14, March 1954, p. 38. At prevailing market prices 1953–4.

considerations of colonial rivalry, internal pacification and the need for administrative cohesion than any assessment of economic potential, which motivated the establishment of a railway into the interior.[1] Begun from Lagos in 1898 the railway reached Ibadan by 1901, Oshogbo in 1907 and Jebba on the upper Niger in 1909, a distance of 302 miles from Lagos. In 1911 the tin mining fields at Jos were connected to the railway at Zaria and in the following year the Zaria-Kano and Minna-Baro sections were completed. Thus in 1912 Nigeria achieved its first two north-south transportation routes, the Kano-Jebba-Lagos railway and the combined river-rail Kano-Baro-Niger artery. Between 1913 and 1916 track was laid from the newly created Port Harcourt to the Enugu coalfields; ten years later this line was extended to Kaduna, giving the country its third north-south artery.[2]

As the production and export of groundnuts, cotton, hides and skins, and tin-ore – the mainstays of the northern economy – did not begin on a substantial scale until after 1912, it is probably not an exaggeration to say that the availability of rail transportation has been the single most important factor in the economic development of Northern Nigeria. In the southern coastal regions, where distances are shorter and population more dense, the principal carrier of goods has been the ubiquitous lorry, integrating local markets and stimulating internal trade as well as carrying much of the import-export trade.

The development of motorable roads followed that of the railways and constituted in the early years a feeder system for the latter.[3] By 1914 there were 2,000 miles of unpaved roads, mostly in the west. After the interruption of the First World War and the diversion of government effort to the construction of the eastern rail line, road building was revived in 1923. It was during this period that the beginnings of an independent trunk road system were laid down. By 1926 the railway was already asking for the restriction of competition in the west where the expanding cocoa crop had given rise to a small but vigorous road transport industry – reported at 218 vehicles in 1933.

[1] The historical account contained in this and the following paragraph is drawn from Gilbert Walker, *Traffic and Transport in Nigeria*, Colonial Research Studies, No. 27, H.M.S.O., London 1959.

[2] 'The simple plan to bring the coal by rail 67 miles to Onitsha and thence down to the Niger . . . was rejected in favour of the more ambitious scheme for a direct line from the coast to the coal and on, across the Benue, to the tin mines on the Plateau. [This northern line from Enugu was in fact a money loser for many years]. The short line to Onitsha would have been much cheaper at the time, and far more economical in the long run, besides serving as an inducement to extend the Lagos railway to Asaba and possibly to bridge the Niger at Onitsha. But the Germans were building from Duala. Strategy, not economics, compelled the choice.' Walker, *op. cit.* p. 64.

[3] Sleeping sickness precluded the earlier development of roads for animal drawn transport in the south, while in the tsetse fly free areas of the north there was no demand for them.

By 1937 the country had 19,450 miles of road and 1,800 route-miles of railways; of the roads, however, over a third were dry season tracks, impassable for nearly half of the year, while only a few hundred miles of the country's carriageways were paved.

Table 12. *Growth in freight traffic*
(millions of ton-miles)

	1939	1953	1960
Rail	246	687	1,103
Water	60	88	120
Road	100	840	2,010
Total	406	1,615	3,233
Combined export-import tonnage (millions of tons)	1·3	3·1	5·9

SOURCES: International Bank for Reconstruction and Development, *The Economic Development of Nigeria*, p. 33, for 1939 traffic; Stanford Research Institute, *The Economic Coordination of Transport Development in Nigeria*, Menlo Park 1961, p. 55, for 1953 and 1960 traffic; Federal Office of Statistics, *Annual Abstract of Statistics 1963*, p. 106, for export-import tonnages.

After World War II the volume of road, rail and water traffic expanded very rapidly reflecting the emergence from a subsistence economy which might be said to have occurred at this time. The further extension of the market and the growth of domestic trade, an indication of increasing economic specialization, is seen in the fact that the volume of freight traffic grew at a considerably faster rate than export-import tonnage.

Of the three transport media, road carriage has shown the most dramatic increases. This was made possible by public and private investment in the following facilities – between 1945 and 1963 the mileage of tarred roads was increased from 533 to 8,000, the mileage of all-surface roads was doubled and the number of commercial vehicles jumped from 1,500 to 24,000.[1] Not only have the lorries been carrying most of the passengers and domestic goods trade, they have also been capturing a proportionally larger share of the export-import business. Over the period 1955–60 road transport's share of import tonnage rose from 25 to 58 % and export tonnage from 20 to 35 %.[2]

For a country its size and at its stage of development, Nigeria is well served by its transportation network. Only along the eastern border – Bornu and Adamawa in the north and along the Calabar-Ogoja axis in the east – can it be said that insufficient transport facilities have held

[1] *Digest of Statistics*, vols. 1 and 13. The Stanford Report estimated the investment per mile of tarred road at £7,300 (valued at 1960 P.W.D. construction costs) and for unsurfaced roads at £1,100. Stanford Research Institute, *op. cit.* p. 139.

[2] Stanford Research Institute, *op. cit.* p. 57.

back development. Roads and railways are now being constructed in these areas. The density of roads relative to area in southern Nigeria is higher than in any other country in tropical Africa and is comparable to that of India.[1] Nor can it be said that Northern Nigeria is served less

Table 13. *The extent of the road transport network, 1963*

	Population per mile of road	Per cent of total area within 1 mile of road (%)	Population per mile of tarred road	Commercial vehicles per 10,000 population
Lagos	2,000	100	2,240	100
West	684	48	1,979	11
East	497	75[a]	5,616	5
North	979	14	8,811	3

[a] Includes an allowance for excessive road density.
SOURCE: Calculated from data in *Annual Abstract of Statistics, 1964* and *Digest of Statistics*, vol. 13.

well by its road network when the low population density (73 people per square mile compared to 298 in the east and 162 in the west), natural resource potential, and *per capita* income level are taken into account.

THE COST OF TRANSPORT

Of the three means of inland transport carriage, water transport is the cheapest.[2] With some eighteen times the carrying capacity per unit of power of the railway and the free provision of 'track' in the Niger and Benue rivers, river convoys are able to overcome the high costs involved in building their own port facilities and in suspending operaions during the low-water period. Fundamental limitations of water transport are geographic inflexibility, seasonality and slow speeds. Although inefficient compared to water carriage, railway trains enjoy economies of motive power relative to the lorry; the lower incidence of wear and tear incurred by a steel wheel running on a steel track means that capital costs per ton-mile are less. Freedom of movement and adaptability in handling different cargoes are the advantages of the comparatively high-cost motor lorry.

All three transport media have benefited from the introduction of important technical advances since 1945. Foremost of these has been the diesel engine, which has reduced fuel cost by 50 to 60 %. In

[1] Stanford Research Institute, *op. cit.* p. 140.
[2] This and the subsequent paragraph are based upon United Africa Company, 'The Co-ordination of Transport in Tropical Africa', *Statistical and Economic Review*, no. 25, March 1961.

addition, for water transport the introduction of 'push-towing' in the early 1950s, adapted from practice on the Mississippi, has increased the capacity of barge trains from 1,400 tons to 3,200 tons. The railroad has benefited from specialized wagons for carrying liquid, refrigerated and perishable commodities, lighter and stronger construction of vehicles, modernization of track allowing higher speeds and greater weights and new communication devices for controlling traffic. The motor lorry is now much lighter in relation to its payload, is fitted out with heavy duty tyres, springs and brakes, and benefits from a much lengthened fatigue-life of all its components.

Table 14. *The cost of transport, 1930–1963*
(pence per ton-mile)

	Water	Rail	Road
1926	...	2·2	...
1933	...	1·4	3·3
1939	1·7	1·7	...
1950	2·2	2·2	3·0–4·0
1963	1·7	2·3	4·0–6·0

SOURCES: For water, Walker, *op. cit.* pp. 168, 170 and Federal Ministry of Commerce & Industry, *Transportation, A Guide to Current Costs in Nigeria*, Lagos 1964, pp. 21–2. For rail, calculated from Nigeria Railways *Annual Reports*. For road, competitive rates cited by Walker, *op. cit.* pp. 171 and 178 and *Transportation, A Guide . . .*, pp. 8–9.

The effect of these technical advances is seen clearly in the above table. Over the past three decades railway and water transport money costs have risen hardly at all, while road charges have gone up by about 75 %.[1] In comparison, the money cost of equipment, fuel and labour, along with the general price level, have risen by some 200 to 300 %.[2] Thus the real costs of transport have fallen substantially.

The dynamic factor in translating the advances of transportation technology into actual practice has been the road transport industry. Despite its higher cost, the latter has captured an increasing share of the country's traffic and in so doing has spurred the railway and water monopolies to introduce all available cost-reducing innovations and to pass these savings on.

The competitive advantage of road transport stems from the small scale of the operational unit. With a carrying capacity of 3 to 5 tons

[1] However, during World War II and the Korean War, when there was a shortage of transport facilities, water and rail rates rose to 3d per ton-mile. A significant factor in keeping the cost of rail and water carriage at its low level has been the increase in average length of haul, as a result of the encroachments of the lorry. The average length of haul on the railway, for instance, rose from 201 miles in 1923 to 588 miles in 1963.

[2] See appendices A and B.

the problem of excess capacity on the return-haul is nowhere as severe as in the case of the railway or barge train where hundreds of tons are required; if a full load cannot be quickly secured, passenger traffic provides a ready supplement. The carriage of goods is door to door: there is no time or expense lost to trans-shipment and intermediate handling. The requirements of specialized cargoes are more easily catered for by the individual lorry transporter. And finally, although there are no inherent technical factors favouring the motor lorry, in practice shippers have found road transport far speedier and more reliable than the railway for long as well as short hauls. A lengthened transit time ties up working capital, incurs interest charges and is likely to place the railway user at a disadvantage *vis-à-vis* his quicker road-using competitors.

Not only has the small scale of its operational unit given road transport greater speed and flexibility, it has also enforced higher standards of efficiency within the industry than are to be found in its rather sluggish competitor, the railway. Because the investment required for the central unit of 'production' is but a few thousand pounds (further reduced by hire-purchase arrangements), entry into the industry is relatively unimpeded. The intense competition resulting from this situation has contributed to the reduction of transport costs in three ways. First, that cost component which represents the return to entrepreneurship and capital has been reduced to its barest minimum. Second, in sharp contrast to the railway, road transporters have exploited the technical capacity of their medium of carriage to its fullest extent and, indeed, beyond.[1] Third, vigorous competition from the road has been responsible (as far back as the first rate reduction in 1927) for far lower railway tariffs than would otherwise have prevailed.

TRANSPORTATION AND NATURAL PROTECTION

Turning from the influence of transportation in determining the overall size of the market, at a more immediate level the cost of carriage provides a substantial measure of protection (or equally, an enlarged market) for many kinds of import substitution and plays a key role in internal industrial location. In general the more fragile or perishable, the bulkier or heavier a product is in relation to its value, the more important will be the transport factor in final cost. The figures below

[1] Drivers and vehicles work long hours, seldom less than 12 a day; the long haul Kano-Lagos route (700 miles) is driven non-stop (2 days as against the railway's 5), the drivers chewing the stimulant kola nut to stay awake. The vast majority of lorries are undermaintained, overloaded and driven at excessive speeds. Not surprisingly, Nigeria is reputed to have one of the highest accident and motor fatality rates in the world. Stanford Research Institute, *op. cit.* p. 191.

indicate the range of 'value added' by transportation for manufactured articles.[1]

Value of Product at:

	Liverpool	(4,210 miles by sea)	Lagos	(700 miles by rail)	Kano
Cement	100		160		254
Flour	100		125		140
Salt	100		121		153
Sugar	100		110		128
Commercial vehicles	100		110		121
Corrugated iron	100		105		113
Textiles	100		105		107

If we allow for an additional 10 % carriage and handling cost as the difference between the ex-factory and f.o.b. value at the point of export, we may say that local industry competing with sea-borne imports enjoys a minimum natural protection of 15 to 70 % of produ-tion cost depending on the commodity in question. The further inland the factory is sited (assuming that the site is approximately co-terminus with the minimum transport point for the market being served), the greater is the additional protection afforded by the cost of land transport.

For the transport-intensive commodities – salt, cement, beer, assembled vehicles – the magnitude of natural protection is such that one would expect, all else being equal, these items to be among the earliest instances of import substitution; equally one would expect local production of such transport-light items as cosmetics, cigarettes, and textiles, to occur comparatively late. Finally the very much higher cost of land transport relative to ocean carriage suggests that the incentive for local processing of exports will be greater the further inland the locus of primary production.

III

The third factor which has a crucial bearing on the size of the market and its relation to the initiation of local production is import taxation. In a more general sphere the level and structure of tariffs are of critical importance to the sequential progress of industrialization.

Until very recently economists have tended to view tariffs primarily from the point of view of international trade theory. As applied to industrialization of underdeveloped countries, the domestic impact of

[1] Adapted from United Africa Company, *Statistical and Economic Review*, no. 19, 1957, p. 12. Points off the railway enjoy still further protection: the cost of carrying cement (salt) 373 miles by road from Kano to Maiduguri is 125 % (54 %) of the Lagos-Kano rail charge.

protective tariffs has been seen in a partial equilibrium context: tariffs are often (*i*) a necessary stimulant and subsidy for the development of manufacturing, and (*ii*) entail a reduction in real output until such time as the price of the home-produced goods falls to (or below) the c.i.f. value of the equivalent import. Further, some consideration is usually given to the effects of protective tariffs on income distribution, with its implications for capital accumulation.

The recent discovery that tariff protection is properly calculated on the basis of net output (value-added), rather than the final value of the product, has highlighted the impact of tariffs on the entire industrial cost structure, and thereby on the possibilities for subsequent industrial expansion. Two further aspects of tariffs, which have so far gone unexplored, are the relationship between pre-existing non-protective tariffs and the size of the market and, secondly, the role of tariffs as a competition-eliminating device for firms attempting to protect valuable markets they have previously supplied from abroad. This latter phenomenon is of central importance in explaining the mechanics of import substitution, the subject of the following chapter.

TARIFFS AND THE SIZE OF THE MARKET

The impact of tariffs on the size of markets is, in one sense, illusory rather than real. A tariff has no influence on the position or slope of the aggregate demand schedule for a given commodity; but it does have an influence on the price that will be realized and hence the quantity actually marketed. This elementary point is of very considerable importance in practice because in many instances, particularly when the government is attempting to determine whether a minimum-sized market has been achieved, the size of the market is measured by the quantity of imports and their c.i.f. value. Where a revenue tariff exists, which is almost always the case, the size of the market is understated by an amount equal to the *ad valorem* equivalent of the tariff.

This understatement of the size of the market, a result of statistical conventions governing the form in which import data are reported, is exemplified in table 10 and the earlier discussion of this chapter, in every official report assessing import substitution possibilities in Nigeria and, indeed, in the writings of virtually every professional economist. In the case of many economists, reliance is placed wholly on import quantities as a means for determining the feasibility of domestic production.[1] This approach violates elementary price theory on two counts: on the supply side it ignores the principle of comparative cost and, on

[1] For example, see A. O. Hirschman, *The Strategy of Economic Development*, New Haven 1958, chapter 7; and Economic Commission for Africa, *Industrial Growth in Africa*, United Nations, New York 1963, chapter 4.

the demand side, incorrectly defines the market in terms of physical quantities.

The simple points to be made are that the size of the market is defined by price x quantity (sales revenue), that price exceeds the c.i.f. import value by the amount of the tariff and any net internal transport advantage enjoyed by a local producer, and that the size of the market varies inversely with the final price – i.e. market demand schedules are downward sloping. To a government attempting to promote industrialization, the consequence of ignoring revenue tariffs, internal transport costs and the price elasticity of demand may be to seriously underestimate the size of the local market and hence the potential viability of the industry in question.[1]

TARIFFS AND THE ELIMINATION OF COMPETITION

More important than its influence on the size of the market available to the local producer, is the tariff's impact on the nature of competition between sellers within the market. Because the intended effect of a protective tariff is to provide local industry with an assured market (i.e. to provide local industry not with equal costs but with a decisive cost advantage *vis-à-vis* overseas suppliers) the imposition of a protective duty establishes the condition for a sharp contraction in competition. In terms of market strategy this means that in the importing or pre-manufacturing period the first seller who is willing to make an industrial investment is rewarded with the effective exclusion of his competitors from the market they were formerly contending for on equal terms.

In so far as the first investment seldom occurs before the market is several times the size required by a single efficient plant, as we shall see in the following chapter, it would seem that the competition-eliminating effect of tariff takes precedence over the market-enlarging effects discussed above. However this obviously does not hold where the government is the investor or is in a strong position to precipitate a private investment: hence the importance of public servants being able to assess accurately the size of the market, taking into account price elasticity, tariff and transport factors.

HOW MUCH PROTECTION?

How much protection can be justifiably extended to a newly established manufacturing industry in an underdeveloped country? We may

[1] Specifically, underestimation will vary with the size of the pre-existing tariff and the degree to which local production will be marketed at prices below the current landed import price (c.i.f.+tariff).

specify four possible grounds for extending protection: disequilibrium in the factor markets, external economies, 'learning' and stimulus to new investment.[1]

The first argument asserts that for institutional reasons (convention, social legislation, trade unions, etc.) urban wages exceed opportunity earnings in agriculture and that consequently tariff subsidization is justified, equal in amount to the difference between actual wage cost and true social opportunity costs as determined by labour's marginal product in agriculture. However, as Myint has observed, the cost of capital and many public services provided to industry are typically undervalued and may more than counterbalance the handicap of overvalued labour.[2]

The second argument for tariff subsidization is to allow the investing firm a monetary reward equivalent to the external economies that its actions create for other producers, i.e. contributing to a pool of trained labour and permitting supplying firms to realize economies of scale. As in the preceding case, it is necessary to set against external benefits any diseconomies created by the actions of the new firm. These include bidding up the prices of scarce resources (e.g. skilled labour, professional services), aggravating bottlenecks in public services (e.g. railway transport, electricity supply) and contributing to the administrative strain and consequent downward pressure on the efficiency of public bureaucracy.

The two preceding arguments for protective tariffs stem from a static divergence between private and social cost.[3] The final two arguments are both 'dynamic'. The 'learning' argument holds that temporary tariff subsidization is justified to partially finance the difference between initial and ultimate labour and managerial efficiency, where the ultimate efficiencies are such that the industry can face world competition unaided.[4] The fourth argument, Hirschman's vertical linkages, states that protection is justified in so far as the initial industry induces further investment in vertically linked industries.

[1] These and related issues are treated at length in chapter 11 in a general equilibrium context. For recent discussions, see H. G. Johnson, 'Tariffs and Economic Development: Some Theoretical Issues', *Journal of Development Studies*, vol. 1, July 1964; and Hla Myint 'Protection and Economic Development' in R. F. Harrod and D. C. Hague, eds., *International Trade Theory in a Developing World*, New York 1964.

[2] Myint, *loc. cit.* p. 312.

[3] The principle which these arguments seek to qualify, comparative advantage, is itself a static construct.

[4] Since the costs involved in learning are no different, save in their time dimension, from any other cost borne by the entrepreneur in anticipation of future gain, there is no *prima facie* reason for subvention. However, since the private investor applies a higher discount rate to future earnings than does society, and since the entrepreneurial loss in the event of the industry's failure exceeds the social loss (there is some gain to the economy in terms of underpriced physical assets and labour skills) partial subsidization can be justified.

It is the writer's tentative conclusion, based on evidence presented in chapters 4 and 9 that in the Nigerian case countervailing disequilibria in the non-labour factor markets offset the over-valuation of urban labour. External economies deriving from new industrial projects have in recent years been more than neutralized by their external diseconomies; however, the physical economies of scale in electricity generation are so great that, despite short-run excess demand and overtaxing of the Electricity Corporation's administrative competence, a reasonable case can be made for a subsidy to new industries with respect to the use of this one input. As for the Hirschman argument, it is valid only to the extent that the induced production does not itself require protection, otherwise the result is still higher prices and further reductions in real income.

For all practical purposes this leaves one viable justification for protection – to subsidize an infant industry during an initial period in which it is achieving cost reductions as a result of learning. The kinds of learning that lead to cost reduction for the typical foreign investor (who has already learned the basic technology) include (*a*) overcoming initial technical, marketing and organization problems of local adaptation, and (*b*) substantial increases in labour productivity as the operations of manufacture become familiar routine; (*a*) and (*b*) permit a reduction in the number of foreign personnel required during the breaking-in phase. In addition, interviewing of managements suggest that in some cases the cost of capital is reduced after the period of prime risk, i.e. the investor's willingness to accept a lower rate of return after capital recovery.[1] By far the greatest part of these cost reductions are achieved within a three- to five-year period; further cost reductions are very gradual and consist primarily in replacing foreign technicians, supervisors and management staff with local personnel.

In practice protective tariffs are generally set considerably higher than 'learning' requirements would seem to justify, unless heavy emphasis is placed upon the need for premium returns for bearing risk and uncertainty. We may consider the case of unbleached textiles (grey cloth), which received protection equivalent to 55 % of the value

[1] The entrepreneurial decision-making criteria implied in the capital recovery notion (payout period), a rule of thumb applied to risky investments, is discussed by William J. Baumol in his *Economic Theory and Operations Analysis*, 2nd ed., Englewood Cliffs, N.J. 1965, chapter 19.

One further source of cost reduction in the typical foreign investment project occurs, not as a result of learning, but through achieving economies of scale which could have been realized immediately. This is related to the investor's desire to minimize the amount of capital he puts at risk: the initial plant is frequently sub-optimal with respect to unit cost, but is subsequently extended when it becomes apparent that the venture is going to be successful. In Nigeria the writer has observed that this 'expansion' usually occurs toward the end of the project's second year of operation.

of the imported product, as a fairly representative case. The production costs are those prevailing after the first year of operation; the investors made an 8*d.* per yard import duty a condition of their investment.[1]

	Cost of production per square yard (*d.*)
Cotton	6·0
Chemicals and materials	0·2
Labour and management	3·3
Electricity, fuel, water	1·2
Spares and maintenance	0·7
Depreciation	1·1
Other	1·5
	14·0
Maximum ex-factory price (import c.i.f. 14·6*d.*+8*d.* duty)	22·6
Profit margin	8·6

The potential maximum profit margin of 8·6*d.* is more than double the return to labour, and even exceeds raw material costs; it would seem hard to justify such a high level of protection, beyond providing a short-run quasi-monopoly return to innovation. Apart from the question of returns to capital, the cost-reducing effects of improved efficiency within the industry are more or less limited to labour and depreciation costs, and in aggregate would be unlikely to surpass 2*d.* per yard.

EFFECTIVE PROTECTION, RESOURCE ALLOCATION AND INDUSTRIAL GROWTH

Consideration of the foregoing data brings out the fact that substantial elements of an industry's cost represent external purchases (e.g. cotton, chemicals, spares and equipment, electricity, fuel) whose contribution to total cost cannot be reduced to any significant degree by improved efficiency within the industry. When those costs which are under the control of the industry are compared to the amount of tariff protection being extended to finance the learning process involved in their dimunition, it becomes clear that effective protection is much greater than it nominally appears.[2]

In the case of grey cloth, for which a tariff of 8*d.* provides a nominal protection of 55 %, the actual *gross* value added by the manufacturing

[1] The tariff was granted, later increased to 10*d.* and then 12*d.* Cost and price data refer to 1961, based on a report prepared by Scheuer Textile Consultants with certain minor revisions as suggested to the writer by the Production Manager of Kaduna Textiles Limited. For further discussion of data and sources, see chapter 4.

[2] This simple but important discovery was first made in 1955 by Clarence L. Barber in 'Canadian Tariff Policy', *Canadian Journal of Economics and Political Science*, vol. XXI, November 1955, pp. 513–30.

processes of spinning and weaving is 7·7*d.* when measured at world prices (see table 11); the actual rate of protection is thus 104 %. Even this understates the effective rate of protection: to find the *net* value added by the textile industry proper we must subtract all externally purchased commodity inputs which go into the spinning and weaving process – starch, electricity, fuel, and capital equipment (depreciation).[1] To the extent that the production of these external inputs is free of import-content and is subject to economies of scale and learning, we may wish to protect them as well; in this case such justified protection would be limited to electricity (which, being an intermediate commodity, must perforce receive any tariff subsidy via protection for its customer industries). At a maximum, protection should be computed on the basis of *domestic* value added.

Given the fact that tariffs have been set on the basis of c.i.f. import values, the divergence of the effective rate of protection from the nominal rate proves to be a matter of considerable importance. Three interrelated effects of conventional tariff-making may be identified: (*i*) it provides excessive protection to individual industries, (*ii*) it distorts investment priorities and leads to a mal-allocation of resources, and (*iii*) it inflates the domestic industrial cost structure so that after the first round of 'easy' import-substitution further industrial growth on the basis of vertical linkages is very difficult. We have demonstrated the first proposition; we now turn to the second.

Again we take as our example the very important case of textiles. Table 15 presents the hierarchy of net output implicit in Nigeria's imports and indicates the extent to which tariffs have increased the maximum value-added limit for each process or group of processes. The cost of cotton is that for Japan; the cost of yarn, grey cloth, bleached cloth and printed cloth are the c.i.f. values of the competitive imports.[2]

The tariffs shown in table 15B are as of mid-1964: the duty on grey cloth had been raised to 12*d.* and that on prints to 16*d*; process (5) is carried out on the basis of Japanese grey cloth imported at a concessionary tariff rate of 1·8*d.* The principal lesson to be learned from Table 15 at this point is that tariff-making of the conventional variety strongly tends to be such as to yield perverse allocational effects: the shallower manufacturing processes receive a proportionately larger protective subsidy than do industries contributing a greater net output.

The fact that the protectiveness of a tariff varies inversely with the value-added/gross output ratio reinforces other reasons why assembly operations and 'finishing touches' consumer goods production tends to

[1] In national income accounting depreciation is treated as part of value added, but this would clearly be inappropriate in the present context.

[2] A more complete discussion and evaluation of these data will be found in chapter 4.

precede intermediate and capital goods industries. The later development of vertically linked industries is made difficult because they must either cut into the subsidy of the first industry, which is likely to be resisted, or result in an increase in tariffs which raises the final price and further constricts the size of the market.

Table 15. *Tariffs, value added and investment priority*

(pence per yard, 1961)

A. *Value-added structure of imported cloth*

Cost of cotton	6·9	Cost of grey cloth	14·6
Value added in spinning	4·6	Value added in bleaching	1·9
Cost of yarn	11·5	Cost of bleached cloth	16·3
Value added in weaving	3·1	Value added in printing	5·5
Cost of grey cloth	14·6	Cost of printed cloth	22·0

B. *Value-added in local production*

Process	Production without tariff	tariff	Production with tariff	Effective Protection (%)
(1) Spinning	4·6	3·5	8·1	76
(2) Spinning and weaving	7·7	12·0	19·7	155
(3) Spinning, weaving and bleaching	9·6	12·0	21·6	125
(4) Spinning, weaving, bleaching and printing	15·1	16·0	31·3	105
(5) Bleaching and printing	7·4	14·2	21·8	191

TARIFF-MAKING AND TARIFF UTILIZATION

It is germane at this point to inquire how protective tariffs are actually set. They are not set by the government acting on its own initiative, but rather by a process of negotiation between the potential investor(s) and public officials.[1] The initiative originates with the former who submits a request for a tariff increase (and perhaps also for duty relief on imported raw materials), supported by an accompanying investment proposal and set of cost estimates. After evaluating the proposal the government usually agrees to some combination of protective tariff and import duty relief, which may or may not satisfy the prospective investor.

There are a number of reasons why the tariff is set higher than the differential costs of production would seem to justify. On the one hand, the investor finds it prudent to pad his estimated costs – the salary and maintenance costs of expatriate personnel, the length of the break-in period, the cost of maintenance and repairs, and such other items as can not easily be verified. For its part the government is not equipped to

[1] The principal ministries involved are Commerce and Industry and Finance. All final decisions are taken by the Council of Ministers.

make a thorough technical investigation; it can do little more than check raw material prices and local wage rates. A desire to increase the tax revenue on the remaining imports of the product in question,[1] the intense political pressure to push through the project from the region of its prospective location[2] and, very occasionally, the corruptibility of individuals in ministerial and junior ministerial positions, also operate to yield an over-generous protective subsidy.

Beyond these inefficiencies in the tariff-making process, there are two structural features of the import substitution situation which have tended to produce the same result. The first is that overseas suppliers are frequently prepared to accept reduced margins, lowering the c.i.f. price, during the infant's critical first year or so, in the hopes of protecting their export market.[3] The second problem is that of 'dumping', which occurs as a result of excess capacity in the exporting country or because some eastern European country may wish to obtain foreign exchange which is freely convertible to sterling. The consequence of these features of the import trade has been that in a number of cases (e.g. cement, singlets, yarn, various metal products, shoes) the initial tariff had to be raised further in order to insure the marketability of local production.

Where high tariff must be imposed (*a*) to keep out competitive imports, (*b*) to correct the balance-of-payments, and/or (*c*) to raise public revenue, it is possible to offset the subsidy this confers upon local producers by the use of excise taxes. This technique of pairing excise taxes with tariff increases was introduced in Nigeria for a wide range of products in August 1964. Although this does nothing to reduce industrial costs it does divert a portion of the monopoly rents to the public coffers.

Our discussion up to this point has been premised on incomplete import substitution: when importation ceases the tariff may no longer be fully exploited in the price-setting of domestic manufacturers and/or their distributors. The mechanism which translates cost reduction into price reduction is competition among domestic producers. It was

[1] As an example of the revenue motive, after granting an additional 4*d*. increase to the pre-existing 4*d*. revenue duty to provide the requested 8*d*. per yard protection on grey cloth in 1956, for revenue purposes the duty on this substantial import was subsequently raised to 10*d*. and then 12*d*. Although the producer agreed not to exploit the higher tariff, the government apparently overlooked the fact that as long as imports bearing the higher duty were still selling distributors would take advantage of the differential and sell the local product at the going price. Similarly, during the first few years of production the Nkalagu cement works allowed its distributors to exploit transport protection prior to introducing regional pricing.

[2] It is a reflection of the intensity of regional political pressure for industrialization that an impartial tariff commission or similar technical body, first proposed in the mid-1950s, has not been established or even seriously discussed.

[3] Occasionally a new industry must also be prepared to wait out the running down of mass inventories imported by the merchants prior to the imposition of the protective duty in anticipation of it.

precisely in this fashion that the great protectionist Friedrich List envisaged infant industries maturing and eventually selling at prices below the comparable c.i.f. import values; the protective tariffs remain, but are not utilized.[1] This ideal pattern of development is shown diagrammatically in figure 2.

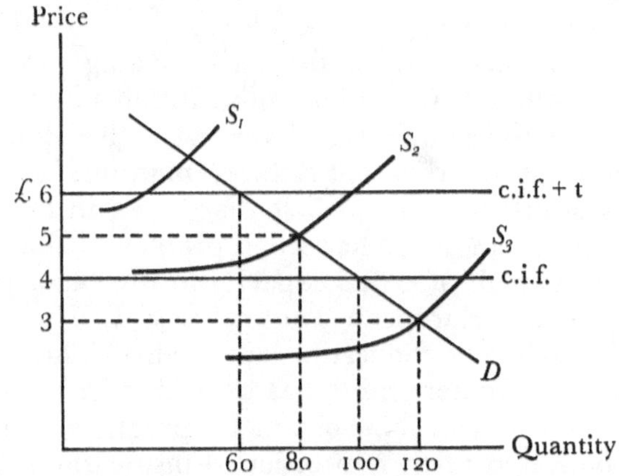

FIG. 2. Infant industry and tariff utilization.

	Total consumption	Domestic production	Price (£)
Pre-tariff	100	—	4
Infant industry (S_1)	60	30	6
Adolescent industry (S_2)	80	80	5
Mature industry (S_3)	120	120	3

If in the practical world tariffs cannot be lowered to induce an ageing infant industry to undertake price reductions, then the stimulation of domestic competition by encouraging as many investors as possible in each industry may well be the best feasible alternative. And in this regard countries with large markets, like Nigeria, are mightily blest. Viewed from this perspective, *if* internal competition is effective, over-generous tariffs are less pernicious in the long run than implied by our earlier analysis; and, *ceteris paribus*, high tariffs are more effective than low tariffs in attracting additional producers.[2] The following two chapters provide some evidence as to what extent and under what circumstances the net benefits of a high tariff policy may exceed those of an allocatively-efficient but promotionally-weak low tariff policy.

[1] Friedrich List, *The National System of Political Economy*, London 1928, Second Book.

[2] The validity of this proposition requires, *inter alia*, that the additional entrants so attracted are 'stickers' who will stay in the market over the long haul rather than 'snatchers' (borrowing J. R. Hicks's terminology) who are in for a quick killing at current prices and out when margins decline.

Part 2

CHAPTER 3

FROM TRADE TO MANUFACTURE: THE MECHANICS OF IMPORT SUBSTITUTION

The preceding chapter considered the critical features of the Nigerian economic environment as it relates to entrepreneurial behaviour. Section I of the present chapter sets forth an hypothesis concerning the primary motive which has channelled entrepreneurial activity into industrial pursuits during the past decade. Section II is a history of the changing market structure of the import merchandise trade over the period 1930–60. Section III reviews the major industrial investment decisions during 1958–65 and the context in which they were made.

I

In a predominantly free enterprise developing economy what are the factors which bring about the transition from importation to local manufacture? By and large, economists have explained this process in a simple and straightforward manner: when the market, as mapped out by imports, has reached or is approaching that size which will support a plant of optimum or near optimum efficiency, an investor who is in search of profitable opportunities will come forward, given appropriate publicity and the provision of reasonable tariff protection and other fiscal incentives. Where, as often happens, markets have reached this critical size and failed to evoke the required investment, the economist takes refuge in *ceteris imparibus*: insufficient publicity or incentive, fear of political instability, foreign exchange restrictions and the like. And indeed in most cases one or more of such impediments are present; yet in other cases (e.g. Brazil, India), where there is no apparent difference in the strength of such obstacles, private foreign investment does occur. The traditional interpretation based on the 'technological threshold' would thus seem to contain a necessary but not a sufficient condition for explaining the investment decision.

An analysis of the history of industrial investment in Nigeria would seem to indicate that the size of the market is indeed an important consideration, but that some 'competitive threshold' as opposed to a 'technological threshold' has been the critical factor. As we saw in chapter 2, prior to the late 1950s few industries serving local demand were developed despite the existence of many markets which would have supported a number of minimum-sized efficient factories. Then, from about 1958 in the face of a gradually deteriorating balance-of-payments position, growing uncertainty about political stability and weakening governmental administration,[1] there was a sharp upsurge in private industrial investment.

The lack of correlation between the technological threshold and the time at which the first import-replacing investment occurs can be seen in table 16. The defective engineering definition of minimum size

Table 16. *The technological threshold and import substitution*

Product and minimum size plant	M.S.P. attnd.	Start -up	Imports at start-up	Add. plants 3 years[a]	Total plants 1965
Asbestos-cement products (17,000 t)[b]	1955	1961	28,359 t	1	3
Galvanized iron sheet (20,000 t)[b]	1951	1964	36,567 t	2	3
Cement (30,000 t)	1923	1957	510,237 t	—	7
Cotton textiles (8 m. yds.)	1890s	1957	156 m.yds.	—	10
Tyres and tubes (2,500 t)[b]	...	1962	...[c]	1	2
Flour (25,000 t)	1953	1962	61,152 t	—	1
Biscuits (2,000 t)[b]	1953	1961	4,000 t	2	3
Leather shoes and sandals (75,000 p)	1947	1963	3·2 m.p.	2	3
Rubber and canvas shoes (250,000 p)	1947	1959	3·6 m.p.	3	6
Paint (120,000 g)	...	1962	...[c]	7	8
Bicycle assembly (30,000)[b]	1946	1958	114,753	2	3
Aluminium holloware (n.a.)	...	1960	470 t	2	3
Enamelware (n.a.)	...	1959	17,300 t	3	5
Gramophone records (50,000 r)[b]	1944	1962	1·3 m.r.	1	2
Steel door/window frames (400 t)[b]	pre-1954	1958	2,700 t	2	5
Candy (500 t)	1947	1959	2,400 t	2	6

t = tons; g = gallons; p = pairs; r = single records; m = millions.
[a] Additional plants established within three years of the first plant.
[b] Announced capacity of first plant to go into production.
[c] Not available in comparable units.

SOURCE: Federal Ministry of Commerce and Industry, *Industrial Directory 1965*, Lagos 1966; Federal Office of Statistics, *Nigeria Trade Summary*, various years.

plant, using physical quantity rather than sales revenue, results in an inflated minimum size. In fact, in the cases of paint, tyres, aluminium holloware and enamelware most of the plants are operating at sub-capacity outputs well below the stipulated minimum – made possible (and probably beneficial in the long run) by 'excessive' tariff protection. The overall picture of import substitution portrayed in table 16 is of considerable 'delay', followed by a sudden cluster of investments in each industry.

The hypothesis offered to explain this observed pattern is that competitive pressures, generated by a rapidly growing demand, have con-

[1] A result of, respectively, the drawing down of foreign exchange reserves from 1955 onwards, internal political problems connected with tribalism and regional separatism, and the rapid expansion of government services coupled with an even more rapid Nigerianization.

stituted the catalyst (for a majority of cases) in transforming ample market opportunities and fiscal incentives into actual investments under the seemingly unfavourable conditions noted earlier. The competitive pressures are of essentially two kinds. The first is related to the number and size of distributive firms engaged in the import trade; the competitive pressure is on the general level of distributive margins. The second kind pertains to specific commodity markets and affects both local distributors and overseas manufacturers; the pressure here is primarily on volume of sales and share of the market. Assuming some *minimum sensible* threshold has been met, the positive entrepreneurial response to both these kinds of 'market threatening' is to protect one's 'stake in the market' by going into local manufacture. The competition from other sellers is eliminated by virtue of the protective tariff.

Thus, as discussed in the last chapter, the competition-eliminating effect of the tariff is a fact of central importance for the individual firm's market strategy. For the price of an industrial investment, including the risk of its possible failure, a seller can transform the competitive market he currently faces into a monopolistic (or oligopolistic) market. In consequence of the elimination of competition a firm will be able to (*a*) expand its total sales, and (*b*) increase net earnings by an even greater proportion as a result of a tariff-enhanced unit profit margin. Not only does the tariff secure the seller who makes an industrial commitment against the competition of similar products, but it also shields him to a substantial degree from technically more advanced varieties or otherwise superior articles which in the absence of fiscal discrimination might pre-empt the market. Hence for both the overseas manufacturer and the distributing merchant firm the optimum solution to mounting competition and threatened markets will often be the establishment of a local factory.

There are a number of implications of the foregoing market protection theory that should be noted. First there is no reason why the competitive threshold of particular product markets should necessarily coincide with the general onset of competitive pressures. Both the beer and cement industries (discussed below) are instances of early market-protecting investments. A second important implication of our thesis is that if market shares of overseas suppliers are atomistically small, and if technical skill barriers are sufficiently high to preclude redeploying merchant firms, import substitution may be long delayed because the interests of no single firm are materially jeopardized. The outstanding instance here is cotton textiles, which had reached the technological threshold before the turn of the century. There is also a question as to what is the relevant market that is being protected. While widening the concept beyond the national market threatens to empty the hypothesis of any operational content, it is nevertheless true that in the cases of beer, tyres, and aluminium rolling, investors were reacting to market strategy factors that were partially external to Nigeria.

It is obvious that this theory will lack predictive power for those investors who have no prior interest in the market. The latter, at least in Nigeria's case, can be classed into three broad groups: overseas manufacturers seeking an outlet for redundant equipment, sellers of new machinery who are prepared to take a small share of the equity in partnership with some other investor (usually the government), and, lastly, the 'unattached' firm or promoter-entrepreneur of economic theory who is simply seeking profitable opportunities wherever they may be. If we hold public investment separate, the quantitative significance of non-market-protecting investment relative to all import-replacing investment is small.

How might we establish a preferential claim for a market protection interpretation, as against the most plausible alternative explanation – that the recent industrialization has been induced by the rise in tariffs and Government promotional and incentive policies? Perhaps the first area of evidence to examine is the public statements of the firms themselves. It is possible to cull from the annual reports of former overseas suppliers statements such as the following, from the parent company of a manufacturer of steel door and window frames in Western Nigeria:

> Our overseas companies have all been established in the normal course of trade in order to protect and exploit the goodwill which we have built up through many years of activity in export markets.[1]

Even stronger support for the market protection hypothesis can be mustered from a major article, 'Redeployment, An Aspect of Development in Tropical Africa', written and published by the largest distributive firm in Nigeria, the United Africa Company:

> Once the development of a country is under way, incomes begin to rise and the demand for consumer goods and services increases. When this happens, the local market comes to assume a growing importance, and new and competitive suppliers of the goods and services in demand are attracted. This is what has been happening in the countries of tropical Africa during the post-war years. Some of the new and competitive suppliers are local traders and wholesalers; others are overseas manufacturers no longer content to leave the local marketing of their wares, as hitherto, to established general merchants, unless on a favoured basis; still others are the new industries that are being developed locally to produce goods and services that

[1] Annual Statement of the Chairman, Crittall-Hope Limited, cited in *West Africa*, 17 July 1966. The occasion for the remark was the recent imposition of discriminatory taxes on foreign investment by the British Government.

previously had to be imported. As many of these new local suppliers are merely taking advantage of the expanding market and are operating on very low overheads, their entry into the field has had the effect of reducing the overall profit margins of the established merchants whose overheads, arising from their world-wide buying machinery and their networks of trading posts, are necessarily on a sizeably larger scale; while the direct incursion of overseas and local manufacturers into the market has detracted from the range of merchandise being handled by the general merchants.

... To withdraw, however, is only in order to reinvest to better purpose. To firms with their sights adjusted to the future, new horizons of opportunity are constantly opening up to replace those which are closing down.

... As produce buying, general retailing and many staples of general merchandising pass into the hands of a multiplicity of new competitors, two broad yet interconnected avenues of development open up. These are:

(*a*) the specialized distribution and marketing of a selected range of merchandise on behalf of, or in conjunction with both overseas and local manufacturers; and

(*b*) the setting up and operation of local industries, sometimes on a wholly-owned basis and sometimes in collaboration with technical partners, to manufacture and process a widening and progressively sophisticated range of goods, many of which hitherto have had to be imported.[1]

A second source of evidence is two questionnaire surveys of foreign-owned manufacturing firms carried out in 1964. In both cases questions were asked about the motivation for investment. In A. N. Hakam's survey of 68 firms the four most frequently cited motives were:

The firm had long held a good market relation with Nigeria. Aiming to preserve the market for the parent company in face of rising duties, possible rise in duties or local competition. [58 %.]

Aim to expand sales into a new market otherwise difficult by just exporting. [30 %.]

As a result of the parent company's strategy of investing in key global areas. Convinced that Nigeria is a very important area and that it might be too late to gain entry profitably into the market if the decision were postponed too long. [28 %.]

Aim at forestalling a major competitor's move or possible move into Nigeria. [26 %.][2]

In Ranald May's survey of twenty-six firms the five most frequently cited motives were as follows: to avoid being shut out by tariffs (15),

[1] The United Africa Company, *Statistical and Economic Review*, no. 28, April 1963, pp. 3, 15, 16.

[2] A. N. Hakam, 'The Motivation to Invest', *Nigerian Journal of Economic and Social Studies*, vol. 8, March 1966, p. 50.

specific invitation from the Nigerian Government (11), long term prospects of the Nigerian economy (9), to take advantage of increased demand (7), and activities of competitors (7).[1] Explaining his results May states:

... The erection of tariff barriers to protect infant industries placed many U.K. companies in a dilemma. In most cases they would have preferred to have continued to supply goods manufactured in this country [England]. Due to economies of scale this could be done in most cases more cheaply. This policy would also considerably reduce the amount of capital at risk overseas. However, the pressure to set up local manufacturing projects was strong. To opt out of local manufacture at this stage would not only mean an immediate loss of export market but make it extraordinarily difficult to re-enter the field at a later stage. . . . The activities of competitors, often European, also influenced a favourable investment decision. This helped to crystallise a decision which might otherwise have been postponed.[2]

Both surveys reveal a considerable preponderance of motives related to protecting a stake in the market. However what is left tangled by these questions-and-response is the causal order: does the high tariff induce the initiation of local production or does the pioneer investment lead to the high tariff? However, elsewhere in their papers both investigators provide an answer, which is in agreement with the discussion of tariff-making in the foregoing chapter:

What was more eagerly sought after [than pioneer income tax relief] was tariff protection, without which many projects would not be able to face competition from imports.[3]

As for tariff protection, infrequent citation of this factor as an investment incentive is due in part to the relatively low duties that Nigeria imposed on most consumer goods up to 1965. As mentioned earlier in contrast to Latin American, Asian and Middle Eastern countries, Nigerian duties in general are only about one-third to half the former, thus often insufficiently protective for a new industry. This was the case with local industries producing paint, perfume, biscuits, beer, enamelware, asbestos cement, butter and radios to mention a few and which have all experienced import competition at least in the short run, because of insufficient duty protection. This protection comes at a later stage, after the firms have been established in the country. Thus the generally low level of duties does not act as an incentive to draw investments into the country, unless there is some definite anticipation of a rise. Furthermore most of the higher duties have been only recently imposed and apply to existing Nigerian industries only.[4]

An interesting evaluation of investment proposals that failed to materialize, primarily American, is provided by a former investment

[1] Ranald S. May, 'Direct Overseas Investment in Nigeria 1953–63,' *Scottish Journal of Political Economy*, vol. XII, November 1965, p. 252.
[2] *Ibid.* pp. 252–3.
[3] *Ibid.* p. 253.
[4] Hakam, *loc. cit.* p. 55.

promotion adviser to the Federal Ministry of Commerce and Industry.[1] The sponsors of these proposals did not spend sufficient time researching and negotiating their project, were typically unwilling to provide detailed cost estimates when requesting tariff protection, and, in general, demanded a rate of return far higher than their successful confrères. And perhaps most to the point, none of these investors had prior contact with the Nigerian market.

In so far as our explanatory hypothesis rests upon the market behaviour of firms, another, perhaps more appropriate test of its validity is to observe the historical behaviour of firms in individual markets as these markets expand and become more competitive. Such an historical recounting is undertaken in the following section.

Before proceeding, however, it is relevant to point out, if only fleetingly, that the logic of the market protection hypothesis suggests that similar behaviour should occur in other countries which possess a large and expanding market. And there is considerable evidence that such is the case. Questionnaire studies have revealed a range of motives very much the same as those uncovered by May and Hakam in Nigeria.[2] In a recent study of the foreign investment decision process as viewed from within the firm, Yair Aharoni identifies four initiating forces leading to the *consideration* of a foreign investment, each of which can be interpreted as a specific kind of market threat.[3] Aharoni formulates the *decision* itself as being a function of the level of the cumulative personal and organizational 'commitment' to making the investment; in all but a few of the cases cited the commitment seemed to vary with the volume of sales involved, i.e. the size of the stake in the market.[4]

II

IMPORT TRADE AND THE EMERGENCE OF COMPETITION, 1930–1960

Following the trade wars and consolidations of the 1920s, the Nigerian market came to be dominated by a relatively small number of large,

[1] Simon Williams, 'Negotiating Investment in Emerging Countries', *Harvard Business Review*, January/February 1965, pp. 89–99.

[2] Lincoln Gordon and Engelbert Grommers, *United States Manufacturing Investment in Brazil*, Harvard Business School, Boston 1962; and Raymond F. Mikesell, *U.S. Private and Government Investment Abroad*, Eugene 1962.

[3] Yair Aharoni, *The Foreign Investment Decision Process*, Harvard Business School, Boston 1966, p. 55: '1. An outside proposal, provided it comes from a source that cannot be easily ignored. The most frequent sources of such proposals are foreign governments, the distributors of the company's products, and its clients. 2. Fear of losing a market. 3. The "band wagon" effect: very successful activities abroad of a competing firm in the same line of business, or a general belief that investment in some area is a "must". 4. Strong competition from abroad in the home market.'

[4] *Ibid.* chapters 5 to 7 and *passim*.

highly integrated merchant firms. These were the United Africa Company (a Unilever affiliate), John Holt, Paterson Zochonis, Compagnie Française de l'Afrique Occidentale (CFAO), Societé Commerciale de L'Ouest Africain (SCOA) and the Swiss Union Trading Company (UTC). Two of the largest of these firms, UAC and John Holt, operated both ocean shipping companies and inland water transport services for evacuating the country's export produce which they purchased and bringing in the country's imports which they sold. The merchants were not only importers and carriers, they operated as wholesalers, as providers of credit and were influential in the retail trade. The high capital requirements of merchandise trading – arising from the maintenance of overseas buying offices, large investment in storage and handling facilities relative to the volume of sales (owing to a geographically extensive but shallow market), the necessity to provide credit and the long trading capital turnover period – imposed a natural barrier to the entrance of potential competitors. To these natural barriers were added a number of man-made impediments to the possible emergence of serious competitors – a conscious policy of pre-empting the market by handling all ranges of merchandise,[1] formal cartel arrangements beginning in 1934, government import-rationing (1940–9) on the basis of a quota system and the overt exercise of market power by the merchants themselves.[2]

Given this stable and highly favourable market situation the interest of the merchants *vis-à-vis* industrialization was a conserving one. John Mars, writing in 1944, analysed their position as follows:

> The attitude of extra-territorial trading companies in this matter of processing and manufacture is understandable, and the motives which inspire their attitude can be briefly stated. The companies do not wish to harm home manufacturers and home processors with whom they have contractual relations or in whose property they are financially interested. They do not wish to lose their import trade in manufactured commodities which compensates them for the low profit on export trade. In addition the import trade greatly reduces the overhead costs on the purchase of goods for export, probably to about three quarters of what they would be for pure importers in comparable circumstances. In so far as an extra-territorial company is also its own carrier as, for example, the UAC and John Holt, the two-way business also helps to keep down costs of carrying. This is, to a smaller

[1] 'If the large firms do not carry a full range of merchandise small-scale and new independent competitors will find it easier to establish themselves in special lines. In this way these competitors may accumulate funds, gain knowledge of the market, and establish contacts with customers. This may enable some of their number to develop into formidable competitors, to enlarge the range of merchandise carried and to extend their activities. Thus the lower costs of more specialized operations may be outweighed by the greater risks of the emergence of new competitors.' P. T. Bauer, *West African Trade*, Cambridge 1954, p. 128.

[2] For a discussion of the actual use of their market power, see *ibid.* chapters 10 and 11.

extent, also true if the extra-territorial company is not its own carrier. If there were no import traffic, the shipping rates on export traffic would have to go up correspondingly.[1]

Mars goes on to point out that by experience and inclination, by skills required and the commitment of long term fixed investment, the merchant firms were ill-prepared to take leading roles in the country's industrialization.

This situation was transformed during the latter part of the 1950s. The rapid post-war growth in imports (from £20m. in 1946 to £166m. in 1958) had a profound effect on the structure of competition. The general enrichment of the market attracted many new sellers and, at the same time, by permitting geographic specialization reduced the capital requirements for entry. These new sellers may be divided into three groups: merchant firms, manufacturers' sales agencies and Nigerian traders.

The first group of importers/distributors who have grown to importance in the Nigerian market, contributing to the rising tide of competition, were in existence prior to World War II but on a very small scale. These are the Indian merchants of K. Chelleram & Sons, J. T. Chanrai & Co., Bhojson, Indian Emporium and Inlaks. By the late 1950s K. Chelleram, for instance, had become Nigeria's fifth largest importer. A second group of new merchants probably quantitatively more significant, are former Greek and Levantine produce buyers and numerous Lebanese retailers who found the import trade more profitable than their previous activities.[2] Outstanding in this group are Mandilas & Karibaris, Nassars, Arab Brothers, S. Raccah and A. G. Leventis. The latter, a Cypriot Greek who started out as a produce buyer in 1938,[3] has developed the importing side of his business to an annual volume in excess of £15m, ranking third only to the United Africa Company and John Holt.

A second important group to enter the import-wholesale trade has been overseas manufacturers. As the economy has expanded the

[1] J. Mars, 'Extra-territorial Enterprises', in *Mining, Commerce and Finance in Nigeria*, Margery Perham, ed., London 1948, p. 68.

[2] The term Levantine is used loosely to apply to some 15,000 Lebanese, Palestinians, Cypriots, Syrians and Greeks whose families came to Nigeria between 1910 and 1940. Initially engaged in transport and small-scale trade (the majority of Lebanese are still in retail and wholesale trade, primarily in Northern Nigeria) the enterprising Levantines have from small beginnings developed many important industrial concerns (e.g. soap, groundnut crushing, plastics, rubber crêping). Levantine enterprise is distinguished from European commercial activity by (*a*) family rather than corporate organization, (*b*) more labour-intensive and smaller scale of operation, (*c*) lower levels of education, and (*d*) quasi-permanent residence in Nigeria.

[3] Leventis, who had begun trading in Africa at the age of 18, had worked his way up to General Manager of G. B. Olivant's operations in the Gold Coast, when the latter was bought out by U.A.C. in 1937.

potential demand for specific products has grown to the point where Nigeria has become a very important concern, to both those manufacturers already supplying the market and for those who are looking for new markets. The traditional stocking and distribution arrangement of the general merchants was no longer adequate; advertising, intensive promotion, specialized distribution and after-service were required to maximize the sales of their particular brand. Many manufacturers—Nestlés, Tate & Lyle, Imperial Chemical Industries, Philips, National Cash Register, British Paints, to name but a few – accordingly set up their own machinery of importation, market promotion and wholesale distribution. Other manufacturers arranged exclusive agencies among established importers, including the general merchants.

A third group who have encroached on the traditional preserve of the expatriate trading companies are Nigerian traders. From a figure of about 5 % in 1949, the Office of Statistics estimates that in 1963 Nigerians were responsible for approximately a fifth of the country's imports.[1] To some extent this has been a result of the gradually increasing skill and capital resources of Nigerian traders. Two other factors, however, have been quantitatively more important in explaining the recorded increase. The first is the growing practice by market-seeking overseas manufacturers of financing the Nigerian importer on the basis of 90-day credit and providing him with the services of a local expatriate confirming and ware-housing agent. Second, since 1958–9, when UAC and John Holt began their withdrawal from general importing as a result of the already intense competition, the latter, presumably to avoid any major dislocations, have provided their former Nigerian customers with clearance, warehousing and credit facilities for a flat 10 % commission. Thus assisted, Nigerian wholesalers have been able to become importers on their own account. John Holt has gone even further and formed these independent traders into trading companies and provided them with managerial assistance – a dramatic example of the indirect benefits of foreign enterprise.

Thus the enrichment of the market attracted a host of new distributors into the import trade. Moreover, the established trading concerns found themselves not only threatened, but at a competitive disadvantage. Carrying with them a country-wide distribution network, foreign buying offices and ponderous administrative machinery from an earlier era when their market position rested upon horizontal integration and self-sufficiency, the general merchants were now burdened with higher overhead costs and less flexibility as they faced intense

[1] Bauer, *op. cit.* chapter 5, for 1949; for 1963, data supplied by the Federal Office of Statistics.

competition from numerous purveyors specializing in specific products and limiting themselves to the richest geographic areas.

A measure of the magnitude of the resultant changes in market structure can be obtained by observing changes in the share of the leading merchant firms in the distribution of imported goods. In 1949 the three largest importers accounted for 49 % of all traded commodities; in 1963 the three leading importers accounted for about 16 %, or one-third of the earlier figure.[1] Similarly with the source of supply: the figures below show that since 1939 British manufacturers have lost over a third of their share in the market to non-Commonwealth suppliers. Coupled with the observation that the number of brands and volume of advertising and promotional campaigning have multiplied in recent years, we may infer that this more than proportionate growth in non-Commonwealth imports has been associated with (*i*) a very much larger number of overseas manufacturers developing a stake in the Nigerian market, and (*ii*) intensifying competition within the individual product markets.[2] It is also to be noted that more than half of this shift in market shares has occurred since 1959, coinciding with the spurt in industrial investments. Taking the Nigerian market as a whole, we may say that the 'competitive threshold' to local industrialization was reached in about 1959.

Table 17. *Imports by country of origin*

(%)

	1939	1949	1959	1963	1965
United Kingdom	55	51	46	34	31
Other Commonwealth	8	8	6	7	7
Rest of the world	37	40	48	59	62
Total imports (£m.)	7	58	178	207	275

SOURCES: Nigeria *Trade Summary* and *Trade Report*, various years.

To recapitulate our discussion of the changing structure of the Nigerian market up to this point, as a result of the growth in the size of the economy many more sellers became interested in entering the Nigerian market. At the same time the ease of so doing was greatly increased: with the bounding growth in purchasing power geographic and commodity specialization became possible, thereby drastically

[1] *Ibid.*

[2] Should the reader doubt that the entry of new sellers has far more than offset the growth in demand with consequent pressure on profit margins, he is referred to company reports (published for the United Africa Company, John Holt, Paterson Zochonis) for evidence on the losses that were made in the general import lines, prior to the merchants' withdrawal from these areas. See also the previously cited article 'Redeployment' in United Africa Company, *Statistical and Economic Review*, no. 28, April 1963.

reducing capital entry requirements. With overseas suppliers demanding exclusive agencies and promotion of specific brands the general merchants' ability to dominate individual product lines was dissipated. The changing composition of demand towards more sophisticated goods requiring maintenance and after-care forced distributors, large and small alike, to move in the same direction, tying themselves to a single supplier. This alignment of specific product brands with particular merchants contributed to the sharpening of competition.

Table 18. *The changing composition of imports – selected commodities*

(%)

	1954	1963
Salt	1·1	1·0
Flour	1·5	0·1
Stockfish	4·6	3·1
Beer	2·0	0·4
Cement	2·7	1·0
Cotton piece goods	14·5	10·3
Rayon piece goods	9·1	2·3
Corrugated iron sheets	3·1	1·1
	38·6	19·3
Drugs and medicine	1·5	2·5
Electrical machinery and apparatus	2·7	4·8
Non-electrical machinery	3·5	8·2
Constructional steel	2·6	5·3
Cars and kitcars	1·9	2·9
Lorries and chassis	2·7	2·2
Other road vehicles and parts	1·3	2·4
Paper and board	0·9	2·5
	17·1	30·8

SOURCE: *Nigerian Trade Journal*, April/June 1956 and 1964.

It is worthwhile to pause for a moment to describe the changing nature of imports just mentioned. As late as 1954 eight staple items constituted 39 % of total imports as shown in table 18. By and large these products require little in the way of specialized storage or handling no after-service and, with the exception of printed textiles, call for no specialized marketing skill. With rising incomes, the growth of more sophisticated urban consumer demands, the need for technically more complex capital equipment, and as a result of import substitution in certain basic lines, there has been a shift towards more complex, sophisticated products. Capital requirements tend to be higher in these non-traditional lines: the urban consumer market, for instance, is served by air-conditioned departmental stores with such features as escalators, self-service, pre-packing, hire-purchase, open refrigerated displays and so on. For vehicles, appliances and all technical items, country-wide facilities for maintenance and repair are required. Extensive advertising, large inventories of spare parts and specialized skills (e.g. pharmacy, electrical engineering) also tend to be associated with these new lines, further adding to capital and organizational requirements.

REDEPLOYMENT OF THE MERCHANTING FIRMS

The merchants' response to intensified competition, adapted as well to the changing character of demand and the political climate of independence, has been to transform themselves from general trading companies handling the full range of merchandise imports into many smaller semi-autonomous specialized marketing and manufacturing units.[1] In so doing they rid themselves of the incumbrances carried forward from an earlier era and at the same time capitalized on their accumulated experience, operating methods, local contacts and knowledge of the market. In terms of market strategy specialized merchanting represents an attempt to concentrate in the least competitive markets, i.e. those lines requiring considerable capital and technical servicing skills, while the establishment of manufacturing, involving greater risks, has the effect of denying the market to competitors altogether.

The area of importing and specialized marketing in which the firms have concentrated are departmental store merchandise, earthmoving and civil engineering machinery, air-conditioning and other electrical goods, office equipment, drugs and pharmaceuticals, and motor vehicles. All these items are imported, advertised, carried to the country's major urban centres and sold from specialized stores directly to the final consumer by the merchants themselves. Technically speaking, the much talked of withdrawal from retail trade in the 1950s may well have been reversed since the end of the decade.[2] The once central

[1] For a detailed discussion of redeployment, framed more in terms of profitable opportunities and comparative advantage than in terms of market strategy, see the previously cited article by the United Africa Company.

[2] The nature of the retail trade is, however, very different in the two instances. In the 1930s and 1940s the firms operated relatively small-scale general trading outlets; re-entry into direct selling since the late 1950s has been limited to lines requiring considerable capital and specialized technical and marketing skills.

In the earlier period withdrawl occurred in two phases. The first followed the 1929 merger which formed UAC and as Bauer has observed 'The fact that a large number of retail outlets were considered no longer necessary after the merger, suggests that the retailing activities of the previously separate firms were to a material extent governed by considerations of market strategy and counter-strategy', *West African Trade*, p. 127.

There was a further reduction of these retail outlets in Ghana and Nigeria from 1,382 in 1939 to 926 in 1952. Fred Pedler, a UAC director, gives two reasons for this second reduction.

import-wholesale trade has dwindled down to a comparatively small fraction of the merchants' turnover, primarily in printed textiles, hardware and construction materials.

But, one may ask, why have not the merchant firms simply shifted over to distribution of locally manufactured products rather than attempt to transform their basic nature? To some extent they have, but here again extensive competition has tended to keep distributive margins fairly small; moreover, the number of locally manufactured products available to the general merchants for wholesale distribution is limited. In highly competitive markets (e.g. beer, soap, tyres) the manufacturers operate their own selling and promoting organizations; for the non-differentiated commodity markets (e.g. flour, cement, enamelware) the very short capital turnover period and minimum handling, storage, invoicing, etc., has enabled low-overhead Nigerian traders, operating on bank overdrafts, to capture the bulk of this trade. The political desirability of using Nigerian distributors has re-enforced market forces. The two main distributive lines where the general merchants are still influential are printed textiles and construction materials for large-scale projects – both instances where the financial ability to carry large inventories, extend credit and maintain a stable price is an important factor.[1]

The second major area for redeployment has been manufacturing. It is through the establishment of local industry that the merchants and other competing sellers have found their most secure and favourable markets. As discussed earlier, the key to this security and high level of profitability is tariff protection. We now turn to an examination of these industrial investments and the context in which they were made.

III

INDUSTRIAL INVESTMENTS OF THE MERCHANT FIRMS

Of all the firms engaged in distribution, not only is the United Africa Company four times the size of its nearest rival, but it has redirected a

'The cost of administering numerous small stores was found to be excessive, while the difficulty of control in remote places led to heavy losses both through the deterioration of stock and through various forms of slackness and dishonesty' and 'A firm which is engaged in wholesaling as well as retailing . . . finds itself competing with its own reseller customers.' F. J. Pedler, *Economic Geography of West Africa*, London 1954, p. 145.

[1] Offset against their low overheads, short-term bank financing dictates that Nigerian traders must turn over their stock regardless of market conditions. In conditions of excess supply where the expatriate firms will withdraw Nigerians perforce continue trading, further depressing the price. When a commodity is scarce, the Nigerian trader will exact the highest price whereas the merchant, who has to consider his long-term relation to his client for a number of goods, pursues a more moderate course. Consequently markets where Nigerian traders are predominant tend to manifest considerable price fluctuation.

higher proportion of its resources into Nigeria's industrialization than any other merchant.[1]

Formed in 1929 after the trade wars of the preceding decade, UAC was the prototype exporter-merchandise importer/distributor-transporter described in section II. From its constituent companies UAC inherited two processing industries which had grown out of the produce trade – a large sawmill at Sapele established by Miller Brothers in 1917 and two (later expanded to six) palm oil bulking plants dating from 1924. In 1948 a plywood factory was added to the sawmill; the resulting company, African Timber and Plywood Ltd., employs fixed capital of £3·om. and a labour force of 3,200 – one of the country's largest industrial establishments. The bulk oil plants, on the other hand, have been gradually nationalized by the Marketing Boards, whose subsidiary the Nigerian Produce Marketing Company took up a third of the capital in 1946 and the other two-thirds in 1961. In 1953, following the lead of John Holt, UAC induced the British construction firm of Taylor Woodrow to come to Nigeria and provided half of the capital; through this holding UAC has interests in three furniture factories (1953, 1955, 1958) and a company producing pre-stressed concrete products (1954).

UAC's first industrial investment other than processing was the Nigerian Breweries Limited in 1949, one of the earliest instances of import-substitution.[2] The primary motive for UAC's initiative was market protection: the company's beer trade had already been displaced in Ghana (1932) and the Congo (1935) as a result of the establishment of local breweries by Swiss entrepreneurs. It was apparent that the Nigerian market would soon be richer than either of these and that unless UAC took the initiative a valuable merchant interest might be jeopardized.

The relatively early date of the investment in beer (the project had been mooted as early as 1937) suggests that the shift from trade to manufacture, which did not become a conscious policy as such until the late 1950s, grew out of earlier precedents. Taking another example, UAC's entry into modern consumer retailing, a field which the company pioneered, developed out of a sudden hunch in 1947 of a visiting London director that a new building with a long frontage on a main street in Lagos, intended as the company's administrative headquarters in Nigeria, should instead be converted into West Africa's first department store, making extensive use of window displays.[3] Over a decade

[1] The primary source of information for section III are interviews with various company officials, carried out in London and Nigeria 1963–5.

[2] Although this is a joint venture with the technical partner, Heinekens, and other merchant firms, the project was initiated and organized by UAC who is also the managing agent.

[3] United Africa Company, *Statistical and Economic Review*, no. 12, September 1953, p. 8.

later this form of merchandising provided a fully explored and proven avenue for redeployment (annual turnover of the Lagos Kingsway having reached £3m.); second and third stores opened in Ibadan in 1962 and in Port Harcourt in 1963.

It was not until about 1957 that conscious redeployment actually commenced. In 1958 the company began its withdrawal from the produce trade and the closing down (or transfer to Nigerians) of small outlying trading stations, and set up its first assembly plants (Bedford lorries and Raleigh bicycles). The movement towards import-substitute industries is reflected in the company's gross capital expenditures in Nigeria over the period 1956–64, as shown in table 19.

Table 19. *UAC's gross investment by sector 1956–1964*

(£000s)

Year ended September 30	Distribution	Industry	Transportation	Plantation
1956	1,186	519	296	100
1957	1,624	552	209	172
1958	1,351	508	635	232
1959	935	563	263	334
1960	1,074	1,224	40	479
1961	1,403	736	82	124
1962	1,368	1,267	48	2
1963	1,293	3,018	37	51
1964	742	1,558	303	74

SOURCE: United Africa Company, *Statistical and Economic Review*, various years; for 1963 and 1964, data supplied by the United Africa Company.

The level of the company's capital outlays for distribution appears to have been little affected by the switch from general to specialized trading. As expected, industrial investment has risen sharply, approximately trebling. On the other hand, there has been a marked reduction in investment in the transport and plantation sectors. With the exception of 1963, gross investment in Nigeria has remained fairly steady, fluctuating between £2·0 and £2·8m. per year.

Table 20 sets forth details of the individual investments in which UAC has an interest. All save one of the twenty-eight projects are directly connected to marketing activities.[1] The production of reconstituted milk, ice cream, meat products and pigs developed from retailing activities of the Kingsway stores. As a general rule of thumb, UAC will only consider an industrial investment if it represents the

[1] The exception was the plastics factory, Nipol, a goodwill venture undertaken in partnership with the Western Nigeria Development Corporation, which was built in advance of the market; losses were made for six of the first seven years of operation. When demand began to develop a Greco-Lebanese firm established and captured the bulk of the market. In August 1964 when the writer visited Nipol the management was instigating major reforms in an effort to put the enterprise on its feet.

protection of an established merchant interest, which is both sizeable and profitable. Production-wise the industry must be within the competence of the company, the Unilever organization, or a principal supplier who can be persuaded to join the venture as a technical partner.

Table 20. *Industrial investments of the United Africa Company*

Company	Product	Year of start-up	Fixed capital[a] (£1000s)	UAC equity %
African Timber & Plywood	Timber and plywood	1948	3,000	100
Nigerian Breweries (3)	Beer and minerals	1949	3,500	33
Taylor Woodrow	Building contractors	1953	500[b]	50
Nigerian Joinery (3)	Woodwork and furniture	1953	100[b]	50
Prestress	Pre-stressed concrete	1954	40	20
Nipol	Plastic products	1957	105	35
Raleigh Industries (3)	Cycle assembly	1958	75	50
Vehicle Assembly Plant	Bedford lorries	1958	500	100
Minna Farm	Pigs	1959	35	80
Northern Construction Co.	Building contractors	1960	100	30
W. A. Thread	Sewing thread	1961	450	20
W. A. Portland Cement	Cement	1961	4,500	10
W. A. Cold Storage	Meat products	1961	250	100
Walls	Ice cream	1961	90	100
Vono Products	Beds, mattresses	1961	80	38
Cement Paints	Cement paint	1962	35	16
Guinness	Stout	1962	2,000	33
Fan Milk	Re-constituted milk	1963	100	45
The Nigerian Sugar Co.	Sugar and by-products	1963	3,800	7
Norspin	Cotton yarn	1963	1,100	53
Pye	Radio assembly	1963	40	50
Vitafoam	Foam rubber products	1963	100	50
A. J. Seward	Perfumery and cosmetics	1964	200	100
Bordpak	Fibre board cartons	1964	800	100
Kwara Tobacco Co.	Cigarettes	1964	500	80
Associated Battery Mfgrs.	Vehicle batteries	1965	65[b]	22
Crocodile Matchets	Matchets	1965	120	51
Textile Printers	Printed textiles	1965	3,250	68

[a] Equity, capital reserves and long-term debt as of 1965.
[b] Author's estimate.
( ) Number of plants.

SOURCES: Information supplied by the United Africa Company, except for 'Fixed Capital' which was compiled from the UAC house magazine, *Link*, press releases and the Registrar of Companies, Ministry of Commerce and Industry.

Such products as cosmetics and meat products are relatively simple to produce and thus could be handled completely by UAC. Ice-cream, packaging materials and (since 1961) plastics are manufacturing activities in which Unilever is engaged and is consequently able to provide the technical know-how. In the case of lager beer, mattresses and beds, yarn, printed textiles, and matchets, UAC was able to persuade one of its suppliers to embark upon a joint venture. For cigarettes and vehicle assembly UAC went out and employed qualified technical managers; this can be a risky practice, as the fate of many government projects attests, because in the event of serious problems there is no reserve of technical knowledge to fall back on, as contrasted to the case of a technical partner where the resources of an entire manufacturing firm can be drawn upon. And finally, in the case of sewing thread, cement, stout, cement paint and radio assembly, it was the manufacturer who took the primary initiative and invited UAC to join for the latter's contribution by way of local knowledge, commercial management and distribution facilities.

Nigeria's second largest merchant firm is John Holt & Company. This family venture was founded in 1867 and is the oldest surviving trading concern in West Africa.[1] Both river and ocean transport interests developed as adjuncts of the merchandise-produce trade soon after the turn of the century.[2] Until just prior to World War II, John Holt differed little from the United Africa Company in its organization and the nature of its activities – only in size, its turnover in Nigeria being approximately a quarter of the latter's. However, in the late 1930s French colonial trade preferences induced the company, which was also trading in the French territories, to establish a French subsidiary; subsidiaries were also established in the United States and South Africa for reasons of procurement. These subsidiaries gradually developed interests of their own independent of West African trade. Thus when the pressure of competition became intense in Nigeria, unlike UAC, John Holt had the option of shifting away from Africa and concentrating on other areas.

Pre-dating UAC's connection with Taylor Woodrow, John Holt formed a partnership in 1947 with the British construction firm Richard Costain Ltd. for a Nigeria venture, to take part in the execution of large-scale construction projects contained in the 1947 ten-year plan; most of Holt's 45 % share was later sold to provide capital for industrial investments more closely linked with its distributive activities. In recent years the company has followed the standard pattern of withdrawal from produce buying, urban concentration and import specialization. The major imports handled are drugs and cosmetics (retailed through its West African Drug Company), automobiles, engineering and electrical equipment and hardware. John Holt is one of the few merchants not to have gone into department store merchandising. On the other hand, the company has redeployed into such activities as shipping and

[1] Much of the following narrative is taken from *Merchant Adventure*, a book published privately by John Holt & Co. about 1950.

[2] The ocean shipping company, Guinea Gulf Line, was sold to Elder Dempster's in 1964 for £1·5m.

travel services, harbour dredging, real estate, insurance, discount banking and stock brokerage.

In the field of industrial processing, from its interest in produce the company has 'backed' into tanning of hides and skins, groundnut crushing (partial acquisition of an established producer) and rubber crêping. Table 21 lists these investments as well as import-replacing industries. A minority share in a biscuit factory (1961), not shown, was sold to the Nigerian Tobacco Company, owing to a conflict of interest in the marketing field.

Table 21. *Industrial investments of John Holt & Company*

Company	Description	Year	Equity capital (£000s)	Holt's equity %
Costains	Construction	1948	400	6
Holt Tanneries	...	1949	150	53
P.S. Mandrides	g-n crushing	1960	625	10
Holt Rubber Co.	Rubber crêping	1962	120	100
Thomas Wyatt	Stationery	1948	220	30
Nigerian Breweries	...	1949	1,500	7
Nigerian Canning Co.	Corned beef	1956	100	30
Critall-Hope	Metal doors, etc.	1958	160	14
Asbestos Cement Products	...	1960	1,000	3
Nigerian Enamelware Co.	...	1961	130	50
Haco	Perfume and plastics	1963	175	51

NOTE: Equity capital is not comparable to fixed investment in table 16, which included capital reserves and long-term debt as well. The 51 % of Haco's equity was purchased for £310,000.

SOURCE: Data supplied by John Holt & Company of Liverpool.

The holding in the Nigerian Canning Company, a project developed by government agencies, parallels UAC's participation in the plastics venture – the factory was built well ahead of demand and, although highly protected, did not get into the black until 1964, still only on one shift a day (a third of capacity). In none of the import-replacing ventures does John Holt provide technical or commercial management and only in perfume and enamelware does the company have a controlling interest.

The principal explanation for John Holt's comparatively limited shift to manufacturing is that the company has had other opportunities in France and England (in the wine and spirits trade, car distributorships) which, although perhaps not quite as profitable, were less risky and did not require a radical break with the company's traditional merchanting activity. It is to these European opportunities that new investment has been directed since 1960.[1] This does not mean that

[1] In the four years 1962–5 proceeds from the sale of capital assets in Nigeria of over £500,000 have been remitted abroad in the form of special dividends.

John Holt may not in the future devote more of their resources to manufacturing. Like the other merchants their knowledge of the local market and of the political-administrative environment, their existing distribution network, etc., are continuing assets which can be capitalized in an industrial venture at any time.

Proceeding to the next largest distributor in Nigeria, A. G. Leventis has, like the others, redeployed from the produce/general import trade to specialized merchandising (six department stores, office equipment, electrical goods, lorries and cars) and industry. The latter include three Coca Cola bottling plants, a vehicle assembly plant, production of industrial gases and a 10 % interest in West African Breweries. Leventis also owns two hotels.

Continuing with industrial investments undertaken by Levantine former produce buyers (later importers), S. Raccah has established a factory producing brass holloware and participated in another making cotton blankets, both articles he had earlier handled as imports. The Gazal brothers shifted from general importing to the production of terrazzo tiles, candles and singlets. The Nassar family, prominent in large-scale food retailing, have established two large biscuit factories. Other redeploying Levantine importer/wholesalers have gone into the manufacture of perfume (4 establishments), hard candy (4), soft drinks, interlock fabric, plastic sandals (2), umbrella assembly, wrought iron and metal furniture (5) and terrazzo tiles (2). In a number of the cases cited the small-scale entrepreneur, suffering from the same pressure on distributive margins as the large trading houses, did not possess the technical competence and was unable to recruit a technical partner to manufacture the article he formerly traded; in these cases the choice of industry was dictated by capital and skill requirements.

While the greatest part of Levantine investment is a reaction to falling margins in the distributive trade, other motives are not absent. In the case of the three out of four Kano groundnut crushers who expanded into import-replacing industry (aluminium holloware, rubber and canvas shoes, soft drink bottling) and Mandilas and Kariberis who participated in a steel rolling mill, the motive was the classical attraction to a profitable market opportunity rather than the compulsion of competition. It would seem significant that none of these ventures, where the entrepreneur lacked an intimate prior knowledge of the product or its market, have been particularly successful.

Returning to the original European merchant firms, Paterson and Zochonis's first industrial investment was in partnership with a Greek soap maker, P. B. Nicholas, in 1949; the motive was the profitability of soap manufacture combined with the assurance of a local source of supply for PZ's marketing requirements. In 1952 the company bought out Nicholas's interest and recruited their own technical personnel; in 1963 operations were extended to include perfume and cosmetics. In 1962 Paterson and Zochonis joined their principal paint supplier in establishing a factory in order to hold their position in that market (four other competing plants were opened in the same year). In 1964 a similarly motivated joint venture began production of galvanized iron sheet (a competing Japanese concern also started up that year).

Of all the merchants the French firms of CFAO and SCOA and the Swiss UTC have gone into industry least – with the consequence that their position in the market relative to the other merchant houses has declined appreciably. Each of the French companies has gone into partial assembly of the lorries they distribute; all three of the firms have made small trade investments (usually less than 10 %) in industries manufacturing products they sell, e.g. metal doors and windows, paint, galvanized iron sheet.[1]

Of the Indian merchants only the largest, K. Chelleram, has so far gone into industry. Since 1962 the latter has bought two factories producing luggage and cosmetics and candles respectively. Chelleram also took minority participation in a varnish factory in 1964. Finally, the smaller merchants and agent/importers have gone into a variety of industries (e.g. proprietary drugs, cosmetics, louvre windows, packing materials), usually as commercial partners with their former suppliers.

INDUSTRIAL INVESTMENTS OF OVERSEAS SUPPLIERS

A number of market-protecting investments by overseas suppliers have already been referred to. (As we will see in chapter 5, a very similar protective, investment-inducing mechanism also operates with respect to export processing industries.) At this point we will review a few of the larger investments of foreign suppliers not already mentioned; the important cases of cement and textiles will be considered in chapter 4.

Beginning with asbestos cement products (flat and corrugated sheets, pipes), over 95 % of the import market was held by two firms, Turner and Newall of England and Eternit of Belgium. Given their large stakes in the Nigerian market and active rivalry between the two firms, both began investigating the possibilities for establishing a plant in the Lagos area in 1959, four years after the technological threshold had been achieved. When Eternit formed a partnership with the Western Nigeria Development Corporation in 1960 to build a £600,000 plant in Ikeja to produce flat and corrugated sheet, Turner and Newall, despite the fact that the market could not at the time support two plants,

[1] For a description of UTC policies and fortunes in recent years see *West Africa's* portrait 'The Family of UTC', 7 November 1964.

went to the east and launched a venture of comparable size at Emene near Enugu.[1]

In early 1964 both firms began constructing £350,000 pipe-forming plants adjoining their existing operations. Later in that year when the Northern Nigeria Development Corporation indirectly let the Ikeja and Emene firms know that it was negotiating with an Indian producer both the Belgian and English companies came forward with counter-proposals; in March 1965 the government of Northern Nigeria announced that an agreement had been signed with Turner and Newall for the establishment of a £400,000 factory at Kaduna.

The establishment of two tyre factories in 1962 and 1963, representing an investment of about £5m., was a dramatic and unambiguous example of manufacturers' market protection. As in the case of asbestos cement products, market shares were highly concentrated, with Michelin and Dunlop supplying about four-fifths of all imports. Both firms had had their own marketing organizations in Nigeria for some years. In 1960 Michelin began discussions with the Federal Government about the possibility of constructing a factory in the Lagos area; a negotiating team from Dunlop arrived soon afterwards. Shortly after Nigeria's severance of diplomatic relations with France over the atomic explosion in the Sahara, Federal approval was given to Dunlop's proposal. The British firm, however, made no move to go ahead with its project, now that the Michelin threat had been turned aside. Meanwhile the latter had quietly approached the Regional Government in Enugu, and in March 1961 Michelin announced that it was beginning construction of a plant in Port Harcourt. Dunlop, despite a statement by one of its directors in the Federation of British Industries investment survey that Nigeria could only support one tyre factory,[2] formally launched its own venture in October of that year.[3]

A majority of the industries listed in table 16 also represent manufacturers' market protection. Perhaps the most spectacular instance was the establishment of five paint factories in a single year, each sponsored by a leading British firm: Imperial Chemical Industries, British Paints, Permacem, International Paints and Pinchin Johnson

[1] Tariff protection was 10 % until 1964; in that year it was raised to 20 %. More important are the following elements of natural protection: transportation costs, 25 %; breakage 10 %; and ship handling, 3 %.

[2] Federation of British Industries, *Nigeria, An Industrial Reconnaissance*, London, February 1961, p. 12.

[3] A revenue tariff of 20 % was raised to 33 % at the request of Michelin, and then 60–70% at the request of Dunlop whose prior share in the car and lorry tyre market was considerably smaller. For bicycle tyres, a field already dominated by Dunlop, no tariff increase was requested.

As mentioned in chapter 3, closing off the importation of used tyres substantially aided the second producer (Dunlop) in getting out of the red by its third year of operation (1965).

(Courtaulds). In 1963 and 1964 the three major suppliers (one British, two Japanese) of galvanized iron sheet began local production. In like manner multi-investments occurred in the cases of Hong Kong enamelware and British metal door and window frames.[1] In other cases, not easily presented in tabular form, single investments were undertaken to hold a market. Such an instance is English Sewing Cotton's West African Thread venture whose purpose was to secure their Nigerian sales from the severe competitive pressure being applied by its chief rival, J. and P. Coates.[2]

INDUSTRIAL INVESTMENTS OF NON-MARKET-PROTECTING FIRMS

We now come to those industrial investments whose sponsors had no prior interest in the Nigerian market. Refining the tripartite breakdown given in the beginning of the chapter, we may divide these investors into five groups according to their primary motive for investing.

1. Large, well established firms, with ample capital resources, which were seeking profitable investment opportunities and which were attracted by the size of the Nigerian market.[3]
2. Individual entrepreneur-promoters who were attracted by the possibility of forming partnership and/or obtaining the financial backing of governmental agencies on terms favourable to themselves.
3. Manufacturers seeking outlets for redundant equipment.
4. Machinery manufacturers.
5. Machinery merchants.

Save for the first group, all the projects of these non-market-protecting investors have required supplementary Nigerian public capital.

Two examples of the first type of investor are Aluminium Ltd. of Canada (Alcan) and Charles Pfizer. In 1961 Alcan began construction of a £1·3m. ingot rolling and finishing mill to produce coils, sheets and circles for subsequent fabrication into holloware and corrugated sheeting. This investment was part of the company's policy to set up operations in the underdeveloped areas as a means for holding its world market share; Nigeria had been chosen over a number of possible

[1] In the case of enamelware the distributive firms and other second parties played an important role in mobilizing the manufacturers to action.

[2] Although English Sewing Cotton's 'Crown' and 'Parrot' thread held 60 % of the market, the competition from Coates' 'Comb' thread had reduced margins to the point where ESC had been making net losses on its Nigerian trade for two years prior to its decision to undertake local manufacture. Coates was supplying the market from a low-cost Indian subsidiary factory, whereas ESC's 'Crown' and 'Parrot' were manufactured only in England.

[3] It is upon the decision-making criteria of this relatively small group that investment incentive policies are predicated.

countries because of its large market, favourable political environment and attractive investment incentive policies.

Charles Pfizer, initially an American producer of prescription drugs, has become a widely diversified international company with plants in twenty-seven countries. The most important attraction for this expansion-bent company to come to Nigeria was the size of the market. A Nigerian subsidiary had been incorporated as early as 1957. The first investment, in 1961, was a £75,000 plant in Aba formulating and packaging antibiotics, a traditional line. In the following year work was begun on an £80,000 plastics factory and two feed mills, both fields in which Pfizer had no prior experience.

Turning to the second group, there are only a few instances of industrial projects being initiated by private entrepreneurs. The first, and most successful, was that of E. A. Seroussi, a former Sudanese textile merchant, who came to Northern Nigeria after having been involved in the establishment of a small perfume factory in Ghana. Mr Seroussi gained the northern Premier's support for a textile venture in Kaduna. To this venture Seroussi and his associates contributed £185,000, a private Nigerian (a Minister in the Regional Government) invested £20,000, and various public agencies provided £430,000 Owing to a series of technical mishaps associated with antiquated equipment and insufficient expatriate supervision, early in 1965 Mr. Seroussi and his associates were forced to sell their interest at a considerable loss to the Northern Nigeria Government, who recruited another firm as managing agent.[1] In the meantime Mr Seroussi was invited by the Regional Government to set up a second textile venture at Gusau; in this project the entrepreneur was careful to avoid his previous mistakes, and the factory achieved profitable operation.

Other private entrepreneurs have proved to be swindlers. According to the verdict of a British court, Ernest Shinwell attempted to promote a clothing factory and a supermarket in Eastern Nigeria in 1963 – using £0·5m. of forged securities as collateral for government-sponsored loans.[2] There was another case in which a group of promoter-entrepreneurs persuaded a regional government of their intention to establish a factory, and on the strength of this obtained an open letter of credit for an amount in excess of a quarter of a million pounds sterling. The fruition of this investment was the arrival in Lagos of unaccompanied crates of junked equipment, later valued at £10,000.

The third group of investors with no prior stake in the Nigerian market are reputable, long-established manufacturing companies seeking an outlet for redundant equipment. The outstanding case here is

[1] The accumulated loss of Nortex at 30 April 1965 was £327,326. Northern Nigeria, *A White Paper . . .*, p. 26.

[2] *West Africa*, 6, 13 February and 15 August 1965.

the American textile firm of Indian Head Mills. This firm promoted a £2.4m. textile venture at Aba to which it contributed £72,000 in cash and forty-year-old machinery officially valued at £688,000 in return for 70% of the equity.[1] Owing to the excellence of Indian Head's management this textile project has proved highly successful despite the old equipment.

The fourth investor category is machinery manufacturers. Of the two largest investments in this category, the machinery manufacturers were not the promoters of the project, but rather were invited to participate by the Federal Government. The first of these projects (discussed at length in the following chapter) was the £2·3m. cement factory located at Nkalagu in the eastern region which commenced operations in 1957. The second was the £3·8m. sugar estate and factory at Bacita in the northern region, in which Booker Brothers, McConnell & Co. was both the machinery supplier and technical partner. Booker's investment in the project is £0·3m., while the value of the installed factory purchased from its equipment-manufacturing subsidiary exceeded £2m.[2] On a far smaller scale, the Swedish shoe-machinery supply firm Skolast has taken a 10 % equity in two shoe factories it has sold to the Development Corporations in Eastern and Western Nigeria.

The final group of investors are machinery merchants.[3] The actual investment made by these firms has been very small – typically 10 % of the equity, which represents 3 to 4 % of the combined equity-debenture capital commitment. Yet the promotional activities of German, Italian and Israeli machinery merchants have resulted in

[1] Information supplied by a principal creditor of the Aba Textile Mills project. Although Indian Head received equity shares valued at $2.1m. (approx. £720,000) the actual cost to the company was only $1.1m. (approx. £390,000) as shown in its 1964 annual report under 'Investments in foreign subsidiaries, at cost'.

[2] The investigation of possibilities for producing sugar was recommended to the Nigerian Government by the 1953 World Bank mission. The government first turned to Tate & Lyle, the principal supplier of Nigeria's imports, who in turn recommended Bookers. After a survey of potential sugar-growing areas in 1957, Bookers and several Nigerian governmental agencies formed a syndicate to conduct growing trials at Bacita. When the trials proved successful, the Nigerian Sugar Company was formed in 1961. In the event serious agricultural problems developed (both the cane output and sucrose yield fell far below the trial results) and by late 1965 the project was facing grave financial problems.

[3] The material in the following five paragraphs is drawn from Federal Ministry of Economic Development, *National Development Plan Progress Report 1964*, Lagos 1965, pp. 20-1; Northern Nigeria, *A White Paper on the Military Government Policy for the Reorganization of the Northern Nigeria Development Corporation*, Kaduna 1966; A. A. Ayida, 'Contractor Finance and Supplier Credit in Economic Growth', *Nigerian Journal of Economic and Social Studies*, July 1965; S. R. Pearson, 'The Political Economics of Nigerian Short-Term Borrowing', *Public Policy*, vol. xv, J. D. Montgomery and A. Smithies, eds., Harvard University, Cambridge 1966; and the following three articles in the March 1965 *Nigerian Opinion*, published by the University of Ibadan: 'Party Finances', 'Mid-West: The Politics of Conciliation', and 'The Ethics of Ministerial Office'.

over £30m. in public investment since 1962, and most of it in uneconomic projects. An incomplete listing of 'turnkey'[1] factory sales of one firm alone, Coutinho Caro of Hamburg, accounts for £18m.: glass factories at Port Harcourt and Ughelli (£1·5m., £1·2m.), a textile factory at Asaba (£4·2m.), a cement factory at Ukpilla (£4·6m.), clinker grinding plants at Lagos and Koko (£0·4m., £0·3m.), a cocoa processing factory at Ikeja (£1·9m.), and a palm kernel processing plant at Port Harcourt (£1·6m.).

The explanation for the rash of 'machinery-sale public-investment' projects is political: prestigious capital-intensive projects can be achieved quickly, they provide well paid directorships for politicians as well as jobs for the unemployed, they are an important source of party finance via the 'kick-back', and they do not require any money down – they are financed on the basis of supplier credit.[2] The drawbacks of this type of public investment are the extensive promotion of political and personal corruption, inflated capital costs (by 100 % or more), serious external debt servicing problems, and money-losing investments.[3] The reasons for this last and economically most damning fault are (*i*) that both the selection of the industry and its location are based upon political grounds and can seldom pass the test of economic viability, and (*ii*) the machinery merchants' method for providing managerial staff to the projects they commission is inadequate to ensure efficient operation.

With regard to the technical characteristics of the equipment supplied by the machinery merchants, two features are worth note. First, while the equipment is always new in the sense of not having been used before, it is usually not of the latest design. Second, the various pieces of process equipment may not be made by the same manufacturer and thus will not be well matched in terms of capacity or rate of throughput. The effect is to make factory operation difficult, to create a serious spare parts problem, and in general to increase the burden on management.

The management factor is of critical importance and is the main reason for distinguishing machinery manufacturers (who also charge lower prices and do less 'promoting') from machinery merchants. The former have a vested interest in the success of the projects they equip – an advertisement for their product – and usually insist that a well established firm in the industry be recruited as the technical partner and managing agent. Individual foreign technicians and managerial

[1] A 'turnkey' project or factory is one in which the seller undertakes to have the factory built and provides management so that the factory is ready to come into operation at the turn of a key.

[2] See Pearson, *op. cit.*, pp. 347-54.

[3] Ayida, *op. cit.*, pp. 181-2; Pearson, *op. cit.* pp. 253-5; *National Development Plan Progress Report 1964*, p. 19.

personnel hired by the machinery merchant are not an adequate substitute: their quality is less reliable, the duration of their tenure tends to be short, they do not have the power to resist pressure to overstaff, and they lack the resources of technical knowledge and organizational strength which are available to a management team which is being 'backstopped' by an entire firm in Europe or America. This is the key factor in explaining why not a single turnkey project in Nigeria was earning a profit as of December 1966.[1]

The discussion of machinery merchants and turnkey projects covers a large part of the state enterprise sector which was described briefly in chapter 1. Recent studies of the regional Development Corporations, the agencies responsible for government-run industrial enterprises, reveal similar tendencies for public undertakings initiated during the 1950s, whether managed by Nigerians or hired expatriates: excessive overstaffing, sluggish response to competition, unresolved technical problems, profitless operation.[2] In marked contrast to these projects, the joint ventures with foreign firms, where the latter undertake both the management and a substantial share of the risk capital, have been highly successful. In the three chapters which follow we shall have occasion to review the performance of a good number of both types of public investment.

IV

Summarizing the principal points of this chapter, the major portion of import-replacing industrialization in Nigeria has been carried out by firms which had a prior interest in the market. The greater part of the remaining import substitution has been effected with public funds. Investments of the latter kind, because of the types of projects selected, high capital costs, methods of financing and subsequent unprofitable operation, have in most cases proved a far less efficient method for industrializing than market-protecting private investment.

Up to this point no attempt has been made to go behind the market protection investment motive and ask whether such a criterion is consistent with rational entrepreneurial behaviour. One can advance at least six reasons why the market protector is more likely to make an

[1] Information supplied by Arthur D. Little, Inc., advisers to the Federal Ministry of Commerce and Industry. The one project which had prospects of soon getting into the black was the WNDC brewery at Abeokuta which had been fortunate enough to recruit the German brewing firm of Henniger as a technical partner (10% of the equity). See p. 96, below.

[2] *Military Government Policy for the Reorganization of the Northern Nigeria Development Corporation*, Government Printer, Kaduna 1966; O. Terriba, 'Development Strategy, Investment Decision and Expenditure Patterns of a Public Development Institution: WNDC 1949–1962', *Nigerian Journal of Economic and Social Studies*, vol. 8, July 1966; and 'New Thinking in Eastern Nigeria', *West Africa*, 25 November 1965.

industrial investment. By virtue of his proximity the 'insider' will note any possible opportunity long before an 'outsider'. Likewise with regard to the cost of gathering information and its reliability, the former has an advantage over the latter. Because of his specialized knowledge of the Nigerian economic environment, the market protector's objective risks of failure are less; for the same reason, his margin of error in quantifying these risks is smaller. The insider can count on lower costs by utilizing his already established distribution facilities, management overheads and connections with the public bureaucracy. Add to these the galvanizing threat of economic loss if such opportunities are not exploited and the market protection hypothesis takes on a high degree of *a priori* plausibility.

In the following chapter the history of four industries will be considered in depth; *inter alia* attention will be paid to differences in behaviour of various types of investors with respect to their requirements for tariff and other forms of subsidization, choice of technology and capital commitment. These findings, along with the evidence of the last twenty pages, will provide material for an analysis in the final section of the efficacy of Nigeria's incentive programme.

CHAPTER 4

IMPORT SUBSTITUTION: CASE STUDIES AND POLICY IMPLICATIONS

The major portion of this chapter is devoted to an analysis of Nigeria's four largest import-replacing industries: cigarettes, beer, cement and textiles. In 1964 these four industries accounted for 40 % of industrial output and 21 % of industrial employment in the sector employing ten or more.[1] Each of the industry studies will be organized around a common set of analytical questions; these include considerations which led to the decision to invest, the choice of technology, industry prices and tariff protection, the profitability of the industry, and its contribution to the development of the economy. A concluding section will deal with the policy implications of our findings with respect to the investment decision and optimal industrial incentive schemes.

I

It is thought that tobacco and the smoking habit were first introduced into Nigeria by Portuguese merchants in the sixteenth century.[2] After that time small crops were probably cultivated by local farmers for their own domestic consumption. Imported manufactured cigarettes made their first appearance during the 1890s. In 1911 the principal overseas supplier, a large British firm, sent out its own representative to supervise and promote the distribution of its products by the established trading firms. Nine years later, in an effort to gain more control over the market and foster its orderly development, the supplying firm set up its own importing agency, constructed depots and formed a sales promotion organization; wholesale distribution, however, was left in the hands of the merchants.

In the early 1930s the supplying company decided to investigate the possibilities for local production. Although competitive pressure may have influenced this decision, the primary motivation was to develop a potentially large demand, rather than to protect the existing market. With the import duty ranging over 100 %, manufactured cigarettes

[1] See table 7.

[2] This historical narrative is based on 'The Tobacco Industry', *Nigerian Trade Journal*, July/September 1963, pp. 119–22, and J. H. Maslen, 'The Tobacco Industry in Nigeria', a talk given over the Nigerian Broadcasting Service, 20 January 1955. Other published works which provided material for this section on cigarette manufacture are 'Tobacco in Nigeria', a booklet published by the Nigerian Tobacco Company in 1960, Annual Reports of the Chairman of the Nigerian Tobacco Company, and J. T. Coppock, 'Tobacco Growing in Nigeria', *Erdkunde*, XIX, April 1965.

accounted for but a small share of all tobacco consumption, the 'primary' market being served by the far less expensive 'black fat' and local tobacco in the form of snuff, chewing tobacco, pipe tobacco and as 'bookies'.[1] The advantages in local manufacture arose not from any difference in the cost of production, but from the preferential tax treatment the colonial government was willing to grant a project which promised agricultural as well as industrial development.

Table 22. *The growth of domestic cigarette production*

(millions of cigarettes)

	Domestic production[a]	Imports		Domestic production[a]	Imports
1939	173	285	1952	1,932	75
1940	...	149	1953	2,126	92
1941	271	224	1954	2,250	64
1942	303	219	1955	2,506	79
1943	411	172	1956	2,650	44
1944	459	160	1957	2,188	64
1945	522	178	1958	2,953	78
1946	559	282	1959	2,749	61
1947	697	430	1960	2,871	104
1948	729	363	1961	3,353	108
1949	739	454	1962	3,488	73
1950	901	494	1963	4,040	104
1951	1,397	247	1964	4,124	74
			1965	4,783	54

[a] Excludes home-made and smuggled cigarettes.

SOURCES: United Nations, *Statistical Yearbook*, various years; and Federal Office of Statistics *Trade Reports*, various years.

By selling their cigarettes at $\frac{1}{4}$*d*, half the price of the cheapest import, the British firm hoped to be able to exploit the major segment of demand. A technical and commercial survey was carried out in 1932. In the following year a small pilot factory was established in an abandoned cotton ginnery at Oshogbo in the western region; at the same time tobacco growing experiments were conducted to find suitable varieties. The cultivation of air-cured Virginian hybrids proved feasible and, with the continuing technical support of the expatriate firm, commercial production was successfully undertaken by peasant farmers in the Ogbomosho area. In 1937 a full-scale factory, employing 160 workers, was opened at Ibadan.

As seen in table 22 the cigarette industry prospered, enjoying a virtually uninterrupted growth in output from 30m. cigarettes in 1934

[1] 'Black fat' is sugar-cured Burley tobacco imported from the United States which is used for chewing and snuff. 'Bookies', home-made cigarettes from local tobacco, derive their name from the 'Holy Book' whose pages originally (*c.* 1900) provided the cigarette paper. In 1964 'bookies' were 10 for a penny.

to nearly 5,000m. in 1965. As a result of overseas wartime scarcities, the local industry was able to firmly establish itself during the 1939–45 period. With increasing protection and sterling area control restrictions on dollar imports the market share of imports had fallen to a negligible level by 1952. A second plant was opened in Port Harcourt in 1956 and a third in Zaria in 1959.[1]

In 1961 the United Africa Company initiated plans to launch the country's second cigarette-producing company; this concern, Kwara Tobacco Company, began production in Ilorin in 1964 with an initial capacity of 360m. cigarettes. In the same year the Premier Tobacco Company was formed by the Western Nigeria Development Corporation, two Nigerian business men and a small American tobacco company to investigate possibilities for growing and curing 'black fat'; this group planned to establish a cigarette factory once the production of 'black fat' was securely established.

While the Premier Tobacco Company grew out of the efforts of the governmental Industrial Promotions Commission at Ibadan, UAC's Kwara venture was a response to the abrupt and very substantial loss of its cigarette trade in 1960. During the late 1950s most large firms went through a process of Nigerianizing their structure and operations in order to conform with the changing political situation. Elements in this process include accelerated Africanization of management, appointment of Nigerians as directors, public relations programmes, local issue of share capital and so on.[2] In 1960 the Nigerian Tobacco Company (as the subsidiary had been called since 1951) ceased distributing through the expatriate firms, and began wholesaling through some sixty independent Nigerian agents. As the principal distributor for NTC, the United Africa Company lost at one blow sales worth £6m. The decision to establish on her own, a decision which accorded with the company's emerging policy of redeployment, was sparked off by a reaction to make good the sales volume she had lost. In an industry where marketing skills are of paramount importance, UAC felt her experience well qualified her to enter the field. Conversely, by building up her own distribution net, which was backed up by the already

[1] Just as in the case of beer, a single large factory, simply by virtue of spreading overheads, would result in slightly lower unit cost. However, since regional markets are large enough to support at least one plant of a reasonably economic size and since Regional Governments wanted their own cigarettes and beer industry, it behove the established producer to build a plant in each region. Tobacco is grown in the west and the north; NTC growing experiments continue in the east where heavy rainfall makes cultivation difficult.

[2] For a full enumeration of the steps taken by the large expatriate firms to conform to the post-independence environment, see F. J. Pedler's contribution in *The Encouragement and Protection of Investment in Developing Countries*, The British Institute of International and Comparative Law, London 1962, pp. 63–77.

existing system of depots, market research and advertising, NTC was unintentionally laying the foundation for her later diversification.

TECHNOLOGY AND SKILL REQUIREMENTS

The manufacturing process employed by NTC is highly capital-intensive, embodying the most advanced technology available in the field of cigarette-making. The purchased tobacco is first conveyed to re-drying plants at the Ibadan and Zaria factories where the moisture content is standardized; after being hydraulically pressed and baled, the tobacco is taken to one of the company's three air-conditioned leaf stores where it is quick frozen to kill any latent insect infestation and then stored to ripen for at least one year at 62°F. and a relative humidity of 62 %. In fact two years supply of tobacco is in store at any one time, a necessary insurance against fluctuations in the size of the crop. Over £750,000 are invested in these facilities alone; well over £1m. is invested in the tobacco inventory itself. Continuing with a description from the *Nigerian Trade Journal:*

> Bales of tobacco of different grades and types are drawn from the leaf stores as required and depending upon the brand of cigarettes to be made. From there it is taken to the primary manufacturing department for cleansing and classifying. There the requisite number of 'hands' of each type of tobacco are stacked on trays to form an appropriate cigarette blend.
>
> These trays are then automatically conveyed to a conditioning machine to soften the leaf. Another machine separates the individual leaves from the 'hands' of tobacco and cuts off the tips. After various other processes in other machines, which process the leaf and the leaf stems separately, the tobacco is eventually cut into the fine shredded form, called 'rag', ready for the actual cigarette making. An average of 45,000 lbs. of tobacco leaf are processed into cigarettes in three factories each day. In the next section of each factory automatic cigarette-making machines receive the cigarette paper and the rag and produce the finished article at the rate of up to 2,000 sticks per minute per machine.
>
> The cigarettes are then conveyed by special trolleys to the packing department where other machines automatically pack them in tens or twenties, as the case may be, and in turn into the bundles and large cartons in which they leave the factory. At the end of this long process the cartons of 10,000 cigarettes each are passed along conveyor belts to a room where Customs officials check for excise duty before leaving the factory.[1]

NTC's choice of technology has been regulated neither by the desire to minimize its capital at risk (not since the experimental days) nor to maximize its profits for a given level of output. Rather the company's choice of technology within the context of Nigeria's well protected

[1] 'The Tobacco Industry', *Nigerian Trade Journal*, July/September 1963, p. 121.

market has been governed by the motive of sales maximization, subject to the constraint of a satisfactory rate of return, i.e. 20 %. The ability to expand output and capacity rapidly, to be able to provide a full range of brands or price lines, to have assured uninterrupted supply – these are the considerations which have counselled management to adopt the most automated production techniques available.

The use of a greater number of older type machines, whose costs do not include a patent component, and the use of labour-intensive handling techniques would reduce both capital costs and the number of senior (still largely expatriate) technicians required to maintain the more mechanized process. On the other hand such a choice would entail higher operative skills, greater reliance on Nigerian supervisors, and greater vulnerability to interruptions as a result of human failure. Added to this in the case of cigarettes – and the same applies for beer – in relation to outlays for raw materials, advertising and selling expenditures, prevailing profit margins and, above all, the tax element, the actual cost of manufacturing is very modest, less than 10 % of the ex-factory price.

One of the chief elements in the infant industry concept is the time required for the development of labour skills. The skilled manpower requirements for running a mechanized cigarette factory would appear rather modest, at least at the operative and junior supervisor level. The educational background of the vast majority of the company's 2,200 employees – general labour, machine operators, machine mechanics, section-men, assistant foremen, foremen, sales personnel – is primary schooling. Training, until 1958, was by working with a skilled operator, rising with seniority, experience and demonstrated ability. In 1958 a training programme was introduced consisting of a number of short (one to three week) formal courses for supervisors; in 1962 courses in the field of machine operation and maintenance and marketing were added. These courses are directed to new employees, poor performers and promotion candidates. Non-routine maintenance and repair is carried out by the factory engineer; the latter is assisted by several craftsmen with City & Guilds qualifications in electrical and mechanical engineering.

At the management level – which includes Departmental Production Assistants, Assistant Factory Manager, Factory Engineer and Factory Manager on the production side – the number of Nigerians has risen from two in 1952 to seventy-two (although half of these were still in training) in 1964. The corresponding number of expatriates in 1964 was sixty-three. Two-thirds of the management candidates have come in laterally or as university graduates; the other third have come up through the ranks. Training consists of rotational assignments in the

Nigerian company and a three month course in the United Kingdom. For the technical managers enumerated above, training in a British plant will be longer, between one and two years.

TAXATION

In order to assess the economics of cigarette manufacture it is necessary to penetrate the 'veil of taxation' which enshrouds the industry. As we have already noted 64 % of the ex-factory price represents 'value added' by import and excise duties. The comparable component of import tariff in landed cost for the imported cigarette is about 80 %. As tobacco taxation has historically accounted for 12–15 % of customs and excise duties, or on the order of 10 % of all public revenue, the Federal Government has been understandably less concerned with the economic efficiency of the industry and its contribution *qua* industry to the economy's development than it has been with maximizing tax revenue.[1]

The calculation of the incidence of taxation and in particular the net protection extended to the cigarette industry is a rather complicated matter. A complex and changing tax structure,[2] an increasing relative content of untaxed local tobacco in the final product and difficulties in reconciling 'progressive' specific and *ad valorem* tax rates with 'average' prices, import duties and excise tax – all these contribute to the hazards, and indeed inevitable imprecision, of the computation given below.

The increasing share of the untaxed local tobacco is to be observed in column A, while the rising rate of import duty on the diminishing import content is shown in column B. Taking 2·2 lb. as the average weight per 1,000 cigarettes, 2·2 × B × A gives the raw tobacco import duty paid per 1,000 cigarettes manufactured in Nigeria. The average excise levy per 1,000 cigarettes, the second tax borne by the local producer, is seen to fluctuate from year to year, according to the composition of output, but with no general upward or downward trend. On the other hand, the tariff on imported cigarettes has doubled

[1] See the Federal Minister of Finance (the Hon. Sam Okotie-Eboh), *The Six Budget Speeches*, Federal Ministry of Finance, Lagos 1964.

[2] The tariff on imported cigarettes was originally a multi-rate specific duty per hundred or per thousand, the rate depending upon unit weight; in 1956 a single specific duty per lb. of cigarettes replaced the old multi-rate duty, to which was added in 1959 an alternative, 'whichever is the higher', specific rate per 1,000. The import duty on raw tobacco has always been a single specific charge per lb. The excise levy on local manufacture commenced in 1939 with two specific rates per 1,000 according to whether the ex-factory price fell below or above a certain value; however, in the 1956 change-over, the valuation basis was altered from a specific quantum rate to an *ad valorem* system with three instead of two categories, according to weight rather than wholesale value. Within the foregoing framework the rate or level of taxation for two of the three levies has been continually rising.

since 1945, and net protection nearly tripled. However, as most imports would have come from the United States, it is quite possible that sterling area restrictions on dollar imports until 1959 provided a uniformly high degree of protection over the whole period. Even since 1959, net protection is a good deal higher than shown in the last column of the table for the simple reason that only the most expensive cigarettes come over the tariff barrier, while the cheaper, more directly competitive imports are effectively excluded by the specific rates.

Table 23. *The structure of tobacco taxation*

	Locally manufactured cigarettes				Imported cigarettes			
	Import contents A (%)	Import duty per lb. raw tobacco B (£)	Excise per 1,000 C (£)	Total producer tax per 1,000 D (£)	Price per 1,000 E (£)	Duty per 1,000 F (£)	Net protection per 1,000 G (£)	G as % of E H (£)
1935	90[a]	—	—	—[b]	0·77	1·07	1·07	139
1945	60[a]	0·15	1·54	1·74	1·28	3·07	1·33	104
1950	50	0·28	1·61	1·92	1·64	3·50	1·58	96
1955	36	0·76	1·39	1·99	1·45	4·14	2·15	148
1960	33	0·76	1·50	2·05	1·55	6·00	3·95	255
1963	16	0·76	1·44	1·71	...	6·25	4·54	293[c]

[a] Estimated.

[b] 1933–6 was a pioneer tax-free period.

[c] As a % of the 1960 price.

SOURCES: For the three most recent years, all calculations based on data supplied by the Nigerian Tobacco Company. The percentage of imported tobacco in the locally manufactured cigarette for 1950 is based upon figures given for 1951 in a booklet, 'Tobacco in Nigeria', published by NTC in 1960. Earlier years are very rough estimates based upon purchases from Nigerian farmers. Import duties are the published rate in the Customs Tariff or, when the latter was not available, duties collected divided by the volume of imports from *Trade Reports*. Excise collected on cigarettes is given in *Trade Reports* 1941–52; cigarette production from the United Nations *Statistical Yearbooks*. The conversion factor of 2·2 lb. for 1,000 cigarettes was supplied by the Nigerian Tobacco Company. This is an average figure. The method of calculation for net protection as shown in the last column is as follows:

$$H = \frac{F-(2.2B(A)+C)}{E}\ 100$$

Since it is virtually impossible to set a tariff which is just high enough to off-set the cost disadvantage of the local industry, the question arises as to how much of the protection is exploited by the local producer in the prices he charges. In the case of cigarettes, tariff increases since the mid-1950s have sprung from the desire for public revenue rather than as a result of pressure from the producer.

Published excise rates, in contrast to average excise duty collected, were located for the years 1945–8 and 1956–64. In the first period for every 1,000 cigarettes at an ex-factory price of £1 2*s*. or less, the fiscal imposition was £1 3*s*.; for every 1,000 above that price, £2 4*s*. In 1956 an *ad valorem* system on a tripartite weight basis was introduced: 30 % of ex-factory price for every 1,000 cigarettes weighing 2 lb. or less, 40 % (raised to 48 % in 1959) for the 2–2½ lb. category and 50 % for all heavier cigarettes. If we take 1960 and assume that 25 % of sales fell into the lowest category, 45 % into the intermediate and 30 % into the highest tax category, on the basis of the average excise charge shown in the table, the average ex-factory price per 1,000 cigarettes was in the neighbourhood of £3·59.[1] Allowing for import duties on raw tobacco we obtain a figure of £3·02 compared with £1·55 for the higher quality imported cigarettes. Thus tariff protection actually exploited in price-setting lies somewhere between 100 and 200 % depending on the price assigned to the lower quality, comparable cigarettes which are being effectively excluded from the market.[2]

The use of several 'progressive' excise rates rather than a single-rated tax has a number of beneficial consequences. First, consumer welfare is increased. Second, by imposing a lower than average tax burden on the cheapest cigarettes, the spread of the smoking habit (i.e. the tax paying habit) is encouraged. Third, the greater prominence of the cheaper cigarette also means that the manufacturer is compelled to use a greater portion of the less expensive (tax free) Nigerian-grown tobacco.[3] Finally, and of particular importance for limiting the exploitation of monopoly conferred by excessive protection, imposing a higher tax on the more price-inelastic expensive cigarettes tends to reduce profits more than it does output and consumption.[4]

[1] The allocation between tax categories is derived from the market share of various priced cigarettes, information supplied by the Nigerian Tobacco Company. In 1959, where published output and sales figures are available, the price per 1,000 was £3·53.

[2] A certain portion of this exploited protection must be attributed to tobacco growing as the Company pays higher than world prices for the grades of Nigerian tobacco it buys, not to mention the cost of its other support activities.

[3] In so far as a progressive excise system only favours the use of Nigerian tobacco as between the three broad categories a more efficient method of encouraging utilization of local tobacco production would be to raise the duty on imported raw tobacco. In particular this would induce the cigarette manufacturer to offer higher prices and take other necessary steps to accelerate production of the flue-cured leaf which is capable of displacing most of the remaining imported raw tobacco.

[4] It would appear that the government was not aware of or concerned with these policy objectives when it increased the intermediate excise rate from 40 to 48 % in 1959. Indeed, because the change resulted in a lower tax revenue per £ of cigarette sales (i.e. consumers shifted to lighter cigarettes), the move was considered a mistake.

> 'It was my hope that by this measure there would be an increase of some £2 million in our receipts from this important source of revenue. Unfortunately, these hopes did not materialise. I must be frank with the House and say that there was undoubtedly some consumer resistance to the higher rate of duty. It was established beyond all doubt that the substantial market in this country is for a cigarette selling at one penny per stick. Consumers were not prepared to stay with the brand to which they were accustomed

AGRICULTURAL LINKAGES

Perhaps no aspect of economic development is more fundamental than the transformation of traditional peasant agriculture – introducing higher value crops, more advanced cultivation practices, more capital equipment and more complex organization. Over the long term it is in this area, in its impact upon the agricultural sector, that the cigarette industry is likely to make its greatest contribution to the development of the Nigerian economy.[1]

As noted earlier the cultivation of a coarse native tobacco both for domestic use and local trade has long been a feature of the traditional economy. The Department of Agriculture first attempted to introduce improved tobacco strains (flue cured bright Virginia tobacco) as the basis for an additional export crop in 1915.

> For several years up until 1926 the Department held annual shows and sales at which it was prepared to buy, at something above its market value, any tobacco offered which was considered suitable for export. Attempts were made in a succession of [northern] villages to grow the crop, but, although the farmers were assisted by an instructor, they all abandoned the attempt and the Agricultural Department concluded that the crop was not then sufficiently attractive to the peasant farmer to warrant any further effort for the time being.[2]

In 1934, having completed its own growing experiments with air-cured tobacco varieties, NTC persuaded a number of farmers in the Ogbomosho area of the western region to plant seedlings provided by the company. The first year 83 acres were sown; production doubled in 1935 and again in 1936. By 1938 over 400,000 lb. were offered by the farmers and purchased by the company – more than the Ibadan factory could use. Leaf production was also successfully introduced in the north using the same techniques: providing seedlings; giving credit for fertilizers and sprays; extending supervision and technical advice on growing and curing; and providing a guaranteed market at specified prices.

Of all NTC's efforts in fostering tobacco cultivation those with the greatest potential significance have been in connection with the flue

and this manifested itself in a decline in the smoking of Bicycle cigarettes . . . While we have not secured the additional revenue for which we hoped and we must now rely upon expanding consumption as a means of increasing revenue from this source, I can frankly say to the House that this has been a valuable experience for us in the Ministry of Finance and we shall be better equipped to meet these difficulties in the future, should the need arise.'

(Chief The Honourable Festus Sam Okotie-Eboh, Federal Minister of Finance, Budget Speech 1960.)

[1] This entire section is based upon J. T. Coppock's very thorough study, 'Tobacco Growing in Nigeria', *Erdkunde*, April 1965.

[2] J. T. Coppock, *loc. cit.* p. 4.

cured crop in the northwest of Western Nigeria. Flue cured tobacco is lighter in colour, milder in flavour and requires considerably more care in growing and curing than the air-cured variety; all imports are of this finer, more expensive leaf. Its cultivation in Nigeria is important not only for import substitution and increased value added, but foı its long-term 'educative effects' in transforming traditional farm practices and economic organization. Coppock's description is well worth quoting in full.

The agricultural landscape has also been transformed by the spread of tobacco production. In place of the fragmented plots and inter-mixed crops typical of peasant agriculture elsewhere in the region, the tobacco is grown as a sole crop in relatively large blocks, comprising as much as 60 acres. This practice has been made possible by the relative abundance of land in this area which has allowed chiefs to make a large acreage available to a group and its associated leaf producers without hardship to the rest of the community. This land is generally cleared of all but the largest trees and then cultivated and ridged. About 15 per cent is currently ploughed by tractor, a task originally undertaken by the Nigerian Tobacco Company, but now done either by the groups themselves, who own three tractors, or on contract by the Ministry of Agriculture and Natural Resources; there is clearly scope, in view of the favourable layout, for a considerable increase in this proportion. These tobacco fields, which ideally consist of multiples of six acres for a first crop and seven for the second (these being the acreages which will feed a single barn) are then divided among the individual farmers who plant, cultivate and reap their own tobacco. The individual plots are in multiples of one-third of an acre and it is generally felt that an acre of tobacco is the maximum practicable for an individual farmer, who is also cultivating food crops elsewhere in the village territory.

The first crop is sown in nurseries in February and is therefore wholly dependent on watering for its supply of moisture during the critical early stages of growth. It is transplanted in April at the beginning of the rains and is then reaped in June and July. The second crop, which, owing to heavy leaching by the first rains, is not as good as the first, is sown in the nurseries in May. It is transplanted to the fields in June and harvested in August and September. Virtually all field activity thus takes place in the wet season and does conflict at many points with the requirements of food crops.

The transformation of the agricultural scene which results from the cultivation of tobacco is only temporary, for once the crop has been reaped the 'field' either reverts to a grass fallow or is recultivated in irregular patches of food crops by the original occupants. But the clearing has, of course, a long-term effect and it is to be hoped that in due course the benefits of mechanical cultivation and sole cropping will encourage farmers to grow other crops in the same way as tobacco and to follow a regular rotation, so that a more rational system of land holding will evolve.

. . . The nurseries, where a large number of girls are employed, are placed near the river, so that the young plants can be regularly watered, water being either pumped from the river or carried by hand. The barn-site, containing three barns and associated buildings such as stringing and grading sheds, is on the outskirts of the village, for a considerable labour force of men, women and children is required for handling and curing the leaf. The tobacco 'fields', are usually at no great distance from the barn-site and vary considerably in size. . .

. . . Flue-curing is an art requiring considerable skill, for not only should the leaf be correctly picked, but it must be heated in barns at specified temperatures for varying carefully defined periods, a task requiring constant attention under wood firing. It also requires considerable capital, for a single barn (which cannot be operated economically by itself), costs approximately £200 and an average barn-site comprising four barns and ancillary buildings represents an investment of some £1,200, a considerable sum for Nigerian farmers. For these reasons, and as experience in rubber and oil-palm production in Nigeria might suggest, it would appear not as well suited to peasant production as the less demanding air-cured crop. Indeed the Agricultural Department thought earlier that flue-cured tobacco was out of the question for peasant farmers and the Nigerian Tobacco Company originally undertook the curing of the leaf, building and operating its own curing barns; it also provided the farmer with plants grown in company nurseries and supervised his cultivation.

Yet since 1954 the company has gradually transferred responsibility for both leaf production and curing to the farmers themselves, beginning with a cooperative at Ilero, and has reverted to its original role as a buyer and manufacturer of tobacco. This has been done by promoting a kind of group farming. Farmers have been encouraged to form either cooperatives or business companies which are registered with the Ministry of Trade and Industry. The Nigerian Tobacco Company will then lend money to such a group for the construction of barns, repayable over a ten year period, and will also provide annual credits, repayable within that crop year, for purchase of seed, fertilizer and additional supplies of leaf. For the members of the group, who are usually the more enterprising villagers and may not even be farmers, are generally not sufficiently numerous to grow all the required acreage themselves and arrange for the balance, which is generally more than half the tobacco needed, to be grown by non-members, known as green leaf growers. These sell uncured leaf to the group at a fixed rate irrespective of quality . . .

In addition to financing new barns, which are now largely built by the Flue Cured Producers (as the groups are known) on plans supplied by the Nigerian Tobacco Company, the company has transferred to producers the barns which it had built and operated itself, so that the groups now undertake all curing. They contract with the company to grow a certain acreage of tobacco, so that there is some control over production, and all this is in turn allocated to individual members and to green leaf growers. The company trains staff for the groups and are continuing to advise and to supervise growing and curing, at least in the early stages of a group's existence. The leaf is cured, graded and baled, usually by hired labour under the supervision of the group's members, and the baled leaf is bought by the Nigerian Tobacco Company, whose officers check all purchases in the presence of group representatives and, if necessary, either regrade bales or, if agreement is not possible, return them to the group.[1]

The growing of the quantitatively far more important air-cured tobacco is less demanding of capital, skill and organization. Production of air-cured tobacco in 1964 was 15m. lb., about equally divided between the west and the north; production of western flue-cured tobacco was 1·6m. lb. For the air-cured crop, seedlings are purchased from commercial nurseries, owned and operated by Nigerians, and planted as the sole crop in many small scattered patches; there is no mechanical cultivation, although fertilizers and sprays are used. The tobacco leaves are dried on the verandah or under the roof of the farmer's home or in simple drying sheds.

An organizational innovation of critical importance is the arrangements NTC has succeeded in establishing for the allocation of acreages and the collection and grading of cured leaf. As a result of over-production in 1958 and 1959,[2] the company assisted the farmers in organizing themselves into associations (28 in the west) which contract with the company to grow tobacco up to a maximum specified acreage. Each member receives an acreage allocation and at the end of the season sells his leaf to the association which grades and bales the cured tobacco prior to sale to the company. As with the flue-cured crop, NTC provides credit for fertilizers and sprays and gives technical advice, working through the associations. In the north similar arrangements are carried out through a system of 'master farmers'.

The effect of these organizational arrangements, in addition to the immediate benefits of stabilizing production and increasing the efficiency of collection, is to give the tobacco-growing industry much greater self-sufficiency. Should expatriate private enterprise be unable to provide the required technical and financial assistance as a consequence of the disappearance of monopoly in the cigarette market, the industry has been brought to such a stage of development that the government, although unsuccessful earlier, could now take over the remaining assistance functions without risk to the industry. And, finally, the degree of autonomy with which NTC's efforts have endowed tobacco growers constitutes a very considerable 'external economy' for NTC's emerging competitors who, able to buy tobacco directly from the

[1] Coppock, *loc. cit.* pp. 301–2.

[2] Owing to insufficient production in preceding years, in 1958 NTC greatly expanded the number of buying points/tobacco stores thereby reducing by many miles the distances armers had to traverse in order to sell their tobacco; this was accompanied by substantial price increases. The success of this scheme lead to acreage restrictions in 1960, and the ensuing farmer protest led to the formation of the associations.

established associations and master farmers, avoid the great cost in time and expense of developing their own local tobacco supply.

There is much room for improvement in both tobacco growing and curing, especially more timely cultivation and greater attention to the firing of flue-cured leaf. Yet when it is considered that in terms of farming technique and commercial organization tobacco is far more demanding than any other crop grown in West Africa and that by and large a satisfactory standard has been attained, NTC's achievement must be judged outstanding. It is particularly so when compared to the time and resources required for government-sponsored endeavours in similar fields. In contrast to research and development activities with palm-oil extraction, fibre processing and gari manufacture examined in subsequent chapters, NTC's research and development was sharply focused on the essential aspects of the problem at hand, it was pursued with urgency and without interruption and the development measures applied were comprehensive.

It is true that NTC's achievement was made possible by the monopoly she enjoyed in the cigarette market, but the critical ingredients have been excellence of management and extensive technical knowledge. The experience of the Premier Tobacco Company illustrates that a favourable market alone is no guarantee of success. A crop failure in 1961 followed by exhaustion of financial resources in the second season resulted in non-payment to a large number of farmers and uncompleted facilities for curing and storing the leaf.[1] In 1964 the company was given a second loan of £76,285 from WNDC; as of mid-1965 Premier Tobacco was still operating in the red.[2]

Similarly UAC's Kwara ran into technical difficulties in achieving cigarette quality suited to the Nigerian consumer. Only in this venture and lorry assembly did UAC deviate from its normal policy of engaging a technical partner in those areas where the Unilever organization did not already have an established competence. Just as with the government turnkey projects, direct-hire technical personnel proved inadequate to the problems encountered, and in late 1966 a substantial share of the equity was sold to the Philip Morris Company, which then took up the management.

OVERALL CONTRIBUTION TO THE ECONOMY

An analysis of the industry's expenditure pattern in 1959 (the only year for which comprehensive data are available) as seen in table 24 shows the relative importance of the various facets of cigarette manufacture so far

[1] Western Nigeria Development Corporation, *Annual Report 1962/63*, pp. 15–16.
[2] Western Nigeria Development Corporation, *Annual Report 1964/65*, p. 59.

discussed and the industry's linkages with other sectors of the economy. Sixty-four per cent of gross income went to customs, excise and income taxes; in 1965 these taxes came to £8·8m. By 1965 tobacco purchases from the agricultural sector exceeded £1·3m., or about 10 % of gross income. However, there is still potential for further import replacement of flue-cured tobacco; in 1964 domestic purchases were £204,000 as compared to imports of four-times that value. The industry's linkages to the utility and transport sectors are negligible. During the period 1959–65 before-tax profits constituted about 11 % of sales.[1] Of these profits, 40 % went to the government in income tax, another 14 % (average 1959–66) has been reinvested in Nigeria, and the remaining 46 % has been paid out in dividends. Until 1960 all dividends were remitted to England; after 1964, following two local issues, 91 % of the dividends were being paid abroad.

Table 24. *Sales and expenditures of the Nigerian Tobacco Company, 1959*

(£000s)

Distribution of expenditure and income		Gross sales
Import and excise tax	£6,067	£10,021
Tobacco		
Imported	570	
Local	488	
Wages and salaries	478	
Depreciation	199	
Advertising and distribution	914	
Other[a]	201	
Profit		
Income tax	462	
Retained	242	
Dividends	400	

[a] Professional services £60,000, Directors' emoluments £45,000, transport £45,000, utilities £21,000, and miscellaneous £30,000.

SOURCES: Nigerian Tobacco Company, *Tobacco in Nigeria*, Lagos 1960; *Annual Report 1960*, Nigerian Tobacco Company Limited; Nicholas G. Carter, *An Input-Output Analysis of the Nigerian Economy 1959–1960*, M.I.T. working paper, mimeograph, 1963, p. 182.

If the actual cost of manufacture is roughly equated with wages and salaries and depreciation, it is evident that (*i*) the influence of the cost considerations in the choice of technique is minimal, and (*ii*) the level of effective protection is very high – even if we include, as indeed we

[1] In 1966 the profit margin rose to 15 %, as reflected in the earnings statistics given below (growth in sales was only 4½ %). A similar jump in prices and profits in beer, treated in the next section, tends to confirm the pattern first observed in the Congo that there is a marked outward shift in the demand schedule for beer and cigarettes in periods of high political tension and social disruption.

should, tobacco growing as an activity to be protected. From our calculation on page 88 we found the tariff exploited in price setting to be equal to 50 to 60 % of NTC's selling price net of import duty and excise; Nigerian tobacco and cigarette manufacturing costs represent about 33 % of this same selling price. Thus the protective subsidy exceeds the domestic value added of the activities to be protected by more than 50 %.[1] A good part of the subsidy must in fact be going to marketing expenditure and enlarged profits.

As a private investment NTC has been very successful. In 1952 the balance sheet showed a paid-up equity of £1m. and no reserves.[2] By 1966 paid-up equity was £6m., there were reserves of £1·8m., a subsidiary investment company had been formed, and dividends totalling £4·9m. had been paid out since 1959 – all financed from earnings.[3] In 1960 NTC offered for sale to the Nigerian public 4 % of its equity at par; in 1964 a further 5 % was offered at twice par value. There was no lack of demand in either case.

Year ended 30 September	Before-tax profits	Issued capital	Capital and reserves	Rate of return on Issued capital	Rate of return on Capital and reserves
	(£000s)			(%)	(%)
1959	1,102	5,000	6,034	22·0	18·3
1960	1,039	5,000	6,228	20·8	16·7
1961	1,143	5,000	6,417	22·9	17·8
1962	1,116	5,000	6,881	22·3	16·2
1963	1,208	5,000	7,015	24·2	17·2
1964	1,442	5,000	7,141	28·8	20·2
1965	1,578	5,000	7,612	31·6	20·7
1966	2,004	6,000	7,833	33·3	25·6

SOURCE: Company Reports.

As a response to the accumulation of excess reserves NTC established a subsidiary investment company in 1963. Marine Investments Ltd.'s first investment (£98,000) was in partnership with the country's leading newspaper publisher, a subsidiary of Cecil King's International Publishing Corporation, to manufacture and print light packaging materials, including cigarette packets. Its second major investment

[1] It is not possible to calculate the effective rate of protection because the value-added structure of potential imported cigarettes is not known.

[2] An annual balance sheet and profit and loss account are filed with the Registrar of Companies for the years 1952–9. Since 1959, these accounts along with the Chairman's statement have been published and distributed to the public.

[3] The statistics presented in NTC's booklet 'Tobacco in Nigeria' (April 1960) comparing 1951 and 1959 suggest that the rate of return on capital was much higher in the early 1950s. Sales were £7·3m. in 1951 and £10·0m. in 1959, fixed assets were £0·4m. and £3·1m. respectively, and equity capital £1m. and £5m. Thus in 1951 the fixed asset/sales ratio was 1 to 18·0 as against 1 to 3·2 in 1959; the respective equity/sales ratios were 1 to 7 and 1 to 2. Even when the more conservative financial structure and greater investment in worker welfare amenities in 1959 are taken into account, the difference remains considerable.

(£116,409) was to buy out John Holt's share in the Biscuit Manufacturing Company, biscuits lending themselves well to NTC's established marketing network. The first investment can be considered as a backward linkage, while the second is best described as horizontal diversification.

II

The beer industry was established in Nigeria in 1949 at the initiative of the United Africa Company which acted, as described in the previous chapter, to protect its merchant interest in the beer trade.[1] After several years of fighting to gain market acceptance,[2] Nigerian Breweries Limited achieved profitable operation in 1952. In order to minimize the chance of a competitor establishing, a second brewery was opened in Aba in 1957 and a third plant in Kaduna in 1963; as in the case of NTC, political considerations influenced the locational decisions.

In 1961 the Irish stout brewer Guinness and its principal Nigerian distributor, UAC, began construction of a brewery at Ikeja, just outside Lagos; after England and the United States, Nigeria was Guinness' largest market. In 1961 the Eastern Nigeria Development Corporation purchased a lager beer brewery from Coutinho Caro which was erected at Umuahia, home of the eastern region Premier; in the following year the Western Nigeria Development Corporation purchased a similar plant from an Israeli machinery merchant which was erected at Abeokuta. WNDC was fortunate enough to recruit the German brewing firm of Henniger as a technical partner (10 %) and A. G. Leventis to assist in the distribution (10 %). ENDC's brewery has suffered from production and marketing problems and excessive employment (in April 1966 100 of its 380 workers were retrenched as 'unnecessary'). As a measure of the immediate commercial success of the Guinness venture, locally issued shares were selling at four times par value in the company's third year of operation.

As can be seen from table 25, by 1964 the industry had built up its capacity some 28 % or about four years ahead of demand. Because Guinness stout only partially competes with lager beer and because of difficulties encountered by Independence Brewery, this excess capacity did not exert the downward pressure on prices which might have been expected in a non-collusive oligopolistic market.

[1] UAC contributed a third of the capital, Heinekens, a third with the balance shared among the other European trading firms (Holt, PZ, UTC, CFAO, SCOA).

[2] After initial technical difficulties (six months) with fermentation and temperature control, the main problem was one of countering the unfavourable demonstration effects of the European community's prejudiced refusal to drink what they dubbed a 'chemical beer'. This negative factor was overcome by an intensive 'Men of distinction drink Star beer' advertising campaign and Star's winning of the first prize at the 1954 Empire and Commonwealth competitions.

As in many other respects, the factors influencing the choice of technology in brewing and bottling are the same as those identified for cigarette manufacture. A well protected market, a low ratio of manufacturing cost to price, and sales maximization constrained by a satisfactory rate of return have led to the adoption of highly automated,

Table 25. *The Nigerian brewing industry, 1966*

	Start -up	Capacity (m. gal.)	Investment[a] (£m.)	Employment
NBL Lagos	1949	5·0	3·5	1,700
Aba	1957	2·5		
Kaduna	1963	1·4		
Guinness	1963	5·0	2·0	650
Independence (ENDC)	1963	1·0	1·0	380
West African Breweries (WNDC)	1964	1·2	1·0	250
		16·1	7·5	2,980
Domestic production (m. gal.)		5·3 (1962)	12·0 (1964)	13·9 (1966)
Imports (m. gal.)		5·0	0·7	0·4

[a] Equity, capital reserves and long term debt.

SOURCES: Federal Office of Statistics, *Economic Indicators*, January 1967, p. 14 and data supplied by the Nigerian Breweries Limited.

capital-intensive technology. The labour skills required in operating a modern brewery are likewise very modest; beyond a relatively small number of senior technicians (maltsters, brewers, production engineers, bottling managers) production workers are not called upon to perform any operation requiring special knowledge or skill. In 1963 eighty foreigners, representing 3·2 % of the labour force, received 37·8 % of the wage and salary payments.[1]

Domestic production of beer has required considerably less tariff protection than cigarettes. In addition to a nominal net tariff protection of 18 to 65 %,[2] international transportation cost adds another 40 %.[3]

[1] Federal Office of Statics, *Industrial Survey of Nigeria 1963*, tables 5 and 6.

[2] The higher protection has occurred in recent years and has not been fully utilized. The important tariff and domestic excise rates per gallon have been as follows:

	Tariff	Excise
pre-1948	2*s*.	—
1948–55	2*s*. 6*d*.	1*s*. 9*d*.
1956–59	4*s*.	2*s*. 9*d*.
1960–61	7*s*. 2*d*.	5*s*. 6*d*.
1962–63	9*s*. 6*d*.	6*s*. 8*d*.
1964–65	15*s*.	7*s*.

[3] A 33 % United Kingdom f.o.b.-Nigerian c.i.f. differential was computed for the years 1957–60. A 7 % mark-up is added to cover the difference between ex-factory and f.o.b. *Annual Statement of the Trade of the United Kingdom*, vol. III, and Nigerian *Trade Reports*.

The information necessary to calculate the value-added by brewing at world prices is not available; however the data in table 27 below suggests it might be on the order of 30 % of the c.i.f. import value. This means that the effective rate of tariff protection is about three times the nominal tariff level, i.e. something over 100 %. For both cigarettes and beer, in Nigeria as elsewhere, the prime value-added components of the product by the time it reaches the consumer are taxation and advertising.

Table 26. *Star beer: prices, output, profit*

	Price per gallon (shillings) (1950 = 100)	Output (1,000 gal.)	Before-tax profits (£000s)
1955	118	1,762	...
1956	130	2,233	...
1957	130	2,407	...
1958	133	3,060	...
1959	155	4,455	745
1960	174	4,459	709
1961	179	4,932	987
1962	192	5,323	359
1963	192	6,822	685
1964	198	7,120	673
1965	205	7,477	1,235
1966	...	8,590	1,598

SOURCE: Data supplied by Nigerian Breweries Limited.

Nigerian Breweries, in operation eighteen years, provides an opportunity to examine the performance over time of an infant industry. Over the period 1949–65 the ex-factory price of Star beer rose 105 %; 43 % of this rise is attributable to excise increases, leaving 62 % to be accounted for by rising wage and workers' amenities costs, growing expenditures on sales promotion, a general inflation of input prices and specific cost increases as a result of backward linkages in respect to the domestic production of bottles, caps, labels and packing materials – items which are nearly as important as manufacturing costs (see table 27). Nor does there appear to be any clear trend for the manufacturer's profit margin on unit sales to fall as greater efficiency is achieved.

Turning to the question of profits, in 1950 Nigerian Breweries' equity capital was £450,000; by 1961 £1,050,000 in retained profits had been capitalized, bringing the equity to £1·5m. In recent years issued capital and reserves have been at about £2m.; however, as a result of inflation and appreciation in urban property land values, the current value of the company's fixed assets in 1964 was £3·2m. Over the six years 1960–65, an average profit of £758,000 yields a before-tax rate of return of 38 % on £2m. It should be noted, however, that Nigerian

Breweries has relied heavily on bank overdrafts to finance all its stock and inventories, whereas NTC has followed a very conservative policy in this area which has substantially lowered its rate of return.[1]

The quantitative significance of the beer industry's potential linkages to the economy is seen in table 27. Forty-three per cent of gross sales goes to the Federal Government as excise and income tax. In 1963 reported wage payments to Nigerians totalled £588,396.[2] Purchases of imported barley malt, the major ingredients, came to £666,000 in the same year. On the basis of present agricultural knowledge and techniques, the potential for the local production of malt is not very promising. Barley can be grown on the Jos plateau, but it is of a poor quality and the yield per acre is about one-fifth that of Europe. The largest single input purchase in beer production is glass bottles – £850,000 in 1963. And in this case a supplier industry has been established.

Table 27. *Distribution of gross income, Star beer, 1964*

	Per cent	Gross sales
Excise tax	36·0	£6·3m.
Advertising and distribution	12·0	
Management overhead	5·0	
Manufacturing cost	11·9	
Malt, hops, sugar	8·5	
Bottles, labels, tops	7·5	
Packing	2·1	
Profit (before tax)	17·0	
Total	100·0	

SOURCE: Data supplied by Nigerian Breweries Limited.

Despite vigorous efforts during 1959–61, neither ENDC nor WNDC were able to interest private investors to undertake or participate in a glass factory. So in 1961 ENDC commissioned Coutinho Caro to establish a £1·2m. turnkey project in Port Harcourt, taking advantage of the area's natural gas and suitable sand resources. However, it is not clear that a minimum sized market existed for a glass factory. Only a small fraction of brewery and soft drink bottle purchases are for *new* bottles: used bottles at 2*d.* each were sufficient to meet 70 % of the bottle requirements in 1963. Locally produced new bottles, selling at 6*d.*, are required only for making good wastage and growth in demand.

Problems on the supply side rendered demand limitations academic during the period under consideration. Much of the Port Harcourt factory's equipment was poorly matched. Of the three moulding

[1] Thus in 1966 NTC's fixed assets, exclusive of goodwill and trade marks, were £4m. as compared to issued capital and reserves of £7·8m.

[2] This and the following 1963 data are drawn from the *Industrial Survey of Nigeria, 1963*, tables 5 and 6 and p. 22.

machines, one was for pharmaceutical bottles for which the annual demand was equal to about one month's production; one of the two beer-bottle moulding machines was of an uneconomically small size. A cracked furnace as a result of the unannounced closing of the gas line during the 1964 general strike, the use of inefficient hand-trucks instead of a gravity-operated silo for charging the furnace, and problems of over-staffing combined with a number of difficulties related to the quality of the glass to keep the Nigerian Glass Company deep in the red. Moreover, the intermediate term prospect for economic production of glass products in Nigeria was further darkened in 1964 when the Mid-Western Nigerian Government placed a £1·3m. order with Coutinho Caro to build a second plant at Ughelli.

III

Of all import-replacing industries none possess so great a comparative advantage as the production of cement. As noted in chapter 2 the cost of carriage to a Nigerian seaport adds some 70 % to the ex-factory price of the overseas manufacturer.[1] Beyond this natural protection, cement has carried the usual revenue tariff which ranged between 9 and 16 % of the c.i.f. value prior to the establishment of local production.[2] For inland producers serving inland markets the cost of land transport provides further protection, the equivalent of 20 % of the cost of manufacture for every hundred miles. Given the size of this transport-savings incentive, it might be expected that the manufacture of cement would be one of the first instances of import-substitution, occurring as soon as the market reached the technological threshold – the capacity of a single vertical kiln, 30,000 tons. In fact, because the industry is characterized by large firms, a market of a mere 30,000 tons is far below the *minimum sensible*; it was not until 1954 when imports were 368,000 tons, thirty-one years after the technological threshold had been reached (1923), that a company to produce cement in Nigeria was formed – and this at the initiative of the government.

As with most other goods, imports of cement were more or less static during the two decades prior to 1945; since then consumption has grown rapidly, rising from 100,000 tons in 1947 to 1,137,000 in 1966. In 1950 the Federal Government invited the British combine Associated Portland Cement Manufacturers (the world's largest producer), who

[1] This figure was confirmed by a major British supplier in 1965.

[2] The import duty per ton of cement has been as follows:

until 1930	– nil	1946–59	28*s*.
1930–7	– 5*s*. 0*d*.	1960–1	20 % *ad valorem*
1937–9	– 7*s*. 6*d*.	1961–3	30*s*.
1940–5	– 11*s*. 3*d*.	1964–6	100*s*.

supplied over half of Nigeria's imports, to establish a local plant. After nearly two years of surveying the country's limestone deposits, negotiating and deliberating, APCM declined to go ahead with the project. Unable to interest private investors, the government determined to undertake the major burden of the investment herself, setting aside £1·2m. in 1952. After two and a half years of searching in Belgium and America for a technical partner, the Nigerian Government finally reached agreement with the Danish firm of F. L. Smidth,

Cement imports

(tons)

1925–45	40,000–80,000	1950	153,861
1946	95,988	1951	261,057
1947	107,306	1952	205,169
1948	131,655	1953	297,436
1949	161,959	1954	368,108

SOURCE: *Trade Reports.*

the world's largest manufacturer of cement-making machinery, and its British associate, Tunnel Portland Cement Company, to join in a venture as consulting engineers and managing agent respectively. Both private firms agreed to take up a small incentive-creating share of the equity capital. The financial structure of the company, located in the eastern region, was as follows:

	Equity (£)	(%)	Debenture (£)
Nigerian Governments*	1,200,000	(68·6)	500,000
Tunnel	93,750	(5·4)	—
F. L. Smidth	93,750	(5·4)	—
Colonial Dev. Corp.	187,500	(10·7)	—
Nigerian public	174,900	(10·0)	—
	1,750,000		500,000

* 65 % contributed by the Federal Government (later sold to the Eastern Nigerian Government) and 35 % by the Eastern Nigerian Government.

Compared to later industrial projects the Nigerian Cement Company was very conservatively financed (low ratio of debt to equity) and only slightly unfavourable to the government who provided 75·5 % of the capital in exchange for a claim on profits (share of equity) of 68·6 %. In contrast, the best terms the Northern Nigerian Government could obtain for the country's first textile firm, a pioneer undertaking of equal risk, was 66·7 % of the equity as against providing 92 % of the total capital.[1] The managing agency fee of £5,000 per annum and 5 % of net profits was also very modest – typically the management fee works out to about 15 % of net earnings.[2]

Once the government shouldered the entrepreneurial risk herself and succeeded in attracting a competent technical partner, APCM was faced with the prospect of losing a large and growing market. As in most of the cases reviewed in the preceding chapter, there was a certain natural disposition to supply Nigeria from APCM's efficient well-written-down home plants. More important the major part of Nigeria's cement consumption was in the Lagos-Ibadan area – markets that could not easily be supplied from the one proven site at Nkalagu in the northern corner of the eastern region. This unfavourable location conjoined with the moderate size of the overall market in 1951 was not attractive enough to APCM to establish a local plant, nor was it likely in the company's judgment to be sufficiently attractive to other investors. Proved wrong by the rapid growth in consumption and by the determined efforts of the government to recruit a technical partner, APCM acted immediately to protect its market lest a second mill be established in the west.

Within a month of the formation of the Nigerian Cement Company APCM set up a syndicate with the Western Nigeria Development Corporation to search for viable limestone deposits. When these were uncovered at Ewekoro in 1957 the West African Portland Cement Company was formed, with the following financial structure:

	Equity (£)	Debenture (£)	(%)
APCM	510,000	1,020,000	51
WNDC	390,000	780,000	39
UAC	100,000	200,000	10
	1,000,000	2,000,000	

In this case of a market-protecting investment, the government did not have to provide any incentive by way of differential gearing. The company's financial structure is geared, for reasons of taxation, but not in such a way as to shift the risk; debenture capital is held only by the entrepreneurs and in proportion to their equity share holding.

[1] Normally non-equity capital bears a lesser degree of risk, but in a pioneering venture where the prime hazard is one of initial lack of viability and where the highly specific physical assets are not saleable, there is a good case for treating all capital as risk capital during the start-up period.

[2] The agreement also provided that F. L. Smidth, as purchasing agent, receive a 5 % commission on all equipment and materials purchased by the company outside of Nigeria, excluding cement-making machinery designed by F. L. Smidth.

Of the two sites Nkalagu would appear to have the advantage on most counts. Being 100 miles further inland natural protection from imports is greater. The limestone deposits are of a higher quality and the Enugu coal fields nearby. As 25 tons of coal are required to produce every 100 tons of cement, the fact that Ewekoro was more than 400 miles from Enugu would have represented a serious handicap to the West African Portland Cement Company if no alternative fuel had been available. The solution to this problem, as well as that of the impure limestone, was to adopt a more capital-intensive 'dry process' which reduces the fuel requirement by a third, oil replacing coal.[1] (Other than the choice between these two processes, there is little possibility for utilizing more labour-intensive techniques in the production of cement.) The only relative advantage enjoyed by the Ewekoro location, and it is a very important one, is its proximity to richer markets, with its corollary of transport savings; Lagos and the west account for over half of the country's total cement consumption.

The manufacture of cement is one of the few cases which conforms to the traditional infant industry concept of a new industry first finding its feet, then expanding and exploiting economies of scale with consequent cost and price reductions. The reasons why cement is exceptional in this regard are that substantial increasing returns to scale do obtain and, more important, production can only be expanded if the transport costs entailed in extending the market are absorbed in the ex-factory price. While the consumer at the periphery enjoys a price reduction only sufficient to induce him to shift his patronage, all other buyers reap a 'consumer's surplus' proportionate to their distance from the periphery.[2]

Regarding realizable economies of scale, the Nigerian Cement Company has estimated that it cost the company approximately £6 to produce 1 ton of cement (exclusive of packaging) when capacity was limited to a single kiln, 100,000–125,000 tons. With two kilns the cost dropped to £5 and with four kilns to £4 per ton.[3] As the factory has expanded from one to four kilns it has to extend its markets toward imports at the coast and towards its competitor in the western region. In the estimates given below we have allowed 15*s.* per ton for packaging.

[1] The dry process involves reducing by half the proportion of water in the mixture of pulverised limestone and clay ('slurry') which is fed into the rotary kiln for fusing into cement clinker. The reduced fuel cost of this dry process is partially offset by increased depreciation charges.

[2] This depends upon the assumption that there is no significant price discrimination against consumers inside the periphery, a condition so far met in the Nigerian case save for one exception.

[3] S. U. Ugoh, 'The Nigerian Cement Company', *Nigerian Journal of Economic and Social Studies*, March 1964, p. 78.

	Kilns	Cost per ton (*s.*)	Price Ex-factory (*s.*)	Price Port Harcourt (*s.*)	Landed cost of import at Port Harcourt (*s.*)
1958	1	135	215	250	204(176)
1960	2	115	205	240	193(165)
1962	2	115	195	230	184(154)
1964	4	95	185+15 155+15	205	238(138)

( ) represent c.i.f. value. There was considerable dumping in 1962 and 1964. In 1962, for instance, slightly more than a quarter of imports was Polish cement at an average c.i.f. value of 107*s.* per ton.

The extra 15*s.* in price in 1964 represents an excise tax which was imposed on local production when the protective import duty was increased from 30*s.* to 100*s.* to protect the coastal clinker plants from abnormally low-priced imports. The second price of 155*s.* pertains only to the Aba-Port Harcourt area (sold ex-depot in Aba at 196*s.*) and was designed to be competitive with imports. This was the first instance of price discrimination against consumers within the periphery. Taking 175*s.* as the average ex-factory price in 1964, there has been a 40*s.* drop in price (18 %) since the plant began operations late in 1957. Because of the richer markets within a 50-mile radius the Ewekoro factory has not had to reduce its price to the same degree as output has expanded – from an ex-factory price of 198*s.* per ton in 1961 to 175*s.* in 1964, 23*s.* as against Nkalagu's 40*s.* – although the former commenced selling at a comparably lower price because of its greater proximity to import competition from the coast.

Table 28. *Distribution of gross income, Nigerian cement industry, 1963*

(£000s)

Distribution of expenditure and income		Gross sales
Wages and salaries	483	4,692
Depreciation	514	
Gypsum	203	
Packing material	180	
Fuel	437	
Electricity	469	
Rents and royalties	214	
Administration and management fee	275	
Profit	1,917	

SOURCES: *Industrial Survey of Nigeria, 1963*, pp. 32–3 and data supplied by the two major producers.

As can be seen from table 28 integrated cement manufacture (quarrying limestone and clay, clinker production, grinding) does not involve extensive inter-sectoral purchases, although the domestic value added is comparatively high. Gypsum, packing material, about three-quarters of capital replacement, the management fee and the oil content of fuel and electricity (up until the end of 1965) represent the industry's primary import components. In addition, a small portion of profits and perhaps a third of the £94,661 expatriate salary payments are remitted abroad. The very sizeable profit margin is a reflection of the industry's capital-intensity. S. U. Ugoh has calculated that local manufacture results in a 20 to 25 % foreign exchange savings.[1]

An import-replacing industry is likely to have positive forward linkages only to the extent the local product is cheaper than imports bearing an equivalent tax burden – otherwise the forward linkage may be of a negative character. Import-substitute production of cement has had negative forward linkages for most of southern Nigeria, and conversely for the rest of the country, owing to transport savings, it has brought about cost reduction in the construction industry and contributed to a higher standard of native housing where concrete has been substituted for mud.

Purchase of electricity represents a major backward linkage in both cement production and (as we shall see) textiles; although it is less important in most other industries, it is nevertheless a pervasive industrial input. As mentioned in chapter 2, given a reasonable degree of geographic concentration of industry, each new industrial customer contributes to potential economies of scale in electricity generation. In 1965–6 large industrial users who had negotiated concessionary rates consumed 19 % of the total electricity supply and an ambiguously described 'small industry' category accounted for 32 %.[2] Since the 15 % increase in 1956 tariff rates have remained stable; over the same period electricity generation has grown an average of 20 % per year. Over the period 1956–65 the cost of production per kWh fell from 3·9*d*. to 3·0*d*., while wage rates and consumer prices rose by 35 to 50 %: the cost of electricity has fallen as predicted.[3]

The cost reduction in the rate per unit of electricity has been partially offset by variations in voltage and unannounced interruptions of supply. Increasing in frequency since 1962, such stoppages have led to lost production and a temporarily idled labour force for many industries; in some cases unannounced electricity interruptions have

[1] S. U. Ogoh, 'The Nigerian Cement Industry', *Nigerian Journal of Economic and Social Studies*, March 1966, p. 109.

[2] Electricity Corporation of Nigeria, *Annual Report 1965–6*, Lagos 1966, p. 10. Concessionary rates range from 2·3*d*. per kWh in Lagos, to 1·4*d*. at Jos, to 3·4*d*. at Kano. These rates are thought to approximate the marginal cost of production in these areas.

[3] *Ibid*. p. 10 and appendix A.

resulted in damaged equipment.[1] Most firms have shouldered additional capital cost by installing stand-by generating equipment. These failings of the Electricity Corporation, stemming from inadequate maintenance and inefficient operation of generating facilities, are attributable at least in part to a rate of growth of output which exceeds the Corporation's managerial and technical capacity. Thus in the short run the full potential of technological economies of scale have not been realized.

Judging by the performance of the Nigerian Cement Company, for an efficient producer cement milling is no less profitable than the other industries reviewed in this chapter. As seen in the figures shown below, during its first eight years of operation the rate of return on equity has averaged 28 %, on equity and reserves, 20 %.[2] Two-thirds of these earnings have been retained with the result that £4·5m. of £6·3m. total capital employed has come from profits. With its pioneer status and depreciation carry-forward, no income taxes were paid until the eighth year.

Year ended 31 March	Net profit	Issued capital	Capital and reserves	Rate of Return on Issued capital	Rate of Return on Capital and reserves
	(£000s)	(£000s)	(£000s)	(%)	(%)
1959	424	1,750	2,027	24·2	20·9
1960	450	1,750	2,302	25·7	19·5
1961	696	2,100	2,789	33·1	25·0
1962	1,021	2,100	3,600	48·6	28·4
1963	826	4,200	5,034	19·7	16·4
1964	916	4,200	5,426	21·8	17·0
1965	874	4,200	5,694	20·8	15·3
1966	1,212	4,200	6,343	28·9	19·1

SOURCE: Company Reports.

So far we have discussed only the two major producers. In 1957 a clinker plant with an annual capacity of 60,000 tons commenced grinding imported clinker and gypsum in Port Harcourt; it closed down for want of technical know-how after three weeks of operation.[3]

[1] To cite one example, R. A. Akinola reported the experience of Nigerian Textile Mills Ltd. as follows: 'Within four months (November 1962 to February 1963), the total loss due to power failures amounted to 250,000 square yards at a cost to the factory of about £24,000. During the same period the damage caused to electrical equipment was estimated at over £21,000. Wages to workers had to be paid at the rate of £50 an hour even when the mill was not working and there was severe disruption of the production programme as well as a failure to meet commitments to customers.' 'Factors Affecting the Location of a Textile Industry—The Example of the Ikeja Textile Mill', *Nigerian Journal of Economic and Social Studies*, November, 1965, p. 255.

[2] In 1966 the Nigerian Cement Company's fixed assets valued at cost were £7·5m.; the depreciated value was £5·6m.

[3] The history of this venture was related to the author by the ENDC Credits Manager and the General Manager of NEMCO, September 1964.

Financed by a £100,000 loan from ENDC, the clinker plant was to constitute the third leg of an integrated cement-sawmill-contracting venture, Nigerian Engineering and Manufacturing Company (NEMCO), organized by one of the region's prominent politician-entrepreneurs. In an attempt to salvage the project the regional government invited a German concern which had been supplying the clinker to join NEMCO as technical partner and managing agent. After six months of restoring the abandoned machinery and reconverting the now petrol drum depot, the clinker plant reopened in 1960. Although temporarily closed down in 1962 as a result of imported Polish cement selling at almost half its own price (the Ewekoro factory stopped production for two months for the same reason), by 1963 the company had covered its past losses. However, with the introduction of the third and fourth kiln at Nkalagu and the consequent extension into the Port Harcourt market, NEMCO was once again driven into the red in 1964, incurring a loss of 25*s*. on every ton produced. The company went into liquidation in March 1965.

A second clinker grinding plant, Anglo-Canadian Cement Ltd., opened in Lagos in 1963. This company, an off-shoot of shipping interests, entered the Nigerian market as an importer of low-priced Polish cement in 1955, and soon moved into the production of pre-stressed concrete products. The decision to establish a clinker plant was influenced by the economies that would accrue to the shipping side of the business: the ability to fill its chartered ships with clinker on the inward voyage greatly enhanced the profitability of the company's principal activity, carrying Nigerian exports.[1] Two other clinker-grinding plants, Lagos Cement Works and the Mid-West Cement Company, joint ventures between Nigerian politician-entrepreneurs and a German machinery merchant, began production in Lagos and Koko respectively in 1964.

Even if the clinker grinding plants could earn a profit, their contribution to the economy would be very marginal, if not negative. The amount of labour employed is small. All the ingredients – clinker, gypsum, paper bags – are imported as, of course, is all the equipment. With no transport savings and the higher cost of purchased clinker, clinker-grinding would appear to be viable solely on the basis of tariff subsidization and guaranteed markets *vis-à-vis* competition from local integrated cement works.

As noted earlier, since 1961 cement mills and glass factories have become important prestige symbols for the regional governments. In

[1] A similar desire to more fully utilize its ships heavily influenced the Southern Star Shipping Line to promote the establishment of a port-side flour mill in Lagos. Its ships bring American wheat in and carry Nigerian produce out.

1962 the Government of Northern Nigeria commissioned Ferrostaal A. G. of Western Germany to install an integrated 100,000-ton cement mill just outside of Sokoto; not only was the location uneconomic, but the machinery installed was unsuited to the local limestone and a second kiln had to be ordered.[1] Similarly, the government in the east in 1964 commissioned a second mill (also supplied by a German firm) to be located at Calabar, despite the absence of demand for additional production. A third integrated cement works, supplied by Coutinho Caro, was commissioned by the Mid-Western Nigeria Government in 1965 to be erected at Opkilla. Even if there were demand for additional local output and there were no technical or managerial problems, only the Okpilla location would possess a viable market; the Nkalagu mill currently supplies the natural markets of the prospective Sokoto and Calabar plants at prices which the latter will not be able to meet without operating at a substantial loss. By the end of 1966, the combined capacity of the two major producers exceeded a million tons, only about 100,000 tons short of total demand.

IV

The last of our industry narratives concerns both the newest and the largest area of import substitution. The cotton textile industry has been one of the major areas of industrialization for nearly every developing country in the twentieth century. There are a number of reasons for this. In low-income societies not only does the purchase of cloth account for a significant portion of all consumer expenditures (about 7 % for Nigeria) but as an import, cotton textiles are the largest single user of foreign exchange – in the case of Nigeria over £21m. as late as 1965. From the supply side, as a modern industry textile production is moderately labour-intensive and yet does not require a highly skilled work force, features which make the industry particularly attractive to countries with an abundance of untrained labour. Excess capacity in both the textile and textile machinery industries in advanced economies means that new and used equipment is available at favourable prices and that competent partners can be recruited. Moreover Nigeria possesses the further advantage of producing some 50,000 tons of high grade, medium staple cotton each year.

There are, however, two factors which have worked against the early establishment of cotton textile manufacturing. The first is the very slight degree of natural protection afforded by transportation conjoined with the existence of highly efficient, low-cost exporting producers in the Far East. Second, and more important, the market-protection

[1] Northern Nigeria, *A White Paper of the Military Government Policy for the Reorganization of the Northern Nigeria Development Corporation*, Kaduna 1966, p. 21.

incentive for the overseas manufacturer to establish locally is not as strong as in other industries. This stems from the fact that the major importing firms maintain buying offices in Madras, Hong Kong, Tokyo, etc., and purchase from a large number of suppliers in each country, and so spread the stake in the Nigerian market over a wide number of producers. Consequently government initiative and special concessions have played a particularly important role in the creation of the textile industry.

Our narrative will begin with an analysis of the demand for textiles; this will be followed by a short chronology of the firms and their sponsors. Using the earlier investor typology as our reference we will examine the equipment policy (choice of technique) and financial structure of the various firms. After a discussion of labour efficiency and locational patterns we will conclude with an assessment of the industry's profitability, government tariff policy and the industry's contribution to the economy.

THE MARKET

The market for textiles in Nigeria is large. Over the last decade imported cotton piece goods have averaged over 200m. yards per year, synthetics 95m. yards and indigenous hand-woven cotton fabrics 50m. yards.[1] Imports of second-hand clothing, singlets and shirts are also significant; in 1959–61 these items accounted for an equivalent of approximately 75m. yards. Table 29 shows the imports of cotton and

Table 29. *Nigerian textile imports, piece goods*

	Cotton		Rayon	
	Quantity (m. yds.)	c.i.f. value (£ m.)	Quantity (m. yds.)	c.i.f. value (£m.)
1937–8	116·4	2·8	9·9	0·5
1946–50	129·1	12·2	10·9	1·8
1951–5	174·8	18·5	72·3	9·6
1956	149·9	14·4	157·6	14·9
1957	156·2	14·5	149·9	11·4
1958	172·5	16·3	151·6	10·8
1959	143·6	14·9	101·4	7·9
1960	210·6	22·4	100·6	8·6
1961	244·8	26·4	89·6	7·4
1962	170·8	18·7	43·7	3·8
1963	206·6	21·4	24·7	2·5
1964	204·2	22·0	28·0	3·5
1965	209·8	21·4	26·1	4·1

SOURCES: Federal Office of Statistics, *Economic Indicators*, March 1966, p. 22; and *Annual Abstract of Statistics*, 1964, p. 83.

[1] The estimate for hand-woven cloth is that of the Federation of British Industries. *Nigeria, An Industrial Reconnaissance*, London 1961, p. 14.

rayon piece goods since 1937; in addition domestic production has grown from 1m. yards in 1957 to 176m. yards in 1966.[1]

Reflecting Nigeria's poverty, *per capita* consumption of cotton and rayon textiles is low; during the three years 1958–60 the average figures were 5·1 and 3·0 yards respectively. For Ghana the comparable consumption rates were 14·8 and 6·5 yards. Measured in fabric weight, Nigerian *per capita* consumption is only two-fifths that of Latin America and one-eighth that of temperate North America.[2] The growth of rayon's share in total imports is attributable to the gradual post-war lifting of exchange controls and import quotas, which in the case of Japan, the principal supplier, had been imposed as early as 1934.[3] The other side of the coin of such low levels of *per capita* consumption, as we saw in chapter 2, is a very high income elasticity of demand.

Table 30. *Textile imports by country of origin*

(£000s, c.i.f.)

	1937	1958	1961	1963	1965
Cotton piece goods:					
United Kingdom	2,964	3,400	4,102	2,186	2,623
India	454	3,091	1,876	1,080	1,209
Japan	66	4,743	12,967	12,997	14,036
China	160	1,265	1,885	929	3,585
Netherlands	137	1,985	3,076	1,793	1,707
W. Germany	86	215	463	642	1,273
Other countries	186	1,596	2,066	1,814	1,895
Total	4,053	16,295	26,435	21,441	26,328
Rayon piece goods:					
United Kingdom	219	184	147	118	...
India	10	312	160	13	...
Italy	140	163	238	86	...
Japan	41	9,302	6,637	2,168	...
W. Germany	258	674	72	31	...
Other countries	83	155	106	110	...
Total	751	10,790	7,360	2,526	3,700

SOURCE: Federal Office of Statistics, *Digest of Statistics*, vol. 13, 1964, no. 2, pp. 43–4.

Almost the whole of rayon imports consists of prints, piece-dyed and colour woven goods, items whose popularity rests upon their considerable price advantage *vis-à-vis* cotton fabrics. This price advantage, however, is offset not only by a certain qualitative preference for cotton but, more fundamentally, by its relative lack of tensile strength (and

[1] The uneven movement of textile imports from year to year arises from the fact that importers must place their orders before the major cash crops are in, with the result that inventory correction may aggravate fluctuations deriving from changes in purchasing power. The local production figure, which includes a certain amount of printing on imported grey cloth (and hence double counting), is given in *Economic Indicators*, January 1967, p. 17.

[2] Scheuer Textile Consultants, Inc., *Feasibility Report for an Integrated Textile Mill in the Eastern Region of the Federation of Nigeria*, Rockefeller Brother Fund, Lagos 1961, p. 27.

[3] Charlotte Leubuscher, 'The Policy Governing External Trade', in Margery Perham, ed., *Mining, Commerce and Finance in Nigeria*, London 1948, p. 159.

hence inability to stand up to the cold water, rock-pounding washing process) which seriously affects durability. The decline of rayon imports began in 1959 with the first tariff increase, losing further ground with each successive hike. The specific duty increases represent a far higher percentage increase for rayon than for the more expensive cotton cloth. The general rise in specific duties on cloth has also resulted in a consumer shift, superimposed upon an overall 3 % growth trend in textile consumption, toward imported used clothing: from 6 % of total textile consumption by yardage equivalent in 1956, this category had grown to 32 % by 1965.[1]

In recent years Japan has supplied from half to two-thirds of all Nigeria's textile imports. Qualitatively her products are superior to

Table 31. *Quantity, unit-price and duty for principal cotton textile imports*

(Q: millions of yards. P: pence per yard. Duty: pence per yard)

	Grey		Bleached		
	Q	P	Q	P	Duty
1956	37·5	12	27·6	22	8
1657	28·0	13	40·3	19	8
1958	25·2	13	43·5	19	8
1959	7·1	13	32·2	19	10
1960	6·6	14	32·9	17	10
1961	8·5	14	48·5	20	12
1962	12·6	17	27·9	21	12
1963	1·2	...	23·5	19	12
1964	1·6	18	24·9	18	15
1965	11·9	...	23·1	19	15

	Prints		Dyed		Colour woven		
	Q	P	Q	P	Q	P	Duty
1956	35·5	25	19·8	26	25·8	29	8
1957	37·8	27	24·8	24	22·4	25	8
1958	49·4	26	29·6	25	21·6	26	8
1959	54·8	26	26·6	25	18·4	27	10
1960	99·0	26	42·2	26	24·0	27	10
1961	104·3	26	47·3	28	30·4	29	12
1962	78·7	25	39·3	27	18·4	30	16
1963	122·0	...	50·5	27	20·3	27	16
1964	97·1	26	50·8	28	22·6	32	24
1965	66·1	27	46·9	29	21·5	31	42

SOURCES: *Trade Summaries* and *Customs Tariff Ordinance 1958*, with revisions.

NOTE: For purposes of calculating protection it should be noted that in August 1964 excise taxes were placed upon local production, 6*d*. per yard for prints and 2*d*. per yard for grey and bleached cloth. A concessionary rate of 1·8*d*. per yard on grey cloth to be used for printing by approved manufacturers was enacted in 1963. This rate was raised to 4. 8*d*. in August 1964.

[1] The corresponding rise in share of expenditures on textile products is 0·8 % in 1956 to 4·8 % in 1965. Data supplied by Arthur D. Little, Inc., advisers to the Federal Ministry of Commerce and Industry, sponsored by the U.S. Agency for International Development.

those of China (Hong Kong) and India, and, although her prints and dyed goods are not quite up to the standard of Dutch and British cloth, on the basis of lower prices Japanese fabrics are highly competitive even in these lines.[1] As a result of Japanese textiles being highly competitive with local production, general balance of payments difficulties and a lopsided trade with Japan in particular (exports of £1·5m. against purchases of £24·8m. in 1962, 70 % of which were cloth), import restrictions were imposed on Japanese products in September 1963. Three months later the Japanese ambassador was informed that if his country could not manage to purchase more of Nigeria's exports, a total embargo might be placed on Japanese goods.[2]

The composition of demand for cotton cloth can be seen in table 31. The greater part of unbleached grey goods are consumed in the Muslim north, providing the material for the traditional 'riga'. In both the south and the north grey or bleached fabrics are used for the trousers and vest. In the south the main outer garment, the 'agbada', is made from prints. Likewise the women's wrap or dress is made of printed fabric throughout the country. In the south each tribe, often each locality, will have its own pattern and colour scheme, some of which date as far back as twenty years. In addition to everyday wear, garments made from special patterns are worn for important ceremonial occasions. In Yorubaland one can observe a wedding or a funeral where an entire clan is clothed in the same pattern, purchased specifically for that event. Most of the less expensive rayon prints are consumed by easterners and by the women in the north.[3] Dyed goods are used for trousers, uniforms of all kinds and household furnishings.

[1] Taking 1961 as an example, the average c.i.f. price of Japanese cotton piece goods was 25*d*. compared to 33*d*. for European suppliers; for man-made fibre piece goods the respective prices were 19*d*. and 54*d*.

[2] *West Africa*, 7 December 1963. Nigeria represents Japan's sixth largest overseas market.

[3] The merchant firms report (*c*. 1960) the following cotton to rayon sales ratio: North 2·1, East 1·1, West 10·1. Scheuer Textile Consultants, *op. cit.* p. 145.

	Nigeria (yards)	Ghana (yards)
Cotton		
Grey	0·7	1·3
Bleached	1·0	1·3
Printed	1·9	10·0
Piece dyed	0·9	1·6
Colour-woven	0·6	0·6
Synthetics	3·0	6·5
Total	8·1	21·3

SOURCE: Nigerian and Ghanaian *Trade Reports* (known as the *Annual Report on Eastern Trade in Ghana*) and the respective approximate population totals of 35m. and 6m. Local production included.

Future growth in the demand for cotton cloth is likely to be concentrated in prints. This is strongly suggested by the experience of Ghana, a country whose basic social and cultural structure is very similar to Nigeria's but where the process of westernization is more advanced and, most important, where *per capita* income is substantially higher.[1] The estimated size of the average annual additon to consumption over the period 1962–72 is placed at 15m. yards, sufficient to support a new plant every year.[2]

HISTORY

Nigeria's first textile plant came into operation in 1950. With technical and financial assistance from the government, Kano Citizens Trading Company, an enterprise formed by leading members of the Hausa trading community in Kano, began weaving operations using fifty second-hand power looms imported from Lancashire. In 1952 a similar mill, J. F. Kamson & Company, comprising sixty looms and a spinning section, went into production on the outskirts of Lagos. This too was a private Nigerian venture extensively assisted by the government. Primarily as a result of bad management, neither of these projects has expanded nor enjoyed any marked degree of success.[3]

Although a number of schemes were proposed in 1952 and 1953, it was not until 1955 that a major project was launched at the initiative of the Regional Government in Kaduna.[4] The capital, about £1m., was provided by the regional Marketing Board and the Northern Nigeria Development Corporation; David Whitehead & Sons of Lancashire, who had recently established a mill in Southern Rhodesia, was approached and subsequently recruited as the technical partner. Production of unbleached grey baft commenced in January 1958; spinning operations, using Nigerian cotton, had begun two months earlier.

Kaduna Textiles Limited (KTL) was an unqualified success. Earning a profit from the first month of operation, an exceptional feat, the factory reached full capacity in the second year. In proving that Nigerian labour was readily adaptable to textile operations and that Nigerian cotton was of the requisite quality without the supplementary

[1] Average textile consumption per person for Ghana and Nigeria over the three year period 1958–60 was as follows:

[2] Ministry of Trade and Industry and Sir Alexander Gibb and Partners, *The Industrial Potentialities of Northern Nigeria*, Kaduna 1963, p. 77.

[3] A more detailed history of these two firms will be found in chapter 10.

[4] The World Bank mission of 1953 advised that a more vigorous effort be made to establish a textile industry in partnership with overseas investors. For a discussion of the earlier proposals see International Bank for Reconstruction and Development, *The Economic Development of Nigeria*, Government Printer, Lagos 1954, pp. 248–9.

use of imported lint, the Kaduna venture had removed major elements of risk for future investors in the textile industry.

The country's second large textile project, Nigerian Textile Mills at Ikeja near Lagos, was also a result of the initiative of a public body, but in this case more than half of the capital was provided by private interests. The Western Nigeria Development Corporation had been trying to interest British and continental manufacturers in undertaking a project in the western region since 1955. It was not until February 1959, more than a year after KTL had begun profitable operation, that an acceptable proposal was received from a consortium of the Trans-Continental Mercantile Company of Milan, Maurer Textile Consultants of Geneva and the Chase-Manhattan Investment Company of New York. Unlike KTL, which only spun and wove grey cloth, NTM undertook the full range of spinning, weaving, bleaching and printing. None of the private investors had a prior interest in the Nigerian market; however, one of the lines of activity of the Milan firm, a co-promoter of the project with WNDC, was selling textile machinery.

NTM opened in 1962. In the following year two more plants began production in Kaduna. The first was Nortex, producing 8m. yards of grey and bleached cloth. Its promoter and principal private investor was E. A. Seroussi, the Sudanese entrepreneur discussed in the last chapter. The second plant was a cotton spinning factory designed to supply (*a*) handloom yarn for the United Africa Company's merchandise trade, (*b*) yarn for conversion into sewing thread in English Sewing Cotton's Lagos factory, and (*c*) cotton cord for Dunlop's tyre factory. The bulk of Norspin's risk capital was provided by UAC and English Sewing Cotton; they also shared the management of the enterprise, with ESC being responsible for the technical side.[1]

Table 32. *Principal Nigerian textile manufacturers at year of start-up*

Firm	Start-up	Capital (£m.)	Spindles (1,000s)		Looms	Capacity (yd. m.)
KTL	1958	1·25	12		288	8
NTM	1962	3·42	15		500	17
Norspin	1963	1·08	26		—	*a*
Nortex	1963	0·64	13		300	8
ATM	1964	2·42	15		380	7, 24p
Arewa	1964	1·50	10		400	10
UNT	1964	0·80	—	(finishing	—	15p
TPN	1965	3·25	—	only)	—	24p
Zamfra	1965	1·10	10		270	8

[a] 5·25m. lb. yarn.
p printing only.

[1] Dunlop initially invested £60,000 in the venture but, following technical difficulties in Norspin's processing of the tyre cord, withdrew in 1965, although still remaining a customer for unprocessed yarn.

As shown in table 32 three more textile plants came into production in 1964 and another two started up in 1965. The first was Aba Textile Mills, designed to produce 7m. yards of grey and bleached cloth, plus printing 24m. yards of imported Japanese grey cloth. The private investor behind this project was the American firm Indian Head Mills whose major capital contribution, as noted in the previous chapter, was redundant equipment from its U.S. plants. The second and third projects, both in Kaduna, were undertaken as part of a move to protect overseas markets of oriental producers. Arewa, with a capacity of 10m. yards grey and bleached cloth, was sponsored by a consortium of ten Japanese cotton spinning firms.[1] United Nigerian Textiles was established by Chinese Dyeworks (Hong Kong) to print 15m. yards of imported grey cloth.

Table 33. *The Nigerian textile industry, 1965*

Product	Plants	Employment	Sales (£000s)	Value added
Total	17	12,117	20,855	9,893
Yarn	1	8·9 %	4·3 %	2·7 %
Woven piece goods, exclusive of prints	7	59·6	47·1	60·4
Prints[a]	2	14·2	34·4	26·2
Towels and blankets	3	11·4	6·9	4·1
Knit piece goods[b]	4	6·0	7·3	6·5
		100·0	100·0	100·0

[a] Includes a plant with non-integrated spinning and weaving facilities.

[b] One of these plants also produces thread, and another fabricates singlets as well as weaving the singlet fabric.

SOURCE: Arthur D. Little, Inc., *The Nigerian Textile Industry Outlook in 1967*.

Two factories began operation in 1965. The United Africa Company and its technical associates, protecting a merchant interest, established Textile Printers of Nigeria at Onitsha to print 24m. yards of Japanese grey cloth.[2] Zamfra, E. A. Seroussi's second joint project with the Northern Nigeria Development Corporation, started production at Gasau, with a planned output of 8m. yards of grey, bleached and dyed cloth. Also in 1965, construction began on Nigeria's first turnkey textile project, at Asaba, sold to the Mid-Western Nigeria Development

[1] As noted earlier, owing to the extreme imbalance in trade with Japan there had been several threats by the Minister of Finance of placing an embargo on Japanese imports (primarily textiles). Quotas were nominally placed on Japanese textile imports in 1965. The Arewa group were actively encouraged in the Nigerian venture by the Japanese Government.

[2] The technical partners, Calico Printers and two Dutch firms, have long printed for the West African market under contract to UAC, using rollers and Japanese grey cloth supplied by the latter.

Corporation by Coutinho Caro; the capacity of this £4·2m. factory (500 looms) was 20m. yards of grey, bleached and printed cloth.

A recent report by Arthur D. Little, Inc. summarizes a comprehensive survey of the textile industry carried out jointly by the Federal Ministry of Commerce and Industry, the Federal Office of Statistics and the Nigerian Institute of Social and Economic Research.[1] By the end of 1965 there were 120,476 spindles in operation (as compared to 21,200 in 1961), 3,252 looms (613 in 1961), and ten roller printing machines (none in 1961). Industry employment exceeded 12,000 and gross output was nearly £21m. The bulk of the industry was located in the cotton-growing northern region: 67 % of total employment, 71 % of the looms, 79 % of the spindles, but only four of the ten printing machines. The breakdown of these industry aggregates by type of product is given in table 33.

The trend to investing in printing, following the government's 1963 decision to allow the use of imported grey cloth for this purpose, can be seen in the production figures for 1965 and 1966:[2]

	1965	1966
Baft and drills (m. yd.)	46·3	51·2
Bleached and piece dyed (m. yd.)	40·8	37·4
Prints (m. yd.)	16·0	87·9
	103·1	176·5

EQUIPMENT POLICY

By virtue of employing equipment of varying age the investor has a choice of techniques (albeit within a limited range) for the mechanized production of cotton textiles. The older the equipment (the oldest in Nigeria dates to 1896) the more labour attendance required per machine and the higher the labour-output ratio (L/O); there is a corresponding lower investment-output ratio (K_s/O). However given the higher productivity and longer life of new equipment, the capital consumption-output ratio (K_c/O) for the older equipment is not always lower, or at least not sufficiently lower to offset the comparative loss in unit labour cost. Thus, in the Nigerian situation at least, the use of second-hand textile equipment maximizes output and employment per unit of capital invested while the use of new equipment maximizes the rate of return to capital.[3]

[1] Arthur D. Little, Inc., *The Nigerian Textile Industry Outlook in 1967*, unpublished report.

[2] *Ibid.* and *Economic Indicators*, January 1967, p. 18.

[3] This of course requires that the supply price of new and used equipment to Nigeria is parametrically given, a not unreasonable assumption.

The first producer, KTL, purchased new, fully automatic looms so as to minimize labour training and maintenance problems; on the other hand, in the less vulnerable process of spinning, fifteen-year old machinery was used. Total investment was kept down by putting in the smallest number of looms and spindles which are compatible with reasonably economic operation, 288 looms and 12,000 spindles.[1] Once the viability of production and market acceptance had been established the capacity of the first mill was doubled, and in the third year construction of a second adjoining plant begun. By 1964 KTL was operating 1,200 looms and 50,000 spindles; in 1966 output reached 40m. yards. With the prospect of competition from 1960 onwards and availability of internal financing, all old spinning apparatus was replaced with the latest, highest speed equipment which reduced labour costs and substantially increased plant productivity, thus enabling the first manufacturer to secure as much of the market as possible before other local production commenced.[2]

NTM at Ikeja installed new spinning and weaving machinery, but its printing equipment was second-hand; unlike other investors with no prior interest in the market, NTM sponsors did not try to hold investment and plant capacity to the barest minimum. In late 1965 NTM announced plans to double its capacity, with primary emphasis on printing.

Nortex and ATM both installed reconditioned machinery which ranged in age from forty to seventy years old. Delivery time for such equipment is some six months quicker, and at a price approximately one-third that of new machines. Because the movable parts of the reconditioned equipment are new and greatly enhance productivity relative to the original design, production costs at Nigerian wage rates are only about 10 % higher than with new facilities. Normally investors utilizing second-hand plant replace their initial equipment with new machines as soon as sufficient depreciation allowances and reserves have accumulated, owing to the difficulty of acquiring spare parts for the older equipment. In the case of ATM, the availability of

[1] Minimum economic size is determined by the smallest cotton blowing machine, one of six steps in the spinning process. Weaving alone can be carried out in very small units, e.g. the two Nigerian mills.

[2] KTL experienced an interesting instance of product specificity or market segmentation. Upon opening the second plant which produced bleached shirting, it was found that the standard quality being produced did not find acceptance with the conservative northern consumer who was accustomed to the cheaper clay-filled Chinese shirting. (In 1961 the average c.i.f. value of bleached shirting from China was 16·3*d*. per yard while that of Japan, consumed by the wealthier southerner, was 22·8*d*. The Chinese cloth accounted for about 43 % of the total market, the Japanese for about 24 %.) When, with some reluctance, the company introduced the finishing process for adulterating the product, the market was quickly captured. Thus even within an apparently homogenous segment of demand there are substantial price and quality variations which increase the risk of failure for the fledgling manufacturer who does not have an intimate prior knowledge of the market.

surplus plant from Indian Head's extensive American operations, its technical expertise and its intimate knowledge of the U.S. used textile machinery market will enable the Aba firm to continue to use old equipment. The Sudanese entrepreneur of Nortex, who lacked the extensive experience and technical resources of ATM, allowed his looms to be installed improperly and then compounded the error by attempting to economize on expatriate supervisors, with the result that all the looms had to be scrapped and new ones installed. In his second mill at Gusau new looms were put in at the outset.

The two market-protecting oriental firms, Arewa and UNT, brought in completely new equipment for all operations, including printing; moreover, both of these producers announced plans to double capacity after twelve months of production. Half of Norspin's spindles were second-hand and some of the equipment in UAC's printing concern at Onitsha (TPN) was used Lancashire plant, although of fairly recent origin.

It is difficult to make generalizations about the pattern of investment in the textile industry for two reasons. First, used equipment covers a wide range, the difference in cost between 40-year-old and 15-year-old equipment being greater than that between 15-year-old and new equipment. Second, the technical advantage of new machines is greater in the case of looms than it is in the case of spindles and printing machines. Taking these qualifications into account it would appear that (*i*) all investors tend to limit their initial investment to the minimum sized plant, e.g. about 300 looms and 13,000 spindles; (*ii*) most investors with no prior interest in the market minimize their capital commitment still further by the extensive use of second-hand machinery; and conversely, (*iii*) investors protecting established markets tend to employ more efficient capital-intensive (K_s/O) processes.

This pattern of investment behaviour is consistent with the implications of our investor typology. Since low cost production is not essential to profitable operation in a monopolistic market, for the outside investor facing a greater risk of failure the capital minimizing technique represents the optimal choice. For the more strongly motivated market protector, with a longer time horizon and a lower risk-discount of future earnings, the more durable and economically efficient capital-intensive technique represents the optimal choice.

CAPITAL STRUCTURE

Analysis of the capital structure of individual firms in an underdeveloped economy is important for at least two reasons: to ascertain the amount of private capital placed at risk and to determine the incidence of taxation on company earnings. In the case of the former, we would expect, once again, differential behaviour correlative with the motive to invest.

The primary characteristics of a firm's capital structure (apart from the important question of the sufficiency of total capital provision) are the relative shares of debt and equity in long term capital, and the proportion in which investors have contributed to these two categories. The debt-equity ratio is related to the subject of gearing or leverage: as borrowed funds are substituted for equity capital, fixed costs are increased owing to debt-servicing obligations; if a reasonable profit is earned the rate of return on the commensurately smaller equity base is magnified.

The conventional trade-off for equity-holders of a greater profit against a higher probability of sustaining a loss is translated into a quite unconventional result when the gearing is extended in risky situations beyond the liquidation value of the firm's assets. When this occurs a second effect of risk-shifting comes into operation: debenture holders and other long-term creditors are in fact providing risk capital without any compensating claim on profits. Given the very limited market for specific industrial equipment in a non-industrial underdeveloped economy, the liquidation value of an industrial project is seldom more than 25 to 30 % of fixed assets.[1] All debt financing above this figure constitutes risk capital. The provision of such non-equity risk capital (or a loan guarantee) is one of the terms a government may concede in order to induce a hesitant investor to go ahead.

The third column in table 34 (*a*) gives the initial debt-equity ratio for eight textile firms. With the exception of UNT, all the firms are geared to have risk-shifting effect to debt-holders. The comparable ratio in U.S. consumer soft goods industries, where both risks and

Table 34(*a*). *Financial structure of selected Nigerian textile firms* (at date of start-up)

	Start-up	Capital (£000s)	Debt/capital (%)	Private investment: Equity (%)	Private investment: Debt and equity (%)	Gearing
KTL	1958	1,250	76	33	8	4/1
NTM	1962	3,416	59	70	53	7/5
Norspin	1963	1,075	53	91	42	2/1
Nortex	1963	635	45	59	32	2/1
ATM	1964	2,424	56	70	31	7/3
Arewa	1964	1,500	53	60	60	1/1
UNT	1964	800	33	100	75	4/3
TPN	1965	3,250	61	83	54	3/2

[1] There are economies of scale here. As the industry grows and with it the demand for equipment, the liquidation value of fixed assets rises.

[2] Eli Schwartz, *Corporation Finance*, New York *1962*, p. 89.

Table 34(*b*).

	Equity (£000s)	Debt
Kaduna Textiles Limited, 1958		
David Whitehead & Sons	100	—
NNDC	100	400
NNMB	100	550
	300	950
Nigerian Textile Mills, 1962		
Amential (Italo-Swiss)	555	93
Chase Manhattan International	425	747
WNDC	420	1,176
	1,400	2,016
Norspin, 1963		
United Africa Company	255	—
English Sewing Cotton	150	—
Dunlop	60	—
NNDC/NNIL	35	175
CDFC	—	400
	500	575
Nortex, 1963		
Sudanese Investors	185	—
Private Nigerian Investor	20	—
NNDC/NNIL	145	185
NIDB/FLB	—	100
	350	285
Aba Textile Mills, 1964		
Indian Head Textile Mills	750	—
Eastern Nigerian Government	321	—
U.S. Export-Import Bank	—	714[a]
Indag	—	150
Taylor Woodrow	—	489
	1,071	1,353
Arewa, 1964		
All-Japanese Cotton Spinners	420	480
NNIL	163	189
International Finance Corporation	117	131
	700	800
United Nigeria Textiles, 1964		
Hong Kong Firm	600	—
NNIL	—	200
	600	200

Table 34 (*b*)—*continued*

	Equity (£000s)	Debt
Textile Printers of Nigeria, 1965		
UAC and Associates	1,045	700
Eastern Nigerian Government	75	75
Indag	130	200
NIDB	—	200
CDC	—	200
Public subscription	—	625
	1,250	2,000

[a] Guaranteed by Eastern Nigerian Government.

SOURCE: Registrar of Companies.

Abbreviations:
NNDC = Northern Nigeria Development Corporation.
NNMB = Northern Nigeria Marketing Board.
WNDC = Western Nigerian Development Corporation.
NNIL = CDC/NNDC joint venture, an investment company.
Indag = CDC/Eastern Nigerian Government joint venture.
NIDB = Nigerian Industrial Development Bank.
FLB = Federal Loans Board.

securities are far more favourable to levering, is 16 %.[2] In order to determine the risk-shifting as between parties (the equity owners may also hold debentures) we must compare the private investors' equity to their combined holdings of equity and debenture. Private investor gearing (p.i.g.) is shown in the last three columns.

P.i.g. is greatest for KTL and ATM – both projects where the private investor had no prior stake in the market. Another 'outside' project, Nortex, was under-capitalized and *de facto* achieved a high degree of leverage on the basis of government-guaranteed revolving short-term credit from the Marketing Board (on cotton purchases) and local banks.[1] By contrast, p.i.g. or risk-shifting is very moderate or non-existent for the four market-protecting investors. The only instance violating the predicted pattern is NTM, which was also the sole exception to the predicted behaviour regarding equipment policy. Whether or not attributable to Chase-Manhattan's entrance into the banking field (Lagos branch opened 1962), Amential and Chase have taken a long term view towards their textile commitment.

The motive for p.i.g. is not so much the 'outsider's' thirst for magnified earnings, but rather, as in the case of equipment policy, it is his reluctance to risk a sizeable investment. As described previously, the prime risk is one of initial viability during the first two years; once

[1] This short-term debt amounted to £301,750 in August 1964. Northern Nigeria, *A White Paper on the Military Government Policy for the Reorganization of the Northern Nigeria Development Corporation*, p. 25.

profitable operation is achieved gearing invariably disappears. As loans are paid back, a corresponding amount of script shares are issued to stockholders which just matches the increase in net worth. No instance of permanent leverage was encountered in the cement, cigarette, beer or any other industries. In the case of textiles, KTL's debenture capital was reduced from its 1960 peak of £1·1m. to £0·1m. in 1964, while the equity base grew from its initial £0·3m. to £1·6m.; all this was achieved without interrupting annual dividend payments of 10 % or more.

We now come to the second motive for gearing, as it is observed among market protectors where there is no risk-shifting to another party. In this case the private investor supplies equity and debt capital in the same proportions as the public partner. This pattern is encountered in Arewa, TPN, West African Portland Cement and Premier Tobacco Company; investor-owned debentures (ranging from 40 to 90 % of long term capital) are also encountered in wholly private companies such as West African Thread, Raleigh Industries and Wall's Ice Cream. The motive in this instance is home country tax avoidance: while local earnings remitted as profits are subject to income tax, when remitted under the form of loan repayments to the parent company they are not. Since interest payments do not qualify for pioneer relief, where feasible the loan from the parent company is interest-free.[1]

There are also a number of lesser advantages to the investor of employing self-held debt capital. 'Ploughing back of profits' in order to effect the loan repayment, coupled with only moderate profit remittances, is more acceptable to the Nigerian Government and public opinion than if the equivalent amount appeared solely in the form of profit on an all-equity investment. Should there be foreign exchange restrictions, debt servicing is unlikely to be curtailed whereas profits are. Lastly, by providing a significant part of his capital in the form of a loan the entrepreneur can limit his loss in the event of business failure – if only because credit losses are tax deductable while losses on equity investment are not.

Returning to textiles, in addition to providing non-equity risk capital, the government has made three other important concessions for the purpose of promoting the establishment of the industry. The first is generous tariff protection. The second is a subsidy to all northern producers to the extent of 10 % of the cost of cotton.[2] Third, the

[1] With reference to the tax treatment of interest-free loan remittances to the home country, U.S. tax authorities apply an imputed interest rule, whereas the British do not.

[2] The Federal Government imposes a 10 % duty on cotton exports, which means that the price received by the Northern Nigeria Marketing Board is 10 % below the world price. The Board sells cotton at this lower price to textile firms located in the north; the Board's price to southern producers is 10 % higher.

majority of firms engaged in printing have been allowed to use imported grey cloth at a price well under that of the locally produced stuff, the difference being borne by the government in loss of tax revenue.

The last point provides another instance of the greater benefits (or the lesser cost) to the economy to be derived from investment undertaken by the market-protector as opposed to the investor attracted solely by profitable opportunity. This concession was granted at the time terms were being negotiated for the first two textile printing ventures. Both the American firm and the United Africa Company contended that the staple of Nigerian cotton was not long enough to be spun to the fineness required for printing at a reasonable cost. To print on imported cloth both producers asked for a manufacturer's concession on the 12*d.* per yard import duty. The American firm requested a reduction of 10·2*d.* as against 6*d.* asked for by the redeploying merchant. Since the Regional Government wanted to have both mills, the higher figure was granted. The American firm made its investment conditional upon receiving pioneer relief from income tax; the market-protector went ahead despite an initial failure to obtain the same exemption.

LABOUR EFFICIENCY AND LOCATION PATTERNS

Because the production of cotton textiles is relatively labour-intensive, the question of labour efficiency is of considerable importance both for the commercial success of individual ventures and for the long term competitiveness of the industry. It has been suggested that a major reason for the excessive protection cotton textile production apparently requires in Africa (Nigeria included) is high labour cost, even where the most modern equipment is used and all economies of scale are realized.[1]

Table 35. *Labour efficiency in two textile factories*

		Spinning		Weaving	
		Spindles/ man	Efficiency (%)	Looms/ man	Efficiency (%)
KTL	1958	500	75	10	80
	1964	1,000	90	12	92
NTM	1964	800	90	14	85
Approx. British Standard		1,600	90	24	90

SOURCE: Data supplied by the production managers of Kaduna Textiles Ltd. and Nigerian Textile Mills.

The facts of the matter are straightforward and do not support the contention. As shown in the figures above Nigeria's labour efficiency is

[1] W. A. Chudson, 'Comparative Costs and Economic Development: The African Case', *American Economic Review*, May 1964, p. 407.

slightly more than one-half that of Britain, and it is improving. On the other hand the average hourly wage, including bonus, for the Nigerian labour force (from sweepers to assistant overlookers) in the two factories was 1*s.* 2*d.* in 1964, as compared to about 7*s.* in the United Kingdom. Allowing for management and technician costs (including housing, etc.) 150 % higher than in the United Kingdom and output per man 50 % lower, unit labour costs are still lower in Nigeria than in Britain.

Although labour costs do not account for the excessive tariff protection,[1] reduced unit labour costs are critical for the long run competitiveness of the Nigerian industry *via-à-vis* Japan, Hong Kong and India – Nigeria's principal suppliers. With lengthening experience and increasing competitive pressures on management to institute separate three month courses for the training of weavers as opposed to instruction on the factory floor (the exposure method), labour productivity will most certainly register further advances.[2]

A more intractable problem with its attendant long term cost disadvantage *vis-à-vis* the Far East concerns the performances of Nigerians at the supervisory and managerial levels. The 1963 *Industrial Survey* reported 208 foreigners engaged in textile production, accounting for 2·6 % of total employment and 29 % of total labour cost;[3] the average salary of expatriates was £2,002 as compared to an average of £899 for twenty-six Nigerians in professional and managerial positions.[4] A certain proportionate reduction in the number of expatriates can be expected in the short run as plant scale is increased and the lowest level of supervisors are Nigerianized: KTL reduced its expatriate-Nigerian ratio from 1 to 25 in 1958 to 1 to 50 in 1964. However a compound of many factors – a general scarcity of suitable Nigerian personnel which leads to competitive bidding and rapid turnover,[5] the difficulty of working constructively under white expatriates in an environment of heightening nationalism, an unfavourable colonial and cultural heritage regarding the acceptance of responsibility and the exercise of initiative – these deficiencies, which are explored more fully in chapter 7, suggest that it will be some time before high-cost expatriate supervision can be dispensed with entirely.

[1] See below.

[2] KTL does have a training school; however up to 1965 it has been occupied with the more pressing need of training loom mechanics and assistant overlookers.

[3] Federal Office of Statistics, *Industrial Survey of Nigeria 1963*, January 1966, tables 5 and 6. Labour cost includes all levels of management, housing allowances, etc. The inclusion of cotton ginning within this category produces a slight understatement of the numerical and financial importance of expatriates in the textile industry proper.

[4] *Ibid.*

[5] Within twelve months of starting a three-year junior management training programme for nineteen carefully selected secondary school graduates, only two remained. The other seventeen had left for government jobs or to pursue a university education.

The location of textile manufacturing in Nigeria is controlled by the locus of the particular market to be served, by political factors and by transport costs.[1] The bulk of prints are consumed in the south while the bulk of grey and bleached piece goods are consumed in the north: three out of four printing firms are in the south while all the producers specializing in grey and bleached cloth are in the north. It is cheaper to transport finished cloth or yarn than cotton lint, thus favouring Kaduna; but for printed cloth the importance of being in close and continuing touch with changing consumer tastes outweighs the transport saving. A southern location has the additional advantages of a more skilled labour force, nearness to a seaport (e.g. time saved in clearing imported machinery and parts, contesting customs valuations) and greater access to the Federal Government in Lagos (negotiation on import duties, excise tax, immigration permits, etc.).

The political factor has two aspects: first if there is to be public participation, which of the regional governments will offer the best terms; second, in the event of regionalized product markets (regionalization already holds in the labour market) there can be no survival unless the plant is situated in the market it is serving. For a firm with many investments, such as the United Africa Company, there is the additional consideration, rising out of the need to maintain good will, that its major projects be apportioned in rough equality between the regions. In the absence of such political factors, the most rational pattern of location would probably have been concentration in two centres, Lagos and Kaduna, with external economies to the industry in labour training, the growth of servicing firms, specialized distribution, etc., that such agglomeration would have brought.

THE ECONOMIC CONTRIBUTION

The textile industry's linkages with the rest of the economy can be inferred from the cost data in table 36. Like cigarettes and beer, textiles are a consumer good sold at a price greater than the import they replaced, thus precluding any forward linkages. The industry's purchase of cotton represents the most important backward linkage; however this does not create a new demand, but simply a diversion from exports (*inter alia*, a loss of foreign exchange) and, with reference to northern textile production, at a price 10 % under the export value. Spare parts, lubricants, shuttles, printing dyes, filling materials as well as supervisory labour, are all currently imported. Of total payments to labour, about 30 % goes to foreign personnel.

[1] A permissive locational factor is the presence of adequate water supplies; KTL uses a million gallons per week, while the printing works use a million gallons per day.

Thus payments to Nigerian labour (£1·2m. in 1963), labour training, purchases of electric power (£296,000 in 1963) and the return to Nigerian capital constitute the contribution of textile manufacture to the growth of the economy. Beyond these resource flows, a modest spill-over of transferable skills into other industries can be expected. There is as yet no indication of any technological transfer, such as occurred with cigarette production and tobacco growing.

Table 36. *Cost of cloth production per square yard*

(pence per yard)

	Grey (1961)	Print (1961)	Grey and bleached (1965)
Cotton	6·0	7·0	6·5
Chemicals and materials	0·2	5·6	1·0
Direct labour and supervision	2·1	3·8	2·8
Electricity, fuel, water	1·2	1·8	1·8
Spares and maintenance	0·7	1·2	2·2
Depreciation	1·1	1·6	
Administrative overhead, etc.	2·7	3·0	2·6
	14·0	24·0	16·9

SOURCES: Data supplied by Kaduna Textiles Limited for grey cloth; Ministry of Trade and Industry and Sir Alexander Gibb and Partners, *The Industrial Potentialities of Northern Nigeria*, Kaduna 1963, p. 249 for prints, with certain revisions as recommended by the management of KTL. The 1965 data were collected by the Federal Ministry of Commerce and Industry and refer to a plant producing 'grey baft, bleached shirting and a small percentage of piece-dyed goods'. See Arthur D. Little, Inc., *The Nigerian Textile Industry Outlook in 1967*.

NOTE: The cost of cotton pertains to the north; because the regional government refused the 10 % export duty rebate to southern producers, cotton costs to the latter (allowing for transport) are about 20 % higher. Higher count yarns required for print cloth account for the higher cotton content.

All evidence suggests that the foreign exchange cost of domestically produced cloth is greater than that of imported cloth. In the most favourable case of grey baft, given the availability of Japanese cloth at 12*d*. or less (10·6*d*. in 1965) and forgone cotton export earnings of something more than 6*d*. there is a net increase in foreign exchange cost if the combined value of depreciation of imported plant and equipment, remittance and import purchases of foreign personnel, management fees, imported materials and profit remittance reach the equivalent of 6*d*. per yard. It is probably very close. In the most unfavourable and increasingly important case of printing on imported cloth, the cost of the imported raw materials alone exceeds the value of the import being replaced![1]

[1] Simon Williams, 'Start-up of a Textile Industry', *Nigerian Journal of Economic and Social Studies*, November 1962, p. 253.

In the long run the picture is considerably brighter. Both the industry's impact upon the economy and its capacity to save foreign exchange should grow. With training and experience Nigerians will account for an increasing share of total wage and salary payments. As managerial deficiencies are overcome, the Electricity Corporation will be able to realize the potential economies of scale. Increased demand from both the textile industry and the industrial sector at large will facilitate local production of chemicals, which should result in a net saving of foreign exchange, although probably to increased cost as well. With the refining of Nigerian crude oil, lubricants and fuel (and hence electric power) will become cheaper, as well as contributing to the balance-of-payments. Finally with the growth in local supply and the emergence of competition, profit remittances to overseas investors should diminish.

Before turning to the last and most important element in the cost of production, the return to capital, it is appropriate to examine comparative data on cotton and labour costs in other countries. The table below presents information collected by the U.S. Department of Commerce and the Economic Commission for Latin America; all figures are in U.S. cents.

Table 37. *Comparative production costs of grey cloth*

(cents per square yard)

	U.S.A. (1960)	Japan (1960)	Chile (1961)	Brazil (1961)	Nigeria (1961)
Cotton	8·61	8·05	10·87	6·57	6·86
Labour	3·92	1·72	4·80	5·16	2·45
Combined cost	12·53	9·77	15·67	11·73	9·31

SOURCES: U.S. Department of Commerce, *Comparative Cost of Fabric Production*, Washington 1962; ECLA, *The Textile Industry in Latin America II Brazil*, New York, 1963; table 36, this chapter.

On the basis of these data Nigeria would appear to have very competitive costs of production indeed, surpassing even Japan. However when the other costs of production are taken into account, all of which are higher in Nigeria than in the other four countries, the picture would be changed substantially.[1] But what does emerge clearly from this comparison is that Nigerian efficiency wages are sufficiently low to

[1] The Department of Commerce report shows that in Japan, Britain and the Netherlands the cost of electricity to textile manufacturers is less than 1*d.* per kWh as against 3*d.* for Kaduna firms. In Japan fuel, water and power costs per yard come to 0·5*d.* compared to Nigeria's 1·2*d*; similarly Japan's depreciation costs are about one-fifth of Nigeria's. With the opening of the Kainji Dam and passing beyond the early period when depreciation write-offs are very high, electricity and capital consumption costs for Kaduna producers should fall considerably.

absorb the high cost of expatriate supervision and still be competitive with labour costs in countries other than India, China and Japan. We will have more to say about the alleged low productivity and high cost of African labour in a later chapter.

PROFITS, PRICES AND PROTECTION

For balance of payments and revenue reasons, the net protection afforded textile manufacture has increased continually since 1959 (see table 31). In most cases the local manufacturers have not exploited the full height of the tariff; however, save where import substitution is virtually complete, distributors have expropriated the difference as a windfall.[1] The mechanics of local pricing are set out in table 38. The competitive imported fabrics being replaced are Indian grey cloth, Chinese bleached shirting and Japanese prints.

Table 38. *Textile prices and profit margins*

(pence per yard at 1961 prices)

	Grey	Bleached	Print
Competitive import fabric, c.i.f.	14·6	16·3	22·0
plus import duty	12·0	12·0	16·0[a]
Landed cost	26·6	28·3	38·0
less cost of production in Nigeria	14·0	16·0[b]	24·0
Maximum profit margin	12·6	12·3	14·0

[a] Effective from 1962, the first year of local production.

[b] Author's estimate, worked from known price and profit margin.

SOURCES: Tables 31 and 36, and *Trade Summary*, December 1961.

The maximum profit margin to the Nigerian manufacturer in 1961 averaged more than 60 % of the cost of production and in the case of grey cloth reached 85 %. These potential margins were further widened, even allowing for excise taxes, by the tariff increases of 1964 and 1965. Thus it is not high labour costs, an overvalued currency or dumping that explains Nigeria's non-competitive performance as a textile producer, as Walter Chudson has speculated,[2] but rather a combination of

[1] See earlier discussion, pp. 49–50. From the point of view of reinvesting the profit surplus it is probably preferable that the manufacturer exploits the full extent of protection. However, for various strategic considerations manufacturers seem to have felt it advisable to share the surplus with their distributors.

[2] 'The position of cotton textiles is worth special attention because their survival (or further development) apparently still requires protection well above the average level of revenue duties even in countries where the size of the domestic market is not a limiting factor in obtaining economies of scale or full utilization of capacity. The subject deserves much closer investigation than it has apparently received. Available information suggests that high labour costs, reflecting a number of features of the Africa labour market, are primarily responsible,

the high cost of capital (or its requisite foreign management) and bad tariff-making.

Until mid-1964 neither KTL nor NTM had raised the prices which they initially established in 1958 and 1962 respectively. KTL sold grey cloth for 21*d.* and bleached cloth for 23*d.* (maximum quantity discount price), while NTM's prices were about 1*d.* higher. KTL's pricing policy was based upon a 7*d.* net profit margin, which has been sufficient to earn a 60 %-plus rate of return on issued capital.[1] While constant money prices imply some reduction in real costs, it is still too early to appraise the extent to which the final consumer price may be expected to fall over the long run.

Table 39 provides a rough measure of the effective rate of protection for various textile manufacturing processes.[2] Part A shows the value-added structure of imports at their Nigerian c.i.f. values; only the cost of cotton is valued abroad (at Japanese prices).[3] In the case of spinning, transportation costs are included in the value added; there is a further subsidy for this process, not shown in the table, by virtue of the 10 % export duty rebate on cotton for northern firms. If the information were available, in order to calculate effective protection for domestic value added, we would net out imported inputs and adjust for a variety of countervailing taxes. Finally, as noted earlier, by 1965 protection was very much higher than shown in table 39, particularly for printed cloth.[4]

The major conclusions that flow from these calculations are that textile manufacture receives excessive protection in general, and

but an over-valued exchange rate cannot entirely be ruled out, nor can some export subsidies in some competing countries. We have here, apparently, largely an "infant industry" situation, but the persistence of non-competitive performance in several countries seems to dramatize the general problem of infant industry productivity in the manufacturing sector under African conditions, even where highly modern equipment is used', Walter A. Chudson, 'Comparative Costs and Economic Development: The African Case', *American Economic Review*, May 1964, p. 400.

[1] In 1963 issued capital was £1·6m. and net profits were £1·050,000 (36m. × 7*d.*) or 63 %. Owing to high leverage in earlier years, the return was probably a good deal higher. The before-tax return on total capital employed (equity, reserves, debt) in 1966 was over 40 %.

Not all technically competent textile producers have been so fortunate, as illustrated by the case of Norspin. A sharp decline in the price of Indian yarn exports resulted in a large increase in Nigerian imports despite a specific duty of 14*d.* per lb. Combined with the weakening cotton grading system of the Northern Nigeria Marketing Board and some technical difficulties, this import competition kept Norspin deep in the red, with an accumulated loss of £430,000 as of September 1965. (Information supplied by E. Hallett of the United Africa Company.)

[2] This table is the same as table 15 in chapter 2.

[3] Taken from table 37 and converted into pence. Because the price of cotton relates to Japan and all later stages are valued in Nigeria, the cost of transport appears in the value added by spinning, which contributes to the apparent lower level of tariff protection accorded to this process.

[4] See table 31.

that the structure of the tariff has perverse allocational effects within the industry. The shallower manufacturing processes receive a proportionally higher protective subsidy; the latter should be either uniform or tapered according to the extent of value-added undertaken. Process group 4, contributing the most real output, enjoys the second least protection, while group 5, with less than half the value added and 100 % based on imported materials, is given nearly double the protection. It is in regard to process group 5, the printing of imported grey cloth, that the error in tariff-making is most damaging. Ignoring the

Table 39. *Value added and the extent of protection in the Nigerian textile industry*

(pence per yard, at 1961 prices)

A. Value-added structure of imported cloth

	(*d.*)		(*d.*)
Cost of cotton	6·9	Cost of grey cloth	14·6
Value added in spinning	4·6	Value added in bleaching	1·9
Cost of yarn	11·5	Cost of bleached cloth	16·3
Value added in weaving	3·1	Value added in printing	5·5
Cost of grey cloth	14·6	Cost of printed cloth	22·0

B. Value added in local production

Process	Production without tariff (*d.*)	tariff (*d.*)	Production with tariff (*d.*)	Effective protection (%)
(1) Spinning	4·6	3·5[a]	8·1	76
(2) Spinning and weaving	7·7	12·0	19·7	155
(3) Spinning, weaving and bleaching	9·6	12·0	21·6	125
(4) Spinning, weaving, bleaching and printing	15·1	16·0	31·3	105
(5) Bleaching and printing	7·4	14·2	21·8	191

[a] A duty of 14*d.* per lb. was imposed in 1964. The spinning factory had been in operation for a year before but made no sales prior to the imposition of this duty and the removal of an excise tax which had been levied in March 1964.

SOURCE: *Trade Summary*, December 1961.

balance-of-payments effect of profit remittances and capital replacement, raw material imports alone for group 5 exceed the value of the finished import being replaced.[1] Yet, because of its enhanced differential profitability as a result of the tariff, it is to this relatively shallow process, with a minimum of linkages to the economy, that investors are being attracted. The Federal Ministry of Commerce and Industry's

[1] Simon Williams, 'Start-up of a Textile Industry,' *Nigerian Journal of Economic and Social Studies*, November 1962.

survey of production costs in 1965 reports the manufacturing cost of printing on imported grey cloth at 7·3*d.* Given net protection of 38*d.*, this would yield a potential profit margin in excess of 25*d.* per yard.

As we saw from our earlier analysis of demand patterns, cotton prints currently comprise the largest single segment of the market and are likely to be of even greater importance in the future. Consequently it is in the production of printed cloth that the future development of the textile industry lies, and unless it is Nigerian cloth which is printed the industry will be a heavy drag on the economy. The grounds on which the concession to import cloth for printing was granted were that medium-staple Nigerian cotton could not be spun sufficiently fine (30's) to weave cloth strong enough for printing. After this concession was given NTM began successful printing operations using Nigerian cotton (narrow agbada cloth woven with 20-count yarn).

The truth in the claim that Nigerian cotton is not printable would seem to be that (*i*) it costs about 20 % more to spin local cotton to 30's than it does to spin long-staple cotton to the same count (slower spindle speeds, more breakages), (*ii*) the cloth produced from Nigerian 30's yarn, owing to certain textural characteristics, is more difficult to print than imported cloth, and (*iii*) Nigerian printed cloth would not be able to displace the best quality imports, representing about 30 % of all prints. Given the more than adequate room for expansion provided by 70 % of the market and the ability of the industry to bear the cost even under much reduced protection, there would seem to be little justification for the concession.[1]

V

We have now completed our historical narrative and analysis of import substitution begun in chapter 2. Having scrutinized considerable evidence pertaining to investment motivation, concessions demanded by investors and the subsequent performance of such projects, it is perhaps appropriate to conclude this chapter with an evaluation of Nigeria's industrialization incentive policies. The policies were described briefly in chapter 1 and have been referred to individually in various contexts during the course of the narration.

[1] The previously cited Arthur D. Little report arrives at similar conclusions. However several officers of the companies involved disagree with the analysis offered here. They argue that the value-added structure implied in imports should not determine the tariff structure (*a*) because the conditions of production in the exporting country are not necessarily related to Nigerian conditions, and (*b*) because some of these imports, in their opinion, have traditionally been sold at less than full cost. They contend that in the absence of experience in Nigeria of weaving on the wide looms required for most print cloth any cost estimates are no more than guesswork. Finally, with regard to profit margins actually set (as distinct from that portion of the potential margin which accrues to the distributor as windfall), they feel insufficient attention has been given to the risks involved.

There is likely to be little dispute about the criterion that should be used in evaluating the efficacy of incentive programmes: maximization of such private investment as is capable of significant contribution to national output and growth, and the attraction of this investment at minimum cost in terms of concessions. Two kinds of promotional choices are involved: the choice of industry and the choice of the investor. The former is a fairly straightforward matter of fact and can be determined by an investigation of comparative cost, the per cent of domestic value added, desirable inter-sectoral linkages and probable educative effects. In theory the Nigerian authorities take cognizance of these considerations in granting pioneer exemptions, import duty relief and tariff protection;[1] in practice, as we have seen, the intense desire for rapid industrialization has all too frequently overidden official prudence.

With regard to the type of investor that is attracted, the desiderata are maximum capital contribution, efficient low-cost production, re-investment of earnings, minimum priced output and minimum tariff protection. The evidence in the preceding eighty pages strongly suggests that these characteristics will be most nearly approximated in the market-protecting investor. Yet the weight of Nigeria's incentive programmes is directed at 'outside' investors who are searching about for profitable opportunities.

Pioneer income tax relief and the provision of risk-bearing debt capital – maximizing short-term profits and minimizing the private capital requirement respectively – are particularly biased toward attracting the high profit-seeking, short-horizoned, risk-averting investor. Tariff protection and import duty relief on raw materials are attractive and necessary to both kinds of investors; however, where excessive, they provide additional attraction to the 'outsider'. Accelerated depreciation, on the other hand, is more attractive to the investor making a large capital commitment, i.e. the market protector.

Every market-protecting investor interviewed by the writer about the pioneer income tax holiday replied that, although it was an attractive incentive, it was not a prerequisite for their investment. Similar findings were reported by Hakam and May.[2] Moreover, because no

[1] *Statement of Policy proposed by the Federal Government on the Report by a Committee appointed to advise on the Stimulation of Industrial Development by affording Relief from Import Duties and Protection to Nigerian Industry*, Sessional Paper No. 10 of 1956; *The Role of the Federal Government in Promoting Industrial Development in Nigeria*, Sessional Paper No. 3 of 1958; *Statement on Industrial Policy*, Sessional Paper No. 6 of 1964.

[2] Hakam, 'The motivation to invest,' *Nigerian Journal of Economic and Social Studies*, March 1966, p. 55. May, 'Direct overseas investment in Nigeria, 1953–63,' *Scottish Journal of Political Economy*, vol. XII, November 1965, p. 253. Most investigators of income tax concessions in other countries have come up with comparable results and have recommended the abandonment of such tax relief programmes. See the literature cited by Aharoni, *The Foreign Investment Decision Process*, chapter 9.

tax-sparing treaties exist, to a considerable extent the pioneer concession goes not to the investor but to the tax authorities of his home country. Some part of the benefit can be retained by the investor through the use of self-held debt or reinvestment of the untaxed profits for expanding productive capacity. Given these facts, a more efficient company income tax policy would be to (*a*) raise the normal tax rate on paid-out profits from 40 to 50 %, (*b*) employ a lower rate for profits retained for reinvestment, and (*c*) abolish the pioneer concession.

Unlike the benefit bestowed by the pioneer concession which is proportionate to the profitability of the industry (i.e. the level of effective protection), accelerated depreciation represents an interest-free loan whose benefit varies according to the size of fixed investment. There would seem little doubt that the latter provides a more desirable basis for an incentive than the former. Accelerated depreciation increases the firm's liquid capital resources which are important for unforeseen contingencies; under certain conditions it also reduces the entrepreneur's risk by permitting a shorter capital recovery period.[1] More important for the market protector who may be going into a market that cannot initially absorb his full output (e.g. Turner & Newall, Dunlop) is the unlimited carry over of losses along with accelerated depreciation allowances for deduction from taxable income in the first profitable years.[2]

In addition to a revision of company income tax rates and the abolition of the pioneer concession, elements of a more efficient industrial incentive programme would include a reduction in the protective subsidy by use of higher excise taxes (or lower tariffs where feasible), a more judicious disbursement of risk-bearing loans and a combination of policies designed to create and then threaten stakes in the Nigerian market. In order to promote maximum employment and training of Nigerians, immigration quotas for expatriate employees have been highly restrictive; this has prevented new exporters to Nigeria from establishing sales offices prior to a possible industrial investment.[3] Every effort should be made to maximize the number of external sources of

[1] Thus accelerated depreciation reduces those risks which vary with time, e.g. breakdown of law and order, the development of competition. Since its benefits can only be reaped if gross profits are being earned, it does not diminish the prime risk of failure to achieve initial profitable operation.

[2] Unhappily the military government in Lagos, under pressure for revenue, virtually abolished accelerated depreciation in late 1966, while leaving the 40 % tax rate and pioneer concessions untouched. This had been one of the recommendations of an IBRD tax consultant who was of the opinion that accelerated depreciation represents a loss of revenue (rather than simply a postponement) and as such the costs exceed the benefit. See Harley H. Hinrichs, 'Mobilizing Government Revenues for Development in Nigeria', xerox, January 1966, pp. 88–90.

[3] Hakam, *op. cit.* p. 54.

supply – and hence internal competitive pressures. If subsequent investment invitations to overseas suppliers fail, market threatening can be achieved by such government-initiated joint public-private ventures as the Nigerian Cement Company or, if need be, by a small turnkey public investment. With time and ingenuity many more such stratagems could be devised.

Part 3

CHAPTER 5

UTILIZING DOMESTIC RESOURCES: PROCESSING FOR EXPORT

The 'valorization' of primary exports follows import-substitution as the second most important area of Nigerian industrial development. The advantages of industrialization based on export processing as compared to import replacement are: (*a*) it is not limited by the size of the home market, (*b*) its import-content of intermediate inputs is typically lower and (*c*) the likelihood of subsidized uneconomic production is significantly less. On the other hand, such industrial development is limited by the quantity of exports and the extent to which they can be processed; moreover its potential growth-inducing effects (linkages to other sectors of the economy) are frequently less than for the import-replacement.[1]

Table 40 shows the number of establishments employing ten or more workers in Nigeria's principal export processing industries. Total employment is in the neighbourhood of 30,000. Groundnut selecting, developed by the same individual who pioneered the crushing industry, is a newly established process in which the best quality nuts are selected and specially packed. Palm oil bulking, which also involves a refining and purifying operation, occurs just prior to ocean loading; as noted in chapter 4 these facilities were developed by the United Africa Company and later purchased by the Marketing Boards. Only in the case of palm oil extraction do smaller firms employing less than ten account for a significant share of processed output. Tanning and cotton de-seeding also take place in small establishments, but in these cases it is solely for the domestic market. Similarly, the £10m. oil refinery, which commenced operations in November 1965 employing 300 workers, will not be engaged in export production.

As seen in table 40 private Nigerian firms play a large role in sawmilling, rubber crêping and palm oil extraction. With the exception of the NNDC's experimental mill, Lebanese and Cypriots dominate groundnut crushing and they are important in tanning, sawmilling and rubber crêping. European firms, larger in scale and more capital-intensive in technique, account for all the output of tin smelting, cotton

[1] While import-substitution can start with the 'finishing touches' (e.g. assembly) and gradually work backwards, progressively widening value added, the multiplicity of particular end-uses and, within end-uses, variations in quality requirements are such that usually manufacture beyond the primary processing stage must be carried out in close proximity to the consumer market, e.g. furniture from lumber, clothing from tanned leather, food preparations from vegetable oils, etc.

Table 40. *Establishments employing ten or more engaged in export processing, 1964*

	Nigerian		Levantine		European		Government		All	Approximate
	10–199	200+	10–199	200+	10–199	200+	10–199	200+	firms	employment
Groundnut crushing	—	—	4	2	—	—	1	—	7	1,800
Groundnut selecting	—	—	—	1	—	—	1	—	2	500
Palm oil extraction	20	—	—	—	—	2	68	—	90	4,000
Palm oil bulking	—	—	—	—	—	—	4	1	5	1,100
Cotton ginning	—	—	—	—	—	13	—	—	13	4,500[a]
Tanning	1	—	2	—	2	—	1	—	6	250
Sawmilling	43	4	5	1	6	7	—	—	51	11,300
Plywood	—	—	—	—	—	1	—	—	1	3,200
Rubber crêping	9	3	6	2	8	4	1	2	35	4,000
Tin smelting	—	—	—	—	—	1	—	—	1	300
Total	73	7	17	6	16	28	76	3	211	

[a] Seasonal employment; year-long employment is 250.

SOURCE: Derived from *1964 Industrial Directory*, Federal Ministry of Commerce and Industries, Lagos.

ginning and plywood, and they play an important role in sawmilling, rubber crêping and tanning.

The major part of this chapter will be devoted to the palm oil industry. Compared to the other processing industries the latter is the oldest, economically the most important and the recipient of the most development assistance. More pertinent to this analysis, because palm fruit is perishable, there is no alternative of exporting an unprocessed primary product: primary production and processing are a compulsory joint product. The other processing activities, all of which are 'optional' and governed by the same principles of location economics, are treated in a final section.

I

PALM OIL: THE BACKGROUND

The processing of palm fruit is the most important processing activity carried on in Nigeria.[1] The end products, palm oil and palm kernels, have traditionally composed 15 to 20 % of Nigeria's exports; in 1965 their combined export value was £40m.[2] In addition, palm oil is an important item in the Nigerian diet (as part of the traditional soap) and is used as an illuminant, cooking fat and soap ingredient; implicit production estimates based on Marketing Board purchases of palm kernels, for which there is little domestic use, indicate that internal consumption ranges from 80 to 150 % of exports.

The wild oil palm is native to West Africa. The area in which it grows, 'the palm belt', covers approximately 70,000 square miles, largely in southern Nigeria. In competition with surrounding vegetation, the wild palm requires about 15 years to rise above the undergrowth (about 40 feet) and commence bearing fruit, as against four years for the plantation-grown tree. The individual palm fruit is oval shaped, about an inch and a half in length and grows in clusters or bunches of several hundred. The fruit is composed of an outer skin, an oil-bearing layer of fibre (the mesocarp) covering the palm nut, and inside the nut, the palm kernel. Compared to carefully bred plantation

[1] The major references which provide the historical and descriptive background for this study are: W. K. Hancock, *Survey of British Commonwealth Affairs*, vol. II, London 1942; Richenda Scott, 'Production for Trade', part II of *The Native Economies of Nigeria*, ed. Margery Perham, London 1946; Anne Martin, *The Oil Palm Economy of the Ibibio Farmer*, Ibadan 1956; United Africa Company, *Statistical and Economic Review*, nos. 7 and 13; S. C. Nwanze, 'The Economics of the Pioneer Oil Mill', *Journal of the West African Institute for Oil Palm Research*, April 1961; Carl K. Eicher and William L. Miller, 'Observations on Smallholder Palm Production in Eastern Nigeria', mimeograph, Economic Development Institute, Enugu, December 1963.

[2] *Economic Indicators*, p. 20.

varieties, wild palm fruit has a relatively large and thick-shelled nut, and a commensurately smaller oil-bearing mesocarp. The difference in yield between a wild palm tree and current cultivated varieties is on the order of 1 to 5.[1] Harvesting is continuous, although there is a sharp seasonal rise from March to May. Wild palm is harvested by climbing the tree with the aid of a rope, cutting the bunches with a machet and letting them drop to the earth. In the case of the much shorter thick-trunk plantation tree (about 15 feet high), the bunches can be cut from the ground by means of a harvesting hook.

It is clear that palm oil production based on plantations has very considerable advantages over an industry based on natural palmeries. In addition to higher oil yields per tree, processing in large plantation mills gives a greater extraction efficiency, a better quality oil,[2] and – owing to planned full-capacity operation – lower processing costs than are obtainable under a peasant smallholder system.[3] Despite these advantages, the colonial administration resisted the determined efforts of William Hesketh Lever in 1907, 1920 and 1925 to establish such plantations in Nigeria. Lever was anxious to secure a raw material supply for the European soap industry. However, upholding the 'dual mandate' the colonial government was even more determined that the agricultural resources of the West African dependencies be developed 'through the agency of their indigenous populations' and that as a 'fundamental principle' no non-native would be allowed freehold land rights.[4] Efforts of the Nigerian Government since the late 1950s to attract foreign investment into the plantation field have been frustrated by the heavy export tax involved in compulsory sales to the Marketing Board; indeed most of the 13,000 acres of palm oil plantation in the hands of expatriates is being replanted with rubber trees, a product not controlled by a Marketing Board.

Since the 1920s informed observers have unceasingly predicted the imminent extinction of Nigeria's native industry by efficient plantation producers. In the pre-war period the Dutch plantations in Indonesia were going to ring the death knell on Nigeria's native industry. 'The West African producers felt, for the first time, the pressure of competition which was growing at a sensational and menacing speed. It was no longer a spirit of greed, but one of fear, which dominated the

[1] 'Notes on Eastern Nigeria Oil Palm Grove Rehabilitation Scheme', mimeograph, Eastern Nigeria Ministry of Agriculture, Enugu 1961; United Africa Company, *Statistical and Economic Review*, no. 25, March 1961, p. 47.

[2] The possibility of obtaining higher quality oil stems from (*i*) processing bunches rather than loose fruit (*ii*) less bruising as a result of the shorter fall, and (*iii*) a closer interval between harvesting and expression.

[3] United Africa Company, *Statistical and Economic Review*, no. 9, March 1952, p. 25.

[4] Hancock, *Survey of British Commonwealth Affairs*, p. 191.

discussion.'[1] Starting from scratch in the early 1920s, in little more than a decade Indonesia had overtaken Nigeria as the world's leading exporter; however after the war and the removal of the Dutch, expansion was replaced by decline and stagnation. In the post-war years Belgian and British plantations in the Congo (concessions granted to Lever in 1911) showed a similarly rapid growth; but once again political disorder since 1960 has converted expansion into decline. The current threat to Nigeria's supremacy, in terms of rate of growth of output, is Malaya; and again political circumstances, whether generated from internal communal stresses or external nationalism, can be envisaged which might disrupt the expansion of Malaya's plantation economy. In short, over the past five decades the economic inefficiency of the indigenous small holder system has been offset by the long-term political vulnerability of the foreign-managed plantation system – and the tropics have yet to operate efficient large-scale plantations on the basis of indigenous managerial resources.

Table 41. *World exports of palm oil*

(1,000 tons)

	1923	1937	1959	1965
Nigeria	128	146	183	156
Indonesia	7	194	102	123
Congo	16	68	181	79
Malaya	—	43	77	138
Other	40	45	18	27
Total	191	496	561	523

SOURCE: Commonwealth Economic Committee, *Vegetable Oil and Oilseeds*, H.M.S.O. London, various years.

The colonial administration, however, did not rest content with just preserving the native small holder system. It set out to increase the technical efficiency of indigenous production and thereby its competitiveness in the world market, by introducing reforms on two fronts, palm grove rehabilitation and improved processing techniques.[2] Although it is the processing aspect which is the subject of our enquiry, for a full understanding of the problems involved it is necessary to review, if only briefly, the principal developments on the agricultural side.

[1] *Ibid.*, p. 191.

[2] *West African Palm Oil and Palm Kernels*, Report of a Committee appointed by the Secretary of State for the Colonies, September 1923, to consider the best means of securing improved and increased production, Colonial Office Report No. 10, H.M.S.O., London 1925.

PRIMARY PRODUCTION

In 1927, after a number of years of experimental breeding,[1] the Department of Agriculture began to distribute free selected seedlings to farmers for the establishment of cultivated palm groves.[2] In 1935 the Cultivated Palm Ordinance provided financial incentive to farmers to undertake such planting by way of a rebate of the export duty. However by 1938 only 5,530 farmers out of nearly 1,000,000 had planted these seedlings, 9,213 acres in all.[3] There were many reasons for this disappointing performance. Principal among these were plot fragmentation and land tenure complications, difficult to administer and inadequate financial incentives,[4] periodic shortages of seedling supplies,[5] the absence of significant price differentials for higher quality oil, and fear that the government would eventually impose a tax on the planted trees as it had done in some cocoa districts.[6] While Professor Hancock has stressed inadequate agricultural extension efforts (p. 245), Richenda Scott points out the then as yet unsolved technical problems:

Over 3,000 acres of palm groves have been planted under the supervision of the Department of Agriculture, but not one has proved a complete success. A serious falling off in yield occurs after the ninth or tenth year, while even peak years have shown yields much below those of the Far Eastern plantations. The cultivated palm tends to exhaust the fertility of the soil more rapidly than the wild palm growing under natural conditions, for in the bush or dense palm grove the nonbearing palms and other trees provide considerable plant nutrients, which they draw from the sub-soil and from which the palms in bearing benefit. This supply is lacking in the carefully spaced palm groves of 60 trees to the acre.... At the present time [1943] Nigerian farmers

[1] A botanical garden was established in Calabar in 1893 by the Consul-General; palm seed beds were started in 1913 and taken over by the Department of Agriculture in 1921. In 1948 the West African Institute for Oil-Palm Research was established by a million pound grant from the Colonial Development and Welfare Act.

[2] Hancock, *op. cit.* p. 240. [3] *Ibid.* p. 242.

[4] 'If a grower registered his plot with the government and the oil produced by him was under 5 % f.f.a., he was then to receive a full rebate of the export duty; if his oil was between 5 and 8 % he would receive nine-tenths of the rebate. But he was only allowed to include the oil produced from the registered palms, and if he was unable personally to plant 15 acres, he had to become a member of a palm oil cooperative society. This scheme, however, proved abortive; though there were a number of planters and societies with sufficient acreage, they were unable to produce oil of the requisite standard as the difficulties encountered were too onerous.' Richenda Scott, *loc. cit.* p. 235. As will be seen later, when substantial price differentials were introduced these difficulties were quickly overcome.

[5] Until 1938 when government supplies became adequate, the United Africa Company provided seedlings free of charge from its plantation at N'dian in the Cameroons. In 1936 the government granted UAC a 6,000 acre plantation concession near Calabar in the hopes that it would have a demonstration effect on cultivation practice in the surrounding areas. UAC has a second palm plantation in the Mid-West which it inherited from a much earlier period.

[6] Richenda Scott, *loc. cit.* p. 236.

are not being encouraged to start oil palm plantations until methods of combating the resultant soil deterioration have been explored.[1]

After the war facilities for research into soil fertility and other problems were greatly expanded by the establishment of the West African Institute for Oil Palm Research. WAIFOR's investigations have added much to the knowledge of environmental factors which shape the oil palm economy and, at the applied level, have recorded significant achievements in the following areas: the breeding of stable hybrid high-yielding palm varieties, large-scale production of selected seedlings for distribution by regional Ministries of Agriculture,[2] disease control, optimum cultivation practice, improvement of soil fertility and more efficient methods of oil extraction.[3] In the field of basic research WAIFOR's investigations have revealed that as a result of comparatively uneven rainfall (i.e. a long dry season), a smaller amount of sunshine and nutrient-deficient sandy soils, Nigeria enjoys a lesser natural advantage in primary production than its major competitors, Malaya and the Congo. Taking an example at the applied level, in the pre-war period the Department of Agriculture recommended the use of manure, lime and cover crops as techniques for maintaining and improving soil fertility, with little success. Later spectrographic analyses of palm leaves revealed 'confluent orange spotting', a result of potassium deficiency. The subsequent use of potassium chloride fertilizers has brought very substantial increases in yield, sometimes as high as 100 %. To cite a second example, a large proportion of the seedlings being distributed by the regional Ministries of Agriculture were failing to survive or showing very poor growth owing to the loss of the ball of earth around the root. WAIFOR discovered in the mid-1950s that by cutting the roots 6 inches from the base of the plant one month before transplanting root growth was sufficiently stimulated to permit long distance carriage and successful replanting without the ball of earth.

A second major post-war development has been the shift in government policy to promote the establishment of large-scale plantations – not by foreign investors but by farm settlement schemes or through the Development Corporations.[4] The first such scheme at Kwa Falls near

[1] Richenda Scott, *loc. cit.* p. 242.

[2] Over the last decade the acreage equivalent of seedling distribution in the east has been about 2,000 acres per year; however only a very small fraction of this is realized in successful plantings.

[3] This paragraph is based on C. W. S. Hartley, 'Advances in Oil-Palm Research in Nigeria in the last Twenty-Five Years', *The Empire Journal of Experimental Agriculture*, April 1958.

[4] The material in this paragraph is drawn from D. L. MacFarlane and Martin Oworen, 'Investment in Oil Palm Plantation Operations in Nigeria: An Economic Appraisal', Economic Development Institute, Enugu, mimeograph, December 1964.

Calabar was initiated in 1948 for the purpose of settling some 20 farming families from the overcrowded areas of the region. Owing to a very low level of grove maintenance, failure to follow the advice given by the Ministry of Agriculture and a general lack of enthusiasm on the part of the settlers the scheme was abandoned in 1955, the land then being used to form the nucleus of the Eastern Nigeria Development Corporation's first plantation. By 1964 ENDC had established five plantations with some 19,000 planted acres. Another 2,000 acres had been planted in the various farm settlement schemes since their commencement in 1961. In the west some 17,000 acres have been planted in WNDC plantations and 3,000 acres in farm settlements. The two older UAC plantations of 6,500 acres each, one in the east and one in the mid-west, are in the process of being replanted with rubber trees.

The third major development in palm cultivation since the Second World War has been the recommencement of a much improved programme for palm grove rehabilitation. In the place of the complicated export duty rebate arrangements of the 1930s, the new scheme, begun in 1954 and financed by ENDC, initially provided direct payment of the following subsidies per acre: 30*s*. on felling and clearing unprodutive wild palms, 30*s*. on the planting of seedlings, 10*s*. a year for four years of satisfactory maintenance – each step to be certified by the Ministry of Agriculture. In 1956, in order to promote greater care by the farmers, the second payment of 30*s*. was divided into 15*s*. on planting and 15*s*. after the following dry season if plant losses were less than 10 %. Although there were many difficulties in implementing this programme, the primary bottleneck appears to have been delay and sometimes failure of ENDC to disburse the agreed subsidies.[1]

Table 42. *Palm grove rehabilitation in Eastern Nigeria*

	Acres planted		Acres planted
1954	97	1960	687
1955	62	1961	—
1956	146	1962	1,761
1957	—	1963	3,793
1958	163	1964	10,480
1959	1,531	1965	13,616

SOURCE: *Annual Reports*, Ministry of Agriculture and unpublished data supplied by the Ministry.

In the 1962–8 Development Plan £1·9m. was set aside for the rehabilitation of 60,000 acres over the following five years. In order to promote consolidation of land holdings a farmer to qualify must have a minimum of 5 acres. The earlier subsidy of £5 per acre cash was

[1] Eastern Region Agricultural Department, *Annual Report 1957/58*, p. 13.

increased to £8 cash and £10 in kind (seedlings, fertilizer, etc.). Only about half the target-acreage figures were achieved in the first two years of the plan, 1962 and 1963. As in earlier years, long delays in payment of the stipulated subsidies were a significant factor contributing to the shortfall.[1] The success of planting in 1964 and 1965 suggest that major inefficiencies in disbursing subsidies and other administrative impediments were overcome.

No less important than the number of trees planted is the standard of cultivation which determines eventual yields. Field observations by C. K. Eicher and W. L. Miller disclosed that the quality of naked-root seedlings varied considerably, that planting and application of fertilizer were untimely and that standards of maintenance were low.[2] In appraising these facts the investigators pointed out that agriculture extension staff responsible for palm cultivation had been deployed without any apparent rhyme or reason; while only four demonstrators were assigned to the three major producing provinces of Uyo, Calabar and Port Harcourt, twenty-one had been posted to the relatively unimportant province of Abakiliki.

It is still too early to judge how successful current measures will be in narrowing the gap in agricultural yields between Nigeria and her competitors. So far large-scale government-run plantations have been only moderately successful; the magnitude of the managerial and technical problems involved are such that it is hard to imagine large Nigerian-owned and -operated plantations making a significant contribution to total output, at least for the next few decades.[3] Farm settlement schemes are likely to be more successful. Regarding the rehabilitation of natural palmeries, in Professor Hancock's opinion lack of funds, personnel and government propaganda were responsible for the little progress achieved during the 1920s and 1930s; deficiencies in these areas have been more than made good in recent years. Equally the scientific and ecological knowledge necessary for a successful transformation is now available. But such qualitative factors as the efficiency with which the Ministry of Agriculture implements its programme and the calibre and motivation of the extension workers could adversely affect the final outcome. Last but not least the level of prices paid by the Marketing Board will have a critical influence on planting and cultivation practices.

[1] Ministry of Economic Planning, *First Progress Report, Eastern Nigeria Development Plan 1962–8*, Enugu 1964, p. 6.

[2] 'Observations on Smallholder Palm Production in Eastern Nigeria', Economic Development Institute, mimeograph, December 1963.

[3] For a discussion of the performance of publically owned plantations, see Lekan Are, 'An Assessment of Some Plantation Problems in Western Nigeria', *Tropical Agriculture*, January 1964; and 'Palm Plantations in Eastern Nigeria', *E.N.D.C. Oils*, Enugu 1964.

PALM OIL EXTRACTION

Having sketched in the major agricultural developments we may now proceed to the processing side of the palm oil industry. As in most earlier instances our method of approach will be to trace the industry's historical evolution with the hope that, in addition to assembling scattered historical facts of interest in themselves, this perspective will give rise to a fuller understanding and a more exact analysis of the problems encountered in the industry's development.

Palm oil extraction involves four steps: (*i*) softening of the palm fruit by heating (e.g. fermentation, sterilization), (*ii*) maceration, (*iii*) oil extraction, and (*iv*) clarification. In carrying out these operations there is considerable choice of both technique and scale of operation. One of the interesting features of the Nigerian palm oil industry is that technically inferior labour-intensive methods have proved economically more efficient than larger-scale, more capital-intensive alternatives.

The traditional methods of extracting palm oil were first described in a series of papers published in the *Annual Bulletin of the Department of Agriculture*, 1922–4.[1] These consisted of the 'hard oil' and the 'soft oil' processes; the former, which produced an oil which is semi-hard at air temperature, is thought to have been the more prevalent of the two up until about 1940.[2] In the 'hard oil' process the fruit bunches are brought to the native's compound, stacked in piles and covered with palm fronds or plantain leaves and left for about four days to loosen. After the fruits are shaken from the bunches they are left to ferment for another six days or so for further softening of the mesocarp. Then, approximately ten days after harvesting, the fruit is placed in a mortar – initially a rock-bottomed wood-lined pit, later half a 44-gallon drum – where it is pounded with long wooden pestles.[3] The macerated pulp is again left to undergo fermentation for twelve hours and then, after adding boiling water, a second pounding is administered. The pulverized fruit is now ready for the third step, oil extraction. This is carried out by applying pressure to the pulp, either by wringing in a net or by treading upon in an inclined open-end 'canoe'. The wrung pulp still contains the nuts which are now separated from the fibre and which later will be individually cracked between rocks to yield the palm

[1] 'Native Methods of Preparing Palm Oil – Parts I, II, III', by J. E. Gray, O. T. Faulkner, C. S. Lewin, A. C. Barnes, in the *Annual Bulletin of the Department of Agriculture Nigeria* (G. P. O. Lagos) for 1922, 1923, 1924.

[2] No records of the quality of Nigerian palm oil exports were kept until the establishment, of the Marketing Boards in 1939.

[3] In two areas in Abak and Okigwi divisions in 1964 William L. Miller reported that the processing was carried out on a considerably smaller scale, the maceration being administered in a small wooden mortar. *An Economic Analysis of Oil Palm Fruit Processing in Eastern Nigeria*, unpublished Ph.D. dissertation, Michigan State University, 1965, p. 35.

kernel. The process of softening, pounding and squeezing is then repeated a second time. The mixture of palm oil and water so obtained is boiled in a large pot and the oil skimmed off.

The 'hardness' of palm oil is determined by its free fatty acid (f.f.a.) content. In its natural state palm oil is composed of glycerides – stable molecules of fatty acids and glycerol. When the fruit becomes over-ripe or is bruised (e.g. in falling from the tree) enzymes present in the cell tissues are activated and, unless destroyed by the application of heat, break down the glyceride molecules into glycerol and free fatty acids. The quality of the oil is inversely related to the f.f.a. content. Because the enzymes are not sterilized in the hard oil process just described and because fermentation for its softening effect is protracted, the resultant oil has a high f.f.a. content, ranging from 20 % upwards, depending upon the extent of fermentation.

To produce an oil with a lower f.f.a. a 'soft oil' process was used, which since the early 1940s has become the only traditional method to be employed. This process differs from the 'hard oil' techniques primarily in that the fruit is sterilized at a fairly early stage. The bunches are left to soften only one to three days after harvesting and then the fruit is picked off by hand and steamed in a pot of boiling water, which neutralizes the enzymes and softens the fruit for pulling. The f.f.a. content of oil obtained by this process can be as low or lower than that achieved by the most mechanized techniques. The disadvantages of the 'soft oil' *vis-à-vis* the 'hard oil' process are that a slightly smaller proportion of the extractable oil is realized, the early removal of fruit from the bunch requires more labour and the initial boiling entails extra fuel costs. Thus it was not until significant price differentials were offered for the better quality oil that the 'soft oil' process became dominant.

In the early 1920s the Department of Agriculture began investigating ways of improving the efficiency of native processing. Improvements on existing practices were effected in the area of ancillary equipment (e.g. drying table, separation boards, barrel halves) and sequence timing. The major advance, however, was the introduction of a screw-press for extracting the oil. After testing a number of makes, the Duchscher press manufactured in Luxemburg, with a 22-gallon capacity and costing £13, was found to be suitable. The press economized on labour time and achieved a substantially higher extraction rate.[1]

The Dutchscher screw-press was first introduced in the late 1920s. Sales of the press were initially slow, but after 1934 hire-purchase terms

[1] The extraction rate is the weight of the oil obtained expressed as a per cent of the weight of the fruit prior to processing. An alternate measure is extraction efficiency which is the weight of the oil obtained expressed as a per cent of the total oil content.

arranged by the Native Administration, associated with higher palm oil prices during 1935–7, resulted in a moderate increase.[1] However with the collapse of prices in 1938 the slow advance of the screw-press was temporarily halted. The Department of Agriculture's *Annual Report* for 1938 explained why depressed prices operated against the more advanced technique, a phenomenon no less relevant in the 1960s.

In spite of the higher proportion of oil which can be produced by means of the press, the owner can seldom make a profit from the processing fee charged for extracting the oil of his neighbours. The market price of fruit approximates closely the value of the oil and kernel which it contains (the labour of extraction by native methods apparently being valued at nil) and the extra oil extracted by the press at low prices barely covers working costs.[2]

Table 43. *Number of screw presses and producer price of palm oil in Eastern Nigeria, selected years, 1930–1963*

	Number of[a] screw-presses	Producer price of palm oil (£/ton)		Number of screw-presses	Producer price of palm oil (£/ton)
1930	24	16	1945	1,300	12
1931	31	6	1947	2,076	15
1932	58	10	1949	2,671	43
1933	76	7	1951	4,481	55
1934	100	5	1953	5,333	75
1935	173	11	1955	...	58
1936	390	11	1960	...	48
1937	734	13	1963	3,893	40

[a] Cumulative sales up to 1953; the 1963 figure is the number reported in use in the east by the regional Ministry of Agriculture.

SOURCES: Richenda Scott, 'Production for Trade', in Perham, ed., *The Native Economies of Nigeria*, p. 237; G. K. Helleiner, *Peasant Agriculture, Government and Economic Growth in Nigeria*, table V-F-6; United Africa Company, *Statistical and Economic Review*, March 1954, p. 7; and Eastern Nigeria Department of Agriculture, *Annual Report 1962–63*.

With rapidly rising producer prices after the war the number of screw-presses grew rapidly. From the original £13, the price of the press rose to £30 in 1948, £65 in 1953, and fell (with commencement of local manufacture *circa* 1954) to £15–£40 in 1964, the price varying with the size of the press. Up until 1953 the figures for the number of presses represent cumulative sales; whether discarded for reasons of age or temporarily out of operations for repairs, the number of presses in use at one time was undoubtedly a good deal lower than the cumulative total.

[1] Richenda Scott, *loc. cit.* p. 236.
[2] Cited in Richenda Scott, *loc. cit.* p. 237.

The 1963 figure is the number of screw-presses reported to be in use in the eastern region by the Ministry of Agriculture.

In the early 1930s the United Africa Company began work on developing a small-scale power unit which would fall midway between the screw-press and the large-scale plantation oil mills. It was felt that the traditional native methods, even when incorporating the screw-press, resulted in relatively low extraction rates, poor quality oil and consumed labour-time which might otherwise be devoted to additional fruit collection.[1] William Lever's experience at Opobo and the government's trial scheme of the late 1920s had shown that 'central factories', the technical equivalent of large-scale plantation oil mills, servicing large areas of wild stands could not count upon a steady supply of fruit at the required volume of intake.[2] UAC's Pioneer mill, as it came to be known, was designed to embody most of the technical advantages of large-scale processing and yet be small enough to be compatible with what was considered a realistic radius of fruit collection – namely, five miles by bush path, seven miles by road and fifteen miles by water.[3] It was originally designed to cost £1,000 and to be owned and operated by local co-operative societies.

The essential components of a Pioneer oil mill are a sterilizer into which the fruit is first fed for sixteen minutes of steaming, a digester (an enclosed set of revolving and fixed arms) which separates the mesocarp from the nut, a centrifugal basket where the oil is spun from the mesocarp, and clarification tanks for the settling out of sludge and other impurities in the oil. Other equipment include a boiler, a steam power unit, a pump for removing the oil from the centrifuge to the settling tanks and an optional nut cracker for extracting the palm kernel. The cost of the first Pioneer mill produced in 1939 was £1,500.[4] It had an extraction efficiency of 85 % and was capable of producing oil with an f.f.a. content of less than 5 %.

Not only did the Pioneer mill fit in with peasant small-holdings and the existing organization of the industry, it also took account of Nigeria's factor proportions:

> ... in designing the mill no attempt has been made to render the extraction of oil and kernels completely mechanical. The stripping of the fruit bunches for the Pioneer mill is still done by hand; so, in many cases is the separation of fibre from nuts, and of shell from the kernels. Arrangements are also made at some mills for selling back the nuts to the African womenfolk for hand-cracking. Bearing in mind that Nigeria is in the main committed –

[1] United Africa Company, *Statistical and Economic Review*, no. 7, March 1951, pp. 3 ff.

[2] Richenda Scott, *loc. cit.* p. 234.

[3] United Africa Company, *Statistical and Economic Review*, no. 7, p. 10.

[4] By 1960 the cost of an installed Pioneer oil mill was £18,000.

according to declared government policy – to peasant development by non-plantation methods, there are grounds for believing that the Pioneer mill is indeed within a measurable distance of being the ideal machine for the job.[1]

This opinion was also shared by the government. After the war, funds were provided to the Department of Commerce and Industries by the Nigeria Local Development Board to establish twelve Pioneer mills on an experimental basis. The first such mill opened in 1946. By 1949 when the regional Development Boards were established five mills had been brought into operation. By 1960 145 Pioneer mills had been erected involving public investment of over £2,340,000.[2] The Pioneer oil mill scheme thus ranks as one of the largest development projects undertaken by the government in the 1945–60 period.

The most recent advance in processing technology was marked by the appearance of the Stork hydraulic hand-press. Designed by a Dutch company in 1959, the press was tested and ancillary equipment developed by S. C. Nwanze at WAIFOR during 1960 and 1961; extraction efficiency was found to be higher than the Pioneer mill and its capacity nearly as great.[3] Yet the installed cost of the Stork press and its equipment (three drums for fruit sterilization, mash reheating and oil clarification) in 1961 was only £560 against £18,000 for the Pioneer. Intended to supersede the screw-press and greatly increase total palm production, 1,000 presses were purchased by the Eastern Nigeria Government in 1962 under Project 31 of the 1962–8 Development Plan at a cost of £400,000.

> ... These hydraulic presses which have an extraction efficiency of 92 per cent [86 per cent was WAIFOR's average, 95 per cent the maximum] will be sold to private entrepreneurs on a hire-purchase basis. The use of these presses will increase the output of palm oil by 30,000 tons as a result of higher efficiency. Government revenue as well as farm income will be directly increased as a result. Maintenance of the presses and technical services will be undertaken by private firms.[4]

Unfortunately the planners' optimism concerning the hydraulic press was not borne out, at least in the short run. When only thirty-one presses had been sold by November 1963 (and of these only ten installed) the regional Ministry of Agriculture requested W. L. Miller of

[1] United Africa Company, *Statistical and Economic Review*, no. 7, p. 11.

[2] This figure includes operational losses for Development Corporation mills in the east (96) and west (17), but not for the north (7). There are twenty-odd privately owned mills in the east.

[3] *Annual Reports of the West African Institute for Oil-Palm Research* for 1959–60, 1960–1 and 1961–2.

[4] *Eastern Nigeria Development Plan*, Official Document No. 8 of 1962, The Government Printer, Enugu 1962, p. 36.

the Economic Development Institute, University of Nigeria, to investigate the matter. Miller's field survey in May 1964 of twenty of the twenty-four presses then in operation revealed that only eight were earning a profit and that ten firms were not even covering variable costs.[1] The average extraction rate was lower than the average for the Pioneer oil mills; average capacity utilization was under 30 %. A certain portion of the failure to achieve test results was attributable to inexperience in operating the new press, failure to reheat the macerated pulp before pressing and inefficient labour utilization. However the prime cause for non-profitable operation was high fruit cost, a factor determined exogenously by competition.[2]

Table 44 summarizes the major operational characteristics of the four technologies in use by 1963. On the basis of simple extraction efficiencies each new method should have displaced its predecessor. And, as we have seen, it has been extraction efficiency which has largely guided government policy.

Table 44. *Four palm oil processing techniques*

	Date of origin	Extraction efficiency (%)	Capacity (8 hours) (cwt. fruit)	Labour force	Investment required (£)
Native method	19th century	55	1–2	2	2–5
Screw press	1930	65	8–16	4	25–50
Pioneer mill	1946	85	96	22	18,000
Hydraulic hand-press	1963	86	68	7	560

SOURCES: *WAIFOR Eleventh Annual Report*, Benin City 1964, pp. 88–95; Anne Martin, *The Oil Palm Economy of the Ibibio Farmer*, pp. 12–13; W. L. Miller, 'The Economics of Field Operations of the Stork Hand Hydraulic Oil Palm Press', pp. 9–11; W. L. Miller, *An Economic Analysis of Oil Palm Fruit Processing, passim*; S. C. Nwanze, 'The Economics of the Pioneer Oil Mill', p. 245.

In the case of the native method and the screw-press, the capacity and investment vary with the size of the maceration vessel and the press.[3] With respect to the labour force, all operations are carried out by women and children in the case of the native method, while only the pressing and a small portion of the pounding is done by men in the screw-press process. Women are employed to separate the nuts from the mesocarp in the Stork process, while all workers are wage-paid males in the Pioneer mills.

[1] William L. Miller, 'The Economics of Field Operations of the Stork Hand Hydraulic Oil Palm Press: Report to the Government of Eastern Nigeria', Economic Development Institute, 31 July 1964, Mimeograph.

[2] Victor Uchendu has informed the writer that all Stork presses had ceased operating by August 1966.

[3] W. L. Miller, *An Economic Analysis of Oil Palm Fruit Processing*, p. 49.

Extraction efficiency, shown in the second column of table 44, is the percentage of the total oil content which is actually obtained; it can only be measured when the total oil content of the fruit being processed has been determined by laboratory analysis. These extraction efficiencies derive from tests carried out by the Research Division of the old Department of Agriculture and, since then, WAIFOR. The extraction *rate* – the form in which extraction data are usually available – is the weight of the oil actually obtained expressed as a percentage of the fruit's weight prior to extraction. If the oil content of wild palm fruit were constant, the extraction rate could be readily translated into extraction efficiency. In fact the oil content of fruit from wild and rehabilitated palm groves varies from as low as 14 % to as high as 25 % (the higher-yielding fruit tends to come from the heavier rainfall coastal areas). Thus the extraction rate achieved by the hydraulic presses surveyed by Miller ranged from 12 to 22 %.[1]

REGIONAL DISTRIBUTION OF PRODUCTION

Before we can proceed to analyse the comparative performance of the various processing technologies, it is necessary to determine the regional distribution of palm oil production. Regional Marketing Board purchases of palm kernel and palm oil for 1955–65 are given in Appendix C. The east and the west are the major producers of kernels; on the other hand, the west supplies very little palm oil for export, and the oil that it does provide is of a low quality. The north is a small export producer of both kernel and oil, the quality of the oil being primarily technical grade I. The east produces some 92 % of all export oil and 99 % of the edible ('special') grade. Thus in terms of value, the east accounts for over 95 % of all Marketing Board purchases of oil. Small tonnages of plantation oil, also of edible grade, come from the east and the west, in about equal measure; because we are interested in the peasant industry, plantation production is excluded from our analysis unless otherwise indicated.

The volume and distribution of palm oil extraction for domestic consumption is much less certain. What evidence there is suggests that in the east and north processed palm fruit is fully utilized, i.e. a conversion factor can be applied to palm kernels to determine the corresponding oil content.[2] In the west, because the oil content and its quality

[1] W. L. Miller, 'The Economics of Field Operations of the Stork Hand Hydraulic Oil Palm Press', p. 9.

[2] For the north, see J. Boston, 'The Igala Oil-Palm Industry', *N.I.S.E.R. Proceedings*, 1962, Ibadan, 1963. Fruit utilization in the east is described in the primary sources cited in the first footnote. The conversion ratios of oil to kernel (130 for the east, 120 for the north, 105 for the west) are derived from United Africa Company, *Statistical and Economic Review*, no. 13, March 1954, pp. 3, 16, 18, 19.

of the dominant wild palm varieties is low[1] and because alternative employment opportunities for men cultivating cocoa are so much more remunerative, a high proportion is not harvested, but rather left to drop and rot on the ground with only the palm kernel eventually being extracted by the women.[2] Working on the assumption that only one-third of the fruit that provides kernels is processed for oil in the west, we arrive at the following estimates of total palm oil production and domestic consumption:

Table 45. *Estimated total palm oil production*

(1,000 tons)

		M. B. purchases of palm kernel	Estimated palm oil production	M. B. purchases of palm oil	Residual domestic consumption
East	1961	208·3	270·8	160·7	110·1
	1962	169·0	219·7	120·9	98·8
	1963	197·0	256·1	139·4	116·7
	1964	203·0	263·9	138·9	125·0
	1965	221·0	287·3	153·6	133·7
West	1961	200·9	70·3	12·4	57·9
	1962	173·9	60·9	7·7	53·2
	1963	197·7	69·2	9·6	59·6
	1964	184·0	64·4	9·0	55·4
	1965	203·0	71·1	10·6	60·5
North	1961	20·8	25·0	0·4	24·6
	1962	19·3	23·2	—	23·2
	1963	18·3	22·0	—	22·0
	1964	15·0	18·0	—	18·0
	1965	25·0	30·0	—	30·0

SOURCE: Appendix C; extracted palm oil as percentage of kernel: east, 130; west, 105; north, 120.

Annual production of palm oil for the three most recent years ranges from 347,000 to 388,000 tons, with internal consumption ranging from 181,000 to 224,000 tons. These figures are consistent with the Eastern Nigeria Ministry of Agriculture's standing estimate of 200,000 tons of palm oil consumed domestically. However it must be admitted that all estimates of total production are to a certain extent guesswork; in our case the 'guess' is the one-third utilization factor for the west.[3]

[1] All the Pioneer mills in the west proved uneconomic for this reason. For the very low extraction rates S. C. Nwanze, 'The Economics of the Pioneer Oil Mill', *Journal of the West African Institute for Palm Oil Research*, April 1961, p. 235. For the very small proportion of special grade oil produced, see *Annual Reports of the Western Region Production Development Board*.

[2] *Report of the Mission Appointed to Enquire into the Production and Transport of Vegetable Oils and Oil Seeds Produced in the West African Colonies*, London, H.M.S.O. 1947, p. 15; and United Africa Company, *Statistical and Economic Review*, no. 13, p. 18.

[3] Based on the assumption that 40,000 to 50,000 tons is a reasonable consumption figure for the west. A significant but unknown share of internal production in the east is exported to the north.

For the purposes of determining output shares of the four processing technologies we shall confine our attention to the east, where production estimates are the most reliable and where some data about processing are available. The total production of oil during 1961–4 by ENDC Pioneer mills ranged between 15,200 and 17,000 tons; it is estimated that oil production of the private Pioneer mills did not exceed 9,000 tons and was probably a good deal less.[1] In 1963 production by the hydraulic presses was negligible; in 1964 it was about 480 tons.[2] Thus, in 1964 the native method and the screw-press, technologically the least efficient processes, accounted for 239,000 tons or 91 % of the total oil processed.

The breakdown of output between the native method and the screw-press is highly problematic. W. L. Miller's sample survey of forty-seven screw-presses in two locations gave an annual average output of 6·2 tons per press; estimates of the number of screw-presses operating in the east range from the Ministry of Agriculture's enumerated 3,900 to Miller's population-based estimate of 17,600. Combining the average output figure with the two extreme values for the number of screw-presses yields 24,000 tons by screw-press and 215,000 tons by native method as the lower limit for screw-presses, and 106,000 tons by screw-press and 133,000 tons by native method as the upper limit. In the only two empirical case studies in the north and the west, it was reported that processing was primarily by the native method.[3] Thus available evidence seems to suggest that the native method continues to be the predominant technology employed in palm oil extraction throughout Nigeria.

We will begin our examination of the Pioneer oil mill's performance by scrutinizing its role in the spectacular improvement in the quality of Nigerian palm oil which occurred during the period that the mills were being introduced. In 1950 less than 0·5 % (300 tons) of the oil purchased by the Marketing Board was of Special Grade quality (f.f.a. content of 4½ % or less); by 1955 Special Grade oil accounted for 70 % (129,500 tons) of Marketing Board purchases.[4] It is commonly claimed that the Pioneer oil mills, in conjunction with the price differentials, played an important part in bringing about this qualitative 'revolution'.[5] That such is demonstrably not the case can be seen from

[1] Interview with Chief Engineer, Pioneer Oil Mill Scheme, Aba, September 1964.

[2] Miller, *An Economic Analysis of Oil Palm Fruit Processing*, p. 73.

[3] Charles P. Takes, 'Socio-Economic Factors Affecting Agricultural Productivity in Some Villages of Oshun Division, Western Region', Nigerian Institute of Social and Economic Research, mimeo, 1963, p. 46; and J. Boston, *op. cit.*

[4] Commonwealth Economic Committee, *Vegetable Oils and Oilseeds*, H.M.S.O., London 1957.

[5] G. K. Helleiner, 'The Eastern Nigeria Development Corporation: A Study in the Sources and Uses of Public Development Funds 1947–1962', *Nigerian Journal of Economic and*

a comparison of special grade oil purchased in the eastern region and the quantity of such oil produced by ENDC's Pioneer mills, the latter being responsible for the great bulk of all centrifuged special grade oil.

Table 46. *Edible palm oil purchases and ENDC ouput*

	Total special grade purchases[a] (tons)	ENDC Pioneer special grade output (tons)
1950	300	300
1951	8,500	700
1952	52,900	4,700
1953	106,800	7,300
1954	124,185	7,400
1955	128,797	15,600
1957	117,133	14,300
1959	135,286	16,300
1961	127,703	14,100
1963	114,000	15,400

[a] 1950–54 figures include small amounts (maximum 1,000 tons) from west and north; thereafter figures are for the east only.

SOURCE: Eastern Nigeria Marketing Board *Annual Reports* and data supplied by the Chief Engineer, Pioneer Oil Mill Scheme, Aba.

At no time between 1950 and 1960 did ENDC own less than three-quarters of all operating Pioneer mills; allowing a 50 % or even 100 % increase on the ENDC figures it is clear that the Pioneer mill's contribution to the transformation in the quality of Nigerian oil has been negligible.

Since the bulk of special grade oil has not been produced by the Pioneer mills, it must have been processed by traditional methods or by the screw-press. Most of the pre-1950 students of the palm oil industry had asserted, like Richenda Scott, that such an outcome was highly improbable:

> . . . it is doubtful if the African producer, utilizing the fruit of the wild palm, will ever succeed in obtaining an oil of a low f.f.a. content on any large scale, or will be able to maintain that standard over a long period by his present crude methods, even with the assistance of the handpress.[1]

This opinion seems to have carried forward, despite proof to the contrary, to much of current literature, including ENDC and other government publications. That the f.f.a. content was solely dependent

Social Studies, March 1964, p. 120; T. C. Mbanefo, 'Pioneer Oil Mills in the Extraction of Palm Oil', *E.N.D.C. Oils*, Enugu 1964; E.N.D.C. *Annual Reports*; S. C. Nwanze, *loc. cit.* p. 233; Frank Fehr and Company, *Annual Review of Linseeds, Oils, Oilseeds and Other Commodities* 1955, London 1956; *Statistical and Economic Review*, March 1951, p. 3 (but recanted in issue No. 13, March 1954, p. 5); Richenda Scott, 'Production for Trade', in Perham, ed., *The Native Economies of Nigeria*, p. 242.

[1] Richenda Scott, *loc. cit.* p. 242.

upon the extent of fermentation (i.e. the speed and care of bringing the fruit to the point of processing) and that the latter could be held to a minimum with the improved 'soft oil' process had already been established by the late 1920s by research officers in the Department of Agriculture.[1] Indeed, experiments conducted in 1963 by T. N. Okwelogu, Chemist of the Eastern Nigeria Marketing Board, suggest that traditional methods, unaided by the screw-press, are capable of producing a higher quality oil than are any of the mechanically-assisted processes.[2]

All available information, then, would seem to indicate that it was the price incentive alone which brought about the qualitative transformation of Nigerian palm oil. Evidence, so far unnoticed, that traditional methods were capable of such achievement is provided by the 1944–9 period when new gradings and increased price differentials were introduced.[3] Over the decade 1939–49 the average f.f.a. content of Nigerian palm oil dropped from 25 to 14 %.[4] The table below shows the response to price differentials for both the earlier and later periods: the earlier categories have been reclassified to fit the post-1950 structure.

The more rapid rate of improvement in oil quality after 1950 is probably attributable to the exaggerated differentials (four to twelve times greater) paid by the Marketing Board relative to the premia given in the free market.[5] This has been possible only because the Marketing Board has set producer prices well below world prices – with its dampening effects on total supply. Total proceeds to Nigeria from palm oil exports would undoubtedly have grown faster under a régime of higher producer prices and smaller differentials.

[1] D. Manlove, 'Palm Oil in Nigeria', *Journal of Tropical Agriculture*, 1931, Trinidad.

[2] Information supplied by the Eastern Nigeria Marketing Board. Technical factors responsible for the potentially lower f.f.a. content of oil produced by non-mechanical means are a lesser degree of heat generated in the extraction process and the absence of contact with oxidizing metals.

[3] During the 1920s and 1930s the writer has been able to find references to only two grades of oil, soft and semi-hard (e.g. *Blue Book*, section 121); 18 % f.f.a. seems to have been the dividing line. Later classifications were as follows:

1939 (%)	1944–49 (%)	1950– (%)
0–10	0– 9	0–4½ (3½ from 1956)
11–25	10–18	4½– 9
25–45	19–27	10–18
Over 45	28–36	19–27 (30 from 1953)
	Over 36	28–36 (not bought after 1951)

[4] Figures for the years 1940–5 are not available. Calculated on the basis of 0·5 % less than the maximum (owing to the middlemen's practice of 'mixing') and 45 % for the 'over 36 %' category.

[5] In 1954 the premium paid in the Liverpool market for every 1 % lower f.f.a. content was 3*s.* 6*d.*; the corresponding premium over the interval between the Marketing Board's Special Grade and Grade I was 60*s.*; by 1964 it had been reduced to 22*s.* *Statistical and Economic Review*, no. 13, March 1954, p. 12.

Why has the Pioneer oil mill, with an extraction efficiency of 85 % been unable to sweep aside pre-existing techniques which attain only 55 % and 65 % efficiency? Why have the ENDC Pioneer mills produced at only two-fifths of their capacity? Why have a large number of the Pioneer mills gone out of operation altogether? Part of the answer

Table 47. *Marketing board purchases of palm oil classified by f.f.a. content*

	Producer price (£ per ton) 1949	1954	1939 (%)	1946 (%)	1949 (%)	1951 (%)	1954 (%)
Under 4½ % (from 1950)	—	61·0	—	—	—	6	61
4½–9 % (from 1944)	42·75	46·0	20	56	66	71	30
10–18 %	37·10	34·0	34	18	15	11	4
19–27 %	33·0	29·0	13	16	13	8	5
28–36 %	—	—	14	9	6	4	—
Over 36 %	—	—	19	1	—	—	—
			100	100	100	100	100

SOURCES: UAC, *Statistical and Economic Review*, no. 1, March 1948; no. 13, March 1954, p. 10; Commonwealth Economic Committee, *Vegetable Oil and Oilseeds*, London 1949 and 1955; Federal Office of Statistics, *Annual Abstract of Statistics 1960*, p. 64.

to these questions was uncovered by S. C. Nwanze, WAIFOR'S industrial engineer, in an investigation into the economics of the Pioneer mills carried out in 1959 and 1960.[1] Mr. Nwanze identified two groups of factors responsible for the disappointing performance, the first related to technical efficiency and management organization, and the second to the supply of fruit.

Regarding the supply of fruit, Nwanze noted the seasonality of wild palm fruit yields; the peak harvesting season occurs between February and June and the supply of fruit tapers off during the latter six months of the year. Where roads are poor, the fruit supply is adversely affected during the early rains, when farmers will only undertake to carry fruit to the mills when they are in especial need of money. Competition from hand-press operators, who show considerable initiative in fruit collection, also restricts the supply to the mills. Finally, the opposition of the women to having to give up their traditional right to the palm kernels has caused the men in some areas not to sell their fruit to the mill.

Underlying all the contributing causes identified by Nwanze is the fruit price that each processor is able to pay; this depends upon the extraction efficiency of the processor's technology, the combined labour

[1] S. C. Nwanze, 'The Economics of the Pioneer Oil Mill', *Journal of the West African Institute for Palm Oil Research*, April 1961.

and capital processing cost and the price received for the end products, the oil and kernels. Nwanze's primary contribution is an analysis of the intra-firm technical and organizational factors that are important in determining the Pioneer oil mill's processing cost per unit of output.

Mr. Nwanze described the faults in design as follows:

> A low installed cost and cheapness of labour were emphasized in the design of the mill and individual equipment conforms to a good but rather rugged standard of mechanical design. It is unfortunate, however, that when all the equipment is assembled the mill does not provide an example of a design giving smooth and unhindered processing. The most important item, which determines the throughput of the mill, is the centrifuge, and all ancillary vessels or machinery might better have been made of the correct size to suit the centrifuge capacity and so prevent bottlenecks in the process. For instance, even when fruit is available, the centrifuge may remain idle because the autoclave and the digester are not producing sufficient fruit to feed it continuously. On the other hand, it is not unusual to find a big pile of fibre still to be separated, because the nut separator cannot deal quickly enough with fibre coming from the centrifuge.
>
> Some of the equipment appears to have been borrowed from other industries without much modification. The fibre separator resembles a cotton ginning machine, the sludge tank and the clarification tanks are reminiscent of the sugar industry, and the digester, which looks like a soap blending pot, has not been steam jacketed in spite of the need for heat to assist in the rupture of oil cells during fruit maceration. The centrifuge is uncovered and considerable heat loss is unavoidable when the basket is spinning. Flow of materials through the various stages of the process is also impeded. The equipment in the mill could have been arranged to make the maximum use of gravity in assisting the flow of materials. A vertical construction would have made the mill more compact and also would have reduced labour since about half of the hands employed do nothing but carrying.[1]

More important than design shortcomings were failings in management organization, especially labour utilization. The investigator's time studies showed that only 7 to 14 % of total workable manhours were usefully employed.[2] Failure to co-ordinate the size of the labour force, raw material supplies and oil evacuation resulted in prolonged stoppages. Supervisors failed to exercise their responsibilities and were often ill-informed about processing technology. There was little rhythm of work, work methods were often inefficient, and many supposedly skilled operators had but a vague understanding of their job. Finally, low levels of maintenance led to frequent breakdowns.

Having diagnosed the difficulties, Mr. Nwanze went on to demonstrate the consequence of applying a few simple principles of industrial

[1] *Journal of the West African Institute for Palm Oil Research*, April 1961, p. 234.
[2] *Ibid.* pp. 238–40.

engineering. Taking a standard model Pioneer mill, he reduced the labour force from 29 to 22, increased fruit throughput from 18½ to 22 centrifuge charges per shift and obtained a 20 % higher extraction rate (by reducing heat loss from the centrifuge) per unit of fruit processed.[1] Taken together these improvements yielded a 96 % increase in output per man. The potential effect of Mr. Nwanze's innovations was to reduce processing cost by a third; however, he calculated that the mills were not an economic proposition unless they achieved an 18 % oil extraction rate and operated at a minimum of 67 % capacity utilization, i.e. 2,000 tons of fruit per year per mill.[2]

Now let us look at the actual performance. The average oil extraction rate for at least twelve of the seventeen mills in the western region in 1954 was 12 %; by 1957, fourteen mills had been closed down. Extraction rates achieved by mills in the east have ranged from 21·5 to 14 %. Regarding the volume of fruit processed, if we take the aggregate annual average for ENDC mills, we see that the scheme has never achieved Nwanze's threshold of economic operation, either in processing capacity utilized or the extraction rate (see table 48).[3] By 1964 ENDC had closed down twenty-nine of its ninety-six mills; of the remaining sixty-seven, fifteen were not earning a surplus over direct costs.[4] Only three were still running in the north and these at a loss.[5] Some twenty-odd privately operated mills (mostly former ENDC mills purchased by the major palm produce buyers) were faring slightly better than their more favourably located publicly owned competitors, largely owing to their greater efforts at fruit collection.

AN EXPLANATORY HYPOTHESIS

What is to explain the competitive superiority of the technologically inferior techniques – an outcome which results in the loss of some 30 % of potential production? Is it only a question of managerial and technical slack in the operation of the Pioneer mills and hydraulic presses, or is it something more fundamental? The explanation to be developed in what follows is that two factors in addition to organizational inefficiency – the small scale of the more primitive processes and the

[1] *Journal for the West African Institute for Palm Oil Research*, April 1961, pp. 250–1.

[2] *Ibid.* p. 247.

[3] Modest paper profits were received in 1955–6, 1958–9 and 1959–60 as a result of underestimating depreciation and omitting administrative overheads. Helleiner ('The Eastern Nigerian Development Corporation: A Study in the Sources and Uses of Public Development Funds, 1947–62', *Nigerian Journal of Economic and Social Studies*, March 1964, p. 19) reports cumulative losses of £378, 400 as of March 1962.

[4] Interview with chief engineer, Pioneer Oil Mill Scheme, Aba, September 1964.

[5] Helleiner, *Peasant Agriculture*, p. 117.

availability of household labour – are responsible for thwarting the introduction of more advanced technology.

Our starting point is the budget studies of Miller carried out in 1964. His findings are summarized in table 49. Only in the case of wages did Miller depart from reporting actual figures. In this instance he sub-

Table 48. *Performance of ENDC Pioneer oil mills, 1952–1964*

	No. of mills	Fruit capacity	Fruit milled	Capacity utilized (%)	Extraction rate (%)
1952	52	156,000	20,646	13	16·8
1953	53	159,000	42,668	27	17·1
1954	70	210,000	47,317	23	16·7
1955	86	258,000	100,051	39	17·5
1956	93	279,000	98,042	35	17·2
1957	95	285,000	102,991	36	17·0
1958	96	288,000	114,784	40	17·1
1959	96	288,000	105,403	37	17·3
1960	95	285,000	121,681	43	17·1
1961	95	285,000	94,682	33	16·8
1962	82	246,000	96,251	40	16·8
1963	78	234,000	101,569	43	16·5
1964	67	201,000	96,371	48	17·2

SOURCE: Chief engineer, ENDC Pioneer Oil Mill Scheme.

stituted 'standard' wages (3*s.* per day for male workers, 1*s.* 6*d.* per day for female) 'because the primary objective [of this study] is to compare the five different processing technologies'.[1] We have discarded his imputed labour costs for the native method and screw-press because these were in fact operated by unpaid family labour. For the privately operated Stork presses the 3*s.* male wage rate is a representative average (range, 2*s.* 7*d.* to 3*s.* 6*d.*); however in the case of the Pioneer mills the basic wage is in fact 5*s.* Indirect labour rates – managerial and skilled maintenance – were estimated at realistic levels.

In terms of the human input, the native method is very inefficient (largely because of the time required at the extraction stage) and the Pioneer mill is very efficient (owing to the mechanization of the maceration stage). The combined labour-capital cost per cwt. of oil for the Stork hydraulic and Pioneer mill are virtually identical at 13*s.* 10*d.* and 13*s.* 11*d.*, respectively. For the native method total annual depreciation is but 5*s.* and, as the items are also used as household utensils, there may be some question as to whether the decision-makers impute any capital

[1] Miller, *An Economic Analysis of Oil Palm Fruit Processing*, p. 40. As a result of using standard money wages – and in general averaging widely differing price relationships into a single constant – Miller's pioneering empirical study is in many respects more nearly a technological than an economic analysis. The fifth technology considered by Miller is a large scale plantation mill factory.

costs at all to processing. The 13*s*. cost advantage of the native and screw-press techniques is partially offset by higher fruit costs and lower total revenue. The latter reflects the absence of a final stage of clarification and bulking in eight-hundredweight metal drums. After allowing for a revenue differential of 5*s*. and the purchase of an additional 0·8 cwt. of fruit (see table 49, third row) at 6*s*. per cwt., the native-method and screw-press processors are left with a surplus or competitive advantage over the next most efficient technology of 3*s*. 3*d*. per cwt of oil processed.

Table 49. *Average operational data per cwt. of oil produced for four processing technologies, 1964*

	Native method	Screw press	Stork hydraulic	Pioneer mill
Firms surveyed	67	47	20	67
Av. annual output (tons of oil)	0·4	6·2	20	248
Cwt. fruit required	6·5	6·6	6·3	5·8
Total labour-hours	9	3·8	3	1·1
Direct labour cost	—	—	7*s*. 2*d*.	3*s*. 4*d*.
Indirect labour cost	—	—	2*s*. 10*d*.	2*s*. 4*d*.
Depreciation and repair	10*d*.	1*s*.	3*s*. 10*d*.	8*s*. 3*d*.
Oil revenue	31*s*. 9*d*.	32*s*.	38*s*.	38*s*. 1*d*.
Nut revenue	14*s*. 4*d*.	15*s*.	13*s*. 2*d*.	13*s*. 2*d*.
Total revenue	46*s*. 1*d*.	47*s*.	51*s*. 2*d*.	51*s*. 3*d*.

SOURCE: Miller, *An Economic Analysis of Oil Palm Fruit Processing*, pp. 37, 39, 40, 43, 44, 50–7, 78, 80, 82.

The introduction of transport costs provides a further, although modest, advantage to the more numerous small-scale processors. Given a weight reduction of about 50 % between palm fruit, on the one hand, and its extracted oil and nut constituents, on the other, there is a transport savings to be earned by processing the fruit as near as possible to the locus of harvesting. The larger the capacity of the processor, the greater the radius over which he must attract fruit. Between the smallest scale native method and the largest-scale Pioneer mill Miller reports a differential of 13*d*. fruit assembly cost per cwt. of oil produced. If the Pioneer mill were to operate at full capacity the additional fruit assembly cost (from 23*d*. to 33*d*.) would be more than counterbalanced by the reduction in fixed costs.[1]

The raw material requirement (the reciprocal of the extraction rate), shown in the third row, is the largest cost item at 6*s*. per cwt. of fruit. Surprisingly (and seemingly unaccountably) the average extractive performance of the native method was slightly greater than that of the

[1] Miller, *An Economic Analysis of Oil Palm Fruit Processing*, chapter 3.

screw-press (15·4 % as against 15·2 %). If average oil content is put at 20 % – the conventional aggregate average for the east – the Pioneer extraction rate of 17·2 % represents an extraction efficiency of 86 % and the 15·2 % of the screw-press technique is equal to a 76 % extraction efficiency.

The apparent discrepancy between this recorded performance differential and the 85 to 65 % test differential reported by WAIFOR is in fact a reflection of the small-scale operator's advantage in obtaining a higher oil content fruit. Not only is the small-scale processor able to inspect the small quantity of fruit he buys much more carefully than his larger competitors, but with no fixed costs he can stop production whenever the better quality fruit is not available. This logical presupposition is supported by all investigators' reports that the small-scale processors do get the premium fruit, and by Miller's findings that these two small-scale technologies have more than double the unutilized capacity of the other two techniques.[1]

Regarding the labour input, there would seem to be little doubt that in the case of the native method, labour time is virtually costless. Miller' studies show that the combined labour time of women and children spent on processing per day ranges between one and two hours.[2] Fitted in between household and farming chores, the time devoted to palm fruit is otherwise 'free time' and does not involve any sacrifice of remunerative employment in another activity. As the wife, in many cases, traditionally receives the kernel-containing nut as payment for her labours, she is quite happy to forgo her leisure. Indeed, the intra-family income redistribution effect of selling fruit rather than its processed constituent parts gave rise to the much publicized female boycotts and demonstrations against Pioneer mills in the early 1950s.

In the case of the screw-press, the amount of time per day devoted to processing is substantial and involves male labour. Data from Miller's survey (table 50) show both the amount of labour expended per day and its distribution among the various stages of processing.

While Miller reports that in his Abak and Okigwi screw-press samples 'since most workers were members of the family they were not paid wages for their labour' (p. 52), in at least two provinces, Annang and Uyo, the workers are commercially engaged, receiving 40 % of the processing fee.[3] In this instance the screw-press owner does not buy the fruit, but merely expresses the oil for a fixed charge; if the proprietor

[1] Miller, *An Economic Analysis of Oil Palm Fruit Processing*, p. 94.

[2] *Ibid.* p. 46. Four child-hours equal one woman-hour equals one man-hour.

[3] Olatunde Oloko, 'A Study of Socio-Economic Factors Affecting Agricultural Productivity in Annang Province, Eastern Nigeria', Nigerian Institute of Social and Economic Research, mimeograph, 1963, p. 61.

of the screw-press is a middleman, he will then buy the oil from its owner. In either case – whether receiving a money wage or not – it is clear from the combined hours of labour time expended per day (34 hours in Abak and 51 in Okigwi) that substantial alternative employment opportunities are being sacrificed and that consequently a real wage is imputed to labour in the case of the screw-press technology.

Table 50. *Average labour requirements per cwt. of oil extracted by screw-press*

(in eight-hour days)

	Abak		Okigwi	
	Female	Male	Female	Male
Sterilization	1·4	—	0·4	0·2
Pounding	0·4	0·4	0·4	0·3
Pressing	0·2	0·3	—	0·2
Separation of nut	1·4	—	1·6	—
Second pressing	0·1	0·1	—	0·1
	3·5	0·8	2·4	0·8
	(cwt.)		(cwt.)	
Average daily production	1		2	
Days in operation per annum	60		94	
Number of firms surveyed	21		26	

SOURCE: Miller, *An Economic Analysis of Oil Palm Fruit Processing*, pp. 51, 61.

This finding alters the ordinal ranking of the technologies as calculated from table 49: the native method is now seen to have a clear competitive advantage over the screw-press. Lending support to this conclusion, Miller reports a net reduction in the number of screw-presses:

Between 1960 and 1964 this [expansionary] trend [in the number of operational screw presses] was reversed. The author became aware of this new trend as he collected the data presented in this thesis. Several screw processing firms were closed, and the owners of these presses indicated they had 'no money to repair them when they broke down'. These firms could not economically invest even the small sum required to repair the press. Some owners of screw press manufacturing plants had changed from manufacturing presses to manufacturing bed frames.[1]

The preceding analysis can be formalized into a simple algebraic expression which has general validity for the determination of competitive superiority among differing processing technologies where the

[1] Miller, *An Economic Analysis of Oil Palm Fruit Processing*, p. 104. Miller interprets this trend as applying to all processing technologies since, with his imputed wage values, the native method emerged as the least efficient technique. On the basis of his calculations, for all techniques average revenue was less than average cost.

prices and quality of the factor inputs are variable as between technologies.

The advantages of the modern, advanced technologies are typically a higher extraction efficiency (more final product per unit of raw material input) and a smaller labour requirement (man-hours) per unit of final product. The countervailing advantages of the primitive technique stem from its small scale. The first is very low wage rates (approaching zero in the limiting case) owing to the availability of household labour with little or no opportunity cost. The second advantage of the primitive technology is its ability to command the best quality raw material input by virtue of (*a*) costless shutdown when the best quality is not available, (*b*) more thorough inspection of the raw material purchased and (*c*) greater local knowledge and contacts. The instance of raw material advantage is but one case of the advantage of costless shutdown and start-up when any condition of production is variable, i.e. intertemporal variation in any item of cost or revenue.

Definitions:

R = Revenue per unit of output
C = Cost per unit of output
L = Labour cost per unit of output
K = Capital consumption and repairs per unit of output
P_a = Price per unit of output of the advanced technology
T = Technology
S = Scale of production
r = Extraction rate
t = Transport cost per unit of output
$Z = P_a - P_p$ (the differential for stage of processing, e.g. clarification and bulking)
Subscript a = Advanced technology
Subscript p = Primitive technology

General relationships:

$C = f(L, K, t, 1/r)$

$L = f(S, 1/K)$
$K = f(T)$
$t = f(S)$
$r = f(T)$

The advanced technology will be able to bid the raw material supply away from the primitive technique when $C_a < C_p + Z$, which occurs when

$$\frac{r_a - r_p}{r_p} . P_a > (L_a - L_p) + (K_a - K_p) + (t_a - t_p) - Z.$$

Conversely the primitive technology will predominate when $C_a > C_p + Z$, which occurs when $\frac{r_a - r_p}{r_p} . P_a < (L_a - L_p) + (K_a - K_p) + (t_a - t_p) - Z$.

In the case of palm oil, given the level of producer prices, the value of the incremental output achieved by the Pioneer oil mills and the Stork hydraulic presses has not been equal to the incremental costs entailed, relative to the more primitive native method and screw-press technique.

ECONOMIC EFFICIENCY: AN OPTIMAL SOLUTION

The existing situation of palm oil processing in Nigeria results in the loss to the economy – both with regard to export earnings and domestic consumption – of thousands of tons of palm oil left in the discarded fruit pulp each year. The loss is equal to the maximum obtainable extraction efficiency (say 85 %) less the weighted average actually achieved by the combined technologies (say a generous 70 %) as a ratio of the latter, times the total oil produced. If the actual production in the east was 287,000 tons in 1965, the recoverable oil lost to the economy was 61,000 tons – worth £5m. at the 1965 export f.o.b. price.

There is another cost to the economy, an unmeasurable social cost, involved in the use of household labour, particularly that of the housewife. Over the long run a socio-cultural transformation involving individual behavioural patterns, motivation and attitudes must accompany or perhaps precede economic growth. A very important element in this process are changes in the pattern of child-rearing. The appropriate education of the mother is half of the matter; release for both her and her children from the long hours of stultifying drudgery involved in processing activities (including preparation of gari) is the other half.

Table 51. *Export and producer prices of palm oil, edible grade*

	Producer price at Port Harcourt (£ per ton)	Export price f.o.b. (£ per ton)
1956	50·0	82·4
1957	50·0	86·0
1958	50·0	75·2
1959	47·8	76·6
1960	47·8	73·9
1961	47·8	82·7
1962	40·0	75·9
1963	40·0	75·3
1964	41·0	80·8
1965	41·0	90·0

SOURCE: Commonwealth Economic Committee, *Tropical Products Quarterly*, various issues.

The remedy to both these losses lies in the Marketing Board's producer price policy. As shown in table 51, producer prices have consistently been set well below world prices; this has been done not for reasons of price stabilization but rather as a means of augmenting public savings.[1]

There are two ways the Marketing Board can assure that all palm produce is processed by the most efficient technologies. The first is by paying a higher price for oil extracted by Pioneer mills and Stork presses relative to that paid for oil extracted by the native method and screwpress. The amount of this 'subsidy' of preferential tax relief would have to be greater than the adjusted cost differential of these two technologies, say 5*s.* for cost equalization and a 2*s.* competitive margin.

The second method, which, unlike the first, would not require any policing or be open to administrative incompetence or abuse, would be for the Marketing Board to raise the producer price for palm oil to that level where the value of the incremental output of the advanced techniques exceeds the adjusted incremental cost. At this point, the advanced technologies could bid away the fruit from the more primitive processors. This required producer price can be determined from the earlier formula. At equilibrium where neither technology is at an advantage,

$$\frac{r_a - r_p}{r_p} . P_a = (L_a - L_p) + (K_a - K_p) + (t_a - t_p) - Z.$$

If P_a is raised, T_a will tend to prevail; if P is lowered, T_p will tend to prevail.

From table 49, $r_a = 0{\cdot}17$ and $r_p = 0{\cdot}15$; the right-hand term of the equation can be estimated at about 10*s.* Then $0{\cdot}133 \times P = 10s$, $P_a = 75s$. Allowing another 3*s.* per cwt. of oil for transport and handling to Port Harcourt (the point at which the producer price is calculated) and 2*s.* as the competitive margin to be paid in higher fruit prices, we arrive at 80*s.* per cwt. of palm oil (or £80 per ton) as the price required to insure that the bulk of palm oil will be processed by Pioneer mills and Stork presses.

Should it be established that the public savings forgone by a reduced tax burden on palm oil would be more beneficial to the economy's growth than the incentive effects of a higher price on palm grove rehabilitation and increased fruit collection, the producer price can be lowered to its previous level once the Pioneer mills and Stork presses have become dominant. This felicitous result is explained by a rising average extraction rate achieved by the two advanced technologies as the better quality fruit comes to them. Owing to their improved extraction rate, the processors can now raise their price for fruit as a proportion of the palm oil price – to such an extent that, above a certain

[1] See G. K. Helleiner, 'The Fiscal Role of the Marketing Boards in Nigerian Economic Development, 1947–61', *Economic Journal*, September 1964, pp. 583 ff.

equilibrium threshold, they can pay more for the fruit than the primitive processors can sell their final products.

The equilibrium threshold producer price can be determined by the same formula as before; the only difference is that now the term $r_a - r_p / r_p$ is considerably larger. If we assume that both technologies now get the same quality fruit, their extraction rates stand in the same proportion as their extraction efficiencies, $(0{\cdot}85 - 0{\cdot}65/0{\cdot}65) = 0{\cdot}310$. The incremental output of the advanced technology relative to the primitive techniques is now more than double the initial 0·133. Substituting in the new value we get $0{\cdot}310 \times P = 10s$, $P = 32s$. If we add our earlier 5*s.* mark-up to cover transport and a competitive advantage margin, we arrive at a minimum producer price of 37*s.* per cwt. of oil (£37 per ton) at which the Pioneer mills and Stork presses would still be able to bid away the raw material supply.

In the preceding pages with regard to both the explanation for the observed output shares of the various technologies and a proposed optimal solution, we have implicitly made the assumption that homogeneous conditions exist throughout the palm industry. In fact there may be considerable geographic variation in (*a*) the division of labour within the family by sex, (*b*) patterns of labour as required by differing food crops and cultivation practices, and (*c*) local customs concerning palm fruit harvesting and processing – all of which, by denying the farmer certain choices, might qualify our analysis for these particular areas. In aggregate, however, such variations are unlikely to modify significantly the workings of the underlying economic relationships. (Nevertheless, this is an important area for further empirical research.) As to the values we have assigned our parameters, by assuming that processing costs will fall only by 10*d.* as a result of full capacity operation of the advanced technology (it could be as high as 3*s.*) and by using the extraction efficiency of the screw-press and the zero labour cost of the native method we have biased our result in favour of the primitive technology. This enhances the probability that the solution producer price will be an efficient one.

Let us sum up the benefits of the policy that has been proposed, considering the situation after the fruit supply has been bid away by the advanced technology and the producer price has been returned to its 1965 level of 41*s.* per cwt. The total output of palm oil has been increased by a minimum of 20 %.[1] Farm household labour time has been freed with no reduction in real income: the value of the 31 % additional oil obtained by the Stork and Pioneer processors allows them

[1] That is, the average extraction efficiency has increased from a maximum of 70 % to 85 %. There is also likely to be an output effect, i.e. increased fruit collection, which would lead to a further expansion in palm oil production.

to pay as much to the farmer for his raw fruit as he could previously get for an equivalent amount of oil and nut.[1] Primary production and fruit gathering are likely to be stimulated as the returns per unit of labour time have increased, *a fortiori* with a rise in producer prices. Even with no change in primary production or fruit collection, tax revenues are augmented in proportion to the advance in the average oil extraction efficiency.

Although there is less certainty about the rate of return to capital in alternative uses, the writer would argue that since most Development Corporation investments are earning negative returns, no more profitable or socially productive investment would be sacrificed as a result of public investment in palm oil processing. For some of the private investment, the existence of the profitable opportunity with its comparatively low capital threshold would induce savings and capital formation that would not otherwise occur; in any case, the private investment will not take place if more remunerative alternatives exist. Lastly, there are two external economies: freeing the housewife and her children from the stultifying drudgery of processing activities as a necessary condition for desirable changes in child-rearing patterns, and the dynamic educative effects of introducing modern technology and organizational skills into the heart of the traditional economy.

II

We now turn to a brief examination of the factors which determine the extent of potential industrial processing for Nigeria's other primary product exports. These include groundnuts, tin, palm kernels, cocoa, logs, rubber and hides and skins. Partial price and cost data have been assembled for all but the last three products. The processing of these products differs in two fundamental respects from palm oil. First, because these products are not perishable and their processing does not involve a weight loss of 50 % or more, there is a question as to whether it is more efficient to undertake processing in the producing country (Nigeria) or in the consuming countries. Second, owing to technological reasons or quality requirements, the primitive-advanced choice of technique does not arise as it does in the case of palm oil. By examining comparative processing costs and transport factors for each product, it is possible to arrive at a rough estimate of the industrial potentialities offered by export processing.

The analysis for determining which geographic location will enjoy a net competitive advantage (and how much of one) involves a con-

[1] Taking 38*s*. as the processor's revenue per cwt. of oil, 31 % is 11·8*s*.; combined with the 5*s*. quality premium, the differential revenue available to cover the entire cost of processing by the advanced technology is 16·8*s*.

sideration of the same cost components as before, i.e. $C = f(K, L, t, 1/r)$. However, given a different pattern of variation among the independent variables – particularly the diminished significance of differential extraction rates and the magnified importance of transport considerations – it behoves us to alter the earlier formulation (balancing incremental revenue against the incremental cost of the advanced technology) to one which simply compares delivered cost from each location to the final consumer.

Definitions:

C = cost of processing per unit of output

t = transport cost per unit of output

u = cost advantage per unit of output which accrues to processors close to the final market

P = net fiscal protection enjoyed by the processors in the importing country

xc = exporting (producing) country

mc = importing (consuming) country

rm = raw material

pg = processed good

Then processing is viable in the raw material producing country when

$$C_{xc} - (t_{rm} - t_{pg}) \leqslant C_{mc} - u - P.^{1}$$

Considering the comparative costs of processing first, the underdeveloped exporting country possesses an important advantage in unskilled labour costs, while the importing country typically enjoys certain economies of scale, cheaper skilled labour and management, and lower capital cost. In some cases processing plants in developed countries achieve a slightly higher extraction rate.

The situation with regard to transport costs tends to tip the scale in the other direction. The processed constituents can usually be transported more cheaply than their raw material equivalent, although special facilities required for the former often mean that the savings is considerably less than the reduction in volume. A second element of transport savings accrues to the raw material producing country when the importing country re-exports a portion of the processed constituents to a third country. Lastly, to the extent that there is a subsidiary domestic market for the processed goods, processors in the producing country enjoy a windfall equal to the cost of transport from the nearest foreign producer.

[1] Or, recasting the formulation in terms of the earlier approach of balancing competitive advantages against competitive disadvantages, processing is viable in the exporting country when $(t_{rm} - t_{pg}) \geqslant (C_{xc} - C_{mc}) + u + P$.

Marketing advantages and net fiscal protection, u and P, both operate in favour of the importing country (save where subsidies in the exporting country exceed protective duties). The marketing advantage lies in the ability of processors at the centre to shift from one raw material to another according to differential commodity price movements (e.g. oilseed crushers, sawmilling); in other cases it is the ability to produce to specific quality standards of individual customers (e.g. cocoa butter, tanning).

GROUNDNUT CRUSHING

The groundnut crushing industry in Nigeria dates from 1941 when a Lebanese produce buyer, Mr. George Calil, established an experimental mill at Kano. By 1953 he had been joined by three other Levantine produce buyers who established their own crushing mills. In late 1964 a fifth mill was opened in Maiduguri. All the firms are of approximately the same size and employ the mechanical expeller method. In 1951, spurred by the example of India and Senegal which had gone into processing on a large scale, the Nigerian Government and the Groundnut Marketing Board commissioned J. C. Gardner, a former official in the British Ministry of Food, 'to make a survey of the economics of local mechanized expression of oilseeds in Nigeria with particular reference to the question whether there is a *prima facie* case for the government of Nigeria and/or the Marketing Board to establish a plant for the large-scale expression of oilseeds in Nigeria'.[1]

In his report Gardner observed that the local market was likely to remain small because the greater part of consumer demand was for groundnut meal (pulverized nuts with only a small part of the oil extracted), and because household oil producers did not have to bear distribution costs (nut collection, bottling, distribution) or employ wage labour. Therefore a large processing plant would have to compete on the world market. The transportation savings to be enjoyed by processing near the source of production were negligible because the extracted constituents composed some 99 % of the weight of the raw nut. The lower capital costs of the European plants, deriving from their large size, were likely to outweigh lower Nigerian labour costs. European mills were often part of a vertically integrated organization. Furthermore as other producer countries began to process their own nuts, Gardner argued, Nigeria would export a growing portion of the world's raw groundnut supply and countries with their own processing plants would become more and more dependent on Nigeria; on the

[1] J. C. Gardner, *Oilseed Processing in Nigeria*, A Report to the Government of Nigeria and the Nigeria Groundnut Marketing Board, London 1952, p. 1.

other hand if Nigeria were to export oil and cake, she would have to compete against a large number of other countries, particularly those in Europe. The largest advantage that accrued to the European mills stemmed from the more varied marketing opportunities available to them. They could, for instance, switch their manufacture from one type of oilseed to another (a not unduly expensive operation for the large European mills) as the conditions of the market dictated.

Despite his advice against the establishment of a public crushing plant, however, Gardner recommended that the private plants be allowed to operate free 'of all forms of control' as an experiment in further determining the feasibility of a Nigerian crushing industry: no quota should be set on the amount of nuts that the mills could buy; the industry should be given Pioneer status; the Nigerian Railway Corporation should extend favourable rates on oil and cake transport; the government should subsidize the local sale of oil and cake; and the Marketing Board should refund the high overhead that it charged against the millers.

Table 52. *Volume of groundnut crushing, 1951–1965*

(1,000 tons)

Year ending October 31	Marketing Board purchases	To crushers	Oil exports	Oil exports/ amt. to. crushers (%)
1951	143	9	3·5	38·9
1952	431	25	4·0	16·0
1953	560	45	9·9	22·0
1954	621	77	18·7	24·3
1955	510	88	30·6	34·8
1956	537	69	33·6	48·7
1957	357	77	35·1	45·6
1958	715	98	38·7	39·5
1959	533	125	39·6	31·7
1960	446	111	47·7	43·0
1961	619	125	46·6	37·3
1962	686	163	45·2	27·7
1963	872	197[a]	62·9	31·9
1964	787	232	69·4	29·9
1965	677	260	79·9	30·7

[a] Of which about 25,000 tons are believed to have been subsequently exported.

SOURCE: Commonwealth Economic Committee, *Vegetable Oils and Oilseeds*, various years.

Although the government only carried out a part of their commended measures, the industry has grown rapidly as shown in table 52.[1]

[1] For a full discussion of government policy, 1951–9, towards the crushing industry, particularly the Marketing Board's reluctance to permit the crushers to expand, see chapter 5 in F. A. Wells and W. A. Warmington, *Studies in Industrialization: Nigeria and the Cameroons*, London, 1962.

A major change in government attitude toward the Kano industry came in 1961 when

The oil extraction rate is approximately 45 %; thus the final column gives a rough (owing to inventory lags) indication as to what proportion of production is sold locally. Taking into consideration the absolute volume, it can be seen that domestic consumption has grown rapidly since 1962 – a major factor in determining the industry's competitiveness.

The competitive strength of Nigerian *vis-à-vis* European and British processors can be determined by considering transportation and actual processing costs. Looking at transportation cost first, in early 1964 railway and ocean freight rates per ton were as follows:[1]

	Groundnuts			Cake			Oil		
	£	*s.*	*d.*	£	*s.*	*d.*	£	*s.*	*d.*
Kano-Lagos	8	6	0	6	15	0	10	0	0
Lagos-Liverpool: freight	5	2	0	3	16	0	4	10	0
insurance	0	1	9	0	4	0	0	7	4

Applying the extraction rates of 45 % oil and 54 % cake, there is a transport savings of 3*s.* on the land haul and 17*s.* on the sea haul. The 3*s.* railway is neutralized owing to the fact that the oil drums constitute 12 % of total weight; tanker cars, which are being introduced gradually, do result in a savings.

As to the actual processing costs themselves, the evidence is fragmentary. Although the mechanical expeller process used in Nigeria is a more labour-intensive process than the solvent method employed in Britain and Europe, and although the Kano millers have replaced capital with manual labour for many materials handling operations, Nigerian labour costs are still only about 15*s.* per ton as compared to 22*s.* in Britain.[2] Capital costs might be a little higher (although Nigeria probably has a higher degree of capacity utilization), while electricity and power costs are definitely greater in Kano. As for supervisory labour and management, the extensive employment of Lebanese and Cypriots in these positions probably results in lower administrative overheads than in Britain.

quotas on the tonnage of nuts the millers were allowed to purchase were effectively abolished and the processors were urged to expand their capacity. Competitive pressures in the interregional race to industrialize were responsible for the change. Earlier reluctance to promote the industry stemmed from the advice of British colonial servants who were (*a*) prone to favour processors in the home country in this rather marginal case, and (*b*) distrustful of Lebanese participation in Nigerian economic life. For a discussion of British colonial discrimination against the Lebanese, see R. B. Winder, 'The Lebanese in West Africa', *Comparative Studies in Society and History*, April 1962.

[1] Supplied by the commercial manager, Northern Nigeria Marketing Board.

[2] Interviews with two of the Kano millers (September 1964) and A. E. Peel, Commercial Director, British Oil and Cake Mills Ltd. (London, July 1965).

Even if Nigerian costs are greater, it is still probable that profit margins in Kano exceed those in England. This is because there is a greater margin between a ton of groundnuts and its processed constituents in Nigeria than in England. This greater value added by processing is attributable to the transport savings and the different extraction rates in the two countries. The latter factor, which can narrow as well as widen the difference in the two margins according to relative movements in cake and oil prices, results from the fact that the solvent process obtains 47 % oil and 52 % cake – which is also less valuable cake because of its lower oil-content.

Table 53 shows the value-added margins in Britain and Nigeria. In both cases valuations are calculated at port. For the United Kingdom we use the price of Indian cake and Nigerian oil, and for Nigeria simply subtract freight and insurance from the c.i.f. values of United Kingdom imports from Nigeria.[1]

Table 53. *Value added in groundnut processing, Britain and Nigeria*

	1961 (£)	1962 (£)	1963 (£)	1964 (£)
At Liverpool c.i.f. prices				
0·52 ton cake (solvent process, Indian)	15·9	17·15	18·1	19·7
0·47 ton oil (Nigerian)	56·8	47·0	45·17	53·5
Value of cake and oil per ton of groundnuts processed	71·17	64·15	63·18	72·12
Less cost of 1 ton of groundnuts	70·1	62·0	62·1	67·1
Value added in Processing	1·07	2·15	1·08	5·02
At Nigerian f.o.b. prices[a]				
0·54 ton cake (Nigerian)	16·1	17·17	18·13	19·6
0·45 ton oil (Nigerian)	51·16	42·16	41·14	48·15
Value of cake and oil per ton of groundnuts processed	67·17	60·13	60·7	68·1
Less cost of 1 ton of groundnuts	65·6	56·16	57·6	62·6
Value added in Processing	1·57	3·97	3·1	5·5

[a] f.o.b. prices were calculated using Liverpool c.i.f. prices with insurance and freight subtracted (£5 4*s.* per ton for nuts, £4 per ton for cake and £4 17*s.* per ton for oil).

SOURCES: Commonwealth Economic Committee, *Vegetable Oils and Oilseeds*, 1965, pp. 44, 230; Northern Nigeria Marketing Board Memorandum No. 6364/LPG/1: *Scheme for Sale of 1963/64 Crop Groundnuts for Local Processing.*

[1] For strict comparability it is preferable to work back to the f.o.b. price from the United Kingdom. However, even if one wished to calculate the value added with reported Nigerian f.o.b. prices, one discovers that in quite a few years the value of the processed constituents was less than the value of raw groundnuts, yielding an apparent negative value added. Thus, in 1961 and 1963 apparent value added was – £1 11*s.* and —£1 17*s.* respectively. As these were both profitable years and factor payments ran into hundreds of thousands of pounds (e.g. in 1964 payments for wages, coal and electricity came to £500,000), one is forced to the conclusion, corroborated by the United Kingdom c.i.f. figures, that the export statistics are unreliable.

Table 53 relates only to the comparative advantage of processing for the British market. Nigeria (along with other producing countries) enjoys additional transport savings *vis-à-vis* processors in the consuming countries whenever the latters' demand for cake and oil do not correspond to the extraction rate proportion of 52/47. For example, in 1963, the most recent year available, the United Kingdom, France, Belgium and the Netherlands exported 42,900 tons of groundnut oil (equivalent to two-thirds of Nigeria's oil exports).[1] Lastly, as already noted, the margin of value added, and hence profitability, of the growing sales to the domestic market is very much greater than for export sales. All in all, despite the advantage of processors in the consuming countries of being able to switch from one oilseed to another, there seems little doubt that Nigerian processors enjoy a stronger competitive position and can expand their capacity to cover the whole of Nigeria's groundnut exports.

Groundnut crushing's linkages to the Nigerian economy consist in its purchase of labour-time, coal and electricity. Total employment, predominantly unskilled labour, is about 1,800. In its use of electricity the industry contributes to potential economies of scale. Domestic sales of cake go to two pig farms, while oil sales are made to a small Kano soap factory, several producers of food preparations and retail distributors.

TIN

Tin ore (cassiterite) has been mined in Northern Nigeria on the Jos plateau since 1909. After reaching a peak of 13·9 thousand tons in 1937, production of ore – by one large and a number of smaller British companies – has remained fairly stable since 1950 at about 11,000 tons. Contributing but 4 % to world output, Nigeria is a high-cost producer owing to low-yield soil, seasonably variable water supply for hydraulizing and high transport costs.

The establishment of a smelting industry in 1961–2 parallels in some respects the start-up of Nigeria's cement industry (and the manufacture of jute sacks discussed in the next chapter). For many years the Ministry of Mines and Power had urged the traditional processor of Nigerian ore, William Harvey and Company of Liverpool, to establish a local smelting plant. Apparently interested in the project, the Liverpool firm continually delayed taking any action. When a Portuguese entrepreneur, connected with smelters in Brazil and Portugal, proposed in 1960 to establish a smelter at Jos based on a new capital-saving electrometallurgical process, the government immediately accepted his offer.

[1] Commonwealth Economic Committee, *Vegetable Oils and Oilseeds 1965*, p. 35.

The Nigerian Embel Tin Smelting Company was to have eight electric furnaces with an aggregate processing capacity of 17,000 tons per annum at a planned investment of £250,000. Despite the fact that the Embel plant had more than enough capacity to smelt Nigeria's entire ore output, Consolidated Tin Smelters Ltd. of London, the parent company of Williams Harvey, announced its intention a few months later to establish a second smelter, Makeri Smelting Company, with a two-furnace capacity of 30,000 tons and costing £500,000.

Embel began smelting in 1961. Theoretically the Portuguese venture possessed a number of advantages over its pursuing rival. Unlike the conventional reverberatory oil-burning furnaces employed by Makeri, Embel's electrometallurgical process utilized only domestic inputs – wood, coal from Enugu, and local limestone. Because of their capacity to reach very high temperatures, the electric furnaces were capable of resmelting the slag, thereby achieving a higher extraction rate. However, owing to the unavailability of sufficient electricity supply, only one (later two) furnaces could be used, and operation of these was hampered because of high silica content in the local limestone. In 1961 only 600 tons of tin metal were produced, the balance of the cassiterite being shipped to Embel's plant in Portugal.

In January 1962 Makeri commenced operations; its output of tin metal for the year was 7,300 tons as compared to ailing Embel's 200 tons. In January 1963 The Nigerian Embel Tin Smelting Company declared itself bankrupt.[1]

The position of Consolidated Tin Smelters was analogous to that of Associated Portland Cement Manufacturers. Given significant diseconomies of small smelters (e.g. those employed by Makeri) and more than sufficient capacity already existing in Britain, Consolidated Tin Smelters was reluctant to make an 'unnecessary' investment and shoulder the risks and inconvenience that a Nigerian smelter involved. Once threatened, to go ahead with such an investment, as it had already done in the case of Malaya, became a requisite of survival. Unlike the British oilseed crushing industry, which has been able to maintain

[1] There is some indirect evidence to suggest that the promoters of Embel did not intend to process all of Nigeria's ore in their Jos plant. The generation of electricity in the Jos area has for many years lagged behind demand; most firms are compelled to install their own auxiliary generating equipment. Embel's smelting process required 250 kW for each of its eight furnaces (compared with 100 kW total requirement for Makeri); yet no auxiliary generators were installed. The plant was inefficient and of old design; even operating at full capacity unit costs would have been far higher than the conventional process which relies on imported inputs. However if Embel had been the only smelter, which its promoters had no doubt anticipated, it would have automatic purchasing rights over all Nigerian cassiterite as was the case in 1961. The unsmelted cassiterite could then be shunted to the home plant in Portugal which, although it enjoys a protected market, has difficulty in securing an adequate supply of ore.

operations near full capacity by substituting U.S. soyabeans for the shrinking supply of raw produce from the former colonial territories, metropolitan tin smelters must take themselves to the producing countries or perish.

Although no actual cost data pertaining to the economies of location were collected, the elements involved are as follows: On the transport side, the weight of tin metal is 72–4 % of its cassiterite source; the full 26–8 % freight saving is not, however, realized because of higher rail and ocean rates on the more valuable tin metal. Against this transport advantage must be set the higher costs of smelting in Nigeria. The latter derive from a sub-optimal scale of operations and a large percentage of high-cost imported inputs. Three aspects are relevant to scale of operations: the size of an oil-burning furnace corresponding to Nigerian ore output (i.e. 15,000 tons per annum) is less than one-half the size of an optimum unit; the necessity to maintain spare smelting capacity and furnace indivisibility means a very high investment relative to actual through-put for a small volume of ore; and the number of metallurgists and other skilled technicians required to operate one furnace is the same as the number required for eight furnaces.[1] The imported inputs for smelting in Jos are Welsh anthracite for use as a reducing agent,[2] fuel oil (produced in Nigeria since November 1965), about fifteen technical and administrative personnel, and, of course, all plant and equipment.

Whether or not the transport savings compensates for the higher smelting cost is not known. However, unlike groundnut crushing, the matter is not decisive for the survival of the smelting industry. It is simply a matter of a windfall loss or gain to the British mining companies. The smelter buys his ore on the basis of its assayed tin content and the spot Liverpool tin price worked back to Jos (i.e. deducting transport, insurance and handling costs on tin ingot), *plus* a deduction for the smelting charge (about £13 10*s*. per ton). Given the excessive year to year fluctuations in tin prices, it is unlikely that the windfall change in earnings will have any effect on production in either direction.

The impact of tin smelting upon the Nigerian economy would seem relatively minor. In regards to the balance of payments, there can be no doubt that far more additional foreign exchange is required for anthracite, capital goods, expatriate salary remittances and repatriated dividends than is saved or earned by lower transport payments and the

[1] Clearly in respect to the diseconomies of small scale, the theoretical advantage of the electrometallurgical over the conventional oil-burning technique is very great.

[2] Nigerian coal from Enugu, 370 miles to the south of Jos, is unsuitable because of its high ash component and general volatility of contents.

value added in processing. Domestic value-added consists of wages to unskilled labour and clerical personnel (about 250 in all), plus that portion of profits going to the government as company income tax. Linkages to other producing sectors (mainly fuel and transport) are fairly minimal both quantitatively and qualitatively.[1]

COCOA AND PALM KERNELS

During 1964 and 1965 five major projects, involving over £7m., were launched for the processing of palm kernels and cocoa. All of these, save one, were government-owned projects. Three plants were being located at Ikeja near Lagos: a £1·9m. 30,000 ton capacity cocoa processing plant, sold by Cutinho Caro to the Western Nigerian Government; a £1·4m. 80,000 ton capacity palm kernel crushing plant, sold by an Italian machinery merchanting firm, Watrade, to the Western Nigerian Government; and a small cocoa processing and chocolate manufacturing plant as a private investment by Cadbury Brothers Ltd. of Britain.

Cadbury, a principal supplier of chocolate and confection to the Nigerian market, had already established a packaging operation, and was now acting to forestall the possible entry of an American firm. The viability of a cocoa processing plant hinges upon developing a local market for cocoa powder; the American firm had proposed to the Western Nigerian Government that a captive market could be created through a government-sponsored school lunch programme, with a tasteful protein-rich cocoa powder-groundnut meal concoction being the main food item.

The fourth project was a £2·1m. combination palm kernel-cocoa processing plant purchased by the Mid-Western Nigerian Government from the previously mentioned Italian firm. The fifth project was a 100,000 ton palm kernel crushing plant at Port Harcourt purchased from Coutinho Caro by the Eastern Nigeria Marketing Board. Because Nigeria accounts for well over half of world palm kernel exports, large scale domestic processing carries important repercussions for overseas firms which have built up a considerable stake in the processing and, especially, marketing of palm kernel oil and cake. At least two of such firms, Cargill of the U.S. and Bunge of Belgium, offered to make major investments in these projects. Despite their poor financial position, these offers were rejected by officials of the regional governments who

[1] It would appear that much the same is true for tin mining as well, probably Nigeria's closest example to an enclave industry. See Edwin G. Charle, Jr., 'An Appraisal of British Imperial Policy with Respect to the Extraction of Mineral Resources in Nigeria', *Nigerian Journal of Economics and Social Studies*, March 1964.

felt such strategic economic activities should be completely free of foreign control. Managing agency contracts, however, were given to Cargill for the Port Harcourt venture, and to Bunge for the Okeja plant.

By virtue of obtaining their raw material from the Marketing Board at 10 % below f.o.b. prices, cocoa processors receive a subsidy which is greater than the value added at world prices, i.e. effective protection of over 100 %. Palm kernel crushers are also exempted from the 10 % export duty on their raw material but, unlike the cocoa processors, they must pay a 10 % duty on all their international shipments of oil and cake. The economics of palm kernel crushing appear very similar to the groundnut case.

The end-uses of the processed palm kernel are virtually the same as for the other oilseeds (e.g. groundnuts, cottonseed, soyabean); the more valuable oil constituent is an ingredient in margarine, compound cooking fats, confections, high grade soap, and synthetic detergents, while the cake is used as an animal feed. The weight loss in processing is about 7 %. The constituents of cocoa are cocoa butter and cake; if all the butter is extracted from the cocoa mass the residue cake is marketed as a low-value animal feed, but when the cake contains 10 % or more butter it can be converted into cocoa powder (used as flavouring, for beverages and as a joint ingredient with cocoa butter in the manufacture of chocolate). The proportion of butter extracted and cake utilization is varied with the changing price relationship between butter, animal feed and various grades of powder. The weight loss in processing (i.e. the shell) is 20 %.

No actual data on the economics of processing palm kernel exports are available. In the case of cocoa, however, a comprehensive study was made for the Federal Ministry of Commerce and Industry by Arthur D. Little Inc. in 1962.[1] The report concluded that processing in the producing countries for the export market (but not necessarily for the home market) was decidedly uneconomic. First, the experience of the two major exporters, Brazil and Ghana, has shown that the cocoa butter produced in the tropics seldom matches the quality obtained in Europe or America, and consequently has sold at a 5 % discount. This fact alone means that value-added in processing at world prices is negative. Second, because cocoa processing is capital-intensive, electricity-using and skill-requiring, processing costs per ton are very much higher in underdeveloped countries. Third, because of extensive vertical integration in the developed countries, processors there have

[1] Arthur D. Little, Inc., *The Economics of a Cocoa Processing Plant for Nigeria*, Cambridge, Mass. 1962.

assured outlets at favourable prices for their cocoa powder.[1] Finally, the A. D. Little report noted that processors in Europe and America enjoy considerable tariff protection, a subject to which we now turn.

PROTECTIVE TAXATION AND SUBSIDIES

Up to this point our analysis of export processing activities in Nigeria has been concerned with the basic economics of location – comparative factor costs, transportation considerations and the influence of existing market organization. Only tangential reference has been made to government interference in the form of fiscal protection, the 'P' of our initial algebraic formulation (export processing is viable in the producing country when $C_{xc} - (t_{rm} - t_{pg}) \leqslant C_{mc} - u - P$).

Table 54 presents tariff data pertaining to the processing industries for which such information is accessible. In every case the processing industry in all the importing countries receives substantial protection, usually in excess of 100 % of the gross value added in processing. Only with respect to the United Kingdom does Nigeria, as a member of the Commonwealth, enjoy an equal footing with the home industry.

Just as with tariffs on labour-intensive manufactured consumer goods, protective import duties on processed raw materials in the developed, aid-giving countries deny primary producers the opportunity to follow their comparative advantage (assuming they possess it in this case), and thus inhibit their growth. There are a number of courses of action open to the individual primary producer. It can attempt to persuade the important consumer countries to remove or lower differential duties, or as in the case of Nigeria and the EEC, to grant admittance into an existing customs union. The latter may not be too difficult where the home industry is primarily concerned about processors in other developed countries. In cases where there is no close substitute and where the primary producers can monopolize supply

[1] The report put particular emphasis on the importance of quality over price with reference to cocoa butter and on the marketing advantages in selling cocoa powder.

> 'Our investigations suggest that the grinding of cocoa beans to make the intermediate products, butter and cake, does not have a clearly identifiable value such as exists when the cocoa-chocolate process is considered as an integrated whole. It is probably true to say that the profitable end of the business is making the final chocolate products, not grinding the beans. That most of the leading chocolate manufacturers do grind beans is probably due more to their desire for control over quality through the use of their own secret recipes and processing techniques than to any value they gain over buying cocoa butter. One leading chocolate manufacturer in fact stated that they could buy butter cheaper than they could grind it, and only ground their own beans to ensure maintenance of the unique qualities of flavour on which their reputation was based. It also appears that those firms which produce butter and powder in Europe are able to do so profitably only because they have traditional outlets for the powder which are not open to new plants in growing countries' (p. 14).

Table 54. *Tariff protection for processing industries in the developed countries*

	United Kingdom[a]	France	West Germany	Netherlands	Italy	EEC[b]	Canada	US
Groundnuts	Free	Free	Free	Free	2·5 %	Free	Free[c]	22 %[d]
Groundnut oil	Free	7·5 %	4 %	4 %	5 %	10 %	10 %	30 %
Palm kernels	Free	3 %	Free	Free	Free	Free	Free	Free
Palm kernel oil	Free	13·5 %	6·5 %	6·5 %	10 %	10 %	10 %	0·5 %
Cocoa beans	Free	...	9 %	2 %	...	5·4 %	1¢/lb.	Free
Cocoa butter	Free	(——	13 % to	20 %	——)	22 %	2¼¢/lb.	6·25 %
Cocoa powder	Free	—	...	...	...	27 %	22·5 %	40 %
Timber	Free	...	...	...	...	Free	Free	Free
Plywood	Free	...	...	...	...	15 %	10¢/lb.	15–40 %

[a] For Commonwealth countries only.

[b] Proposed rates effective 1970.

[c] 12.5 % for uses other than industrial processing.

[d] 41 % for uses other than industrial processing.

SOURCES: Commonwealth Economic Committee, *Vegetables Oils and Oilseeds*, 1965, appendix VI; *West Africa*, 2, 30 May 1964; 20, 26 February 1965. Arthur D. Little, Inc., *The Economics of a Cocoa Processing Plant for Nigeria*, pp. 8–10.

(either by acting collusively or in response to similar pressures to establish industries) the processing industry in the consuming countries is simply starved to death, e.g. tin and possibly cocoa in the future. Although groundnut and palm kernel crushing could be monopolized by producing countries, the availability to crushers in the developed countries of numerous other oilseeds processed for the same end-uses would doom Nigeria to subsidized uneconomic processing in the absence of access to an unprotected market. Given the extreme scarcity of such markets, duty-free access to British consumer industries is an asset of no mean value.

CHAPTER 6

UTILIZING DOMESTIC RESOURCES: APPLIED INDUSTRIAL RESEARCH

Applied research into the industrial processing possibilities of domestic resources represents a potentially powerful technique for creating new manufacturing industry and augmenting national output. Moreover such industries are likely to have strong linkages to the agricultural sector. There are three areas to which research can be directed: the development of improved processes to replace primitive cottage production, the development of new industrial uses for existing agricultural crops or for their unutilized by-products, and the development of industrial uses for technically feasible primary products not yet in commercial production.

It has generally been recognized that returns to such research activities are likely to be high. W. Arthur Lewis wrote in 1955: 'There is no doubt that one of the main deficiencies of underdeveloped countries is their failure to *spend* adequately upon research, and upon the development of new processes and materials appropriate to their circumstances.'[1] In this chapter we shall review the history of Nigeria's principle institution for applied industrial research. We shall see that, just as in other developmental efforts, careful organization, the recruitment of appropriate personnel and judicious selection of projects are likely to be of greater importance for success than the volume of financial resources that are expended.

HISTORICAL BACKGROUND

One of the functions of the Department of Commerce and Industries as originally established in 1946 was to conduct small-scale experimental schemes with a view to their subsequent development by private entrepreneurs. When the Department was reorganized in 1949 the research and development function was divided into three separate activities and made the prime objective of the Industries branch.[2] The three activities were investigations, experiments and pilot operations.

The first research project which was not associated with the development of an already established crop was an investigation of wild fibres

[1] W. A. Lewis, *The Theory of Economic Growth*, London 1955, p. 175. Italics added.

[2] The next most important task of the Industries Branch was the management on a commercial basis of various processing schemes initiated by the Agricultural, Veterinary and Forestry Departments. These included fish farming, mechanized palm oil extraction, several dairy schemes, pig production and rice milling. By the mid-1950s most of these projects had been transferred to regional agencies.

as a basis for a sack (produce bag) industry. This survey commenced in 1948. In the following year three other projects were initiated: a dye chemist was recruited to investigate potential local dyestuffs in connection with the textile programme (see chapter 10); the services of two expatriate shipwrights were obtained to design and construct in-shore fishing vessels and cargo-carrying creekcraft; and a number of small power-driven mills for the expression of ground-nut oil were ordered for use in the north. In 1950 two pottery specialists began an investigation of Nigerian clays in conjunction with a scheme to develop the indigenous pottery industry and possibly brick production. In the same year experiments were conducted on the mechanical drying of conophor nuts, canning of clarified butter and citrus fruit, charcoal production from coconut shells and brick-baking. In 1951 consultations were initiated with two engineering firms in England for the acquisition of a coconut fibre decortication plant; experiments to mechanize the production of gari were also begun in that year. A preliminary survey of the possibilities for paper manufacture was added to the list of the Ministry's research activities in 1952.

As a result of the Nigerian Government's invitation to the World Bank in September 1952 to conduct a comprehensive economic survey, it was decided to abstain from any new research undertaking until the Bank's recommendations were received. The latter were transmitted to the government exactly two years later. In the sphere of industrial research the IBRD Mission observed

> . . . industrial research in Nigeria today is, with a few noteworthy exceptions, not a systematic development effort. Much of it is devoted to a search for solutions of technical difficulties which in some cases could have been forestalled before the projects were launched. Sometimes it may be carried on in conjunction with other, incompatible efforts, such as a pilot factory, a straight forward profit-making venture or a training school. Research personnel work singly or in small groups and have no regular contact with each other. Equipment cannot be shared from day to day. There is no adequate technical reference library.[1]

To remedy these deficiencies the Mission recommended that all research activities be centralized in a semi-autonomous institute of applied technical research. This institution would be manned by a full complement of scientists, technologists and supporting staff. The Bank's prescription was accepted by the government and £260,000 was allocated for construction and equipping of the Institute in the 1956–7 Federal budget.

[1] International Bank for Reconstruction and Development, *The Economic Development of Nigeria*, p. 234.

In 1956 the Federal Institute of Industrial Research (FIIR) was formally inaugurated.[1] The functions of the Institute were:

i. To carry out basic research into the raw materials available in Nigeria for use in industry, and the processes which can be used most effectively to convert them;

ii. to carry out pilot-scale trials of process found in the laboratory to be technically feasible;

iii. to calculate by means of larger-scale tests or otherwise the probable viability of such processes if established on a commercial scale.[2]

Initially housed in temporary quarters, it was not until 1961 that the permanent physical facilities of the FIIR were completed. These included engineering workshops, a pilot plant development building, air-conditioned laboratories, an administration-library block and supplementary buildings. The senior personnel establishment was sixteen in the first year; by 1960 the figure had risen to thirty-two.

The FIIR has not opened up any major fields of research; rather efforts have been directed toward the expansion and further development of activities already under way. As of 31 March 1966 the Institute had published reports on twenty-two major experiments or pilot operations and another twenty-seven technical memoranda summarizing known facts about specific projects. The most important of these are:

Manufacture of Gari from Cassava (6 reports)
Fibre Investigations
Suitability of Nigerian Raw Materials for Paper-making (4 reports)
Utilization of Cashew Apples
Possible Uses of Jatropha Curcas Oil
Cashew Nut Oil Expression
Occurrence and Utilization of Plant Gums
The Preservation of Palm Wine
Fermentation of Coffee Pulp
Production of Methane from Farm Waste
Medical Plants of Nigeria
Rubber Production, Costs and Utilization
Background to the Development of Leather Industries in Nigeria
Tar Sand Deposits
The Mechanical Extraction of Coir Fibre (2 reports)
Estimates for Rubberized Coir Fibre Plant
Utilization of Coir Fibre Trash
Production of Desiccated Coconut

[1] During its first year the Institute was known as the Institute of Applied Technical Research.

[2] *Annual Report of the Department of Commerce and Industries*, *1956–7*, p. 26.

Work for which no formal reports were issued include leaf protein, protein fortification of starchy foods, salt production from sea water, utilization of solar heat and the manufacture of hardboard from vegetable wastes, fish drying, vegetable oil and oilseeds, mangrove bark tannin, and clay and ceramics.

What has been the fruit of these eighteen years (1948–66) of research effort? As a preface to any assessment of the productivity of research, a distinction must be made between an end-result leading to a practical industrial application and an intermediate-result, either positive or negative in character, which contributes to the success of later research. In economic terms the latter represents an investment whose gestation period and return is unknown. The relative importance of such intermediate results, which are extremely difficult if not impossible to evaluate in any satisfactory manner, declines as the duration of research activities lengthens. In the case of end-results the question to be posed is, given the opportunities for research and development, resources available and time, has there been a reasonable number of successful projects?

The answer is as follows: commercial projects have been launched in five areas in which government research has been carried out. Fibre processing as a rural industry, citrus fruit and meat canning, and coir extraction have been established as a direct result of such research and development work; large investments in sack production, ceramics and paper manufacture were made prior to any positive findings from on-going research. To the latter three industries reference will be made subsequently; however in the case of the directly research-promoted projects it will be helpful to give a capsule statement of their performance to date.

Fibre processing into rope, twine and matting is carried on as a cottage industry in Western Nigeria, largely as a result of the supervision and support of the regional Ministry of Trade and Industry; owing to its haphazard organization and the varying quality and limited quantity of output, the industry cannot yet be considered viable. A £580,000 citrus fruit canning factory owned by the Western Nigeria Development Corporation, although modestly successful in its initial pilot stage, has run at a sizeable loss every year (cumulative loss of £488,371 as of 31 March 1965) since its establishment in 1954. For the twelve months prior to the writer's visit to the factory in September 1964, output averaged 5 % of capacity. The sources of trouble in this project include an inadequate supply of citrus fruit, excessively high priced fruit and quality problems in relation to the export market.[1]

[1] It should be pointed out that in 1953 both the Federal Ministry of Commerce and Industry who developed the project and the IBRD Mission recommended against the then proposed expansion. The decision to go ahead was taken on political grounds.

A meat canning plant in Kano, established jointly by the Northern Nigeria Development Corporation and two private firms in 1955, after a long process of market development, aided by a 50 % protective tariff, earned its first profit in 1964. A small coir extraction mill purchased from the FIIR by the Egun Awori Local Council was an immediate success; however, for want of entrepreneurship the industry has failed to spread.

When one considers that over £600,000 and eighteen years have been devoted to industrial research, these results appear rather meagre. They are even less impressive when it is realized that one of the two clear successes, meat canning, is only to a limited extent a result of applied research: it is a case where existing machinery was employed in a proven process to convert known raw materials. It could be argued that this project might just as easily have been pioneered by one of the Development Corporations.

Such a verdict, indeed any negative verdict, is open to objection on the grounds of insufficient time. While there may be a certain degree of validity in this reservation, a review of the major research activities will indicate that the chief explanation for disappointing results lies elsewhere.

FIBRE RESEARCH

The first government-sponsored research began in 1948. As described in the departmental report of that year,

> The main item of the year's research . . . has been that carried out by the Fibre Officer in the *utilization of fibres* belonging to the jute class. A series of fibres has been examined and the production areas surveyed. It has been established that there are valuable textile fibres in Nigeria, other than cotton, which are both capable of a more extensive cultivation and useful for a variety of purposes. This examination brings into view the possibility of a valuable light industry for the making of produce bags; hessians and similar cloths; ropes, twines and cordage; matting; and possibly paper.[1]

In 1949 several fibres, notably a 'rama' fibre (*hibiscus cannabinus*) and 'bolo bolo' (*clappertonia ficifola*) were sent to the United Kingdom for testing; neither was found to be as suitable as Asian-grown jute for produce bags, although the 'rama' – because of its greater resistance to insect attacks – was stated to be the better of the two. In the same year the Fibre Officer began teaching cottage industry techniques of spinning

[1] *Annual Report of the Department of Commerce and Industries, 1948*, p. 5. In fact the Ministry of Agriculture had carried on growing trials between 1939 and 1943 of ten different fibre crops, including most of those the FIIR subsequently worked with. Because many of the trials were poorly controlled and/or poorly documented, very little of this earlier experience was utilized in the efforts following 1948.

and weaving coconut fibre into rope, twine and matting. In 1950 similar instructions, using 'rama', were carried out in the north. Work with coconut fibre in Badagri, one of the two major coconut growing areas, suggested the possibility of establishing a coir extraction plant to produce mattress stuffing for the export market; accordingly, with the aid of two British engineering firms plans for such a factory were begun.

The Department's annual report for 1951–2 contains two surprises. The value of the preceding three years of investigation was thrown into doubt by the statement:

> The industrial value of these fibres, both soft and hard, has yet to be established and the commercial potential has yet to be assessed. The arrival in December 1951 of an officer qualified more especially in the *utilization of these fibres* enables a small beginning to be made in tackling this problem.[1]

The second surprise was the announcement of a £1m. sack factory to be established in Onitsha by the Colonial Development Corporation in conjunction with the produce Marketing Boards, using the already rejected or untried 'rama' fibres (*cannabinus*, *saddariffa*, *asper* and *urena lobota*). Indeed the report states problems of retting this new production and of turning out a fibre of uniform quality suitable for the manufacture of bags have yet to be solved'.[2] The report could also have pointed out that the annual growth of such fibres was insufficient to meet the raw material requirements of the factory and that no marketing arrangements existed for their collection. The project collapsed the following year entailing a loss of some £300,000.[3]

During 1953 and 1954 investigations focused on retting techniques and trial cultivation of some twelve varieties of hard fibres. The earlier decision of the Colonial Products Laboratory concerning the superiority of 'rama' over 'bolo bolo' as a sack yarn was reversed, on the grounds that the latter could be produced more cheaply. Twenty acres of swamp and bush were cleared and planted with cuttings in order that large-scale retting trials could be conducted the following year. In the event the plantings failed as a result of abnormal flooding of the Cross river. In the field of coir extraction, after two years of inactivity, it was announced that small-scale trials were held in the United Kingdom and

[1] *Annual Report of the Department of Commerce and Industries, 1951–2*, p. 35. Italics added.

[2] *Ibid.* p. 36. Retting is a process whereby ligneous particles adhering to the fibre after decortication are removed by bacteriological action promoted by steeping the fibre in warm water for some days and then washing.

[3] John Adler, Chief Economist in the 1953 World Bank Mission, gives two additional reasons for the project's abandonment: 'It was conceived during the Korean boom when jute prices were abnormally high; when prices went down the basis for any competitiveness simply disappeared. Moreover the Financial Secretary told the promoters of the scheme that he would have to collect an excise tax on each bag equivalent to the duty on imported bags!' Letter to the author, 26 June 1964. See also International Bank for Reconstruction and Development, *The Economic Development of Nigeria*, p. 232.

that the necessary machinery for further experiments were being sent to Nigeria. Trials in Nigeria the next year, 1955, revealed that the quality of the fibre so produced was unacceptable in the brush bristle export market.

In 1955 all field trials connected with jute-substitutes at Samaru in the north and Itu in the west were discontinued. Experiments, however, were revived by the northern Regional Government at Mokwa in late 1957. In 1959 the government formed a consortium with the United Africa Company and a Dutch firm, Vereenigde Klattensche Cultuur-Maatschappij (VKCM), for the purpose of undertaking kenaf (*hibiscus sabdariffa var, altissma*) planting trials as a preliminary step to the establishment of a plantation and sack factory; two years later the experimental trials were moved to Jema'a to take advantage of the better soil there. In 1962 a UAC-VKCM evaluative report concluded that 4m. bags could be produced at a cost of 3*s*. 8*d*. per bag (including a 10 % profit) with a combined factory and plantation investment of £2·2m. Since the world price of bags was about 2*s*. 6*d*., some sort of protection would be needed; the report suggested that the most satisfactory arrangement would be for a government purchasing agency to subsidize the plant directly.[1]

In late 1962 the northern government dissolved the consortium and began planning a new scheme based on peasant farm production with the aid of a 700-acre seed distribution plantation and technical assistance. On the basis of newly developed decortication and ribbon weaving machines, Mr. O. E. Nasse, an adviser to the Northern Nigerian Development Corporation, proposed the use of unretted kenaf ribbons (thereby avoiding peasant retting) as the weft in the manufacture of sacks, while using imported fibres for the warp. However in 1964 the northern government began negotiations with Pakistani firms and in 1965 an agreement was reached with Nasreddin and Company to establish a £1·7m. sack factory at Jos. This project, which had not come into operation as of December 1966, was to be based on imported jute from Pakistan for the first few years while surrounding farmers were being taught to grow and ret kenaf. In the meantime, apparently unconnected with any previous research, the western Regional Government contracted with Gardella and Company of Genoa to establish a £1·5m. factory at Badagri.[2] This project, utilizing the newly developed decortication and ribbon weaving machinery mentioned above, began production in 1966 on the basis of locally-grown

[1] Ministry of Trade and Industry, *Industrial Potentialities of Northern Nigeria*, section on fibres.

[2] The originally published capital cost of the project was £875,000 with Gardella contributing £147,000. The usual 'inflation', mostly non-economic, brought the final cost up by over £600,000.

unretted kenaf. Whether or not the sack industry will eventually be successful (i.e. be able to operate without protection), its establishment would appear to be largely unconnected with FIIR research activities.

Returning to the FIIR, although all fibre growing experiments were discontinued in 1955, investigation of various retting techniques proceeded, and in 1959, with the aid of the Professor of Bacteriology at the University in Ibadan, a thermophylic bacterium process considerably superior to the anaerobic method was developed. Apparently, however, this development came to no practical use. Until 1957 considerable research was undertaken on sun hemp and pineapple leaves as possible fibres for the cottage production of rope, twine and matting. Specimens of sun hemp were also dispatched to England for testing as a possible paper-making material. Experiments with these fibres were continued for two and a half years despite the knowledge that neither could be grown economically on any significant scale. Finally, during the second half of the decade new methods were developed, simple machines tried out and instructions given for hackling, spinning, dyeing and weaving fibres for the hand-production of matting, ropes and cordage. These activities, however, had little lasting impact.[1]

Two definite successes which resulted from the fibre research were the development of improved retting procedures and the mechanized production of mattress-filling from coconut fibre.[2] As previously recounted, the latter appeared to have run into a dead end in 1955 when the quality of the coir proved unacceptable for export. The project lay dormant until 1959 when two mattress factories were opened in Lagos; in this case the coir was suitable for the type of mattresses produced and found a ready market at 3*d.* per lb. The pilot plant, processing one ton of coir per day with the possibility of producing charcoal as a by-product, was reassembled in Badagri and run for a three month trial by the FIIR until the Egun Awori local council assumed both the ownership and responsibility for operating the mill. The latter was already operating a copra exporting co-operative society and consequently was in a position to organize the collection of coconut husks. When the venture proved profitable a request was received from the Eastern Nigeria Development Corporation to advise on the purchase and assembly of a much larger unit for its nascent coconut plantation at Bonny. As of the end of 1966, as far as the writer could determine, the Badagri mill had not expanded and the Bonny project was still on the drawing board. The problem here was one of entrepreneurship, not one of technical knowledge.

[1] Interview with the Acting Director, FIIR, October 1964.

[2] The process involves acquiring discarded coconut husks which are successively soaked, burst by a hammer mill and the fibre sifted, separated and dried.

PULP AND PAPER

The course of the pulp and paper-making project has followed a similar path to that of fibre research. The first 'preliminary investigation' was carried out in 1951–2. In the following year data were collected on the pulping, bleaching and paper-making qualities of various cellulose materials; by the end of the year, based on advice received from three British firms, it was reported that the viability of a paper-making industry appeared to be contingent upon the development of a local source of the requisite chemicals. During 1953–4 overseas counsel was sought on the feasibility of using imported pulp or a combination of imported and local materials; various fibres and non-resinous soft woods were also tested, using improvised equipment.

For four years all investigations and enquiries on the subject were suspended. Then in 1958 a true pulp and paper testing laboratory was ordered;[1] testing of fibre cellulose materials started once again. No activity was reported the following year, but in 1960 the test equipment arrived and, with the help of a specialist seconded from the London Tropical Products Institute, was installed. The 1960–1 annual report began its review of work in this field with a sentence ominously reminiscent of another statement made in the third year of fibre research:

> Although there are many materials in Nigeria suitable for paper-making, no systematic practical investigation has been carried out.[2]

By mid-1963 three timbers and one fibre (sorghum) had been fully investigated while another four potential pulp materials had been partially tested. The best material found was *gmelina arborea*, an Asiatic specimen similar to poplar and suitable for writing paper.

In 1963, although the testing of indigenous pulp and paper materials was not completed and work had not begun on developing required pulp wood plantations, the Federal Government contracted to purchase a £2·3m. paper mill from the firm of Coutinho Caro and Company of Hamburg (the latter contributed £100,000 of what worked out to be an investment of £3m.).[3] Despite the fact that all the raw materials have to be imported and that over half of all paper products are purchased in Lagos, the factory was located at Jebba in the northern region – apparently for political reasons. By the end of 1966 the mill,

[1] The pulp equipment consisted of a rotating autoclave, a wet disintegrater, a strainer, a ball mill, a laboratory beater, a 12-inch laboratory refiner and a standard pulp evaluation apparatus including a disintegrater, a sheet maker and a freeness tester. The equipment tests for thickness, moisture, folding endurance, tensile strength, tear resistance, etc.

[2] *Annual Report of the Federal Institute of Industrial Research, 1960–1*, p. 10.

[3] This paragraph is based on information supplied by Arthur D. Little Inc., and Scott Pearson, 'The Political Economics of Nigerian Short-term Borrowing', *Public Policy*, vol. XV, p. 350.

embogged in a financial crisis, had still not come into production. All the classical ingredients of a turnkey project were present: a market too small for the types of paper that the equipment was capable of producing, uneconomic location, over-spending, illegal diversion of funds, and inability to obtain competent technical management.

THE MANUFACTURE OF GARI

Next to fibres, the manufacture of gari has been the subject of the most extensive investigation. Started in 1951, the process was still not completely worked out by 1966. Unlike the history of fibre research where human culpability in the form of oscillating policies, lack of research perseverance and apparent technical incompetence seemed to be the key factor in shaping the outcome, the gari story highlights the purely physical-technical complexities that can arise when developing an apparently simple and straight-forward process.

Gari, a flour prepared from the cassava root, is an important staple of southern Nigeria.[1] In 1957, the most recent year for which figures are available, some 4·7m. tons of cassava valued at £45m. were consumed in the form of gari or akpu.[2] The justification for undertaking research on the mechanization of gari-making was given in the *Annual Report of the Department of Commerce and Industries 1950–1*:

> The production of gari is a laborious process. The cassava root has to be washed, dried, grated, sifted and dried again; and many hours a day are spent in its preparation. It must be dried soon after it is taken from the farm or the resultant gari will be inedible. With a growing urban population, combined with the present tendency on the part of farmers to neglect the cultivation of food crops for the more profitable business of producing and selling for the export market, the supply of gari is becoming precarious and prices have risen steeply.[3]
>
> In order to alleviate this situation, to enable preparation of the food to be carried out under more hygienic conditions and to afford relief from wasteful and time-devouring labour, the Department has undertaken investigations into the mechanization of cassava processing (p. 30).

The first step was to develop a simple, inexpensive power-driven grating machine. This objective was obtained in early 1952. Efforts were made in the following two years to mechanize the other steps in gari preparation by finding suitable standard machinery and thus avoid the cost and delay in developing specialized equipment. In 1954 full mechanization on a laboratory scale was attained; unfortunately,

[1] Although cassava is an important staple in many parts of the tropical world, gari is found only in West Africa.

[2] (E. F. Jackson and) P. N. C. Okigbo, *Nigerian National Accounts, 1950–57*, p. 47.

[3] During the period for which price data are available (1955–65) the price of gari has risen less than the average urban consumer price level.

however, the end-result was not recognized as gari by the consumer. 'This indicated that the Department's knowledge of the chemistry of the process was incomplete.'[1] Accordingly fundamental research was undertaken to discover the biochemical changes which accompany the conversion of cassava pulp to gari. At first it was thought that two yeast agents and a cocus were the critical taste-formers, but by 1957 it was clear that the transformation was more complicated.

Experiments showed that the fermentation process which takes place in the cassava pulp and produces gari in the ultimate frying is more complex than was earlier thought. It now appears that the fermentation takes place in four stages, the first of which is a biochemical and the last three micro-biological operations. The object of these complicated studies was the production of an agent capable of producing an acceptable product in a shorter time than by the traditional means. There is reason to hope that the achievement of this aim will not be long delayed.[2]

Somewhat surprisingly, even though the physical chemistry of the process was not yet known, detailed plans for a pilot plant were begun in 1954. But owing to lack of funds, implementation of these plans was abandoned the following year. Apparently in lieu of the mechanized unit, it was decided to develop a completely hand-operated process which would be superior to existing village methods.

The prototype consists essentially of a hand-operated grater or rasper, with a moving perforated grating surface which will treat approximately four cwt. per hour; a simple hygienic press for squeezing out the fruit water; and a multi-pan frying range which reduces the frying time by about half. The unit, which produces a far cleaner product, is so designed that it can be copied by any village craftsman.[3]

In 1957 Patrick Collard, the same Professor of Bacteriology who contributed to the solution of the fibre retting problem, determined the full sequence of chemical changes in the fermentation of cassava pulp which culminates in esterification of the fatty acids, producing the characteristic taste of gari.[4] Armed with this knowledge the FIIR was able to develop a 'seeding' technique which is suitable for use in large-scale mechanized production. The 1954 pilot plant proposals were revised and equipment ordered. The first trials were held in 1960.

The engineering problems of developing an efficient production process have proved no less difficult and protracted than the earlier

[1] *Annual Report of the Department of Commerce and Industries, 1953–4*, p. 28.

[2] *Ibid., Annual Report of the Department of Commerce and Industries, 1956-7*, p. 29.

[3] *Ibid.* According to officials of the Eastern Nigeria Development Corporation, whose loans for the purchase of gari graters have largely been defaulted, the apparatus was poorly designed. See Helleiner, *Peasant Agriculture*, p. 264.

[4] For the Professor's full exposition, see *Annual Report of the Department of Commerce and Industries, 1957–8*, p. 30.

fundamental research. The process used in the pilot plant was as follows: The cassava root was placed in a water-filled concrete mixer adapted with wooden mixing arms; when the arms were set in motion, the rubbing of the roots against one another and against the side wall 'peeled off' the cassava's outer skin. The roots were then finely grated on a small 'Protessor', a machine with fast-rotating cutting blades. The resultant mash was put into aluminium tanks, seeded with four-day-old cassava liquor and left for 24 hours to ferment. Next the mash was centrifuged for 20 minutes to reduce the moisture content to about 50 % and then granulated to separate the particles and to remove as much of the fibre as possible. The particles were 'garified' or partly gelatinized and dried to a 6–8 % moisture content in a rotary kiln. Lastly, the gari was run through an adapted coconut sifter.[1]

A number of changes have since been made in this process. The Protessor has been abandoned because it has been found that a simple hammer mill, at one-tenth the capital cost, can do the same job slightly better and handle five times the through-put. The seeding technique of fermentation was abandoned in 1962; the amount of hydrogen cyanide gas released during fermentation was excessive, fermentation was not homogeneous and seeding gave the gari a flat rather than the preferred customary tart taste. Fermentation is now done in the traditional way, by allowing the mash to ferment for three days without the aid of a catalyst. The mechanized peeling process has also been abandoned; it removed the outer skin, but not the cortex which during the drying stage released phenolic compounds that combined with the cyanide to form a discolouring agent. All in all, not a great deal of the labour-saving mechanization remains in the modernized process. Peeling is now done by hand at the rate of 1 ton of gari (i.e. about 4 tons of cassava roots) per eighteen man-days; it has been estimated that women could do this operation in half the time, although the loss in weight to the end product would be some 15–20 %.[2]

As of 1964 there was one unsolved difficulty remaining: the rotary kiln used in the garifying and drying stage was not completely satisfactory; not only was it expensive in heat and electricity,[3] but it provided insufficient heat and removed too much moisture.[4]

[1] I. A. Akinrele, *et al.*, *The Manufacture of Gari from Cassava*, FIIR Research Report, No. 12, Lagos, May 1962, pp. 5–7.

[2] Interview with O. Adeyinka, August 1964. The mechanical method of peeling allows a processed gari: raw cassava root yield of 27–8 %; factory hand-peeling allows 23–4 % and village peeling 20 %.

[3] I. A. Akinrele, *et al.*, *Gari Pilot Plant (1 ton a Day): Results of 3 Month Trial Run*, FIIR Research Report No. 13, Lagos, May 1962, p. 7.

[4] The moisture content after drying was 6–8 % as compared to about 15 % in the village method. To compensate for this, water had to be added to the factory-produced gari to raise the content to 10 %.

Beyond the extensive technical problems involved in developing mechanized gari production, there is the further question of economic viability. The Institute's practice, and earlier that of the Industries Branch of the Department of Commerce and Industries, has been to assess the extent of the market and the probable costs of production. The latter are determined more exactly as a project progresses from experimental to pilot to 'works' scale. However the method of calculation leaves much to be desired.[1] In the case of gari production, the economics of a 10-ton per-day plant were based on the results of the 1-ton plant's three month trial run. For the 10-ton plant, total costs exclusive of cassava purchase and transport were to be £12 5*s.* per ton of gari.[2] Cassava costs were to be an additional £10 to £13 6*s.* 8*d.* At the assumed market price of £30 per ton of gari, profits would thus be £4 8*s.* 4*d.* to £7 15*s.*

These calculations are questionable for a number of reasons. Costs were based on all gari produced, including waste gari. No cost at all was allowed for the jute bags in which the gari was stored, on the unlikely grounds that all bags would be returned to the plant.[3] The gari yield was to be 30 %, although it had been only 23–4 % in the 1-ton plant. The factory was to run at full capacity, although the 1-ton plant had run at only 52 % capacity.[4] Direct labour costs were greatly underestimated. In the 10-ton per-day plant they were to be only £1 4*s.* 6*d.* per ton of gari yet they had been £28 17*s.* 10*d.* in the 1-ton plant; nor could the latter's undercapacity be used as the reason for even part of this phenomenal drop in cost, for idle time had accounted for only 2 % of all indirect labour costs. Finally, if only a result of transport costs, the price of cassava could rise well above the £3 to £4 that the FIIR anticipated when demanded in the large quantity necessary to supply a factory producing 10 tons of gari daily.[5] As an alleviation to possible high costs and also to the uncertainties of fluctuating supply, it has been suggested that the FIIR establish a cassava plantation to provide the factory with one-third or one-half of its cassava input.[6] However both wage labour and cultivation costs would be higher there than on the family farm. Also, the investment in-

[1] All costing data below are taken from Akinrele *et al.*, FIIR Research Report No. 13 and L. Banks *et al.*, *Estimates for a Factory Producing 10 Tons a Day of Gari*, FIIR Technical Memorandum No. 14, Lagos, July 1962.

[2] i.e. £1 4*s.* 6*d.* for direct labour, 19*s.* 5*d.* for indirect labour, £7 4*s.* for supplies (except cassava) and £2 17*s.* for depreciation and insurance (1*d.* error due to rounding off).

[3] Cost for bags for 1 ton of gari is £1 13*s.*

[4] The 1-ton plant was in operation for 60·5 days and produced 31·63 tons of gari, including an unspecified amount of waste gari.

[5] Interview with Adeyinka, August 1964, and FIIR Technical Memorandum No. 14, p. 6.

[6] The plant would require, at a 30 % gari yield, 10,000 tons of cassava annually. Transport costs would be high not only because of the large acreage necessary to supply such a quantity as cassava, but also because of the scattering of the small cassava plots over the countryside.

volved in a plantation would be many times the size of the investment in the factory itself.

In 1965 the FIIR loaned its 1-ton plant to a group of Yoruba entrepreneurs in Ijebu-Ode. Beset with rising cassava prices, difficulties in the drying process and frequent breakdowns, the factory was returned to the FIIR in 1966. The Institute remained hopeful that the more economical ten-ton plant might be given a trial under more favourable circumstances.

Until the technical process is fully worked out and the costs of production more exactly determined, no definite judgment on the potential value of the gari manufacturing scheme is possible. However, on the basis of the general principles that were outlined in the previous chapter, we can make a few observations. The advantages of factory production of gari are a higher gari yield, a smaller labour-time requirement and a superior end-product. However, the last of these advantages (greater cleanliness, uniformity of taste and quality) is but little valued by the consumer and receives only a small, if any, premium. The savings on labour-time is nullified by a much greater differential in labour price, so that labour costs are actually higher for the factory. Only the first advantage is of major importance and it would seem to be considerably outweighed by the disadvantages of factory production. These disadvantages are (*a*) higher labour cost, (*b*) a higher raw material cost owing to the greater distance over which the larger volume must be attracted (the weight loss in processing is 75 %) or higher cassava costs if reliance is placed on a plantation, (*c*) administrative and marketing overheads not borne by the village producer and (*d*) an inability, given the importance of fixed costs, to start and stop production according to changes in market conditions.

A strong case based on the foregoing economic arguments can be made that, in the light of alternative research opportunities a majority of the projects in the field of processing, canning and preserving of foodstuffs should not have been undertaken. Indeed the Department of Commerce and Industries recognized the need for caution at an early date in the case of canning.

In Nigeria, canning is by no means a cheap method of preserving food and it is probable that the process will only be used where large quantities of a valuable foodstuff would otherwise go to waste. Canned foods can make a useful contribution to the local diet, which is generally short of animal protein, but if they are to do so within the price range of the average consumer, the cost of raw material will need to be extremely low.[1]

[1] *Annual Report of the Department of Commerce and Industries, 1951–2*, p. 29. In terms of import substitution, although the total volume of imported canned goods is considerable, it is spread over a wide variety of foodstuffs which are either exotic to Nigeria or of a very much higher quality than the local product.

Unfortunately the wider validity of this injunction was not appreciated when new areas of investigation were selected. As for protein fortification, development activities in this field should have awaited upon the successful completion of field trials by nutrition specialists. Independent of any cost considerations, a fortified staple food with reasonable chances of being assimilated into Nigerian dietary patterns has yet to be identified.

The decision to enter other fields of investigation might well be judged faulty in relation to an assessment of the risks involved and probable economic returns. This is most apparent in the case of various local vegetable seeds and vegetable oils (cashew nuts, cashew apples, melon seed, kolanuts, conophor oil, jatropha oil, plant gums). These were instances of virgin experimentation with industrially unknown materials; to bring any one of these projects to fruition would require the determination of the materials' properties, development of an efficient processing technique and finding an industry where the Nigerian product would be competitive with existing raw material inputs.

CONCLUSION

To conclude our analysis, criticism of applied industrial research in Nigeria can be summarized under three major headings. First, at no time has there ever been a research plan, listing topics to be dealt with and assigning relative priorities to them. Projects have been widely scattered and the magnitude of research and development work to be done has seldom been considered before the work is begun. Second, insufficient attention has been paid to the economic, as opposed to the technical, aspects of the projects being investigated. Such important factors as the logistics of raw material supply, the size of markets as compared to efficient scale of plant, the effect on prices of the implementation of the project and the net advantage of displacing cottage industry are given only cursory, if any, attention. Thirdly, research in any individual field (e.g. fibres) is seldom conducted in a systematic and thorough manner, but rather has tended to be sporadic and incomprehensive, following the path of least resistance.

Beyond all these immediate causes for the meagre research results so far achieved, there are important organizational considerations which have materially contributed to the situation described. The chief of these have been acute staffing problems, insufficient co-ordination and lack of whole-hearted government support.

Since 1948 there has never been a time when more than 60 % of the established research posts were filled: in relation to the funds available the industrial research effort has been operating at half speed. Initially, qualified scientific and engineering personnel were in extremely short supply as a result of the reconstruction of war-torn England and Europe. From 1952 to 1954 there was a staff freeze pending the recommendations of the IBRD Mission. The establishment in 1954 of three regional Ministries of Trade and Industry in addition to the Federal Ministry further aggravated existing staff shortages. Despite the recommendations of the World Bank, FIIR salaries for research personnel remained tied to the government scale until 1957. Even after the shift to individual contracts, Nigerianization policies prevented the FIIR from guaranteeing duration of employment to expatriates beyond 18 months. Moreover salaries were still too low, just as in the case of technical education instructors discussed subsequently, largely because of a Nigerian reluctance to pay expatriate specialists as much as or more than a minister's salary.[1] As for attracting qualified Nigerians, higher paying industry and more prestigious positions at the universities have tended to monopolize the meagre supply.

The last two organizational difficulties – insufficient coordination and lack of whole-hearted government support – are interdependent. Because no permanent channels exist for communication between the FIIR and many of its potentially most important consumers – the regional Development Corporations and Ministries of Trade and Industry – these regional bodies have little knowledge and less interest in the activities of the FIIR and they have generally opposed plans to devote more resources to the FIIR. There has also been a lack of continuous communication between the FIIR and other research bodies – the universities, the geological survey unit and the various agricultural research centres. In sum, the FIIR has suffered from its relative isolation – isolation both from agencies most in need of its immediate services and from important sources of knowledge relevant to its own work.

All three of the underlying organizational impediments to effective industrial research are amenable to correction. A comprehensive and well adapted set of coordinating institutional arrangements, centring around a national research council, was developed by a Ford Foundation

[1] In attracting and retaining the best scientific personnel from abroad, energetic and highly motivated, the developing country suffers from an inherent disadvantage. Administrative inefficiency, over-burdening bureaucratic procedures, lack of funds, shortage of needed junior skilled staff and many other built-in features of the underdeveloped country thwart and impede effective action. In the case of the scientist or engineer who is concerned with physical problems, this pervasive and largely unexpected intrusion of manifold non-technical difficulties which embog him at every step lead to severe frustration. He feels he is operating at a small fraction of his normal productivity. The outcome is easily predicted. The work-oriented technologist resigns after his first tour while those who value the material benefits of a higher salary, free housing, etc. and who are able to adapt themselves to the 'low productivity environment' remain and rise to the senior decision-making positions.

team in 1963.[1] On the personnel side, the scarcity of qualified Nigerian science graduates seems likely to be overcome within the next decade. In the meantime the introduction of three tour (five year) contracts for expatriates as of late 1964, and financial and recruiting assistance from UNESCO, AID and the Ford Foundation should be sufficient to bring scientists from abroad who have the requisite qualities to select and execute appropriate research projects and who have the prudence to seek guidance from the lessons of FIIR's past history.

[1] Mogens Host and Haldor Topse, 'Memorandum Concerning Applied Research in Nigeria', mimeograph, 1963.

Part 4

CHAPTER 7

THE SUPPLY OF LABOUR

An adequate supply of labour, amenable to supervision and responsive to economic incentives, is clearly a prerequisite for any sustained industrial growth. The existence of such a supply of labour in Africa has often been questioned. It has frequently been alleged that the individual African's labour offer curve for wage employment is backward bending at an early stage and that while employed his work performance is sadly wanting. In this chapter we shall examine evidence relating both to the supply and the productivity of Nigerian labour. Our analysis of productivity will be with reference to the general quality of labour and organizational factors; in the following chapter the specific issue of skill formation will be taken up.

I

DEMOGRAPHIC ASPECTS

Nigeria's human resources amounted to some 39·4m. people in 1966. In the census year 1953 the population was distributed as follows: Lagos 0·9 %, western region 19·9 %, eastern region 23·5 %, northern region 55·7 %.[1] With 44 % of the population under 15 years of age, Nigeria is a young and rapidly growing nation: despite a very high infant mortality rate, annual population growth is estimated to be 2 %. The regional age distribution in 1953 was as follows:

Age group	West (%)	East (%)	North (%)	Nigeria (%)
Under 2	12·3	10·2	10·8	10·9
2–6	17·8	18·4	17·0	17·5
7–14	17·5	17·3	14·6	15·8
15–49	45·1	48·4	48·2	47·8
Over 50	7·9	5·0	9·4	8·0
	100·0	100·0	100·0	100·0

SOURCE: *The Census, 1952–3.*

Because birth dates are largely unknown, it was necessary to employ very rough standards of age determination (see *Census* appendix, 'Instructions to Enumerators'). Two observations on the above figures may be made. First, the mortality loss between the 'Under 2' group and

[1] Department of Statistics, *Population Census of the Western Region of Nigeria, 1952* (Government Printer, Lagos 1956); Department of Statistics, *Population Census of the Eastern Region of Nigeria, 1953* (Government Printer, Lagos 1955); and Department of Statistics, *Population Census of the Northern Region of Nigeria 1952* (Government Printer, Lagos 1956). Hereafter referred to as *The Census, 1951–3.*

'7–14' is greater than half. Should these figures be only approximately correct, a very severe population problem is likely to develop as public health programmes begin to have greater effect. Second, on the basis of the first three age groups it would appear that population growth is greatest in the west.

The economically active population in 1953 was given as 14·5m. or 47·8 % of all inhabitants; this represents a median participation rate among developing countries.[1] Of this labour force over three-quarters (78·2 %) were employed primarily in agriculture, with common secondary activities in trading and crafts. Economically active females (41·2 %) were classified only in agriculture (5m.) and in trading and clerical work (1·4m.).[2] A more detailed breakdown was attempted for the male labour force.

Occupation	Per cent of 1953 male labour force (total: 8m.)
Farming and fishing	78·6
Admin., professional and technical[a]	2·8
Trading and clerical	5·8
Production workers and craftsmen	6·1
Other occupations[b]	6·7

[a] Including teachers and all government employees.
[b] 'Drivers, domestic, dock workers, miners, quarry workers, etc.'
SOURCE: *The Census, 1952–3.*

Of the total labour force, only a small proportion are wage-earners. In 1962, the most recent year for which figures are available, the Federal Office of Statistics estimated that 630,000 persons were employed in establishments of ten or more.[3] If a generous allowance of an additional 300,000 is made for wage-paid employment in small-scale establishments in agriculture, industry, services and distribution, the total number of Nigeria's wage-earners in 1962 amounted to 930,000 or about 5 % of an estimated economically active population of 17·6m.[4] This represents only a slight proportionate gain over the 157,500 reported by Major Orde Brown in 1938.[5] Nor is it clear from the figures

[1] Some comparative figures are India 40 %, Brazil 33 %, Egypt 36 %, Japan 46 %, Thailand 52 %, and Turkey 61 %. See International Labour Office, *The World's Working Population*, Geneva 1956, p. 159.

[2] An unknown number of women engaged as teachers, nurses, administrators, etc., were classified as being outside the labour force in 'Other females'.

[3] Federal Ministry of Labour, *Report on Employment and Earnings Enquiry 1962*.

[4] At least several millions are involved full-time or part-time in these activities, but the overwhelming majority represent self-employed, unpaid family labour and apprentices. The 300,000 figure is an educated guess based on the writer's impressions gained from supervising small scale industry enumerations in the country's major urban areas in 1961–2.

[5] *Labour Conditions in West Africa*, Cmd. 6227, H.M.S.O., 1941, p. 79, cited by T. M. Yesufu, *An Introduction to Industrial Relations in Nigeria*, London 1962, p. 13. Of this 157,500 (exclusive of the Cameroons) mining accounted for 48,600 and government for 65,700.

below that there is any significant growth trend in the size of the wage-paid labour force.

As seen in table 55 the public bodies – Federal, Regional and Local Governments and public corporations – account for well over half of all enumerated employment. This fact is of controlling importance in the areas of wage determination and industrial relations, discussed subsequently. Turning to the distribution of employment by sector of activity, on the assumption of a uniform degree of understatement, construction and services contribute more than half of the total. The fastest growing sectors over the period 1957–62 were manufacturing and processing, utilities and services. The introduction of more capital-intensive techniques is responsible for the decline of employment in mining, construction and commerce. In 1956 women, largely in the services sector

Table 55. *Reported employment in establishments of ten or more*

(1,000s)

Type of employer	1956	1957	1958	1959	1960	1961	1962
Government	...	...	198	210	213	184	195
Public Corporations	...	...	76	67	73	51	324
Private	...	...	167	147	179	188	...
Total	416	439	441	433	500	423	519

Industry sector	1957[a]	1962
Agriculture and forestry	42,600	31,300
Mining and quarrying	53,700	47,800
Manufacturing and processing	31,600	53,100
Construction	111,200	100,800
Utilities	8,900	16,500
Commerce	56,500	38,900
Transport and communications	45,000	49,800
Services	126,000	180,500
	475,600	518,800

[a] Includes 36,600 employed in the Southern Cameroons, mainly in Agriculture and forestry and Services.

SOURCE: Federal Office of Statistics, *Reports on Employment and Earnings Enquiry.*

(teaching and nursing), accounted for 2·1 % of total employment; this figure had risen to 6·9 % in 1962.

MIGRATION AND LABOUR COMMITMENT

There are two types of labour migration in Nigeria. The first, seasonal migration is governed by the farming cycle and is well known in other parts of the continent. The second, of greater quantitative significance, consists of more permanent movements from the homeland.

The great bulk of seasonal labour originates in Northern Nigeria, north of the 10th parallel.[1] A very short wet season in this area means that during large portions of the year, the primary economic activity, farming, can only be carried on on a very limited scale. Thus it is to be expected that many will seek work elsewhere during the dry season. Indeed throughout the north seasonal migrants are referred to as masu cin rani, 'men who while away the dry season'.

From October 1952 to April 1953 the Federal Office of Statistics undertook a survey of migration from Sokoto Province; the latter contains some 30 % of the country's population living north of the 10th parallel. The total number of migrants recorded was 259,000 of whom 73 % were natives of the province, representing from a quarter to a third of the male labour force. Of the other 27 %, Africans from French territories accounted for 17 % and other Northern Nigerians, 10 %. The motivation for leaving home in 92 % of the cases was to supplement income, for the purpose of securing food and consumer goods. Forty-two per cent were headed for the cocoa harvest in Western Nigeria and Ghana, 18 % were destined for Eastern Nigeria for purposes of trade, 2 % were going to French territories, and the remainder – 38 % – were bound for the tin mining and cotton and ground-nuts growing areas in the north itself.

Eastern Nigeria also supplies labour migrants of a relatively short-term character (six months to two years) to the plantations in the Cameroons and Fernando Po. The number of easterners who are recruited to work in Fernando Po ranges from 7,000 to 9,000 per annum.[2] Although far less than in the pre-independence days a substantial number of Ibo and Ibibios still seek work on plantations in West (formerly Southern) Cameroon.

However, by far the most significant labour movement is migration of a much more permanent nature. This migration, of southerners to the north and easterners to all regions, takes precedence over the seasonal movements because of its longer duration, greater numbers and higher skill content. Although the regional government policy of 'Northernization' sharply restricted the flow, the more educated, technically advanced southerners were still important in 1965 as clerks and skilled labour in the large firms, public corporations, small-scale industry and the service sector. Table 56 sets forth the over-all situation of population movement as it was in 1952–3.

Three principal population flows can be identified from table 56.

[1] The following discussion is drawn from R. M. Prothero 'Migratory Labour from North-western Nigeria', *Africa*, July 1957; and Federal Office of Statistics, *Report on Labour Migration, Sokoto Province*, Lagos 1955.

[2] See *Annual Reports*, chapter II, of the Federal Ministry of Labour.

Unskilled northerners moved south seeking casual employment in various forms of arduous physical labour.[1] This movement was more than counter-balanced by southerners going to the north in search of

Table 56. *Nigerian population movements, 1952–1953*

	East	West[a]	North	Total
Northerners	20,525	57,190		77,715
Hausa	14,879	45,217		60,096
Nupe	2,859	7,422		10,281
Kanuri	2,300	1,318		3,618
Tiv	487	3,233		3,720
Westerners	16,766		66,302	83,068
Yoruba	12,340		54,364	66,704
Edo	4,426		11,938	16,364
Easterners	36,094	115,463	136,486	288,043
Ibo	25,794[b]	108,876	123,727	258,397
Ibibo	10,300[b]	6,587	12,759	29,646
Net Population movement	−251,025	+89,585	+124,673	

[a] Includes Federal Capital.

[b] Migrants to Southern Cameroons. The figures exclude resident border minorities and wandering pastoral tribes.

SOURCE: *The Census, 1952–3*, table 6.

clerical and artisan employment. And finally, easterners have traditionally migrated to the Cameroons, the west and Lagos in search of wage-earning employment, primarily at the semi-skilled and clerical levels.[2]

As seen in table 56 migration of Ibo and Ibibio is greater than for all other tribes combined. Several examples (*circa* 1960–2) will serve to indicate the importance of easterners in the industrial labour force throughout the Federation: a brewery in Kaduna, 25 %; four baking firms in Ibadan, 28 %; a timber and plywood plant in Sapele, 55 %; a Lagos soap factory, 47 %; a brewery in Lagos 52 %; the Ebute Metta Railways Workshop, 30 %; and the Nigerian Port Authority, 35 %.[3]

The well-spring of Ibo-Ibibio migration is easily identified: population pressure. Apart from the small territory of Burundi, Eastern Nigeria has the highest population density of any area in Africa. Migrants move from the over-populated east to the relatively under-populated north and west and to Lagos. That the ratio of migration to

[1] It has become a tradition that Hausas seek very arduous or unpleasant work which other Nigerians are not willing to undertake. Their daily earnings on a piece-rate basis range from 10*s*. to 15*s*.; on the other hand, Hausas do not usually work continuously.

[2] As an indication of the number of easterners living abroad, over 700,000 repatriates had registered with the Rehabilitation Commission in Enugu by November 1966. *West Africa*, 26 November 1966.

[3] Figures for Railways and timber and plywood taken from Yesufu, *op. cit.* p. 119. Total employment for all establishments is approximately 12,000.

the west and north is not proportionate to the relative population densities as shown below is attributable to higher *per capita* incomes and greater economic opportunities in the west and the federal territory of Lagos.

Population density per square mile[1]

	North	West	East
Average density	60	134	245
Highest province	204	365	537
Lowest province	25	81	107

And finally, there is intra-regional migration, a large part of the labour force in each town having their own home in outlying provinces. Thus of 250 apprentices interviewed in 1961 by Archibald Calloway in Ibadan, 60 % came from provinces within the western region other than Ibadan; 10 % came from other regions and 30 % from Ibadan itself.[2] Of forty-six employees interviewed by the writer in 1960 in four bakeries in Ibadan only eight were from Ibadan province whereas twenty came from western provinces other than Ibadan. Intra-regional migrants accounted for 40 % and 59 % of the labour force in the Sapele timber and plywood plant and in the Ebute Metta Railway workshop respectively.[3]

What is the effect of this 'migrant' pattern on labour commitment and labour performance? Does it lead to high rates of labour turnover and consequent low productivity? Research has shown that although the Nigerian wage-earner persistently remains a 'migrant', refusing to settle permanently in the towns, he nevertheless remains fully committed to wage-earning. This is substantiated by the absenteeism and turnover figures to be reviewed subsequently. If this is so, the question arises, in what sense is the Nigerian worker a migrant? Yesufu writes:

> ... no matter how long the Nigerian worker may have remained in wage employment or even with the same establishment, he retains a continuous link with his village home or town. He spends his holidays, more often than not, in that village – when he will take the occasion to plant cash crops like cocoa, to build houses, and to marry and to perform burial or other ceremonies. His wife goes home for confinement. He sends some of his money to his parents and relatives [in the order of 10 %] and, in return, sometimes gets food from them. In a period of protracted unemployment he goes back there, and if he works to an old age, he retires from the city to his village.[4]

[1] *The Census 1952–3*, table 2.

[2] Archibald Callaway, 'Nigeria's Indigenous Education: the Apprentice System', *University of Ife Journal of African Studies*, July 1964, p. 6.

[3] Yesufu, *An Introduction to Industrial Relations in Nigeria*, p. 119. [4] *Ibid* p. 213.

Of no less importance in this continuous contact are the Village Improvement Unions, which exist in every major town 'abroad'. As Josef Gugler describes them:

Improvement unions perform 'urban' roles: they give assistance in litigation, illness and death; they are a channel of information on urban conditions, in particular employment opportunities; they act as arbitrators between members; under particular circumstances they may even provide educational facilities. However, the main concern of the unions is with the affairs of the home community. In Eastern Nigeria decisions on village affairs are not taken by the village residents but by the people living in the towns. If many a union calls itself Improvement Union, this refers to the improvement not of urban living conditions, but of the home area represented by this union. These unions transmit new ideas and aspirations and at the same time effectively contribute finance and counsel to the realization of such improvements, e.g. the building of roads, schools, maternity homes, in a few instances even secondary schools and hospitals.[1]

The persistence of these close connections of the urban wage-earner with his rural origins is partially based on economic consideration, as implied in the passages cited. In an economy characterized by extensive unemployment and an absence of social security arrangements the wage-earner faces grave risks – the possibility of redundancy or dismissal, serious sickness and old age.[2] The substitute for a public social security system is the solidarity of the village community. Not only may the loyal son expect to receive personal care and maintenance in the case of emergency or old age, but his inalienable rights to the use of communal land represents a subsistence-yielding asset of the last resort.

But more fundamental than the economic basis of the migrant's attachment to the place of his origin, the village and the culture it embodies remain the source for many of the social and moral values which sustain the town dweller. It is communal responsibility and traditional status, based on the village unit, which provide the points of stability in the process of adapting to a modern, urban, wage-earning way of life. That this factor of social continuity operates to keep the wage-earner a migrant rather than a permanent settler in the towns can be seen in the case of the highest income groups who have no need of the economic insurance provided by the rural attachment. Gugler's investigation included such a group, university educated civil servants of the Eastern Nigerian Government in Enugu. He sums it up thus:

[1] Josef Gugler, 'Life in a Dual System', *East African Institute of Social Research Conference Papers*, January 1965, mimeograph, p. 6.

[2] In fact a compulsory National Provident Fund was established in 1961 and by December 1965 513,191 employees in firms employing ten or more had been enrolled with total contributions of £13·7m.

The majority of urban well-to-do maintain their attachment to the villages where they were born. They care about the opinions people in the villages hold of them. It would seem that the man who has won success in town plays a very similar role to that of a man prominent in the traditional context. Like his counterpart he is flattered by the prestige he enjoys in the eyes not only of his relatives but of all villagers. This prestige is based on the fact that he is not only rich by customary standards but displays his wealth in visible ways – in a large car and an impressive house (occupied only during vacations), in generosity and hospitality and in contributions to village improvement. His standing gains most vivid expressions in the number of dependents who gather round him. In short, he has attained rural status through urban achievement. And the only possible explanation is these urban dwellers continue to think of themselves as part of their home community.[1]

URBAN UNEMPLOYMENT AND ECONOMIC GROWTH

The existence of urban unemployment in Nigeria's major towns is a phenomenon of considerable economic, social and political consequence. While it is extremely difficult to get a useful statistical measure, all observers agree that by the early 1960s apparent unemployment had reached significant proportions and was growing. Only one unemployment survey has been taken, in 1963, and it reported average unemployment in twenty-seven towns of 14 %.[2] Of the unemployed, 89 % were males between the ages of 14 and 30; 62 % had no previous working experience.

As described in chapter 1, on the order of half the labour force in the small industry and service sector do not receive a regular wage: a considerable proportion of such persons are former seekers of high-wage employment forced by lack of success and their desire to remain in town to accept some form of marginal employment, i.e. employment which yields a product substantially less than opportunity earnings in agriculture. It is the combination of a fairly modest degree of open unemployment with a high degree of underemployment that makes any meaningful assessment of the unemployment problem so difficult.

Can industrialization be expected to absorb the urban unemployed? The answer is an unambiguous no. In a careful study, Charles Frank has shown that even on the most favourable assumptions about the growth of GDP and government employment, non-agricultural wage employment will grow at a slower rate than the urban labour force – unemployment will increase.[3] This finding, reflecting the capital-intensity of

[1] Gugler, *op. cit.* p. 9.

[2] National Manpower Board, 'Urban Unemployment Survey, 1963', mimeograph, Lagos 1964.

[3] Charles Frank, Jr., 'Employment and Economic Growth in Nigeria', AID Summer Research Project, mimeograph, August 1966.

modern technology, conforms to the general experience of contemporary developing countries that wage employment grows at less than half the rate of GDP.[1]

This means that labour absorption will have to take place in the rural sector, urban unemployment being ameliorated by a reduction of migration into the towns. A full discussion of the causes and cures of unemployment, and its impact on labour remuneration outside the organized labour market, is undertaken in chapter 9. We now turn from aggregate participation in the manpower market to a consideration of the employed worker's labour supply schedule.

II

THE SUPPLY OF EFFORT

As we noted at the beginning of this chapter, the conventional image of the African labourer, in terms of his willingness to work and his proficiency, is very unfavourable. The studies which are responsible for this image have depicted a situation of excessively high rates of absenteeism and turnover, lack of punctuality, and inefficiency and inaptitude in the work place.[2] The following conditioning factors are cited as being responsible for this outcome:

i. In the traditional subsistence milieu, work for individual gain is unknown.

ii. Work is an aspect of communal activity intermittently performed for immediate and limited ends.

iii. Division of labour does not go beyond sex and age.

iv. There is no other discipline than that imposed by the rhythm of the seasons.

Any incentives to work, including the wage itself, are of limited effectiveness because, 'an absence of conscious need, contentment with little, and consequent improvidence typify tribal life everywhere in Africa south of the Sahara'.[3] Nor was Nigeria exempted from this pattern: 'In Nigeria, again, the African people are satisfied with such a low level of subsistence that the necessity of wage earning does not arise. Wage-earning is in a sense a luxury and is often used for the provision of luxuries.'[4] A quotation from the I.L.O.'s *African Labour Survey* completes

[1] W. Baer and M. Herve, 'Employment and Industrialization in Developing Countries', *Quarterly Journal of Economics*, February 1966, pp. 90–1.

[2] P. de Briey, 'The Productivity of African Labour', *International Labour Review*, August-September 1955; Inter-African Labour Institute, *The Human Factor of Productivity in Africa*, Bamako, 1956; International Labour Organisation, *African Labour Survey*, Geneva 1958.

[3] Inter-African Labour Institute, *The Human Factor of Productivity in Africa*, p. 35.

[4] W. Hudson, 'Observations on African Labour', *Journal of the National Institute of Personnel Research*, Johannesburg, March 1955, p. 13.

Table 57. *The supply of labour*

Establishment	Year	Employment	Standard	Overtime	Total	Hourly wage	Incentives	Gross absence	Gross turnover
SOUTH									
(*i*) Nigerian			(*hours*)	(*hours*)	(*hours*)	(*d.*)		(%)	(%)
Bakery	1959	38	54	—	54	5	—	2	10
Textiles (L)	1964	100	45	—	45	9	—	5	...
Printing (L)	1964	45	45	18[a]	63	8	—	1	7
Bakery	1964	30	54	3	57	5	—	2	2[b]
Leather shoes	1964	30	50	—	50	5	—	7[c]	nil
Singlets	1964	40	47	24[a]	61	5	T	6	1[b]
Rubber processing	1959	220	45	32	77	5	—	3	23
Rubber processing	1959	200	45	32	77	4	—	8	94
(*ii*) Levantine									
Soap	1964	120	45	5	50	7	—	3	8[b]
Iron fixtures	1964	25	45	18	63	7	—	10	7
Rubber processing	1959	120	45	24	69	5	T	5	15
Rubber processing	1959	330	45	23	68	6	T	4	...
(*iii*) European									
Cigarettes	1964	2,200	45	2	47	10	—	2	5
Plastic utensils	1964	127	45	4	49	10	—	2	4
Steel rods	1964	200	48	8	56	7	SB	3	4
Paint	1964	40	44	10[a]	54	8	T PR	1	7[b]
Cement	1959	380	48	—	48	6	—	2	4
Plastic utensils	1964	85	48	—	48	10	SB	2	nil
Cement	1964	92	48	—	48	9	—	1	nil
Tyres	1964	600	42	—	42	10	—	1	7
Vehicle assembly (L)	1964	350	44	20[a]	64	10	—	2	4
Brewery (L)	1964	500	44	—	44	12	—	3	2
Brewery	1959	396	44	2	46	6	—	2	4
Soap (L)	1959	636	44	1	45	10	—	2	7
Construction	1959	135	45	—	45	5	—	2	...
Joinery (L)	1959	400	45	—	45	8	—	3	5
Rubber processing	1959	90	42	12	54	8	SB	3	7
Timber and plywood	1959	3,200	48	—	48	6	—	3	12[b]
Coal-mining	1959	8,000	48	—	48	9	PR	12	4
Harbour management	1959	8,900	45	—	45	7	—	3	6
NORTH									
(*i*) Levantine									
Ceramic tiles	1964	105	45	10	55	6	PR	3	5
Enamelware	1964	500	48	—	48	5	—	2	10
Rubber shoes	1959	270	47	20	57	6	PR	6	4
Ground-nut crushing[d]	1959	1,000	48	—	48	5	—	3	...

Table 57 (cont.)

Establishment	Year	Employ-ment	Stand-ard	Over-time	Total	Hourly wage	Incen-tives	Gross absence	Gross turn-over
NORTH									
(*ii*) European			(*hours*)	(*hours*)	(*hours*)	(*d.*)		(%)	(%)
Textiles	1964	350	48	—	48	8	PR	4	2
Textiles	1964	2,750	48	—	48	10	PR	3	9
Cigarettes	1959	180	45	—	45	7	EB	2	4
Canning (w)	1964	200	48	4	52	6	—	5	2
Perfume (w)	1959	140	42	4	46	5	—	2	4
Tin-mining	1959	3,500	45	—	45	5	—	6	8

(L) = Lagos location (w) = predominantly women ... not available

[a] Seasonal, between three and six months of the year.

[b] More than half as a result of management initiative.

[c] Confined to unpaid apprentices.

[d] Four firms. F. A. Wells and W. A. Warmington, *Studies in Industrialization: Nigeria and the Cameroons*, London 1962, chapter 6.

T = task PR = piece rates SB = shift bonus EB = efficiency bonus

the elaboration of the African worker as he is portrayed in this conventional image.

What has emerged is that, while it is accepted that there is no scientific basis for the proposition that any initial incapacity in the African rests on any difference in hereditary biological constitution between him and members of any other racial group, it is a fact that by tradition and background the African is singularly ill-adapted for assimilation as an effective element in a wage economy on the modern pattern, that the reason that leads him to seek wage-paid labour heavily influences his attitude to work and his response to incentives and that his reactions differ widely from those of the European worker, whose background and aims are so different. It also has emerged that the African's work performance is at present unsatisfactory in many respects by European standards; that in quantity and quality it is often inferior; that the African sometimes lacks pride in his work; that he is often unstable and restless and prone to absent himself apparently without valid reasons. (p. 169)

Various sources of error in this portrayal of the African worker in terms of the geographic areas and industries surveyed, methodology and racial bias have been identified elsewhere.[1] More important recent field studies have shown the traditional appraisal, whether valid or not in an earlier time (pre-1939), to be totally fallacious today.[2] In the

[1] Peter Kilby, 'African Labour Productivity Reconsidered', *Economic Journal*, June 1961, pp. 275–6.

[2] Y. Glass, *The Black Industrial Worker: A Social Psychological Study*, Johannesburg 1959; R. Poupart, *Facteurs de Productivité de la Main-d'oeuvre Autochtone à Elizabethville*, Institut de Sociologie Solvay, Brussels 1960; Peter Kilby, *op. cit.*; C.C.T.A. Report of an Investigation into Absenteeism and Turnover in Selected African Countries, Sixth Inter-African Labour Conference, March 1961, Bamako.

following section we shall present primary data pertaining to absenteeism, labour turnover, hours of work and response to incentive wage schemes. From these findings and other collaborative evidence regarding consumer behaviour we will attempt to make appropriate inferences regarding the slope and position of the individual Nigerian's labour supply schedule.

Data in table 57 were collected by means of management interviews in early 1960 and late 1964; in a number of cases the information was extracted from attendance registers and wage books. The forty-three firms were classified into three groups (Nigerian, Levantine and European)[1] and by region. The general wage level, which provides the context for evaluating individual establishment wage rates, is higher in European firms, higher in the south and higher still in Lagos. The magnitude of geographic differentials is best judged by the minimum Federal wage rates prevailing in these areas in 1964: north, 4*s.* 3*d.* per day (6·4*d.* per hour); south, 4*s.* 11*d.* per day (7·4*d.* per hour); and Lagos 5*s.* 10*d.* per day (8·8*d.* per hour).[2] For the employer groups the difference in average wage level between the third and the two lower paying categories is greater than indicated by the minimum rates shown. First, 'learners' on 2*s.* 6*d.* constituting as much as 10 % of the labour force in many Nigerian and Levantine firms were passed over, starting instead with the lowest paid operatives. Second, more extensive job-grading in European establishments means that average earnings are a good deal further above the minimum rate than in Nigerian and Levantine firms; a similar differential obtains for fringe benefits: as against one or two paid public holidays and perhaps one week's paid vacation in the first two categories, the European employers very often provide full medical benefits, subsidized meals, uniforms, eleven paid public holidays and a vacation travelling allowance.

It is evident from table 57 that absence and turnover are low, particularly when the total number of hours worked is taken into account. Just how low these figures are can be seen by comparing them with performance in Britain and America:[3]

[1] Three public enterprises (coal mining, rubber processing, and the 350-man textile establishment) are included in the European category.

[2] These rates, as well as those in the table and throughout the text, are 'pre-Morgan' and were in effect until mid-1964. Similarly the 1959 figures are 'pre-Mbanefo'. The comparable Federal rates in 1959 were 3*s.* 6*d.* north, 4*s.* 1*d.* south and 4*s.* 8*d.* Lagos.

[3] For average hours worked, Ministry of Labour, *Statistics on Incomes, Prices, Employment and Production*, December 1964, table D. 6. and Bureau of Labour Statistics, *Employment and Earnings*, January 1965, table C. 2. For turnover *Ministry of Labour Gazette*, January 1965, p. 35. Absenteeism from H. Behrend, 'Voluntary Absence from Work', *International Labour Review*, February 1959, p. 171.

	Average total hours worked	Gross absence (%)	Gross turnover (%)
Britain	48	5	35
United States	41	4	47

Such figures provide scant support for the contention that the African 'is often unstable and restless and prone to absent himself apparently without valid reason'. Inasmuch as the results of the CCTA studies in eight other African countries were identical with the above findings for Nigeria, we may dismiss a number of problems commonly claimed to be impeding the progress of industrialization in Africa. These include problems of labour recruitment, partial commitment to wage-earning, adverse effects of labour migration, impaired productive capacity as a result of excessive absenteeism, and barriers to the development of a skilled labour force as a result of labour instability.

ABSENCE AND TURNOVER

Turning to a closer examination of absence and turnover, making allowance for cases of high redundancy or dismissals and the special working conditions associated with coal mining,[1] it can be seen from table 57 that variations, particularly in the case of absenteeism, tend to be related to the wage paid and the hours of work. This important fact, that performance is dependent upon working conditions and not on any inherent attitudes of the African or cultural factors, is more clearly seen by an examination of three firms.

Figures for the Nigerian Ports Authority pertain to the permanently established staff of about 4,100. The minimum wage was 7*d.* an hour; fringe benefits and conditions of work were also favourable. The extremely low net absence rate is explained by lenient sick-leave requirements and liberal vacation and holiday provisions. The unestablished staff, who are not paid sick leave, exhibited a 50 % lower sickness rate. The Lever Brothers factory employs 650 established workers. Its minimum hourly wage of 10*d.* was the highest among the firms surveyed in 1959. Enforcement of rigorous standards results in minimum levels of sickness and voluntary absence. As with the Ports Authority, labour turnover was very low for a long established employer whose labour force is comparatively old.

Turning from the highest paying to the lowest paying establishment (4*d.* per hour), the Edokpolo factory employed 200 workers processing rubber crêpe. No distinction was made in the wage register between

[1] Nigeria's absence rate of 12 % compares favourably with 16 % for coal mining in the United Kingdom. *Ministry of Labour Gazette*, January 1965, p. 36.

Table 58. *Absence and turnover in three firms, 1959*
(monthly percentages)

Nigerian Ports Authority			Lever Brothers soap factory			Edokpolo Rubber crêping factory	
Sick	Absent	Left	Sick	Absent	Left	Absent	Left
3·1	0·08	0·4	0·3	0·7	1·0	7·4	4·6
3·8	0·10	0·5	0·5	1·3	0·1	12·1	9·7
2·7	0·08	0·4	0·4	1·8	0·6	16·1	17·0
2·7	0·07	0·6	0·4	2·5	0·2	12·7	5·9
3·1	0·06	0·5	0·6	2·0	0·8	7·8	11·1
3·8	0·07	0·3	0·3	1·5	0·6	9·7	11·3
1·9	0·04	0·5	0·5	1·7	0·8	7·5	6·7
2·4	0·04	0·3	0·9	1·6	1·2	5·3	10·4
2·6	0·06	0·5	0·7	1·9	0·8	5·7	6·8
2·3	0·02	0·8	0·7	1·3	0·2	5·5	2·1
2·3	0·03	0·4	0·3	1·6	—	4·8	3·0
2·8	0·04	0·3	0·4	1·2	0·9	16·4	5·0
Annual turnover		5·5			7·2		93·6

sickness, compassionate leave or unexcused absence – all were treated the same, no work no pay. The factory operated seven days a week, as did the other Nigerian rubber processing firm, 364 days a year, and only Christmas was excepted. There was no annual leave, save for about ten of the clerical and supervisory staff. Indeed the employer treated his work force as casual labourers and was not concerned with high rates of absenteeism or labour turnover – these were not the limitational factors on his factory's productivity. His attitude was similar to that reported by Wells and Warmington for the Kano ground-nut crushers:

There was a large pool of labour to draw upon, and no firm, it appeared, had any difficulty attracting workers at existing wage-rates. We also found a tendency to assume that labour instability was not seriously detrimental to productivity (p. 98).

Table 59. *Distribution of absenteeism in the WNDC rubber crêping factory*
(June 1958–December 1959)

	Weekly hours index	Wage rate index	% of the work force	% of total absence
Artisans, clerks, storekeepers, engine minders, foremen	100	100	30	11
Packers	116	60	12	6
Crêpers	121	62	32	41
General labour	104	60	26	42

In a similar rubber crêping plant run by the Western Nigeria Development Corporation it was possible to obtain a breakdown of absenteeism by type of workers. The better paid skilled workers show the lowest rate of absence; the unskilled and relatively low paid packers are only slightly more absence prone. On the other hand, comparatively high absenteeism is recorded in the low paid, long working (in the case of crêpers), arduous jobs of crêping and general labour. Again, the objective factors of wages, hours and the nature of the work are seen to be responsible for varying rates of absenteeism.

Table 60. *Labour turnover in five firms*

	Paint factory (1964)	Textile mill (1964)	Timber and plywood (1959)	Rubber crêping (1959)	Rubber crêping (1959)
Average employment	40	2,750	3,200	90	120
Gross turnover	7 %	9 %	12 %	7 %	15 %
Cause for separation:					
Management termination	100 %	41 %	66 %	65 %	74 %
Retirement or death	—	1 %	12 %	2 %	14 %
Voluntary leaving	—	58 %	22 %	33 %	12 %
	100 %	100 %	100 %	100 %	100 %

Labour turnover is composed of separations as a result of retirement, serious sickness, death, redundancy, breach of discipline, inefficiency, excessive absenteeism, theft and voluntary leaving. It is only in the last case that the initiative lies with the worker; it is to such voluntary quitting that labour instability and net absenteeism refer. For the five firms where a breakdown of turnover is available, only in one case does voluntary leaving constitute as much as a half of gross labour turnover, while in three cases it is less than a quarter. In terms of productivity and wastage of training, it is relevant to note that by far the greater part of labour turnover is confined to the lower ranks of unskilled and semi-skilled workers.

Regarding overtime, it should be observed that most progressive managements do not favour a policy of working substantial overtime hours on a continuous basis, despite pressure from their employees to do so. If the need to work more than the normal eight hours appears likely to persist, a second or third shift is recruited. These employers operate on the principle that if they are utilizing their labour force at maximum efficiency for the standard eight hours, productivity is bound to fall with any substantial increment. There is also a cost consideration. The European employer (and the Government) by tradition pay time-and-a-half for overtime, whereas Nigerian and Levantine employers of whom public opinion is less demanding here as in other matters, pay the normal rate, save on Sunday. The latters' overtime policy is justified economically only if productivity per man hour falls no more than that amount which will just compensate for the extra costs of employing additional labour (e.g. administrative expenses, fringe benefits).

There are two final pieces of evidence relevant to the number of hours a Nigerian labourer is willing to work. The first is the practice of 'moonlighting'. In interviewing workers in the baking and rubber crêping industries in 1960 and in various establishments in 1964 it often came out that the employee was engaged in some kind of part-time after-hours employment to supplement his primary wage. In the only case where an exact count was made, the Guinness brewery in Lagos (paying 12*d.* per hour), 26 % of the labour force were engaged in other gainful pursuits after-hours.[1] The second piece of evidence is the number of hours worked in the small industry sector. The writer's investigations in 1961 in connection with A.I.D. surveys revealed that a ten to eleven hour day (exclusive of lunch) is worked six days a week. These figures are supported by Callaway's findings.[2]

RESPONSIVENESS TO INCENTIVE SCHEMES

The elasticity of supply of effort in respect to monetary incentive is to be seen not only in the willingness of Nigerian labour to work long hours but also in their response to payment-by-results.[3] In every incentive scheme investigated, save one, management reported that productivity had risen substantially since payment-by-results had been introduced. In the case of textile manufacture where piece rates were part of the wage system from the beginning, management was of the opinion that a shift from piece rates to straight time rates would lead to a sharp fall in output per man. In the one textile firm not employing piece rates (but also poorly managed) productivity was very low. The only instance where a production bonus scheme did not succeed was in a semi-automated sequence in a cigarette factory; the bonus scheme had very little applicability and the basis on which it was calculated was not fully understood by the operatives.

A few examples may be cited. As would be expected, incentive schemes contribute the most when the prime requisite is effort rather than skill and where there is no 'pacing' already provided by a machine or interdependence with other phases of production. Thus output per

[1] H. Dieter Seibel, 'Industrial Labour in Nigeria', mimeograph, 1963, p. 34.

[2] Archibald Callaway, 'Nigeria's Indigenous Education: the Apprentice System', *University of Ife Journal of African Studies*, July 1964, p. 9.

[3] Workers are also induced to greater exertion by the promise of promotion and overtime to those who perform well.

man-day in a Kano tile factory shot up from 70 terrazzo tiles to 200 with the introduction of a piece rate system. In a luggage factory in Apapa daily output rose from 20 units per operative to 85 as a result of payment-by-results. In the case of processes involving manually controlled machines or where there is extensive group interdependence the possibilities are less spectacular. In an Aba plastic utensil factory output rose by 17 % when inter-shift competition for a monthly production bonus was inaugurated. In the WNDC rubber crêping plant the introduction of a bonus system raised productivity by a quarter. As already mentioned piece rates are considered essential to the level of performance attained in the textile industry. In all these cases productivity gains have been achieved without any loss in quality and without additional supervision, by using a system of financial penalties. And finally, throughout Nigeria all very arduous or particularly unpleasant labour is performed by casual Hausa labour working exclusively on piece rates.

The fact that payment-by-results is eagerly received in Nigeria whenever it permits the worker to increase his average earnings, in contrast to the tendency to abandon incentive schemes in developed countries, is strongly connected with, if not wholly a result of, the greater desire of the very much lower paid Nigerian worker to increase his wage earnings. At his level of income the utility of additional money far exceeds the disutility of extra exertion, possible group tension, difficulties in distributing the 'paying' jobs and potential inequities in rate setting which appear to be tipping the balance against payment-by-results in high-wage countries.

THE DESIRE FOR MONEY: THE CULTURAL CONTEXT AND CONSUMER ASPIRATIONS

We have reviewed the evidence pertaining to the shape of the individual's labour supply curve and other aspects of his response to monetary incentive. What are the motives which lie behind the observed behaviour? Clearly the limited wants and high valuation on leisure postulated in the traditional protrayal are incompatible with the empirical findings. Our re-appraisal will concentrate on the Nigerian's motive for desiring money; this will include traditional factors, status-recognition and the financial requirements for consumption needs.

Far from emphasizing non-material values and minimizing the need for money, and thereby slowing down and impeding the transition to a wage-earning money economy, culture has, if anything, encouraged and facilitated the process of change. Customary practices have come into contact with the new life, have gone through a process of monetization and have been integrated into the new pattern. The bride-price, once a certain number of goods and services, is now a sum of money which continues to serve its stabilizing function as of old, as well as offsetting the father's expense in educating his daughter and equipping her for married life (sewing machine, household implements, bicycle). The situation is similar regarding initiation rites, honorary orders, chieftancy and funeral ceremonies. The more elaborate the trappings and the more opulent the celebrations, the larger is the reward within the traditional context. Even the intricate and far-reaching code of hospitality has to a considerable extent become monetized. Not only is the food and beverage proffered bought by money, but when the latter is not at hand money may be given in its stead. The importance of financial remittances by 'sons abroad' to their traditional village home has already been discussed. The customary practice of gift-exchange provides a pervasive traditional motive for wage-earning; this practice is particularly significant among the Muslim Hausa, where it accounts for nearly one-quarter of all expenditures.[1]

> Hausa practice gift-exchange in set kinship contexts such as child birth, naming, circumcision, marriage and death, and in others which establish special social relations such as bond-friendship or clientage. Islam proves another frame for transfers and exchange at fixed festivals, such as Id-el-Fitr, Id-el-Kabir, or on the tenth day of Muharram.... The Islamic emphasis on charity is perhaps most clearly expressed among the Hausa in the institution of Koranic schools, in which both teacher and pupils depend for their subsistence largely on alms from neighbours.
>
> ... Taken together, these customary transfers form a separate system and express certain interdependent values, especially those of religion, kinship and community. These values are not insulated from Hausa commerce. Kinship and religion provide frames of reference in which customary and commercial exchanges are both consistent and complementary. So too with the political system, which itself involves another set of transfers. Some political transfers, such as tribute or tax, are obligatory and enforceable. Others, such as gifts, express relations of patronage and dependence inherent in Hausa political organization. In other contexts, such as the Sallan festivals or accession to office, gifts are transferred ceremonially to declare or to strengthen solidarity.[2]

Independent of meeting traditional obligations, status recognition provides another motive for the individual to maximize his money income. To repeat an appraisal given by the writer in 1961, 'An impressive house, numerous servants, generosity to relatives and friends, lavish tipping and, above all, a big car are the hallmarks of the

[1] M. G. Smith, 'Exchange and Marketing Among the Hausa' in *Markets in Africa*, P. Bohannan and G. Dalton, eds., Evanston 1962, p. 312.

[2] *Ibid.* pp. 311–12.

Nigerian who has arrived. The measure of a man is the money he has; and money is valued for what it will buy and not, as in developed countries, as a yardstick of his capabilities or attainments. The successful politician, shrewd trader, civil servant, football-pool organizer or money-lenders are all equal in the eyes of the community as long as the external manifestations of their affluence are equal. In short, money is status.'[1] While this description may do an injustice in ignoring the status accorded certain occupational achievements, it is by and large supported by sociological investigations. Gugler's description of how successful urban sons gain rural status by the display of wealth and the maintenance of a large number of dependents will be recalled. Even in traditional Ibo society wealth was a dominant factor in determining an individual's status.

> The most characteristic feature of the Ibo status systems, although not found everywhere, was the title society. This consisted in its most developed form of a series of ranked titles, the entry to which was contingent upon acceptance by existing title-holders, payment of a set entrance fee, and providing a feast for members of the society. Membership was open to anyone of free birth, but the fees and feasts effectively limited title-holding to those of some wealth. This was increasingly the case as one progressed to higher titles. Membership in the society entitled one to share in the entrance fees paid by new members and to enjoy the prestige of title-holding. In many areas the title society also constituted a political oligarchy in the village or village group, controlling the making of decisions even at public meeting at which all men had a right to speak and in which decisions were formally imposed by the heads of descent groups. The most important were not inherited but fell vacant upon the death of a title-holder.
>
> The title society was thus a means by which the wealth of a man could be translated into social and political status, ultimately the highest status which the local social system had to confer.[2]

Among the Tiv a man's status was related to his wealth as measured by the size of his farm, in turn related to the amount of labour expended by the farmer and his family.[3] Even in the country's least materialistically oriented community, the Muslim Hausa, money is an important status factor.

> ... customary exchange marks wealth and its pursuit as legitimate at the same time it demonstrates status and affirms prestige. The generosity of wealthy men evokes admiration for wealth and emulation in its pursuit. It also leads Hausa to set high value on the freedom to pursue wealth, within limits set by Islamic on the one hand and customary norms on the other.

[1] Kilby, 'African Labour Productivity Reconsidered', *Economic Journal*, June 1961, p. 283.

[2] Robert A. LeVine, *Dreams and Deeds: Achievement Motivation in Nigeria*, Chicago 1966, p. 34.

[3] Paul Bohannan, *Tiv Farm and Settlement*, H.M.S.O., London 1954, p. 51.

Thus Hausa admire industry and commercial display by which this wealth and status is demonstrated. The prominent man has many dependents and makes generous outlays, and his means of obtaining his income is socially legitimized thereby.[1]

The third and quantitatively most significant motive for acquiring money is the desire to obtain goods and services for personal consumption. Sometimes referred to as the 'revolution of rising expectations' or the 'demonstration effect', the Nigerian lives in poverty and he is conscious of it. He seeks wage-earning employment not just to obtain a shirt, bicycle or watch but to buy more and better food, decent clothing, electricity for his dwelling, a radio, schooling for his children and

Table 61. *Urban income-expenditure patterns*

(monthly, at 1959 prices)

	1953–1956[a]		1959[b]	
	Labourers	Artisans	Labourers	Artisans
Household income	238*s*.	459*s*.	316*s*.	592*s*.
Wage earnings	136*s*.	283*s*.	185*s*.	395*s*.
Wage earnings/income	60 %	69 %	58 %	67 %
Individuals per household	3·1	4·1	3·6	5·1
Expenditure per person on goods and services	67*s*.	86*s*.	69*s*.	90*s*.
Remittances	—	30*s*.[c]	19*s*.	36*s*.

[a] Lagos 1953–4, Enugu 1954–5, Ibadan 1955, Kaduna and Zaria 1955–6.

[b] Lagos 1959.

[c] Refers to Kaduna and Zaria only; the breakdown between artisans and labourers was not shown in the earlier surveys.

SOURCE: Federal Department of Statistics, *Urban Consumer Surveys in Nigeria* (Lagos).

members of his extended family, medical attention and so on. His horizons are defined not only by his western education and want-creating advertisements but by what he personally observes, what he hears on the radio and what he sees in films. As a result of these influences and because the material standards of developed countries are achieved by a sufficient number of expatriates and Nigerians – in the large firms, in the higher civil service and in politics – the aspirations of the average urban-dwelling Nigerian are not very different from those of Europeans or Americans.

The income-expenditure patterns revealed in the urban consumer surveys provide collaborative evidence regarding the worker's need for money and explains both the length and the slope of his labour offer curve. Wage-earnings do not meet family requirements. And the lower the wage the greater the proportion of income to be secured in other ways: part-time after hours work, trading and borrowing. Similarly the size of remittances to the home village varies with the level of income.

[1] M. G. Smith, *loc. cit.* p. 313.

Approximately three-quarters of all households resided in a single room.[1]

We saw in chapter 2 that the individual's consumption behaviour as income rises is the same as that observed elsewhere: there is a shift to less starchy, more expensive foods, and more than proportionate increases in expenditure on clothing, other soft goods and consumer durables. In short there is nothing to suggest limited wants or approaching satiety.

From all this, it is manifestly clear that the Nigerian's demand for money is not terminal at an early stage. His demand for goods and services is only limited by his purchasing power, in turn limited by his income pössibilities. Having a greater desire for money and a lesser means for earning it, it is not surprising that his willingness to work exceeds that of his European and American counterparts.

III

PRODUCTIVITY AND THE QUALITY OF LABOUR PERFORMANCE

The determinants of output per man viewed at the macro-level of the economy is none other than the problem of economic development itself. Our interest is quite different, it is both static and micro: given technology, a certain quantity of capital equipment and a constant set of external influences, what are the determinants of factors controlling labour productivity at the establishment level. In attempting to answer this question we shall first discuss the proficiency of Nigerian workers at various jobs and then look at several case studies where quantitative productivity and performance measures have been taken to see whether labour proficiency or some other input is the limitational factor.

Our scrutiny of labour proficiency is perhaps best begun by a recitation of all published evidence on the subject.

At the cement works at Ewekoro in Western Nigeria it has been reported that the filter press machine was the same in Nigeria as that in the associated company in the United Kingdom. In both countries 4 presses are run by 4 operators and each operator undertakes 16 processes. Most of the operators in Nigeria are illiterates who were trained, in Yoruba, for a period of 3 weeks. It was observed that their productivity was exactly equal to, and sometimes better than that of their U.K. counterparts, in a timed operation requiring regularity of sequence rather than particular skills.[2]

[1] Sixty-seven per cent of all Lagos residents share a 10-foot square one room dwelling with an average of two other people. Federal Office of Statistics, *Lagos Housing Enquiry*, June 1961.

[2] *Report of the National Seminar on Productivity*, Lagos, February 1963, p. 4.

... the makers of the perfume bottling machines estimated the maximum output at 3,000 bottles per hour, but one Hausa woman regularly did 3,600, and there were others almost as good. [Average output was 3,200 in this Kano firm as against 2,900 in Switzerland.][1]

In factories making window and metal door frames and corrugated roofing, Nigerian workers on machines requiring repetitive movements, such as a corrugating machine, press brake machine and metal guillotine, are almost as productive as workers on the same machines in the United Kingdom. However, productivity falls off considerably where metal hand work is involved in addition to machine work. On nail machines in a factory operating for only a few months, productivity per worker is presently estimated at 65 % to 70 % of what it is in Germany.

Labour productivity in a Nigerian luggage factory, where employees are paid by piece rate, is greater than in Europe according to the plant supervisor. Productivity in another factory, which has been in operation only a few months assembling a popular household machine, is already almost 60 % of what it is in a similar plant in the United States.

Two companies have recently started manufacturing tyres in Nigeria and it is already evident that Nigerian workers will compare favourably with workers in Europe. The normal output per worker on a tyre machine in the United Kingdom is twenty tyres a day after an average training period of three months. Six months training is necessary for a Nigerian to meet this output. It was pointed out that Nigerian labour does an equal, and in many cases a better job of verifying the tyre faults than labour in European plants.

With adequate supervision, productivity of Nigerian labour in such routine jobs as packaging and bottling is about equal to what it is in Europe. For example, at an ice cream plant, Nigerian workers employed as packers, mixers and freezermen are as productive and in some cases more so, than, workers on the same machines in the United Kingdom, according to the production manager. Packers at a factory making ethical and proprietary drugs are as productive as workers in either the United States or in the United Kingdom, and furthermore will perform the same task for a much longer time.

Productivity is more difficult to judge for skilled jobs. A well-known office machine company gives a five year training course for Nigerian mechanics. To date 150 have been trained and about 10 % are as efficient on a broad range of office machines as a European or an American. This company's experience shows that it is much easier to train a mechanic on one machine than a variety of machines.[2]

The information gathered by the writer during the course of establishment interviews in 1960 and 1964 was very similar to the instances cited above. Nigerians were usually judged superior to European labour in

[1] Wells and Warmington, *Studies in Industrialization*, p. 103.

[2] Federal Ministry of Commerce and Industry, *Industrial Labour*, Lagos 1963, pp. 15–16.

most jobs with an invariable sequence or that required great physical exertion; it was also asserted that Nigerians would sustain a given level of productivity in these positions for a longer period of time. Digital dexterity was also reported to be high, especially among women. However where more than two or three operations had to be co-ordinated and judgment was required, performance was often a good deal lower. Yet in the newer industries it is still too early to make a fair judgment.

In general employers seem to agree that Nigerian workers, especially southerners, absorb knowledge up to a certain point more rapidly than comparable English workers and that in the exercise of specific skills they are equal to Europeans, but in non-routine situations requiring analysis and judgment (i.e. understanding the underlying mechanical principles) Nigerian performance usually falls considerably short.[1] The explanation for this short-coming would seem to be a combination of cultural factors, deficiencies in training and existing employer policies regarding the organization of work.

As Robert G. Armstrong has pointed out, for various ecological reasons the simplest mechanical principles embodied in the wheel, the inclined plane and the lever never found their way into traditional West African societies.[2] In so far as these principles are even now only occasionally to be found in the rural environment where most children's perceptions of the physical world are formed, it is not surprising that the individual fails to integrate later technical knowledge into a set of principles which would enable him to apply his acquired mechanical skills in unstructured situations. Secondly, in traditional society most of the working situations which would otherwise require analysis and judgment have already been anticipated and appropriate responses prescribed by custom. Needless to say, to prove or measure the impact of such culture inheritances is extremely difficult, if not impossible.

The contribution of training to poorly developed analytical abilities in the work place is related to the omnipresent problem of communications[3] and, very often, the instructor's failure to provide sufficient supplementary background information. Regarding the second point, Hudson has described one typical pattern:

Unsatisfactory work performance can in many instances be laid at the door of the trainer or supervisor. The African operative is required to be accurate,

[1] See also International Labour Office, *African Labour Survey*, p. 143.

[2] R. G. Armstrong, 'Some Technical Gaps in the Nigerian School Curricula', *Proceedings of the West African Institute of Social and Economic Research*, Ibadan 1953.

[3] As English is always a second or third language among Nigerians, failures of comprehension are frequent. Nigerian workers are notoriously reticent to say they do not understand or to ask their superior to repeat instructions.

to follow certain specifications. He follows his instructions precisely, but finds that the European supervisor pays less heed to accuracy than to speed of performance. The European supervisor may be correct in doing so since he realizes the relative value of each step in the processing of the article and is aware of the characteristics of the material. But the African worker is likely to be in ignorance of all that, and to become confused by contradiction between precept and practice, until his own work performance deteriorates.[1]

The above quotation suggests a final source for poor performance of complex operations. In the era prior to World War II when the experience background and general educational level of the labour force was very much less sophisticated than it is today, employers had no choice but to practice job dilution. In conjunction with this policy of breaking each job into a series of simple steps which the operative learned by rote (in contrast to the much more difficult and time-consuming technique of teaching the individual the principles involved and the nature of his job's interdependence in the production process), all workers were instructed to stop their machine and call the European supervisor should any irregularity arise. Because this policy is easier to implement and because competent Nigerian supervisors, who would have assisted the worker in his learning process, have been slow to develop, a significant proportion of expatriate firms have carried on the traditional approach of job dilution and suppression of worker initiative. While such a policy is often necessary to get a new industry started, its continuance retards the development of labour skills and leads to high labour costs (e.g. the employment of European supervisors).

This brings us to a category of human proficiency that properly belongs to management rather than labour: supervision. With few exceptions among firms employing over twenty-five, the inadequacy of Nigerian supervisory performance was reported by management to be their chief problem in the labour field.[2] Three particular weaknesses were cited in virtually every instance.

i. Lack of surveillance and intervention in the work process and unwillingness to establish a work pace.

ii. Poor diagnostic and organizational ability in non-routine situations.

iii. Reluctance to accept responsibility (for faulty work of subordinates, for preventing damage to machinery, for maintaining the flow of production, etc.)

In general supervisors tend to identify with the workers rather than with management and although the racial factor undoubtedly contributes to this identity of allegiance, it is also found to a certain degree in Nigerian

[1] W. Hudson, 'Observations on African Labour', *Journal of the National Institute of Personnel Research*, March 1955, p. 78. [2] Also reported by Wells and Warmington, *op. cit.* pp. 37 ff.

firms. Other faults frequently but by no means universally alleged were arbitrary and inconstant treatment of subordinates (at one moment protective and in the next, wielding the 'big stick') and the showing of favouritism concerning discipline and promotion along tribal and village lines.

Of well over fifty firms which were studied only three were encountered where the performance of Nigerian foremen and supervisors was deemed completely satisfactory: a Nigerian jobbing printer John Okwesa and Co. in Lagos, the Nigerian Canning Company in Kano and the Permacem paint factory in Port Harcourt. The first two were managed by a Nigerian and Englishman respectively, both of whom were strong personalities and had worked long hours on the shop floor, and who personally selected and trained the current supervisors; a feeling of personal responsibility and loyalty to the firm was in evidence among the workers as well as among the supervisors. In the case of the two-year-old paint factory the labour force was small (40) and the manufacturing operation very simple; the two foremen were energetic and technically competent and appeared to have identified their own long-term interests with the success of the company.

Some of the conditioning factors relevant to supervisory performance would be the same as in the preceding case involving judgment and analytical abilities. Regarding organizational powers and surveillance, a simple technology and little division of labour in traditional agriculture provided meagre scope for the development of such abilities. Again, for the individual who attains superior position in tribal society the prerogatives of status receive greater stress than do the obligations of performance. And to the extent that the role of a Nigerian foreman is translated, both for him and his subordinates, into that of a senior brother in the kinship system, there is a reluctance to 'drive' and a resistance to being 'driven'.[1]

PRODUCTIVITY MEASUREMENT

We now turn to two case studies carried out by the author in 1960.[2] The first study is an inter-temporal analysis of various productivity

[1] It may be that this factor is also operative in producing the situation described for the large timber and plywood firm. 'The dearth of African supervisors was due not merely to the shortage of men with appropriate technical qualifications. Even more important than these were the want of willingness to take responsibility and ability to exert authority. The foremen, it was said, tended to be too much like their men. An African trying to impose discipline in the interests, as it would appear, of a European management, attracted animosity. The men might "gang up" against him, applying subtle pressures, or perhaps by bringing accusations of receiving bribes, which could mean the foreman's dismissal.' Wells and Warmington, *op. cit.* pp. 37–38. It hardly needs saying that the fact that many supervisors do accept bribes further undermines their authority.

[2] A shortened presentation of these studies appeared in Kilby, 'African Labour Productivity Reconsidered', *Economic Journal*, June 1961.

indices of the West African Institute for Oil-Palm Research. The second is based upon inter-firm comparisons for five rubber crêping processors. In these two studies we will attempt to identify the limitational factors in determining labour productivity, and specifically to see to what extent labour proficiency figures in this category.

The West African Institute for Oil-Palm Research, located near Benin, was established in 1948 as a semi-autonomous corporation. It was supported, until 1964, by fixed annual contributions from the four former British West African territories. The plantation labour force had fluctuated between 600 and 800. The minimum hourly wage in 1959 was 4½*d.* However in addition to the wage, the workers were provided with bungalows, electricity and water at a nominal fee, free education for children, medicine and recreational facilities. This 'wage package' compared favourably with alternative employment opportunities in the area.

The work consisted of general plantation labour: clearing heavy forests, cutlassing of undergrowth, lining out planting stands, planting, fitting of wire collars, labelling, ring-cutlassing and harvesting. These operations would classify as semi-skilled labour. A system of work was employed whereby a certain number of acres to be cleared, seedlings to be planted, etc., was specified at the beginning of the day as the requirement for that day; when this task was completed, the labourers were free to go home. Work was carried out in gangs of twenty and upwards.

	Absenteeism		Dispensary attendance	
	1953 (%)	1959 (%)	1952	1959
April	19	4	717	441
May	10	3	789	493
June	9	6	422	505
July	10	7	370	560
August	9	6	642	571
September	9	6	732	422
October	9	7	816	369
November	15	9	806	375
December	9	5	1,047	393
January	6	6	369	215
February	2	6	462	258
March	10	4	643	242

As seen from the figures above, over the period 1953–9 the annual absence rate was reduced from 8·6 to 5·0 %, increasing the utilization of potential labour time from 91·4 to 95·0 %. Similarly dispensary attendance was halved. In the earlier period 80 to 90 % of those who went to the dispensary with an alleged illness were found to be fully fit and ordered back to work; in the meantime several hours of working time had been lost. It is this component of dispensary attendance, subject to abuse by the workers, which contracted sharply.

Table 62. *Selected intertemporal productivity measures, WAIFOR plantation*

(*a*) Harvesting

Year	Average daily attendance	Acres	Tons harvested	Tons/man index
1952	758	968	1,047	100
1953	694	1,052	1,944	149
1954	783	1,126	1,920	130
1955	729	1,153	2,600	190
1956	745	1,272	2,673	191
1957	829	1,345	3,401	218
1958	753	1,438	2,807	198
1959	743	1,523	3,986	285

(*b*) Maintenance man-days/acre

Year	Older areas	Younger areas	Combined index
1954	2·90	4·20	100
1958	1·73	2·40	172
1959	1·66	2·09	190

(*c*) Man-days required for clearing and planting heavy forest

Year	Man-days/acre	Index
1955	96·2	100
1959	63·0	135

Not only have the number of man-days from a given labour force been increased, but as can be seen in table 62 output per unit of labour time has also registered striking gains, from a minimum of 35 % to a maximum of 185 %. What are these gains to be attributed to? The degree of mechanization remained constant during the period. Although labour skills may have improved somewhat with experience, given the relatively modest skills entailed it would seem likely that the greater part of such improvement would have already occurred in the preceding four years. A minority portion of the increase in harvesting productivity was probably a result of higher tree yields per acre. However this still leaves the major part of the productivity advances unexplained.

It is possible to select four principal causes. The first was a continuing increase in supervision in both its extent and in its intensity. This was achieved by management pressure on the overseers and by holding out promotion opportunities for the latter to artisan pay scales when their performance so merited. Second, tasks were enlarged. Third, greater incentives, both positive and negative, were given to the workers: promotion to junior supervisory grades, closer enforcement of penalties for failure to complete task and selective dismissals during times of seasonal redundancy. The latter measure coupled with a generally more rigorous approach to labour discipline was responsible for the decrease in absenteeism and dispensary attendance. Finally, improved work methods and better control contributed to increased efficiency; the first consisted in the introduction of harvesting chisels and harvesting hooks, the second in the organization of felling heavy timber.[1]

The foregoing analysis indicates that the achievable productive capacity or the proficiency of Nigerian labour was not the limitational factor on labour productivity at the WAIFOR plantation. Rather, a number of management functions – the provision of adequate incentive, supervision, work methods and organization – appear to have been the key factors inhibiting higher productivity.

The second case study concerns five rubber crêping firms. All these firms were located within a thirty-mile radius of one another and drew upon the same labour force. Of the two firms in Benin, the establishment hereafter referred to as Firm III was owned by the Western Nigeria Development Corporation and was managed by an experienced Nigerian university graduate, assisted by a European chief engineer; the other, Firm V, was owned by a Nigerian formerly engaged in supplying rubber lumps (the raw material) to other processors, and managed by the proprietor (part-time), his chief clerk and a supervisor. The other three firms were situated around Sapele, thirty miles to the south of Benin. Firms I and II were owned and operated by Greeks, while Firm IV was one of several processing enterprises owned by the Mid-West's most prominent businessmen; the latter was managed by one European for the first seven of the eighteen months covered. The entrepreneurs of all three of the Sapele firms had previously been in the produce trade.

The operations of a rubber crêping factory can be divided into five stages, as follows:

(*a*) The purchase of rubber lumps and their inspection for excessive adulteration.
(*b*) Soaking of lumps in water tanks to soften.
(*c*) The crêping process.
(*d*) Drying of crêpe sheets in steam-heated sheds.
(*e*) Brushing and baling of sheets for export.

The crêping process itself consists of feeding the rubber lumps (later pulp) through a series of dual, intermeshed, water-washed corrugated rollers which macerate, clean and form the pulped rubber into long sheets. Each set of rollers is tended by one man who feeds in the pulp and guides out the sheet at the other end. The machines used in the five firms were identical (only one manufacturer) and plant layouts

[1] These reforms were instigated after top management became concerned about cutting costs as a result of budgetary pressures.

were very similar. The least capitalized firm, Firm I, had the least efficient layout in that (*i*) the crêping rollers were too close together, hampering freedom of movement; (*ii*) the rollers were not raised on concrete mounts, forcing the operator to bend down; and (*iii*) the sequence of buildings did not conform to the sequence of production, necessitating extra handling and carriage.

Table 63. *Rubber crêping inter-firm productivity comparisons*
(18 months)

Firm I		Firm II		Firm III		Firm IV		Firm V	
Hours/ ton	Tons/ machine	Hours/ ton	Tons/ machine	Hours/ ton	Tons/ machine	Hours/ ton	Tons/ machine	Hours/ ton	Tons/ machine
194	23·6	183	20·9	244	13·6	373	11·1	426	12·5
187	24·7	159	21·5	231	13·9	382	12·0	324	7·5
184	27·2	185	17·7	233	14·4	422	13·6	343	6·3
167	29·1	236	16·9	238	14·7	387	16·0	316	7·9
155	29·6	198	20·8	199	17·4	272	19·8	308	8·3
169	28·6	161	23·0	198	20·7	276	19·2	359	6·9
174	25·8	155	25·2	207	18·4	242	20·1	374	6·5
166	26·2	136	28·1	208	13·9	203	20·9	381	6·0
144	22·6	143	27·7	208	13·3	314	15·1	326	7·1
115	23·2	151	25·9	201	14·4	393	12·1	293	8·4
103	28·7	161	23·7	179	17·9	303	16·8	314	8·0
103	29·7	180	22·2	181	18·5	231	20·5	325	7·5
109	30·4	188	22·0	213	16·6	227	20·8	350	7·3
108	29·8	188	23·6	182	19·3	224	19·5	334	6·5
106	28·8	172	26·8	141	24·5	227	18·0	288	6·7
112	30·1	153	28·1	157	23·0	212	19·9	241	7·8
112	32·0	151	27·2	187	17·8	224	18·8	222	8·0
107	32·9	151	26·7	197	16·3	251	16·5	236	8·0
				18 month average					
140	27·9	171	23·6	200	17·1	287	17·3	328	7·6
				(Index)					
100	100	122	85	143	61	205	62	234	27

Despite the disadvantage in layout, Firm I recorded the highest productivity, whether measured by man-hours required per ton or by tons produced per machine per month.[1] This was achieved by highly efficient organization, including an hourly quota system for each machine operator, and the personal supervision in the production area of one of the Greek managers at all times. Firms II and III were also well managed although control was not as rigorous. The pace of work in Firms IV and V was very erratic and stoppages were frequent. For

[1] Unlike man-hours per ton, output per machine is influenced by the number of hours worked per month. Firm III worked six 21-hour days per week, Firms I and II six 24-hour days per week, and Firms IV and V seven 24-hour days per week. As later indicators will suggest Firm II was at least as efficient as Firm III, but being a Government establishment carried a larger labour force (clerical and maintenance staff) than was necessary.

example, in Firm IV an examination of the records for two months showed that the crêping machinery had been out of operation for 156 and 180 hours due to various mechanical mal-functionings and lack of lumps.[1] The following description is taken from working notes made while observing operations in this firm.

> There is no lump shed nor are lumps stocked against the future. In fact operations are often halted for lack of lumps. .... The tempo of work in the crêping mill appears to be about one-third that of Firm I. Supervision is practically nil. The most senior man is the tally clerk; the production manager spends most of his time doing administrative work and attending to matters other than in the crêping mill. Men on the machines stop and talk or argue with others around them.
>
> In the baling shed there is a hydraulic press. Although only one year old it has been out of operation for the last three months as a result of careless handling (lack of supervision). Spare parts from England are still awaited. In general work was more continuous here than in the crêping mill.
>
> ... There is little specialization of labour. Not only do they rotate jobs – from machine to machine, to server, to cart pusher, to loading lumps – but the labour force in the baling shed rotates weekly with the crêping mill gang. The wage rate is based on the individual and not on the job he performs...

It is possible to quantify in a rough manner the extent to which the various sources of low productivity described above have contributed to the final performance of each firm. The degree of fluctuation in unit labour requirements from one month to the next gives a fair measure of management's ability to plan and coordinate such elements as customers' orders, funds to provide for the required quantity of rubber lumps, sufficient capacity of the physical plant in working order and recruitment of labour, particularly skilled labour. The measurement for the five firms is seen below. Firm I shows the best performance. Firms II and III exhibit a fluctuation some 75 % greater than Firm I, and Firms IV and V a fluctuation some 300 % greater.

Average monthly change in unit labour requirement

	Man-hours
Firm I	9
Firm II	17
Firm III	15
Firm IV	35
Firm V	36

The graph of daily fluctuation in output for the five firms during December 1959 shown in figure 3 may be said to measure three potential

[1] It must be remembered however that there was no Sunday rest-and-maintenance period (equivalent to 96 hours per month) in this firm. Nevertheless labour continued to be paid during stoppages.

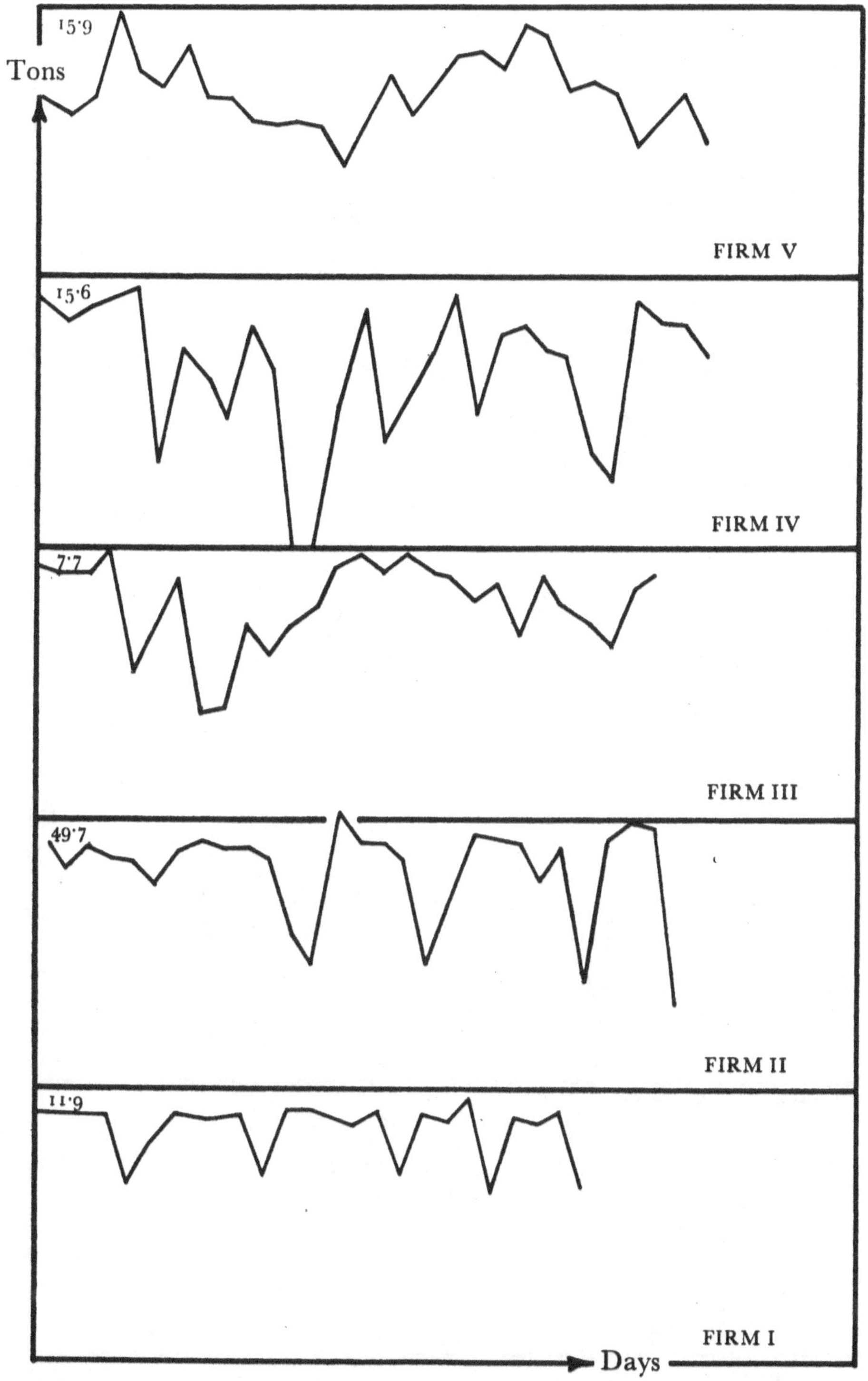

FIG. 3. Fluctuations in daily production: five rubber crêping firms, December 1959.

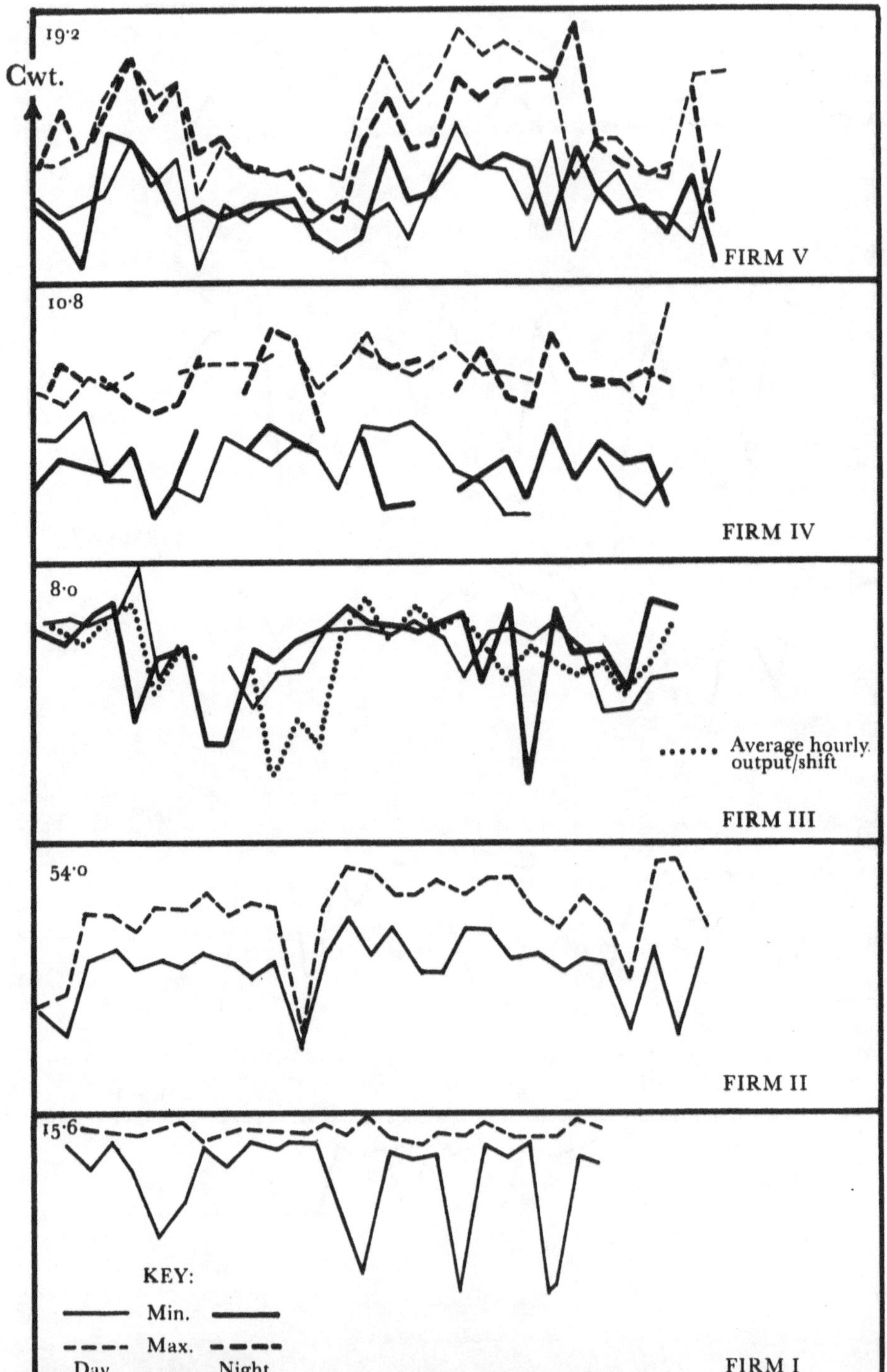

FIG. 4. Minimum-maximum hourly output: five rubber crêping firms, December 1959.

weaknesses: failure to provide for continuing maintenance and for the availability of spare parts, failure to set daily production quotas which ensure that daily output will in fact approximate maximum capacity, and failure to stockpile sufficient amounts of unprocessed rubber.[1]

A final index of management performance is minimum and maximum hourly production – again the data are for December 1959. There are three significant things to be observed in figure 4: the average level of hourly production, the degree of fluctuation in this level and the discrepancy between minimum and maximum hours. The first measures the quality of supervision, while the second and third indicate its constancy.

The conclusion to be drawn from this interfirm comparison is similar to that in the WAIFOR case: organization and supervision are the effective limitational factors on labour productivity and not the proficiency of the Nigerian labourer. As for the standard-setting factories, Firms I and II, both general managers stated that, with the exception of the mechanical staff, in their opinion output per man was at least as high as it would have been with European labour. In particular, regarding the arduous and monotonous crêping working itself, they doubted European labour would allow themselves to be pushed at the pace which the Nigerians had accepted without complaint.

What little other evidence is available (e.g. C. S. Nwanze's study of ENDC Pioneer oil mills) likewise indicates that improvement in management techniques has a far greater contribution to make to advances in productivity than changes in labour proficiency. That managerial input should be of over-riding importance in smaller scale Nigerian establishments, as has been documented in the case of the baking industry,[2] is not very surprising; it is more surprising when UAC's African Timber and Plywood Company, one of the country's most efficiently run firms, discovers that, as a result of the organization of work, capital utilization in certain of its operations is as low as 50 % of capacity.[3] There are exceptions of course, current standards of loom tending in the textile industry being the outstanding case. Weaknesses in Nigerian supervisors may often have unfavourable effects on productivity, especially in Nigerian firms, but we have argued that these are more properly treated as managerial deficiencies of Nigerians rather than as a problem in general labour performance.

[1] The ceiling is set on the basis of the highest output achieved that month by the individual firm, rather than on the basis of a standard output per roller. Only half of Firm V's rollers were operating throughout the month.

[2] Peter Kilby, *African Enterprise: The Nigerian Bread Industry*, Stanford 1965, chapter 5.

[3] Wells and Warmington, *op. cit.* p. 34.

CHAPTER 8

EDUCATION AND SKILL FORMATION

Just as economic development is accompanied by a transformation in the structure and nature of the economy, so too must the character of the labour force change if economic growth is to be sustained. The most fundamental of these alterations are changes in the occupational distribution and a substantial improvement in the skill endowment and quality of the work force. While the first is more or less automatically brought about by market forces, except perhaps in under-populated countries or in cases where there are unusually severe institutional impediments to labour mobility, the second depends upon the development of appropriate educational arrangements.

This chapter reviews the efforts of Nigeria to develop these educational arrangements. Section I outlines the over-all structure of the educational system and appraises the major features of its performance; section II describes the institutions which provide technical education and training in both the public and private sectors. Within the context of this institutional framework the following subjects are examined: difficult decisions as to the exact functions of a system of technical education, administrative problems of organizing all the necessary inputs for its efficient operation, awkward adjustments of supply to demand, and the pitfalls in the hazardous business of assessing long-term skill requirements.

I

THE OVERALL EDUCATIONAL STRUCTURE

The basic educational structure of Nigeria is seen in table 64. Primary education represents a course of eight years in Lagos, six years in the west, six years in the east (seven years prior to 1962) and seven years in the north. The age of entry is five or six years. After a very rapid expansion during the 1950s, primary school enrolment (1m. in 1951) has been held at the 3m. mark since 1960.

At the secondary level government and missionary-operated grammar schools pursue an academic course of five to six years; their purpose is to prepare students for the sixth form (two years) and thence for the university. In the final year of grammar school (fifth form) students take the West African School Certificate (WASC) examination (coordinated with the University of Cambridge), which is the equivalent of the University of London's General Certificate of Education, Ordinary Level, which is taken by candidates not currently enrolled in a recognized institution, i.e. those who have previously failed the WASC and correspondence students. Sixth formers take the Cambridge Higher School Certificate, and non-enrolled candidates take the London General Certificate of Education, Advanced Level. Commercial schools, which are all private and generally of a lower standard,

Table 64. *The Nigerian educational system*

	1957	1960	1965
Population	34,000,000	35,100,000	38,600,000
Primary school	2,498,491	2,912,619	2,911,742
Secondary school	96,218	167,953	225,134
Grammar	67,250	55,235	132,973
Commercial		3,874	9,964
Modern		75,899	47,130
Teacher training	23,186	27,908	26,260
Craft schools	2,831	1,247	3,167
Trade centres	1,596	1,679	2,623
Technical institutes	1,355	2,111	3,017[a]
Higher education	4,661	6,558	16,497
Sixth form	206	899	5,097
Universities, home and abroad	4,455[b]	5,659[b]	11,400[c]

[a] 1963 enrolment.

[b] Includes Nigerian College of Arts, Science and Technology; enrolment abroad estimated at 3,000.

[c] Estimated from number of 1965 and 1966 graduates, as reported in Federal Ministry of Education, *National Register of Students, 1966* (Lagos).

SOURCES: Federal Education Dept., *Digest of Statistics*, 1957; Federal Ministry of Education, *Statistics of Education in Nigeria*, 1963 (Lagos); data for 1965 supplied by the Federal Ministry of Education.

offer courses in bookkeeping and accounting, secretarial skills and commerce; students graduate after five years and take one of the Royal Society of Arts examinations. Secondary modern schools, which are both public and private, were initiated in 1955 to provide a three-year terminal general education with a semi-vocational bias for primary school graduates who could not enter a grammar school.

As is generally the case in tropical Africa, the primary school base is out of all proportion to the secondary and tertiary levels of the pyramid: enrolment in secondary schools in 1965 is only 8 % of that in primary, while the corresponding figure for higher education is 0·5 % (or 7 %

of secondary enrolment).[1] While the aggregate secondary enrolment has grown at an encouragingly brisk pace, technical education (craft schools, trade centres, technical institutes) has grown only moderately. Higher education, on the other hand, has grown very rapidly.

More meaningful than the national aggregates are the regional breakdowns. Since we are primarily interested in the wage-earning population, the relevant educational statistics are those pertaining to males.[2] Table 65 shows the respective proportions of school enrolment for the primary and secondary school age groups in the three regions (mid-west is included with the west) and Lagos.

Table 65. *Educational enrolment ratios, 1960 and 1965*

		Lagos (%)	West (%)	East (%)	North (%)
Males age 6–14 enrolled in Primary School	1960	90	86	77	11
	1965	100	73	71	17
Males age 13–18 enrolled in Secondary School	1960	24	17	5	1
	1965	43	13	7	1

SOURCES: Federal Ministry of Education, *Digest of Educational Statistics, 1960*; 1965 figures supplied by the Federal Ministry of Education; *Census of Nigeria, 1952–3*.

At the primary school level there is a sharp contrast between the south, where universal primary education programmes launched in the mid-1950s have succeeded in enrolling the bulk of school-aged children, and the Muslim north where large-scale government educational endeavour has only begun in the last decade and where the establishment of Christian mission schools – still the foundation of the primary

[1] Nigeria's position relative to other African countries can be seen from the following comparison of educational enrolment ratios:

Per cent of relevant age group of population in school

	Primary (%)	Secondary (%)	Tertiary (%)
Gabon	90·2	6·6	—
Ghana	75·7	27·7*	0·3
Liberia	37·3	5·2	0·3
Niger	9·8	0·5	—
Nigeria	40·4	4·8	0·1
Togo	56·9	3·3	—
Kenya	63·7	5·5	0·6
Tanganyika	27·3	2·2	—
Egypt	71·4	20·1	5·4
Algeria	56·2	4·1	0·3

* Of which 86 % is enrolled in Secondary modern schools.

SOURCE: *Report of the Director-General*, ILO Second African Regional Conference, Geneva 1964, p. 36.

[2] Females constitute less than 10 % of the enumerated wage-earning labour force. On the other hand, many girls do work in the unorganized sector. It should also be remembered that the population figures are tentative, and that there is a high dropout rate.

educational system in the south – has been proscribed. At the secondary school level the south is far less advanced, although still many years ahead of the north. It is primarily from this, the secondary level, that Nigeria must recruit her skilled labour and potential technicians.

It is worth pausing to consider the social and economic repercussions of a situation where the combined enrolment of secondary and tertiary levels is less than one-tenth that of the primary level. On the positive side, primary education serves important functions in communicating new ideas and widening intellectual horizons, in breaking down prejudices and, generally, in promoting the transformation of traditional society. Equally, primary education provides the basis for further training and the acquisition of specific skills. But when enrolment in primary schools expands very rapidly in a short period of time, as has been the case in most of Africa during the 1950s, a number of problems emerge. First, there is a sharp rise in primary school leavers not matched by a proportionate increase in secondary education; as a result large numbers of vocationally unequipped persons, no longer satisfied with their rural condition after their glimpse of the attractions of modern life during their schooling, enter the already saturated urban employment market. Government wage policy, a disproportionate share of the tax burden on the agricultural sector and the urban bias of economic development programmes co-operates with universal primary education to produce rural exodus and urban unemployment, one of the major socio-political problems facing virtually every newly independent African country.

The over-expansion of primary education also reacts upon the educational system itself. The quality of education at all levels is adversely affected: the rapid primary school expansion is purchased at the price of scholastic dilution, the effects of which necessarily carry forward to the higher levels of education and, through its impact on teacher training, to future educational standards. The quantity of post-primary educations is also curtailed to the extent that the resources which could have been devoted to this have been absorbed instead in primary education. In sum, a level of primary school output which exceeds the combined absorptive capacity of the modern sector and the educational system creates serious problems for further healthy development. That these problems have not proved more serious for Nigeria is largely attributable to imperfections in the university graduate labour market, discussed subsequently.

This brings us to an examination of the qualitative performance, or some notion of efficiency performance, of the Nigerian educational system. The true measure of performance would be the success of the system in promoting the country's social and economic growth. As a far more limited but quantifiable measure, we can examine such internal norms as student wastage, examination passes and teacher qualifications which give some indications of the system's 'academic efficiency'.

Table 66 summarizes available statistics on student wastage during recent years. Reasons for the very high drop-out during primary school are the financial costs to the parents in books, fees and uniform of £7 to £10 per year and the inefficacy of a primary education (especially if obtained from a poor school) in enhancing a person's employment opportunities.[1]

Table 66. *Primary and secondary school student wastage rates*

	Wastage (%)
Eastern Region	
Primary – Generation 1954-60	66
Western Region	
Primary – Generation 1959–64	52·5
Generation 1960–5	55·4
Grammar – Generation 1960–4	30
Generation 1961–5	24·4
Modern – Generation 1960–4	10·3
Western Region	
Grammar – All classes, 1962	15·9
All classes, 1965	10·3
Modern – All classes, 1961	3·2
All classes, 1964	25·8

SOURCES: Western Region Ministry of Education, ILO Educational Adviser; P. N. C. Okigbo, *Nigerian Public Finance*, Evanston, 1965, p. 177.

Even among those who remain in school to finish their course, the toll taken by final examinations is severe. In 1963 only 63 % of the candidates passed their primary school leaving exam; 44 % of the candidates in the secondary modern schools were successful.[2] In both cases exam standards were considerably lower than they had been prior to 1958, the year when the impact of universal primary education was first manifested in final year students. In teacher training colleges, the pass rate averages about 40 %.[3] For commercial, academic and technical secondary schools final examinations are external; in these cases there has been no diminution of standards.

Approximately 60 % of final year grammar school students pass their WASC; this represents about 40 to 45 % of the number who

[1] Field survey findings of ILO Education Adviser to the Western Nigeria Ministry of Education, 1965. It was precisely the fact that primary education was a guarantee to employment in the late 1940s and early 1950s that led to the massive popular pressure for the primary school expansion. See International Bank for Reconstruction and Development, *The Economic Development of Nigeria*, p. 367.

[2] Federal Ministry of Education, *Statistics of Education in Nigeria* 1963, table 22.

[3] *Ibid.*

started. The pass rate is drastically lower for sixth formers, a situation which has worsened with rapid expansion in enrolment: a larger absolute number passed four subjects in 1959 when enrolment was 716 than in 1965 when enrolment was five times as great.[1] The situation is somewhat improved by virtue of the GCE exams which provide a

Table 67. *External examination results*

	Candidates				Percentage passes			
	1957	1959	1963	1965	1957	1959	1963	1965
WASC	3,563	5,127	10,766	12,888	72	51	62	71
GCE (O+A)	6,348	6,096	22,244	...	15	21	...	...
HSC	...	310	1,223	1,874	{ 4 sj:	21	1	1
					{ 3 sj:	49	35	30
RSA	747	938	1,388	...	10	7	12	
C. & G.: Intermed	...	509	1,183	...	...	30	44	...
Advanced	...	43	162	...	...	19	30	...
Univ. of London (external)	264	396	454	...	24	17	17	...

SOURCES: Federal Education Department, *Digest of Statistics*, 1957, 1959 and 1960; Federal Ministry of Education, *Statistics of Education in Nigeria*, 1963; 1965 figures supplied by Federal Ministry of Education; City and Guilds figures supplies by Norman Schmidt, ILO.

second and third chance to convert failures into passes. The number of candidates and percentage passes for commercial school, technical training and external (correspondence) students of the University of London speak for themselves. In all of these cases the exam can be taken more than once.

The most important reason for the low quality of much of Nigeria's education and indirectly contributing to the high wastage factor is the quality of the teaching. The situation described by the Ashby, Banjo and Dike Commissions in 1960 and 1961 was decidedly unencouraging.[2] Few teachers had been instructed in the art of teaching. Far worse, many lacked the basic factual knowledge: 'Sometimes the teacher

[1] In 1963 sixth form enrolment was 3,621; in 1965 it was 4,140. To pass the HSC exam, candidates must pass a General Paper and obtain a minimum of five 'points' in single subject exams, with Principal subjects counting as two points and Subsidiary subjects as one. Assuming that of those candidates who pass four subjects equal numbers pass no, one, two, three and four Principle subjects, 80 % will pass the exam; only those passing no Principal subjects will fail the exam. Similarly, assuming random distribution of Principal and Subsidiary passes among those candidates who pass three single subjects, 50 % will pass the exam. Applying these ratios to the figures given in table 67, we may estimate that the portions of total candidates who passed the HSC examination in 1959, 1960, 1963 and 1965 were 43, 35, 18 and 16 %, respectively.

[2] E. Ashby *et al.*, *Investment in Education: The Report of the Commission on Post-School Certificate and Higher Education in Nigeria*, Federal Ministry of Education, Lagos 1960; S. A. Banjo *et al.*, *Report of the Commission Appointed to Review the Educational System of Western Nigeria, 1961*, Government Printer, Ibadan 1962; K. O. Dike *et al.*, *Report on the Review of the Educational System in Eastern Nigeria*, Government Printer, Enugu 1962.

makes his first acquaintance with the subject matter just when he is preparing the lesson: and without clearly understanding it he goes to teach it.'[1] In primary school the amount and quality of learning that can be achieved under these conditions is further diminished by the shift from the native tongue to English after the third year, the student being taught in a foreign language by a teacher who himself is only semi-literate in the second medium.[2]

Table 68. *Teachers, by qualifications*

	Number				Per cent qualified			
	1957	1960	1963	1965	1957	1960	1963	1965
Primary schools	86,960	98,960	94,176	87,074	21	31	63	71[a]
Grammar schools		3,098	5,281	7,320		48	66[b]	68[b]
Commercial schools	3,535	239	431	541	34	16	46[b]	47[b]
Modern		3,558	5,193	2,158[c]		3	5[b]	5[b, c]
Teacher training	1,760	1,657	1,978	1,713[c]	21	47	42	61[c]

[a] Estimated.

[b] Teacher training Grades I and II, grouped in the same category in the source, were divided on the basis of 1960 ratios of Grade I: Grade II.

[c] Mid-West excluded.

Qualified teachers were defined as follows:

Primary school: Teacher Training Grades I, II and III; WASC and equivalent; Secondary Modern School Certificate.

Secondary Grammar, Commercial and Modern Schools: Graduate teachers; NCE, ULIE and equivalent; Teacher Training Grade I; HSC and equivalent.

Teacher training colleges: Graduate teachers; NCE, ULIE and equivalent.

SOURCES: Federal Education Dept., *Digest of Statistics*, 1957 and 1960; Federal Ministry of Education, *Statistics of Education in Nigeria*, 1963; 1965 figures supplied by Federal Ministry of Education.

However the situation has quite unexpectedly improved as evidenced by maintained standards in the face of very large increases in enrolment (tables 64 and 67) and a higher ratio of qualified to unqualified teachers. This latter improvement in the teaching qualifications is shown in table 68 where 'qualified' is generously defined as

[1] S. A. Banjo *et al.*, *op. cit.* p. 47.

[2] *Ibid.* p. 8. A useful perspective on the Nigerian situation is provided by contemporary reports on American school instruction during the 1820s and 1830s. 'President Duer', on the New York state school system in 1837, found the 'teachers inexperienced and transitory, snatched up for the occasion . . . paid by salaries which hardly exceed the wages of a menial servant; and as a necessary consequence, ignorant and disqualified.' James Carter in 1826 reported that 'The country schools are everywhere degraded. . . . It is thought a mean thing for a man of competent estate, or for any but the mechanic, artisan or the labourer, to send their children to them for their education. . . . The teachers of the primary schools have rarely had any education beyond what they have acquired in the very schools where they begin to teach.' Stanley Lebergott, 'Labor Force and Employment, 1800–1960', in D. S. Brady *et al.*, *Output, Employment, and Productivity in the United States after 1800*, National Bureau of Economic Research, New York 1966, p. 125.

having any schooling beyond the level at which the individual is teaching (e.g. an unqualified primary school teacher is himself only a primary school graduate).

The improvement in teacher qualifications has been greatest at the primary level, rising from 21 to 71 % from 1957 to 1965 – thus more than recovering the ground lost during the earlier student enrolment expansion. While teaching qualifications in secondary modern schools have remained at a very low level, there has been great improvement in commercial schools and teacher training colleges. Most spectacular has been the rise in qualified teachers in grammar schools from 48 % to 66 % from 1960 to 1965 occurring simultaneously with a 70 % expansion in the number of teachers. The chief factor responsible for this outcome – an outcome which suggests that Nigeria's most severe skilled manpower shortage will soon lie behind her – has been the recruitment of 2,000 university graduates as grammar school teachers (including about 500 Peace Corp Volunteers). This 'windfall' of talent to the educational system has occurred because rigid salary scales in the civil service, public corporations and expatriate firms precluded the employment of large numbers of university graduates in these sectors.

It would seem that there has been an unanticipated re-allocation of high-level manpower away from current production to the educational system as investment in future productive capacity. While this particular short-term outcome may represent something of an optimal choice with respect to the economy's growth, wage and salary rigidity in the long run can only lead to the inefficient deployment of skilled manpower, to slowed economic growth and to distorted income distribution with resultant political tensions.

Finally mention should be made of the quantity of resources devoted to education. Statistics are available for public expenditures over the period 1950–61. Recurrent and capital expenditures by Federal and Regional Governments rose from £3·4m. in 1950 to £28·1m. in 1961, ranging from 22·5 to 13·3 % of all government expenditures for individual years.[1] It is impossible to determine with any reliability whether or not such magnitudes of expenditures on education represent an efficient allocation of investment resources in the absence of a measure of the marginal social product of this and alternative investment opportunities. While one can only conjecture that there may have been over-investment in formal education as a whole, it is clear that relative under-investment in grammar schools has had the effect of creating negative or zero marginal products for investment at the primary level and, as we shall see subsequently, for technical education since 1963.

[1] G. K. Helleiner, *Peasant Agriculture*, table V-E-7.

II

TECHNICAL EDUCATION

The conscious planning of a system of technical education in Nigeria dates from 1946 when it was given a major place in the Ten-Year Plan for Development and Welfare. During the previous half century the colonial government's attitude was that the provision of technical education for Nigerians (beyond very limited artisan training for government departments) was neither necessary nor feasible. Even as late as 1942 education officials were unable to recommend the establishment of a single training institution.

> It is doubtful whether a big trade school or a technical college is necessary at the present stage. Such a school would be extremely expensive to build and equip, require a large European and African staff and there would be no great demand for its products when trained.[1]

Thus it was decided that the need for technical education for the next decade would be served by an expenditure of £73,600 for the training of handicraft instructors.[2] Moreover, prior to 1945 there were only three schools in the entire country whose curricula included a science course.[3]

The Commission on Higher Education in West Africa of 1945 marks the beginning of constructive policy. Dealing only with higher education, it recommended that the Higher College at Yaba be converted into a technical institute to produce the technicians that the country's economic development and eventual political independence would require. It also stressed that provision should be made for the systematic training of skilled labour at the lower levels.

The following year these proposals were implemented in the Ten-Year Plan for Development and Welfare. The latter called for a tripartite scheme of Handicraft Centres, Trade Centres and Technical Institutes with the respective functions of prevocational training in the manual arts, the training of skilled craftsmen and the training of technicians. A Colonial Development and Welfare grant of £401,000 was extended to pay for the first five years of the programme.

One of the chief motives in launching the handicraft scheme was to help break down the colonial prejudice toward working with one's hands, to instil in every boy as part of his general education a respect for manual skills and technical achievement. At their inception it was also intended that the Handicraft Centres would help 'to develop a

[1] *Ten Year Educational Plan*, Lagos 1944, p. 18. [2] *Ibid.* p. 19.
[3] *Report of the Commission on Higher Education in West Africa*, p. 33.

critical sense of quality' as a prerequisite for raising the very low standards of craftsmanship then prevalent.[1] Scattered throughout the Federation these Centres have provided thousands of primary school children with training in woodworking and metalworking and to a lesser degree in such traditional crafts as weaving, leather-working and smithing.

In 1962 the Northern Nigerian Government transformed its craft schools from adjuncts of the primary school system into three-year post-primary 'pre-vocational' schools, similar to the secondary modern school in the west and Lagos. In 1964 the Eastern Nigerian Government expanded the number of its craft schools and changed them into three-year post-primary 'Technical schools'. In late 1965 all these developments were coordinated in a common three-year syllabus, which in the third year provides for two streams: one with an academic bias for those suited to enter grammar school and one with a technical bias for employment as an artisan or entry into a Trade Centre.[2]

The Trade Centres, of which four were to be constructed in the first place, had as their purpose the training of high-grade craftsmen under ideal conditions. It was hoped that these master craftsmen, strategically placed in government and industry, would exert a potent upward pressure on the general level of skilled labour performance.[3] Although there has been heated dispute over the years as to the proper function of these Trade Centres, their basic pattern has altered but little. Candidates, in most instances, are chosen from primary school graduates; a three-year residential course is followed by two years of apprenticeship with the employer, after which time the candidate sits for the London City and Guilds Intermediate examination.

The functions of the Technical Institutes were more varied. They included the provision of theoretical training for Trade Centre students (an arrangement subsequently dropped), sandwich courses and night classes for artisans employed in industry, and the full-time training of candidates for the British Ordinary National Certificate. The latter consists of two years of post-secondary course work and one year of on-the-job training. Owing to the lack of interested secondary-school graduates with a science background, a junior technical course was inaugurated. This consists of a five-year secondary course with a technical bias (woodworking, printing, drafting, commerce or engineering principles) which leads to the West African School Certificate.

Although only two Trade Centres and one Technical Institute had

[1] *Memorandum on Educational Policy in Nigeria*, Lagos 1947, p. 48.

[2] Skapski *et al.*, *Report of the Comparative Technical Education Seminar Abroad*, mimeograph, Lagos, June 1966, p. 7.

[3] *Memorandum on Educational Policy in Nigeria*, p. 50.

produced any graduates ten years after the programme had been launched (1955), by 1965 there were ten Trade Centres and five Technical Institutes (renamed Technical Colleges in 1964) in operation.[1]

Table 69. *Enrolment in Government Trade Centres*[a]

	1957	1960	1963	1965[b]
Motor vehicle electricians	—	—	—	58
Electrical installation	—	—	—	310
Fitter/machinists	156	162	346	310
Blacksmiths and welders	114	91	150	111
Sheetmetal workers	134	108	110	90
Plumbers	33	70	71	73
Instrument mechanics	21	14	36	—
Electricians	74	135	332	293
Auto/diesel mechanics	240	229	340	353
Cabinet makers	161	133	173	234
Carpenters and joiners	162	132	230	261
Wood machinists	109	40	33	15
Motor body builders	19	57	66	55
Bricklayers/masons	110	151	170	140
Shipwrights	12	22	—	—
Painters and decorators	114	120	100	112
Leather workers	12	24	—	—
Radio/telecommunications	—	—	185	192
Others	—	—	90[d]	417[c]
Total	1,471	1,466	2,432	3,024

Enrolment in Technical Institutes and Colleges

	1957	1960	1963	1965
Junior				
Technical, Commercial and WASC/GCE	337	431	716	883
Part-time	—	—	907	270
Total	337	431	1,623	895
Senior				
Mechanical engineering	—	50	107	128
Electrical engineering	—	53	107	142
Civil Engineering	—	—	121	181
Building and architecture	—	—	82	63
Quantity surveying	—	—	13	—
Town planning	—	—	14	17
Commercial	283	14	153	145
Art	—	—	28	27
Telecommunications	—	—	33	64
Laboratory technicians	—	—	24	—
Printing	—	—	29	199
Others	—	176[g]	113[f]	131[e]
Part-time	662	1,025	540	713
Total	945	1,749	3,017	2,106

Footnotes for table 69 are on p. 245.

[1] The Trade Centres are located in Yaba, Enugu, Sapele, Ijebu-Ode, Oshogbo, Owo, Oyo, Ilorin, Bukuru and Kano. The Technical Institutes are located in Yaba, Enugu, Ibadan, Kaduna and Auchi.

In addition to the system of technical education sponsored by the government, the major employers of technical labour have operated their own schemes to train artisans and craftsmen. These employers include government departments, public corporations, foreign firms and small-scale Nigerian employers.

Government departmental training schemes were initiated as follows: Land and Surveys 1908, Marine (later Ports Authority) 1928, Public Works 1931, Post and Telegraph 1931, Railways 1942; the combined output of these schemes up to 1945 was about 300 artisans and craftsmen.[1] Messrs. Caunce and Cottier reported enrolment in regulated apprentice schemes in 1961 as follows: Railway Corporation, 750 in twenty-five trades; Electricity Corporation 80; the Ports Authority, 300 in seventeen trades; Federal Ministry of Works and Surveys, 60 in seven trades.[2] Only the Ministry of Post and Telegraph carries on training at the technician level (in tele-communications); all other departments sponsor students in the Technical Institutes to meet their requirements at this level.

The first recorded apprentice training by an expatriate company was that of John Holt's in the early 1930s; in 1939 a formal school, with places for twelve, was established in Warri for selected company employees.[3] However the major development for firm-sponsored technical education dates from the opening of the United Africa Company's first training school at Burutu in 1954; by 1959 the Company had five schools in operation with a total enrolment in excess of 500.[4] Of total

[a] Excluded from the table are 2,596 women enrolled in 1963 in House-keeper/Matron, Needlework and Embroidery, Secretarial Course and Copy Typist; and 3,936 women enrolled in 1965 in House Craft, House-keeper/Matron, Needlework and Embroidery, Secretarial Course, Business Studies and Trade School Course.

[b] Mid-West not included.

[c] 54 agricultural machinists, 45 in business studies, 20 in pre-foreman course, 24 booster refrigerator and maintenance fitters, 26 in special course (trade and technology), 240 in general course (mechanical and electric), 8 installation machinists.

[d] 72 in draughtsmanship in the East and 18 in agricultural mechanics in the West.

[e] 112 Mechanical/Electrical, 19 Technical Assistants.

[f] 39 Assistant Technical Officers, 8 Technical Assistants and 66 Engineering Assistants, all in the North, no doubt at the Technical Institute at Kaduna.

[g] 143 Technical Officers, Technical Assistants and Engineering Assistants of the Public Works Department at the Technical Institute at Kaduna plus 33 enrolled in a five-year course in Engineering Institutions at the Technical Institute at Yaba.

SOURCE: Federal Ministry of Education, *Statistics of Education in Nigeria*, various years, and information supplied by the Ministry.

[1] *Report of the Commission on Higher Education in West Africa*, H.M.S.O., London 1945, appendix V.

[2] F. Caunce and W. L. Cottier, *Report on the Development of Technical and Commercial Education 1961–76*, U.K. Technical Assistance Programme, mimeograph, 1961.

[3] Department of Labour, *Quarterly Review*, September 1944.

[4] United Africa Company, *Statistical and Economic Review* (London), No. 22, January 1959, p. 24.

enrolment, five-year apprentices accounted for 358 in seven trades, two-year artisan trainees for 124 in six trades and various employees in five 'booster' evening courses for 194. In 1958 the Shell-B.P. Petroleum Development Company established a trade school at Port Harcourt with places for 130 apprentices in five trades. In 1959 the Swiss firm, Union Trading Company, opened a school for thirty motor mechanic apprentices at Enugu. The expatriate firms, like the goverment departments, have sponsored their employees or students at the Technical Institutes to meet their technician needs.

The last source of technical training is the apprentice system of the indigenous enterprise sector. If the proprietors of indigenous business firms are excluded, apprentices and 'learners' comprise well over half the labour force of this sector.[1] Although partially a manifestation of underemployment, these arrangements are capable of imparting modest artisan skills and have done so on a vast scale. The limitations of the indigenous apprenticeship system – with its resultant inability to produce skills capable of innovation that would facilitate the active expansion of the small-scale industry sector – was well stated by the 1966 Comparative Technical Education Seminar:

> [Apprentices] never learn from their 'masters' anything more than practical manual operations. More often than not these operations are, in fact, incapable of high productivity and often are carried out with inappropriate tools or with unsuitable methods. The apprentices are thus conditioned to stick to the old ways. Without knowledge of the technological principles which underlie their respective trades, even the most able of the artisans cannot introduce innovations which might improve the quality and quantity of their product. What is more, having neglible general education, which seldom exceeds a few years of primary school, or no education at all, they have little possibility of improving themselves through reading.[2]

III

THE CONTENT OF TECHNICAL EDUCATION

There has been much debate over the years as to what the exact form and content of Nigerian technical education ought to be: particular

[1] Peter Kilby, *The Development of Small Industry in Eastern Nigeria*, p. 11; Federal Office of Statistics, *Lagos Pilot Survey of Small-Scale Industry*, Lagos, 1966, p. 2.

The age of entering apprentices ranges from 12 to 20 years. The majority have had several years of primary schooling, but are not fully literate. Relatives tend to start at an earlier age and serve a longer term. For non-relatives, apprenticeship lasts from three to five years and requires a premium or learning fee varying from £5 to £15, depending upon the trade and the length of the agreed term – the shorter the term the higher the fee. A modest apprentice remuneration – pocket allowance, subsistence or use of facilities for after-hour jobs – occurs in most cases.

[2] Skapski *et al.*, *op. cit.* p. 58.

skill levels to be aimed at, course curricula and examination standards. Regarding general education, on the other hand, participants and outside observers alike have agreed upon the need to introduce practical subjects into the primary school syllabus and more of the physical and social sciences into secondary school courses. This reform of traditional academic curricula, which had already begun as of the late 1950s, has been recommended not only to provide a viable base upon which technical education can build but, more fundamentally, as a means for making the individual's education more relevant to the contemporary Nigerian environment and its problems. In what follows we shall concentrate on technical education, treating the reform of general education as a settled issue.

To begin we must define the four basic skill levels which constitute the traditional occupational hierarchy of technical labour - artisan, craftsman, technician and technologist. The *artisan* possesses specific practical skills developed on the job, usually by working with craftsmen; he lacks any theoretical knowledge and requires close supervision. The *craftsman*, who is capable of independent work, possesses manual skills, can interpret technical drawings and perform all the calculations relating to his trade; he also has sufficient knowledge of elementary science to understand the materials and processes with which he works. With an entry requirement of six to eight years of schooling, training consists of a regulated five-year apprenticeship combining formal instruction and supervised on-the-job training. The *technician* combines a sub-professional knowledge of applied theory with the practical qualifications of the craftsman; he carries out the technologist's plans and exercises supervisory responsibility. With an entry requirement of secondary education (WASC or GCE, O), training consists of two years of formal instruction in theoretical and practical subjects. The *technologist* is a professional engineer or applied scientist who is responsible for the application of scientific knowledge and method to industry; the minimum qualification is a bachelor's degree.

We have already described the philosophy which lay behind the Trade Centres – forming master craftsmen to be strategically placed in government and industry and, through their impact on the artisans attached to them, to exert an upward pressure on the general level of skilled labour performance. It was just this master craftsman concept which the World Bank Mission of 1953 questioned:

> The Mission regards the trade centre programme in its present form as unsound. It believes that the objective of producing a highly skilled artisan of limited theoretical knowledge and without organizational skills is too limited to be of significant practical benefit in meeting Nigeria's problems of trained manpower for industry. The programme of apprenticeship under

trade centre instructors consumes much time and fails to give students the vigorous and exacting experience they would get in on-the-job training in an industrial or commercial firm. The numbers trained are too few to make a significant contribution to the serious shortage of skilled artisans. The fact that students even after five years of training do not have the basic knowledge required eventually to become foremen, a pressing need of industry, constitutes a major weakness.[1]

In the place of the master craftsmen, the Mission recommended that the Trade Centres 'produce people soundly trained in technical skills who can act as foremen and can discharge supervisory responsibilities'.[2] To this end the Mission recommended that the training programme be reorganized, starting with two years of general instruction in English, mathematics and the social sciences, followed by three years of specialized training on a six-monthly rotation between residential instruction and on-the-job training. As for the problem of craftsmen, this was to be left to in-service training by the employers themselves.

A Federal Advisory Committee was formed in December 1955 to review the International Bank's proposals and to suggest measures for implementation. Although the Committee agreed with the Bank on a number of minor points, the latter's basic position was rejected.

We are unanimous in our belief that training in supervisory techniques should not be introduced until after the period of apprenticeship has been completed and should be given only to those who, subsequent to the ending of their apprenticeship training, show that in addition to having attained a high standard of skill, they possess the requisite personal qualities.[3]

To deal with supervisory training the Committee recommended that a separate series of short courses should be organized and attached to the Technical Institute. This was subsequently carried out. For training skilled workers who require a less rounded background than the full craftsman, the Advisory Committee recommended that 'artisans' should undergo a year of instruction and then a two-year period of training within industry; this recommendation was never implemented. In 1959 A. P. Straker, a British consultant, was commissioned by the Federal Ministry of Education to make a survey of technical manpower requirements. Mr. Straker reported that large public and private employers were increasingly producing their own craftsmen.

Even in the most favourable conditions, it must be difficult for Government Trade Centres to produce craftsmen of the standard to be expected from training in industrial surroundings. Nor are Trade Centres as attractive as

[1] International Bank for Reconstruction and Development, *The Economic Development of Nigeria*, Federal Government Printer, Lagos 1954, p. 379. [2] *Ibid.* p. 378.

[3] *Report of the Federal Advisory Committee on Technical Education and Industrial Training*, Federal Government Printer, Lagos 1959, p. 9.

those provided by the best of the private schemes, because of the more certain future provided by the latter.[1]

Mr. Straker concluded that Trade Centre graduates were destined to join the smaller firms engaged primarily in maintenance work; accordingly he recommended '. . . that the whole conception of the Government Trade Centres should be revised, on the lines of two year basic courses, consisting mainly of practical work, theory being reduced to a minimum'.[2]

Regarding the need for technicians Mr. Straker found that most of the technical work being done in Nigeria was concerned with machine maintenance.

Such industrial processes as exist require for their performance only semi-skilled, or unskilled, labour, using plant designed abroad. In such circumstances only a few professional engineers are required, whose duties consist mainly of management and control. Under present conditions in Nigeria, these professionally qualified managers require under them good general foremen, not the technicians required in a true manufacturing industry. The real need is for better craftsmen and better foremen, drawn from the ranks of the craftsmen. Only in certain cases is there any need for these foremen to be also technicians.[3]

The well-known Ashby Commission of 1960 took a very different view of the need for technicians, although the empirical underpinnings of their estimates (reaching 2,500 new technicians per annum) were considerably more impressionistic than those of Mr. Straker's four month field survey.[4] However it has been the spirit of the Ashby Commission

[1] A. P. Straker, *Survey of Technical Manpower Requirements*, mimeograph, August 1959, pp. 25–6.

[2] *Ibid.* p. 27.

[3] *Ibid.* p. 25. 'We have found objections to using the Technical Institutes as a means of producing supervisors on the grounds that boys from that source feel that they should be managers at the end of their course. It was said that many boys do not understand that book learning is not enough. . . . Such technical training is perhaps essential for supervision in certain highly technical fields, but it is not necessary for supervision of the general run of work being performed in Nigeria. A great deal more needs to be done to train intelligent shop floor workmen whom it is intended to promote, and existing foremen, on day-release courses, either within their own organizations or at Technical Institutes, in the principles and practice of supervision. . .. We have found amongst employers more interest in this project than in the idea of increased facilities for the education of technicians' (p. 34).

[4] 'Every employer of technical and scientific manpower who has given evidence to the Commission has complained in forceful terms of the dearth of Nigerian technicians qualified to fill the middle grades of industrial employment, and of the inadequacy of the facilities for training them. A serious consequence of this, we are informed, is that in many cases professional engineers are being uneconomically employed upon duties which could be adequately performed by well qualified technicians. We are convinced that Nigeria's most urgent task in the field of technical education is to remedy this dangerous defect.

'We are unable to estimate with any certainty the desirable rate of flow of technicians of various kinds, but it is the general experience in other parts of the world that, although the

Report that has guided the current and prospective expansion of Technical Institutes.

In 1962 Adam Skapski and Michael Goldway shared many of the same observations and reached similar conclusions in reports submitted to the western and eastern regional governments respectively.[1] They were both of the opinion that training in a significant number of the crafts was more extensive than that required by employers. Dr. Skapski's solution was to reduce the length of the course to two years, while Mr. Goldway proposed that the number of trades taught should be reduced, which would then free the Trade Centre 'to provide advanced training for carefully selected workers to prepare them for higher grades or supervisory functions'.[2] Mr. Goldway made the more general argument that apprenticeship training was becoming outmoded owing to the bias of modern automation technology; the latter places a premium on the single-skilled operative and the technician, while diminishing the need for craftsmen and general labour.[3]

Both reports noted that the Technical Institutes had great difficulty attracting full-time students, and that those who were enrolled had not done so with the intention of training to be a technician. Dr. Skapski described the situation at the Ibadan Technical College in 1961:

> Over 600 applications were received, and about 350 applicants who were considered qualified were invited for the entrance tests. Of these 184 appeared at the testing date, and 72 were eventually selected. But when the courses opened, only 45 students actually came. [And later:] Most of the students

proportion varies as between different industries, at least five or six technicians are, on the average, required for every professional engineer or technologist. We see no reason why this ratio should not be valid for Nigeria, and as Harbison has estimated that professional engineers or technologists should be produced at the rate of some 500 per annum, we suggest that plans should be made for the development of a pattern of courses gradually building up to a production of about 2,500 technicians per annum.

'We are aware that there are those in Nigeria who will maintain that this is an overestimate – that there will not be occupations for this number of technicians trained to the level implied by the above definition. We believe that this view cannot be justified except by looking only to the short-term needs. We are obliged by our terms of reference to look further ahead, and we entertain no doubt that the industrial development of Nigeria will demand a progressive expansion of the facilities for the training of technicians to a capacity no less than that which we have suggested.' Sir Eric Ashby *et al.*, *Investment in Education: The Report of the Commission on Post-School Certificate and Higher Education in Nigeria*, London, 1960, pp. 95–6.

[1] Adam Skapski, *The Development of Technical Education and its Relation to the Educational System in Western Nigeria*, multilith, May 1962; Michael Goldway, *Report on Vocational Education in Eastern Nigeria*, Enugu, 1962.

[2] Skapski, *The Development of Technical Education*, p. 15.

[3] Both reports also note the inappropriateness to the tropics of a number of subjects that are required by the London City and Guilds syllabus, e.g. wallpapering and open hearth indoor fireplaces. However these anomalies were removed in 1963 when the London City and Guild Institution adapted its overseas examination standards in consultation with the Technical Education Committee of the West African Examinations Council.

who are enrolled have done so for lack of university tuition; they treat their technician studies as a step toward professional engineering.[1]

Nor was the Technical Institutes' situation in this regard appreciably changed by late 1965.[2] While Skapski proposed that technicians should be accepted as a 'dynamic group' (continually turning over membership) for the time being, Goldway pointed out the structural feature that the *de facto* entry requirements for Nigerian universities and Technical Institutes were the same, yet it takes at least one year longer to obtain full sub-professional qualification of the Higher National Diploma than it does to achieve graduate professional status. Goldway recommended that the entry requirements of the technician course be lowered by a year or more.

In his draft plan of 1964 the Federal Adviser on Technical Education, John W. Gailer, also recognized the technician defection problem and, like Skapski, recommended that no bars be placed in the student's way to transfer to the university.[3] For the Trade Centres, Gailer proposed a tripartite scheme of (*i*) an 18-month basic trade course proceeding to (*ii*) a senior trade course of at least one year's duration with graduates going into industry as prospective craftsmen and (*iii*) an advanced trade course leading to an instructor's qualification with candidates being chosen from the most promising craftsmen in industry.

With the exception of Gailer, all advisers have proposed a shortening of the traditional apprenticeship craftsman training and abandoning the London City and Guilds exam for the local Federal Ministry of Labour Trade Test. The employers, however, have continued to give preference to the more rigorous and comprehensive London examinations. The United Africa Company has stated its position as follows:

> But the successes which have been achieved in modifying and adapting the training of semi-skilled and skilled workers should not obscure the fact that as far as the higher technical skills are concerned, it is doubtful whether the period of apprenticeship can be shortened without a comparable drop in standards. It is certainly the view of the Company's own experts that five years is still the minimum length of time required to master the basic principles and practices of civil, mechanical or electrical engineering. The 1957 Inter African Conference on Education, while registering its approval of the useful social purpose fulfilled by accelerated training schemes and of the high standards achieved despite the limited period available, recommended that the longer courses should remain as the normal means of providing a fully balanced scheme of craft education and training.

[1] Skapski, *The Development of Technical Education*, pp. 60, 108.

[2] Skapski *et al.*, *Report of the Comparative Technical Education Seminar Abroad*, mimeograph, Lagos, June 1966, p. 44.

[3] J. W. Gailer, *A National Plan for the Development of Technical Education in the Federal Republic of Nigeria*, a draft, mimeograph, Lagos, August 1964.

Three further points may be made in this connection. First, unless high standards of proficiency are aimed at from the outset, human nature being what it is, the standards ultimately achieved are likely to be mediocre. Second, there is the important psychological consideration that trained persons do not like to feel that their level of attainment is inferior to that acquired in other countries – a mere 'second best'. Moreover, completion of a recognized apprenticeship of five years is usually a prerequisite for those wishing to proceed to higher technical qualifications. . . . Third, there is the point that the amount of supervision needed by fully-trained men is much less than that required where the level of skill is of a lower order.[1]

The Nigerian Employers Consultative Association ratified a similar statement of policy in 1961.[2] And even after 1962 when, as a result of intensifying competition, the United Africa Company and other large merchant firms were compelled to cut back on their costly training programmes (e.g. UAC closed down two of its five schools in 1962–3 and halved total enrolment), they continued to stand by the City and Guilds standards.[3] As to the bias of modern technology, study groups of the ILO have gone on record with the opinion that automation and other forms of technical progress have increased rather than diminished the importance of apprenticeship training.[4] E. H. Phelps Brown has appraised the traditional apprenticeship as follows:

It has been attacked, moreover, as inadequate to the needs of the day – as being spun out for longer than is needed to shape a workman by intensive training and as ill-suited to the trades where the learner must be instructed by intensive training in an advanced technology. It has become costly, and only the bigger firms can maintain it. But it has held its own, and in contemporary discussion of vocational training as a means to economic growth it appears to have gained acceptance as a major agency. This may be attributed to two considerations. First, it is a form of training on the job, in which the schoolroom is an actual workshop and the teacher a craftsman such as the pupil himself aspires to be; it is therefore likely to keep more closely up to date, provide more equipment, and above all motivate the pupil and keep his interest more surely than would courses in the classroom alone. Second, though apprenticeship is a cumbrous method of teaching particular operations, it provides the range of experience that alone will give the pupil the versatility that is the hallmark of the true craftsman. It is the aim of versatility, with the independence and initiative which make it possible, that

[1] United Africa Company, *Statistical and Economic Review*, no. 22, January 1959, pp. 46–7.

[2] Conference proceedings of the Nigerian Employers Consultative Association, November 1961, as reported in *Inter-African Labour Institute Bulletin*, November 1962.

[3] Interview with the Technical Training Advisor to the United Africa Company, London, February 1965.

[4] International Labour Office, *Problems of Apprenticeship, Vocational Training and Retraining in the Textile Industry*, Geneva 1963, p. 13; *Report of the Director-General*, Report I, Part I: *Automation and other Technological Developments*, Geneva 1957, p. 48.

marks off apprenticeship from the other forms of training on the job whose only aim is to practice in particular operations that will be carried out under supervision.[1]

Perhaps an even more vital consideration favouring the five-year apprenticeship is its contribution to the diffusion of technical knowledge, its percolation through the economy as a prerequisite for significant structural change. Whether it be after hours, by retirement or by job migration, a class of craftsmen gradually carry their technical knowledge and understanding of how it can be applied beyond the walls of the foreign-owned factory, to the indigenous enterprise sector, to household industry, to agriculture. No comparable transfer is possible where production processes are characterized by artisan skills and job dilution; in this case technical knowledge is not transmitted to any domestic factor of production. Thus, even in instances where the firms and government corporations find the use of artisan skills to be the efficient solution, if the applied technical knowledge involved has relevance for other sectors of the economy, the alternative employment of craftsmen may well be justified on the grounds of horizontal and intertemporal external economies.

While economists are now quite rightly sceptical about accepting an inefficient deployment of resources on the basis of alleged and immeasurable externalities, the most superficial observation of the progress of the indigenous economy reveals that the transfer and imitation of the production and organizational techniques of the foreign firms has constituted a major, if not the principal element in this process. And the carriers of this technical knowledge have been, virtually without exception, the trained employees of the foreign firms.[2] Devoting the same resources to a fuller and more comprehensive training of a limited group of craftsmen will create a far greater technology-carrying capacity than training a larger number of artisans who lack an integrated knowledge and command over the processes they are trained to perform.

The educational implication of the foregoing is to leave the government Trade Centre programme as it is. Given the fact that large numbers of Trade Centre students never sit for the City and Guilds[3] and that of those who do 55 to 75 % fail to pass (see table 67), the existing system is *de facto* already producing the artisans and sub-craftsmen called for in the proposed reforms. Indeed most of these trainees who

[1] E. H. Phelps Brown, *The Economics of Labor*, Studies in Comparative Economics, New Haven 1962, p. 67.

[2] The author discusses this subject in relation to indigenous manufacturing in *African Enterprise: The Nigerian Bread Industry*, chapter 9.

[3] Interview with the Acting Principal of the Yaba Trade Centre, September 1964.

do not obtain the City and Guilds Intermediate Craft Certificate obtain, by sitting the Ministry of Labour's examination, qualification as Artisan Grade III and II. At the same time, the normative standards toward which students strive are kept high, giving the system a built-in potential for raising the average level of skilled labour attainment.

Turning to the question of technicians, it would appear that this skill category has been given a distortedly high priority by manpower forecasters and educational planners. The divergence between a rather casually assessed 'need' and effective demand is dramatically revealed by the extreme difficulties that the Technical Institutes have experienced in attracting candidates and the subsequent problem of defection. Beginning with the Ashby Commission, all reports since 1960 have called for increases in technicians' salaries and other measures to enhance their status recognition, but in vain.

The underlying forces at work are not hard to discern. While the grammar schools are now supplying an aggregate number of graduates sufficient to the needs of the post-secondary educational system and direct employment requirements, there still remains a severe shortage of graduates possessing a qualification in mathematics and science (physics, chemistry, technical drawing) which is an entry prerequisite for both the Technical Institutes and applied science majors at the university. Given a shortage of science students, the universities have permitted direct entry to candidates with mathematics and science, substituting in place of the sixth form an additional year at the university; as a consequence Technical Institutes are denied all but the 'special circumstances' candidates.

Three phases can be expected in the development of this situation. In the first phase the great majority of graduates will take up employment as engineers, architects, university teachers, *et cetera* with the high-salary employers. The second phase takes over when the vacancies in the high-salary sector are exhausted and the 'excess' graduates turn to teaching positions in the grammar schools. Increased science and mathematics teachers in these institutions now leads to an expansion of qualified secondary school graduates, thus relieving the original bottleneck. In the final 'equilibrium' phase only the best science and math graduates proceed to the sixth form and university, while the remainder provide an ample supply of candidates for the Technical Institutes – the pattern obtaining in most developed countries. Nigeria would appear to be nearing the end of phase one.

The Nigerian College of Arts, Science and Technology, which opened its doors in 1954, was designed to provide for all post-secondary professional and sub-professional technical education not catered for by the Technical Institutes or the University College of Ibadan. In response to the same pressures that have operated on the Technical Institutes, by 1958 more than half of the students enrolled were in an 'intermediate' course studying for the GCE, A level, while the bulk of the remaining students were pursuing B.Sc. degrees, an option made possible by the establishment of a special relationship with the University of London.[1]

The Ashby Commission, while recognizing the College's contribution to sixth form education, was less pleased with its performance at the technician level:

> But in engineering the College has deviated from its original purpose, by allowing itself to be drawn into degree work and concentrating its efforts at that level. In consequence there has been virtually no provision in Nigeria for training men to the level of Higher National Certificate. In each region there are now technical institutes and the hope for sub-professional technical education now rests with these institutes.[2]

As a result of the Commission's recommendation, the branches of the Nigerian College were subsumed into the various regional universities in 1961. In light of the Technical Institutes' subsequent record it seems clear that the College was successfully (its students pass rate was far higher than that of the Technical Institutes) carrying out those functions which had the highest priority.

A basic question remains as to why, if their need is so great, technicians' salaries have not been raised to a level approaching that of the technologists. The answer would appear to be that in most instances investigators have equated technicians' skills with a capability to act in supervisory capacities. Yet in most instances the technical knowledge requirement for such foremen and supervisors does not exceed that of the experienced craftsmen. This was the writer's finding from interviews with commercial and manufacturing firms in 1959–60 and 1964, and is borne out by salary data collected in January 1965.

The educational attainment of a copy typist is two to three years of post-primary vocational training, and for a clerical position, the WASC (i.e. five years of secondary school). A craftsman's training duration is the same as the clerical, while a technician's is an additional two to four years longer.[3] As can be seen from table 70, the maximum salaries paid to technicians and foremen is not only not near the £2,500-plus maximum for engineers, but it falls within the same range as the clerical positions (maximum salary average: Clerical £798, Technician

[1] *Report of the Visitation: Nigerian College of Arts, Science and Technology*, March/April 1958, London.
[2] E. Ashby *et al.*, *op. cit.* p. 5.
[3] The junior Technician qualification, the Ordinary National Diploma, is taken after two years of theoretical and practical instruction, and the Higher National Diploma after a further two years of full time study.

£766, Foreman £741). The obvious conclusion is that Nigerian technicians and foremen, at least in the private sector, have been drawn from the ranks of experienced craftsmen and that – in accord with A. P. Straker's analysis in 1959 – effective demand for the technician's special skills is far more moderate than usually supposed.[1]

This leaves the problem of supervisory skills, skills which are not

Table 70. *Annual salary ranges for selected occupations, January 1965*

(£s per annum)

Industry (no. of firms)	Copy typist min/max	Clerical min/max	Technician min/max	Foreman min/max
Metal and steel (7)	144/300	120/725	196/810	300/660
Cement and asbestos-cement (5)	108/361	240/808	360/522	360/948
Food and vegetable oil (4)	120/294	446/840	219/810	308/920
Rubber and shoe (4)	144/400	324/800	246/800	240/800
Tobacco (2)	189/251	384/850	189/773	384/773
Paper products (3)	168/269	360/1008	300/864	360/864
Brewing (1)	172/266	760/1200	—	334/597
Paint (1)	240/360	500/800	240/480	240/480
Textiles (1)	204/204	420/420	—	—
Motor trade (5)	156/252	312/840	372/840	279/600
Tech. sales and service (8)	134/418	237/725	237/815	249/1155
Advertising (2)	162/249	260/725	—	308/440
Oil marketing (3)	168/350	360/750	168/1085	360/505
Timber (4)	96/204	180/382	180/540	180/900
Air transport (2)	—	504/840	—	—
Shipping (3)	162/362	304/1020	219/810	308/758
Merchandising (14)	120/334	240/840	168/810	180/720
Average	155/305	350/798	238/766	293/714

SOURCE: Nigeria Employers Consultative Association, *Wage and Salary Survey 1965*, p. 21.

attached to any one occupational grouping, but which are required in varying degree at all levels, from skilled labour up to the factory manager. Following the recommendation of the Federal Advisory Committee which reviewed the International Bank's proposals, a series of three week courses (supervision and management, foremanship, office supervision, higher management) were inaugurated in

[1] This rather heretical conclusion is further confirmed by a survey of 124 firms, representing 65,000 employees, carried out by the National Manpower Board in July 1966. Of 4,404 persons in the intermediate category, only 475 possessed two years or more of post-secondary technical education, and very few of these individuals had significant supervisory responsibilities. On the other hand, for 2,924 persons listed as 'junior administrative, supervisory, foremen' 85 % had no more than the equivalent of secondary education, and only 5 % had attended a Technical Institute. With regard to manpower forecasting and the use of rigid educational requirements discussed subsequently, the survey reports that 43 % of the employers were willing to accept substitution of experience and in-service training for formal education. National Manpower Board, '1966 Survey of Educational and Training Content of Occupations', mimeograph, Lagos 1967, pp. 19–21 and table 1A.

July 1959 in a special division of the Yaba Technical Institute. These courses have proved popular and continue to be offered. In 1963 the United Africa Company opened its own supervisory training school at Igbobi near Lagos, also operating on the basis of three week courses. The teaching methods employed at both schools are those of the case study and role-playing. Decision-making based upon analysis, effective communication, systematic methods of control and good human relations are stressed. Although commonplace in Europe and America, such instructional techniques represent a healthy break with the expository teaching methods which predominate in Nigeria. Many of the larger firms have their own staff development schemes, based on periodic reporting and evaluation of individual supervisors' performances.

While training can contribute materially to the development of supervisory skills, it is unlikely that deficiencies in this area – which constitute the principal 'drag' to improving Nigerian labour efficiency – can be wholly remedied in the near future. It would seem that the weaknesses in supervisors reported in the preceding chapter are part of a set of personality characteristics which manifest themselves in the entrepreneurial sphere, in the performance of the civil service and in the ability of Nigerians to carry out large-scale agricultural projects. Although the socio-cultural environment and child-rearing practices which at least in part form this disposition are themselves influenced by economic forces and are amenable to policy intervention, change will undoubtedly be fairly gradual.

SUPPLY AND DEMAND FACTORS

We have already seen how, despite the investment of very considerable resources, the production of trained technicians has not succeeded because, so far, it has not been consonant with Nigeria's relative skill scarcities. The importance of carefully determining effective market demand, and adapting educational planning accordingly, can hardly be over-emphasized. Indeed, one of the principal reasons why even the Trade Centres took over a decade before achieving a significant output of craftsmen was lack of applicants.[1] Although a demand of sorts existed, it was spread very thinly over the country and over a wide variety of organizations. 'In such conditions there were no stable employment opportunities for skilled men or engineers; there were no fixed rates paid and no fixed conditions of service which could be offered to these people. Therefore it seemed to them that they were committing themselves to a career in which the rewards were very

[1] J. E. Richardson, 'Technical Education in Nigeria', *Journal of the Royal Society of Arts*, London, March 1957, p. 317.

uncertain and would vary from place to place.'[1] By contrast, the training schemes launched by the large firms attracted large numbers of applicants for the very reason that subsequent employment with the company was guaranteed.[2]

Recognition by educational planners of the influence of market demand on student motivation and the ways in which it is likely to operate will most probably be a critical factor in determining whether the environmentalistic-vocational reforms now being introduced into general primary and secondary education will in fact take hold. The importance of this point can be more fully appreciated by considering the process which shaped the 'literary' educational system that Nigeria now has.

As in most other underdeveloped countries, it has generally been accepted that the prime fault of Nigeria's educational system is its literary orientation, and that the major thrust of reform should be to inject technical and vocational elements into the curricula. The origins of the literary tradition in West Africa are traced to the culturally-blinded evangelist missionary who, although ignorant of educational theory, laid the foundations of the educational system in the nineteenth century.[3] The work so begun was consolidated in the early twentieth century by the arts degree holders of Oxford and Cambridge who constituted the colonial administration and who set the standard for the emerging westernized élite. Thus the Ashby Commission interpreted the failure of technical education to take hold in the following terms:

> Unfortunately other forms of education beyond secondary school have developed less favourably. There is a profound reason for this. It is one that has to be reckoned with in any planning of Nigerian education. The reason is that the first Western schooling brought to Nigeria was a literary education, and once civil rule was established the expatriate administrators were graduates, most of them graduates in arts. And so the literary tradition and the university degree have become indelible symbols of prestige in Nigeria; by contrast technology, agriculture and other practical subjects, particularly at the sub-professional level, have not won esteem. It is small wonder, then, that training for qualifications other than degrees, especially in technology, is not popular (p. 5).

Recent historical research of J. F. A. Ajayi and others has shown this interpretation to be rather wide of the mark.[4] From the time the

[1] Comments of A. G. Pointon, United Africa Company, on Mr. Richardson's paper, *ibid.* p. 330.
[2] *Ibid.*
[3] See, for example, Margery Perham, *Native Administration in Nigeria*, Oxford 1937, p. 280.
[4] J. F. A. Ajayi, 'The Development of Secondary Grammar School Education in Nigeria' and 'Henry Venn and the Policy of Development', *Journal of the Historical Society of Nigeria*, December 1963 and December 1959 respectively. Also in the same *Journal*, J. B. Webster,

first schools were established in the late 1840s until 1930 the missionary societies gave primacy to a practically oriented educational system, stressing agricultural and industrial skills. However technical schools consistently failed for want of patronage, while the literary grammar school, pioneered by 'renegade' African clergymen, flourished despite official disfavour. And the reasons were not dissimilar to those which have determined the course of events in the post-World War II era.

> The most promising routes to success, wealth and distinction lay through teaching and service in the Church, commerce or professional training in bookkeeping, medicine and so on. And the key to these was grammar school education. Carpenters, masons, coopers, blacksmiths, tailors, mechanics and other artisans were needed and were encouraged, but they were almost always servants of the successful clergyman, merchant, doctor or lawyer. Industrial education taught skills; literary education taught knowledge and knowledge was power. Literary education was therefore superior.[1]
>
> ...The truth was that in those years when the administrators were lecturing the missionaries about the virtues of technical education, the government gave little thought to industrial or technological development. Rather, they discouraged the little there had been. In the middle of the 19th century, the missions, by sending people abroad for technical training, and even more by encouraging the training and employment of educated Africans in diverse trades and professions, had given an impetus to some technological development. In the 1860s and 1870s, development was very much in the air. There were Nigerian engineers building roads and bridges on their own, architects, master masons, printers, sea captains piloting their own vessels from Lagos to trade on the Niger. There were vague dreams of establishing factories in Lagos and building ships on the Niger. But these were quickly shattered in the 1890s first by the persecution of educated Africans on the Niger by the Royal Niger Company, and secondly by the discrimination against them in employment in the administrative and professional grades of the new Civil Service. Only a few African carpenters and builders were required on the few public works. The Railways, the Survey Department and other technical branches of government made arrangements for training their artisans specifically for work in their own Departments. The few artisans were denied the incentive of possible progress to the professional level. Ambitious Africans, able to afford the costs, aimed at the professions of law and medicine. Others became clergymen, and could hope with a degree from Fourah Bay and with the right demeanour to become an archdeacon or assistant bishop. Technical education continued to be praised in theory and discouraged in practice.

'The Bible and the Plow', December 1963. Similar findings are reported for Ghana by P. J. Foster, 'The Vocational School Fallacy in Development Planning' in C. A. Anderson and Mary Jean Bowman, eds., *Education and Economic Development*, Chicago 1965.

[1] J. F. A. Ajayi, 'The Development of Secondary Grammar School Education in Nigeria', *loc. cit.* p. 522.

The real anxiety of the early colonial administration was not how to produce enough artisans or technically competent Nigerians, but how to provide enough clerks of the right quality and efficiency to keep the administration going. It was the Age of Clerks.[1]

ADMINISTRATION

Turning from questions concerning the external matching of skills produced with skills required, we now consider the internal efficiency of the system's operation. Aside from the post-Ashby trend to build more training institutions than are required, the major source of inefficient performance has been the poor quality of instruction, which is reflected in the low pass rate. In this case the instructors are not Nigerian, but rather (in the typical case) young, pedagogically inexperienced Britishers who come to Nigeria for one eighteen-month tour, who themselves are studying for a final professional exam to be taken on their return to the United Kingdom.

We have already noted the small proportion of Trade Centre students who sit for and pass the Intermediate certificate exam of the London City and Guilds. The situation is much the same regarding the Technical Institutes; the following figures relate to enrolment in senior courses at Yaba and the number who sit for the external O.N.C. examination.[2]

	Full time	Part time	Total	O.N.C. exam Sat	O.N.C. exam Passed
1962	189	371	560	37	17
1963	358	305	663	74	19

By contrast, an ILO-sponsored 1963–6 instructor training scheme at Yaba, manned with qualified teaching personnel, achieved for 115 enrolled an 87 % pass rate for the difficult Final certificate examination of the London City and Guilds.[3] This pass rate is three to four times higher than that typically achieved by the Trade Centres; even after discounting for special circumstances, the implication concerning the quality of Trade Centre instruction is clear.

Recruitment of inexperienced, continually turning over expatriate personnel is the result of a persistent refusal by the Nigerian authorities – despite the urgings of every one of the reports previously cited – to offer competitive salaries and other conditions of service to attract seasoned instructors. This same refusal to follow the called for 'high

[1] *Ibid.* pp. 527–8.

[2] Compiled by the author from returns submitted by the Yaba Technical Institute to the Federal Ministry of Education.

[3] Nigeria Employers Consultative Association, *NECA News*, February 1966.

wage policy' has obtained with regards to the Federal Institute of Industrial Research, with similar results. Beginning with AID staff support of the Ibadan Technical College in 1960, various foreign aid agencies have increasingly stepped into the breach and provided the personnel to fill the empty places. The only drawbacks to this arrangement have been lack of teaching continuity and (when not British) unfamiliarity with the U.K. system. The situation regarding the recruitment of qualified Nigerians is much the same: salary and promotion prospects are more favourable with the Ministry of Works and the private firms.

Related to instructor shortages, Trade Centres have in a number of instances (e.g. cabinet-makers, shipwrights) continued courses when there was not currently any demand for the product, previous graduates being unemployed or having gone into other fields. The cause for this has been inability to recruit instructors in alternative crafts, combined with ministerial pressure on the Trade Centre principals to maintain maximum aggregate enrolment.

Another inefficiency in the administration of the technical educational system has been a tendency, which has become more pronounced since independence, to indulge in prestige expenditures on the latest equipment and facilities regardless of their usefulness in the Nigerian context. For instance, a portion of the Shell-B.P. £500,000 independence gift to the Yaba Technical Institute was used to buy equipment which was far too sophisticated for training purposes, and which, for want of an adequate ministerial budget allocation for maintenance, has since become unusable. Likewise much of the investment since 1963 in the renovation of old and building of new Technical Colleges – given the unavailability of instructors and the absence of qualified student entrants – must be placed on a par with government-sponsored glass factories and cement mills.

To what extent do the foregoing problems and pitfalls constitute a natural and unavoidable set of impediments which are inherent in the development of a young economy? In fact many of these inefficiencies could be resolved, or at least reduced to more manageable proportions, by giving the private sector a larger role to play in the training process. Such a change would result not only in the increased efficiency of technical training, but the cost per student would be materially reduced and the government's administrative burden lightened.

Consider the case of craftsmen. By virtue of their closer contact with the market, an employer-operated system would be more efficient in its selection of trades. Less encumbered by formal regulations and bureaucratic procedures, private firms can establish, expand, adapt or discontinue training courses with greater speed and at lower cost. Training orientation and content are automatically brought into close harmony with the requirements of the workplace, and student motivation to effectively integrate theory with practice is enhanced by greater proximity to the actual working situation and the immediate presence of a prospective employer. Moreover, after the first year the trainee's contribution to output usually offsets his maintenance costs, which represent a significant share of the total training cost.[1]

However, it is in the realm of instructor recruitment that the large firms possess their greatest advantage over alternative methods for organizing technical training. By drawing instructors from their own career technical staff on a rotational basis – a long established and proven practice – the firms face neither a shortage of instructors nor the necessity to pay the substantial scarcity and tenure-compensating salary premia.[2] This system of instructor recruitment has the additional merits of ensuring that training will be kept abreast with the most recent developments in applied technology and, by familiarizing the senior technical staff with the special problems of comprehension and communication that arise in the learning process, it improves the latters' managerial effectiveness upon their return to regular duties.[3]

Administratively, shifting most of the trade training and the basic engineering technician courses to the employers (including government departments and public corporations) would involve government subsidization. Such subventions could be partially recovered, if deemed advisable, by imposing some form of *per capita* 'apprentice tax' on all (or some) employers of skilled labour. In any event, the net savings to the public purse would be substantial.

MANPOWER FORECASTING

This brings us to our last subject, forecasting the economy's future skill requirements. Nigeria's first attempt at such an exercise occurred as a result of the appointment of a commission by the Federal Minister of Education in 1959 to investigate the country's needs in the field of post-secondary education. The commission, headed by Sir Eric Ashby, requested Professor Frederick Harbison to estimate the economy's needs for post-secondary school graduates by 1970. Professor Harbison's estimated minimum targets, 35·9 thousand university graduates and 55·4 thousand subprofessional graduates (two to three years post-5th

[1] United Africa Company, *Statistical and Economic Review*, January 1959, no. 22, p. 43.

[2] *Ibid.* p. 31.

[3] *Ibid.* p. 32. A certain portion of UAC's instructors receive pedagogical training in the United Kingdom; half of their instructors are Nigerian.

form education), provided the quantitative basis for the Ashby Commission's recommendations.[1]

Although the GDP grew at Harbison's predicated rate of 4 % per annum, his projections proved inaccurate. By January 1963 recorded high-level manpower exceeded the 1970 target of 91,100 by 5,000.[2] A certain share of the underestimation is no doubt to be attributed to greater coverage in 1963 as compared to the 1958 employment and earnings data Professor Harbison was forced to rely upon. However, the greater part of the error attests to the fundamental falsity of the implicit assumption which such long-term projections are based upon, namely that there exists a fixed relationship between the stock of skilled labour and the growth in national output. Not only is there substitution as between technologies and between factors of production under a given technology, but within the labour category itself there is considerable room for substituting for a given quantity of skilled labour a larger quantity of less skilled labour. As we have previously indicated and as suggested by the following table, such substitution is particularly possible in the intermediate-technician category.

Table 71. *Skilled manpower projections*
(Employment, in thousands)

	Intermediate		Senior	
	Non-graduate qualified teachers	Other intermediate	Graduate teachers	Other senior
Harbison's figures				
1958 (actual)	4·0	8·7	1·3	11·7
1960 (estimated)	4·3	11·1	1·7	13·7
1970 (target)	18·0	37·3	7·0	28·9
Manpower Board				
1963 (actual)	25·7	48·8	3·6	17·9
1970 (min. target)	...	83·4	7·2	28·3

SOURCES: E. Ashby *et al.*, *Investment in Education*, pp. 61–2; National Manpower Board, *Nigeria's High-level Manpower 1963–70*, Manpower Study No. 2, p. 23.

As revealed by the manpower survey of January 1963 the massive unanticipated increase occurred almost entirely in the intermediate category. Although a superficial inspection of post-secondary school enrolment, much less examination passes, shows that these accretions cannot represent *educationally* qualified individuals, both Professor Harbison and the National Manpower Board insisted that two to three

[1] E. Ashby *et al.*, *Investment in Education*, pp. 61–2.

[2] National Manpower Board, *Nigeria's High-level Manpower, 1963–70*, Manpower Study No. 2, p. 23.

years post-secondary training was the 'normal standard' and that such training must be provided for a 12 % annual accretion if a 4 % growth in GDP is to be sustained. These estimates have served as the official justification for building more Technical Institutes and a projected five-fold increase in teaching staff by 1968, despite the prior existence of substantial excess capacity.[1]

Even if one suspends an adverse judgment on the basic question of fixed educational growth coefficients,[2] three serious problems remain. First, the simple educational enrolment totals, which are all that the manpower planners have so far used, cannot be validly equated with skill attainment. The latter is traditionally measured by passing the final qualifying exam – which a rather high proportion of students fail to do. This implies that enrolments must be expanded still more. If a less rigorous rule-of-thumb approach is taken, where can the arbitrary line be drawn, and can one rule out promotion from below (probably the predominant qualification of current personnel in the intermediate category) – at which point the formal educational requirement tends to dissolve altogether?

Second, there is a problem of over-shooting educational supply: starting off from a deficit position in terms of a graduated average annual output sufficient to meet the seven or ten year requirement, the educational system ends up with excess capacity for the period immediately after the target year.[3] Third, and perhaps related to Professor Harbison's under-estimation, many skill-requiring government activities cannot be considered as contributing to or entrained by the growth in national income. Just how important a consumer of skilled manpower government is can be seen in table 72.

Public agencies accounted for 78 % of all intermediate level employment in 1963 (57 % of senior level).[4] Moreover the public employers forecast a skilled manpower growth rate seven times greater than the private sector. Even though the latter's projected requirements seem rather low (shifts in activities and towards more capital-intensive techniques) it is hard to give full credibility to the public agencies' estimates (e.g. a 200 % increase in junior managerial and administrative staff). Another imbalance which suggests that such a large

[1] National Manpower Board, *op. cit.* table 23.

[2] The formula applied by the National Manpower Board, and which has been used elsewhere, is that total employment grows half as fast as national income, intermediate manpower grows three times as fast as national income and senior-level manpower grows twice as fast as national income. This formula was supplemented with employers' forecasts for the year 1968. See *Nigeria's High-level Manpower, 1963–70*, p. 12.

[3] The initial deficit derives from the fact that the educational system is contributing only a part of the accretion in the reported skill categories, but is expected thereafter to contribute the whole of the accretion.

[4] National Manpower Board, *op. cit.* table 14.

accretion to intermediate level manpower is not required for growth is the distribution between sectors: the directly productive sectors of agriculture, power, transport and communications, commerce, construction, mining and manufacturing reported additional needs by

Table 72. *Employer survey of intermediate manpower requirements*
(excluding teaching and research)

	Public		Private	
	1963[a]	1968[b]	1963[a]	1968[b]
Junior managerial and administrative staff	7,446	14,000	1,164	133
Nurses and midwives	4,834	2,179	856	164
Surveying assistants	793	265	18	−4
Engineering technicians and assistants	6,025	2,884	1,033	−131
Draughtsmen	418	202	89	17
Radio and telegraph operators	415	246	51	−42
Accounting and audit assistants	1,311	240	1,106	−366
Cashiers, bookkeepers and storekeepers	440	600	1,126	146
Secretaries	405	229	545	−32
Agricultural extentionists	2,853	2,197	874	−619
Foremen and supervisors	5,130	−1,015	2,364	−1,180
Other[c]	4,053	1,315	814	2,892
Total	34,123	23,342	10,040	978

[a] Actual.
[b] Additional number required by 1968 as given by the employers.
[c] Medical technicians, laboratory technicians and assistants, artists, journalists, actors and musicians, library assistants, salesmen and insurance workers, forest assistants, statistical assistants, housekeepers and catering officers, other.

SOURCE: National Manpower Board, *Nigeria's High-level Manpower 1963–70*, table 15.

1968 of 3,170 as compared to 20,000 for the services sector (exclusive of education).[1] In sum, it would appear that much of the projected shortage of intermediate manpower arises in connection with non-essential government services.

Finally, an intuitive assessment of many of the occupations listed in table 72 supports our earlier contention that for performance of most technician-intermediate jobs there is no minimum threshold of required technical knowledge which can be equated to two or three years of post-craftsman (or post-fifth form) formal education. Instead, experienced individuals with these latter educational backgrounds can perform as technicians, albeit with somewhat lower productivity. That this process of substitution has operated and that no bottleneck has in fact developed is borne out by the comparative stability of technician salaries. As the shortages at the professional and technologist level are made good, the 'senior courses' in the Technical Institutes may be expected to fill and graduates from these courses will then displace the lesser qualified current incumbents.

[1] *Ibid.* table 13.

For educational planning in general, far more attention should be given to price signals emanating from the private sector, with less reliance placed on highly questionable manpower coefficients. While government salary levels may thwart price signalling of developing skilled labour surpluses, no such constraint prevents the signalling of genuine scarcities.

CHAPTER 9

INDUSTRIAL RELATIONS AND WAGE DETERMINATION: FAILURE OF THE ANGLO-SAXON MODEL

In this chapter we shall examine the character of industrial relations in Nigeria and the nature of its influence on the country's political economy. Section I describes the institutional setting and the structural features of the trade union movement, and reviews certain aggregate measures of the system's performance. Section II presents an analysis of wage determination in Nigeria and the role of unions and collective bargaining therein. Section III is descriptive and historical; by scrutinizing what are thought to be the critical features of Nigerian industrial relations it attempts to lay bare the underlying dynamics of the transplanted British system. Section IV, based on the preceding analysis, sets forth a general interpretation of why the Anglo-Saxon model has failed to function as it was intended, both in Nigeria and in the underdeveloped world at large. Section V suggests some alternative arrangements and considers certain aspects of incomes policy.

I

Total *wage-paid* employment in Nigeria in 1962 was in the neighbourhood of 930,000.[1] Of these about 300,000 or 2 % of the economically active population belonged to a trade union. Unionization is limited to the civil service, public corporations and the European firms – those areas where wages and conditions of service are most favourable. The small-scale sector, where wages are low, has remained largely unorganized. Another important feature of the labour market setting is that the government and public corporations, whose wage-setting decisions are most subject to non-economic considerations, employ over half of all unionized labour. Consequently the government's behaviour as an employer, quite independent of its policy objectives in the labour field, exerts a powerful influence on industrial relations throughout the economy.

The non-unionized firms are usually small Nigerian and Levantine concerns (five to forty employees) which operate in highly competitive markets. Interviewing on the subject revealed that workers accept low wages and determined hostility towards union from 'a private man' as natural and in the order of things, if regrettable. 'Government' and

[1] See section I in chapter 7.

'expatriate firms', on the other hand, whose plants are not only much larger but also much more capital-intensive are seen as vast impersonal organizations with unlimited ability-to-pay. The result is a sharp dichotomy of expectations on the part of wage-earners about pay and conditions of service in smaller individually-owned firms as contrasted to other types of employment.

THE INSTITUTIONAL SETTING

The year 1938 is commonly designated as the beginning of organized industrial relations in Nigeria.[1] In that year the British colonial government enacted the Trade Union Ordinance which endowed labour unions with legal status and laid down a minimum code of conduct for union administration. To assist voluntary negotiation between trade unions and management, conciliation and arbitration machinery was established in 1941. The Wage-Fixing and Registration Ordinance of 1943 empowered the Governor-General upon the advice of the Labour Advisory Board (the Wages Board after 1957) to set minimum wages in those industries where collective bargaining did not exist and where wages were unreasonably low. In 1942 a Department of Labour was established and in 1946 a special trade union division was created in the Department. Staffed with professional trade unionists seconded from the British T.U.C., this unit assisted in the formation of new unions, advised existing unions on their administrative problems and conducted various programmes of trade union education. Extensive overseas scholarship programmes for trade union officers were operated by the Ministry of Labour and the Railway Department during the 1940s and early 1950s.

Taken together these legislative and administrative measures represent a reproduction of the metropolitan institutional framework corresponding to a mature system of industrial relations and wage determination which had evolved over a long period. The system has as its objective that the conditions and terms of employment be settled by a process of negotiating and collective bargaining. On the one hand, the Anglo-Saxon model differs from the unorganized free market, where workers individually settle on terms with the employer, by virtue of labour's greater bargaining strength achieved by combination into a single bargaining unit. On the other hand, the British prototype is distinct from external political or administrative regulation of con-

[1] Prior to 1938 three unions were in existence: the Association of Nigerian Civil Servants, the Nigerian Union of Teachers and the Railways Workers Union. The first two of these groups were more concerned with maintaining professional standards of their members than agitating for higher wages and improved conditions of employment. The Railways Workers Union was active in pressing its claims and is discussed subsequently.

ditions and terms of service in that the issues are resolved on a private and voluntary basis by those directly involved – those who presumably possess the most intimate knowledge of the problems to be settled and who will be most affected by the settlement (broadly alluded to as 'industrial democracy'). There are two major requirements for the system's effective operation: that both parties possess the capability and the willingness to negotiate, 'to give and take', and that in the final resort, if all else fails, there exists the freedom to strike and to lock out.

In addition to those enactments designed to promote voluntary collective bargaining between organized labour and management, a wide range of protective and minimum welfare legislation was passed during the 1920s and 1930s. These included prohibition of forced labour, minimum conditions of recruitment and long-term contract, protection of wages, minimum age, paid maternity and sick leave, control of apprenticeship and workmen's compensation for accident and death. During the 1950s this legislation was revised and extended. To these enactments was added the Factory Ordinance in 1955, laying down minimum safety standards for all establishments employing ten or more. In 1961 a compulsory retirement benefit scheme (the Provident Fund) was enacted.[1]

It has consistently been the government's policy that free negotiation within the established institutional framework should be the central regulating principle of industrial relations. A complete statement of the government's philosophy was given in early 1955 by the Prime Minister on the occasion of delivering a rebuke to the Action Group-controlled Western Nigerian Government for its use of wage increases as a vote attracting device – a stratagem his own party was to use in 1964:

> Government re-affirms its confidence in the effectiveness of voluntary negotiations and collective bargaining for the determination of wages. The long term interest of Government, employer and trade unions alike would seem to rest on the process of consultation and discussion which is the foundation of democracy in industry. Government intervention in the general field of wages should be limited to the establishment of statutory wage-fixing machinery for any industry or occupation where wages are unreasonably low by reference to the general level of wages. Any other policy would seem likely to lead to political influences and considerations entering into the determination of wages with effects that might be ruinous economically, and which would have serious adverse consequences for the development of sound trade unions.[2]

[1] For a detailed discussion of Nigerian labour legislation see 'The Influence of International Labour Conventions on Nigerian Labour Legislation', *International Labour Review*, July 1960.

[2] Reprinted frequently in Ministry of Labour *Annual Reports* and the *Handbook of Commerce and Industry*.

At about the same time the Federal Minister of Labour, then chief Okotie Eboh, was addressing a conference in Geneva; in this instance adherence to the British model – which also underlies the ILO labour conventions – was made explicit:

Can the various types of collective bargaining familiar to older industrial societies thrive in the different conditions of underdeveloped countries today? This is an important question which in the view of my government permits of only one answer. We have followed in Nigeria the voluntary principles which are so important an element in industrial relations in the United Kingdom.... There is little doubt that Government intervention in the field of wages can have very adverse effects, in developing countries at least, on trade union development and therefore on labour-management relations, unless it is carefully restricted to those fields where collective bargaining is either non-existent or ineffective. Equally it is my view that compulsory arbitration must inevitably have adverse effects on the seriousness with which both parties enter into the earlier stages of negotiation. Compulsory methods might occasionally produce a better economic or political result, but labour-management must, I think, find greater possibilities of mutual harmony where results have been voluntarily arrived at by free discussion between the two parties. We in Nigeria, at any rate, are pinning our faith on voluntary methods.[1]

Continued adherence by the government to the Anglo-Saxon model was expressed both before the Morgan Commission in 1964 and after the General Strike in 1965.[2]

And in practice the government has, with one important exception, lived up to its declared policies. No attempts have been made to influence the outcome of private negotiations. Statutory wage-fixing has been infrequent and limited primarily to a few Nigerian-operated industries in Lagos.[3] The one failure of the government to honour the voluntary principle has been in wage determination in the public sector; wage and salary changes have occurred not as a result of collective bargaining but on the recommendation of specially constituted tribunals.

It only remains to note that both employers and organized labour have long accepted the principle that voluntary negotiations and collective bargaining are the best means of determining wages and conditions

[1] Ministry of Labour, *Quarterly Review*, June 1955.

[2] Government statement before the Morgan Commission. *Report of the Commission on the Review of Wages, Salary and Conditions of Service of the Junior Employees of the Governments of the Federation and in Private Establishments 1963–4*, p. 3. This report will be referred to hereafter as *Report of the Morgan Commission*. The 1965 statement was made by the Federal Minister of Labour in the House of Representatives, 7 April 1965. Reproduced in Nigeria Employers Consultative Association, *NECA News*, May 1965.

[3] Minimum wages have been decreed for Lagos only in the following industries: tailoring 1944 and 1947, printing 1946, motor repair 1949, stevedore and dock labour 1949, catering 1950, retail distribution 1960. Only twice were wages fixed for employment outside of Lagos, for rubber tapping in the Benin Province 1947 and tin mining on the Jos plateau 1948.

of employment – with the caveat for the labour movement that free bargaining should be supplemented by minimum wage legislation.[1]

GROWTH AND STRUCTURE OF THE TRADE UNION MOVEMENT

From fourteen registered trade unions with a membership of 4,600 in 1940, the movement had grown to 642 unions with a membership of about 400,000 by the end of 1965.[2] Taking the 1962 estimated employment figure of 630,000, it would appear that something like 60 % of employees in establishments of ten or more are members of a union.

Table 73. *The structure of Nigerian trade unions*

Membership	Number of unions				Distribution of membership (%)			
	1948	1953	1957	1961	1948	1953	1957	1961
–50	26	26	69	75	0·8	0·5	0·8	1·6
51–250	42	35	92	120	6·3	3·3	5·8	7·3
251–1,000	24	24	37	69	12·1	9·9	8·5	13·3
1,001–5,000	7	14	29	40	13·6	23·1	31·3	31·8
5,000+	6	6	8	8	67·2	63·2	53·6	46·0
Unknown	22	26	45	48				
	127	131	270	360	100·0	100·0	100·0	100·0

SOURCE: Federal Ministry of Labour, *Annual Reports*.

Distribution of membership by size of union remained fairly stable throughout the period 1948–61, with the exception of an increase in the 1,001–5,000 category at the expense of the over-5,000 grouping. Unions of under 1,000 account for 70 % of all unions and of these three quarters have a membership of less than 250. The eight unions in 1961 with over 5,000 members were the Teachers (54,000), Railway and Ports Workers (11,000), Public Utility Workers (11,000), Local Government Staff (10,000), Civil Service (9,000), the Northern Mine Workers (12,000), Plantation and Allied Workers (10,000) and the

[1] Virtually every labour union federation since 1943 has supported voluntary collective bargaining. For a historical review of central trade union organizations and their policies see, Ministry of Labour *Quarterly Review*, March 1960, and for recent evidence see *Report of the Morgan Commission*, p. 33.

[2] The growth in unions and union membership has been as follows:

	No. of unions	Membership
1940	14	4,600
1946	100	52,700
1950	140	110,000
1955	177	165,100
1960	347	259,100
1964	540	367,200
1965	642	...

SOURCES: Federal Ministry of Labour, *Annual Reports* and *NECA News*, May 1966.

United Africa Company African Workers (6,000).[1] Only the last three of these unions are in the private sector.

An important qualification to the picture presented by table 58 is that some 20 % of the organizations registered under the Trade Union Ordinance are not in fact labour unions.[2] Under the permissive terminology of the statute such traditional associations as the Ote Tomo Native Herbalist Union and the Gbongan Mud Builders' Union are able to achieve the same legal status as labour unions. More important however are trade associations of independent Nigerian business men in such fields as carpentry, tailoring, fishing, building, baking, truck pushing, and timber selling. Three of the organizations registered under the Ordinance are employers' associations primarily concerned with labour relations.[3] Three-quarters of all non-labour unions have a membership of less than 250; hence, not only is the number of unions slightly overstated but so is the preponderance of small unions.

Despite this inflation, it remains true that Nigerian unions are very small, particularly in the private sector. As a very rough indication, the average union size in the United Kingdom is twenty-five times that of Nigeria.[4] In the absence of a significant number of skilled craftsmen in the early stages of industrial development, it is not surprising that development of unions takes place initially on the basis of the place of employment, in contrast to the economically stronger craft-protective unionism of nineteenth-century England and America. What is more surprising is that despite all the efforts of the Ministry of Labour and the various central labour organizations, 'house' unions, once firmly established, have not been able to co-operate and consolidate in order to achieve stronger bargaining units in the form of industry-wide organizations.

At least four conditioning factors in the failure of the industry-wide union to merge can be identified. The first is the physical consideration: the size of the country, distances between centres of employment and problems of communications make the organization and administration of nation- or even region-wide unions a difficult task. Second

[1] Federal Ministry of Commerce and Industry, *Industrial Labour*, Lagos 1963, p. 22.

[2] Excluding the Cameroons, in the last year that the names of individual unions were recorded (as at 31 March 1955) 22 % were other than labour organizations. Inspection of new registrations reported in the *Quarterly Review* indicates that this proportion has declined slightly.

[3] These are the Nigerian Mining Employers Association, the Nigerian Society of Master Builders and the Nigerian Employers' Consultative Association. The latter was established in 1957 at the instigation of the Ministry of Labour (*Annual Report* 1957–8, para 20); it includes the country's largest employers in almost all industries.

[4] In 1964 there were 591 unions in the United Kingdom with an overall membership of 10,065,000. (*NECA News*, May 1966.) The comparable figures for Nigeria are 540 unions with 367,200 members.

and third contributing factors to an atomized trade union structure are the tribal rivalry inherent in any larger grouping and the reluctance of paid union secretaries to see themselves consolidated out of a job. It is a rare instance of union dissension or disintegration where either tribalism or personal competition between paid officials is not to be observed.

A final factor which may have inhibited the development of industry-wide unions was the disposition of employers before independence. Lack of any organization among employers or, indeed, even informal co-operation prior to the government-requested establishment of the Nigerian Employers Consultative Association (NECA) in 1957, together with its cause – the desire for maximum individual autonomy on the part of the foreign firms – may have constituted an indirect deterrent to intra-industry co-operation among trade unions. In addition, a significant number of unionized firms were, often as a result of past experience with professional secretaries, reluctant to deal with union officials unless employed by the company. It is difficult to judge how large a role management has played in discouraging amalgamation. In most instances, the first three causes appear to have been sufficient to produce the result. However, since 1962 NECA, in an all-out effort to forestall political wage-fixing, has formed its members into 'trade groups' for intra-industry consultation on such bargaining issues as job classification, terms of service and appropriate negotiating procedures.

Despite the establishment of these 'trade groups' in 1962, despite the wave of labour solidarity following the general strike of 1964, and despite employer and government effort to make National Joint Industrial Councils operational during 1965, the formation of house unions continued unabated and any amalgamations were more than offset by comparable dissolutions.[1]

THE SYSTEM'S PERFORMANCE

One conventional index to the success of a system of industrial relations is the extent of industrial unrest as measured by the number of strikes and total man-days lost therein. By this criterion Nigeria's labour-management relations have been very good; Nigeria's proportionate loss of total working time to industrial stoppages (about 0·07 %) has averaged less than half that of the United Kingdom or the United States – a fact the government has naturally been quick to point out.[2] (See table 74.)

[1] Federal Ministry of Labour, *Quarterly Review*, December 1965.

[2] Federal Ministry of Commerce and Industry, *Industrial Labour, An Introductory Guide for Prospective Investors*, Lagos 1962, p. 25. On 14 February 1959 the Federal Minister of Labour commented in the House of Representatives as follows:

The first observation about such an appraisal is that the official statistics are incomplete. An unknown but probably significant number of disputes are not registered with the Ministry of Labour. The year 1960–1, the year after the Mbanefo Award looks particularly suspect: it is the only one of four years following a wage increase in the public sector in which strikes demanding implementation of the award in the private sector have not resulted in at least half a million man-days lost.[1] Moreover, sit-down strikes and go-slows are apparently not treated as stoppages.[2] Concerning the general strike of June 1964, the actual time lost was more than 722,000 man-days.[3] All in all, it is quite possible that comprehensive and accurate reporting would reveal Nigeria's performance with regard to strikes was no better than that of England, America or many other countries.

A second observation on the relatively small number of strikes is that made by T. M. Yesufu: the high degree of labour utilization lies less with industrial harmony than with the incapacity of unions to call successful strikes.[4] The basis for this argument is that both workers and their unions lack the financial resources required to abstain from employment. A review of this history of strikes in Nigeria would seem to suggest that any such constraint has operated only in the case of the smaller private establishments. For the larger, more conspicuous European firms and government establishments, where management tends to be more tolerant and where public opinion and political factors often favour the workers, the record indicates that unions have not hesitated to call out their members.

'I am deeply conscious of the interest of Members of this House in the maintenance of good relations in industry, an interest which is bound to grow with our increasing industrialization. . . . It is unfortunate that the occurrence of a strike in a key industry tends to becloud the progress which this country is making in the field of labour-management relations. I have some cold facts and figures which place this age-old phenomenon of the strike weapon in perspective, and dilute the drama (with) which periodic incidents are presented to the public. For example in terms of production, the cost of one public holiday is one hundred times more expensive than the total loss through strikes in the past year. This is a startling fact which members of the public may wish to bear in mind when next they enjoy a public holiday.' (Cited by Yesufu, *An Introduction to Industrial Relations in Nigeria*, p. 35.)

[1] The corrected figure for man-days lost in 1964–5 is 1,181,877, discussed below.

[2] For a recent example, the March 1965 *Quarterly Review* notes that the abortive JAC go-slow strike of 29 December–6 January involved large numbers of government employees in Lagos, Ibadan and Enugu, and yet it is not included in the official statistics of industrial disputes.

[3] The *Quarterly Review* of June 1964 (and subsequent issues) shows industrial stoppages for the quarter of 1 April–30 June as having involved 3,097 workers with 6,198 man-days lost; elsewhere in the same issue it is stated that 76,528 had taken part in the strike of 1–12 June for a total of 722,114 man-days lost. In April 1965 the Minister of Labour informed Parliament that 122,870 workers had participated in the 13-day strike for a total of 934,615 man-days lost. This would raise the number of man-days lost for 1964–5 from 253,460 to 1,181,877.

[4] Yesufu, *op. cit.* p. 56.

A related and final observation about the strike statistics concerns the exceedingly short duration of the average stoppage (see the last two columns of table 74). An inspection of individual strike summaries in the appendices of the Ministry of Labour's *Annual Reports* and in the *Quarterly Reviews* discloses that about three-quarters of these stoppages have ranged from three hours to two days. While a certain portion of

Table 74. *Reported labour disputes*

	No. of disputes	No. of strikes	Per cent strikes	Men involved	Man-days lost
1946	16	10	63	6,485	...
1947	59	28	48	17,721	...
1948	...	21	...	6,839	...
1949–50[a]	86	46	54	50,043	577,000
1950–51	46	19	41	35,573	286,351
1951–2	...	38	...	6,930	20,243
1952–3	...	26	...	12,455	59,847
1953–4	52	33	64	9,990	26,874
1954–5	50	30	60	6,473	12,200
1955–6[a]	76	43	57	89,522	901,000
1956–7	98	30	31	23,623	61,297
1957–8	136	49	36	21,797	63,410
1958–9	129	53	41	19,046	73,095
1959–60	131	54	41	23,250	70,862
1960–1[a]	140	65	46	36,667	157,373
1961–2	127	58	46	18,673	57,303
1962–3	...	...	...	...	...
1963–4	...	...	...	45,409	96,621
1964–5[a]	...	195	...	73,447	253,460

[a] Years following a major wage award in the public sector.

SOURCES: Federal Ministry of Labour, *Annual Reports*, 'Summary of Disputes'; and Ministry of Labour, *Quarterly Reviews*, 1964 and 1965.

such strikes can be attributed to weak unions or to the skilful intervention of the Ministry of Labour, the most frequent cause has been precipitous action on the part of the union leaders. Once the management has been fully informed about the claim or grievance, such 'disputes' have been quickly settled. In so far as unions are prone to strike too readily, it could be argued that strike statistics over-state the disharmony of Nigeria's industrial relations.

II

WAGE DETERMINATION

The major test of any system of industrial relations is how effectively it deals with the central issue of the labour-management relationship, wage determination. Despite the carefully constructed institutional framework and the avowed commitment of all parties concerned, voluntary collective bargaining has failed to function as a significant mechanism for fixing wages.

In Nigeria [in 1962] employers still fix wages and conditions of employment without reference to labour unions and it is not common practice for unions and employers to negotiate and sign contracts which fix wages and other conditions of service for a given period of time.[1]

In place of voluntary collective bargaining, wage rates in the unionized sector of the labour market have been determined by means of independent commissions in which neither workers nor employers have been represented. Prior to 1954 these commissions were set up in response to pressure from government employees suffering from an erosion of their real wage; since 1954 the 'pull' of electoral politics has re-enforced the 'push' of rising prices in bringing about wage tribunals and wage awards.[2] Unions have played an important role in transmitting these pressures to the government, and have made clear to the contending political parties the electoral benefits of pre-election wage awards. Government pay rises have been transmitted to the unionized segment of the private sector both by a tradition that European employers should pay no less than the government and by a wave of strikes which such expectations, if not immediately fulfilled, give rise to.

The unorganized segment of the labour market is generally semi-modern, labour-intensive, and atomistically competitive. Employers in this sector offer wages closely approximating the marginal supply price of labour. There are a number of difficulties in selecting a representative minimum wage rate, the two most important of which are the conventional problem of 'compensating differences' and payment-in-training. The latter explains the wide-spread employment of low-paid apprentices and learners in industries not characterized by significant capital entry barriers (e.g. tailoring, tinkering, carpentry, motor repair); current sacrifice of part or all of the wage constitutes an investment in a secure future earning-capacity operating one's own enterprise. In those industries where there are appreciable capital requirements (e.g. singlets, baking, building construction) the incentive to serve as an apprentice or learner is far less and their presence is seldom observed. Employers in these industries have a correspondingly greater capacity to engage paid labour because competition is less intense.

If we take industries characterized by significant capital require-

[1] Federal Ministry of Commerce and Industry, *Industrial Labour: An Introductory Guide for Prospective Investors*, Lagos 1963, p. 23.

[2] For a full discussion of the political factor in government wage fixing over the period 1954–60 see Yesufu, *op. cit.* pp. 141–8.

ments, we find that the minimum wage was about 5*d.* per hour in early 1964 (see below, table 75). A highly simplified explanation of the process by which this minimum wage is determined is set out in figure 5. D_O and D_U represent the demand schedules for labour in the organized and the unorganized sectors respectively. The supply schedules

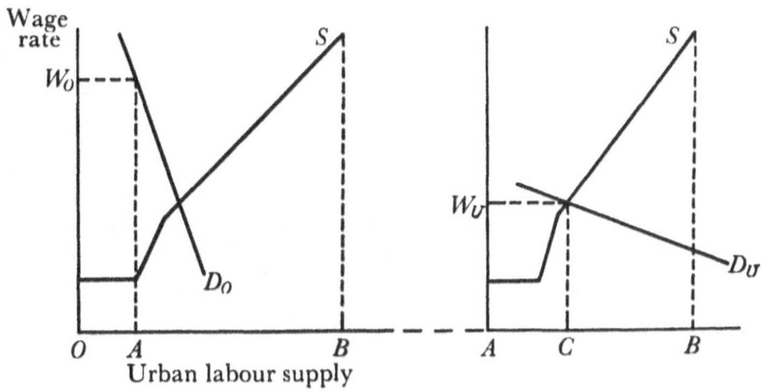

FIG. 5. Wage determination in the unorganized labour market.

exhibit a positive slope because individuals (*a*) have differing income opportunities back on their village farm or in terms of support from their urban relatives, (*b*) attach differing values to their leisure, and (*c*) have differing risk preferences for holding out for a certain period of time for the chance of a high-paying job before accepting employment at the going-rate in the unorganized sector. On the basis of the simplifying (but not too unrealistic) assumption that unskilled labour is homogeneous, the labour supply to the unorganized sector is the same as that to the organized, less those actually employed in the organized sector.

At a given point in time the labour force *OB* has or is seeking employment. *OA* obtain employment in the organized sector, *AC* are engaged in the unorganized sector, and *CB*, whose reservation wage rates W_U, are voluntarily unemployed.

Turning from the static to the dynamic situation, over time both the demand and supply schedules shift outwards. Shifts in the demand for labour depend upon the growth in demand for goods and services (as a result of population growth and advances in *per capita* income), adjusted for increases in productivity.[1] During the period for which statistics exist (1957–62), annual growth in employment averaged 1 to 1·5 % in the organized sector.[2] No figures are available for the unorganized

[1] This subject is thoroughly discussed by Charles Frank Jr., 'Employment and Economic Growth in Nigeria', AID Summer Research Project, mimeograph, August 1966.

[2] *Ibid.* p. 13 and table 10.

sector; however one would be inclined to guess, on the basis of near static productivity and a reasonably high income elasticity of demand for its products, that the growth in employment in this sector was considerably higher, perhaps approaching 4 to 5 %. Assuming that shifts in the supply schedule are directly and proportionately related to growth in the urban population, we may use the conventional estimate of 6 % outward shift per annum.[1] The ordinal consistency of these shift estimates appears to be borne out by a decrease in the real wage in the unorganized sector and an apparent increase in unemployment.

It is clear from the foregoing that the critical determinant of the wage rate in the unorganized sector (W_U), as well as the extent of unemployment, is the rate of flow of labour from the country-side into the towns. The prime variables controlling the rate of flow are economic, and are capable of being manipulated by appropriate public policies.[2] These economic variables are the institutional wage in the organized sector (W_O), the corresponding opportunity earnings in agriculture (W_A), the weighted average of perceived probabilities (P) of obtaining high-wage employment by potential city-bound migrants for any given W_O, and the capacity of those gainfully employed in the towns to support unemployed kinsmen. Unemployment supportive capacity can be taken to vary with W_O if we assume that D_O for labour is relatively inelastic. Then we can write the urban labour supply function as follows $S_L = f(W_O, P, W_A)$, where $\frac{\partial S}{\partial W_O} > 0, \frac{\partial S}{\partial P} > 0, \frac{\partial S}{\partial W_A} < 0.$

Government's capacity to influence all three of these variables is considered in a later section of the chapter. What is relevant in the present context is that every increase in the government minimum rate (W_O) will tend to depress the ruling wage in the unorganized sector (W_U) and to increase unemployment.

Fragmentary information concerning the course of the money wage in the unorganized sector since 1953 gives some support to the fore-

[1] Actually the rate of urban influx is (we argue subsequently) determined in part by changes in W_O and thus the estimated annual 6 % shift should represent an average in which inflow rates for the later years are higher than in the earlier years.

[2] This is not to deny that there are strong sociological preferences for town life. More exactly the willingness to take up employment in town at a wage lower than opportunity earnings in agriculture can be attributed to an 'implicit wage supplement' deriving from (*a*) free urban amenities which are a result of public expenditure, i.e. a government subsidy on top of the employer's wage, and (*b*) the comparatively diverse attractions and leisure-time opportunities inherent in town life. Save in so far as (*a*) is an economic policy variable, the implicit wage supplement is of a once-and-for-all nature and has no effect on changes in the rate of urban influx.

going analysis: while the real wage rate in the organized sector has risen by over 50 %, it has actually fallen in the unorganized sector.[1]

Table 75. *Minimum unskilled wage rates*

A. Southern Nigeria (Lagos excluded), April 1964, hourly rate

Government	7*d.*	European	
Nigerian		Cigarettes	10*d.*
Bakery	6*d.*	Steel rerolling	7*d.*
Shoe manufacture	5*d.*	Plastic-ware	10*d.*
Singlet	5*d.*	Paint	8*d.*
Tyre retreading	7*d.*	Cement	9*d.*
Levantine		Tyre manufacture	10*d.*
Soap manufacture	7*d.*	Plastic-ware	10*d.*
Wrought iron	7*d.*		

B. Lagos only, daily rate

	Government	European firms
1938	1*s.*	1*s.* 2*d.*
1945	2*s.*	1*s.* 9*d.*
1950	2*s.* 8*d.*	3*s.* 5*d.*
1957	4*s.* 8*d.*	4*s.* 9*d.*
1960	5*s.* 10*d.*	6*s.* 1*d.*
1964	5*s.* 10*d.*	6*s.* 10*d.*
1965	7*s.* 8*d.*	7*s.* 8*d.*

SOURCES: Data in A collected by the writer, establishment interviews 1964. Data in B, Ministry of Labour, *Quarterly Reviews* and information supplied by the United Africa Company and the Nigerian Tobacco Company. See also the *NECA Wage Survey*, January 1965, p. 14.

As seen in table 75A rates of pay range upward in a continuous spread from W_U to the government rate, to the rate paid by the 'premium' private employers. The spread is further increased when the fringe benefits given by employers at the higher end of the range and the presence of sub-minimum wage 'learners' and apprentices employed by firms at the lower end of the range are taken into account. The explanations for this spread include ability-to-pay, differential labour quality requirements, the employer's public image and union activity.

The pattern of unskilled wage rates as between government and foreign firms shown in table 75A depicts but one phase in a continuing process of narrowing and widening differentials. The government rate remains stationary between its widely separated jumps, the jumps being a function of some combination of politics and inflation. The high-paying European firms' wage rates jump so as to be at a par with

[1] During the period the writer had personal knowledge of the unorganized labour market, late 1959 to late 1964, there was no change in W_U. Several correspondents, a bread producer in Ibadan and a singlet manufacturer in Aba, reported that W_U still had not risen as of early 1966; they also reported that the minimum daily wage rate they offer has risen no more than 6*d.* since 1953. Consumer prices have risen some 40 % over the same period.

government, but they also move upward (for causes discussed hereafter) with rising prices during the intervals. In early 1964, five years after the Mbanefo award, the European firms' wage rates had risen by a considerable margin above the government rate; just after the wage award in 1964 the gap between the two rates was closed.

Regarding the wage structure with respect to skills, government, here as elsewhere, has set the pattern. Beginning with 'General Labour', the scale ranges upward in even and continuous steps through three grades of semi-skilled 'Special Labour', then through three 'Artisan' grades and ending with craftsman. Because the lowest grades of labour have always received the largest proportionate wage increase, there has been a gradual compression of skill differentials as the wage level has moved upwards. This trend is seen in the figures below which express the last step of Artisan Grade I as a per cent of the first 'step' of the federal 'General Labour' grade.

	Lagos (%)	Ibadan (%)	Kaduna (%)
1947–9	368	671	760
1955–9	343	392	457
1959–64	317	366	424
1964–5	274	351	411

General Labour and the three grades of Special Labour vary geographically (based on cost-of-living considerations) whereas all higher grades are constant throughout the country – hence skill differentials vary geographically.[1] In 1963 the maximum rate for Craftsman Grade I was 830 % of the General Labour rate.[2] On the clerical side, chief clerk and senior secretary-typist are in a comparable range with Craftsman Grade I.[3] A very similar wage structure prevails in the private sector as indicated by table 70 in the previous chapter.

Dividing the yearly Federal minimum area wage rates by urban consumer price indices we arrive at an approximate measure of the movement of real wages in the organized sector. These indices are

[1] The actual rates are as follows:

	Artisan Grade I		General Labour, first step		
	Bottom	Top	Lagos	Ibadan	Kaduna
1947–9	8*s.*	9*s.* 6*d.*	2*s.* 7*d.*	1*s.* 5*d.*	1*s.* 3*d.*
1955–9	14*s.*	16*s.*	4*s.* 8*d.*	4*s.* 1*d.*	3*s.* 6*d.*
1959–64	16*s.* 2*d.*	18*s.* 6*d.*	5*s.* 10*d.*	4*s.* 11*d.*	4*s.* 3*d.*
1964–5	17*s.*	21*s.* 11*d.*	7*s.* 8*d.*	6*s.* 3*d.*	5*s.* 4*d.*

Federal Ministry of Labour, 'An Outline of the Development of Wages and Wage Structures in Nigeria', mimeograph, February 1966, *passim.*

[2] Federal Ministry of Commerce and Industry, *Industrial Labour*, appendix VII.

[3] *Ibid.*

given in table 76 along with available figures on movements in Nigeria's national *per capita* income over the same period.

Real wages in the organized sector have increased at more than twice the rate of *per capita* GDP. What has been the influence of collective bargaining in bringing about this outcome? Trade unions have played an important role in mobilizing, magnifying and channelling the discontent of government employees suffering a gradual erosion of their money wage; these union activities have resulted in more frequent

Table 76. *Urban wages and national* per capita *income*
(indices)

	Urban real wages				*Per capita*
	Lagos	Ibadan	Enugu	Kaduna	GDP
1953	100	100	100	100	100
1956	117	139	121	128	106
1959	105	141	113	123	110
1962	118	139	111	127	118
1965	146	185	164	159	126[a]

[a] Estimated.

SOURCES: Federal Office of Statistics, *Annual Abstract of Statistics 1964* and *Economic Indicators*, January 1967 for urban cost-of-living indices and Gross Domestic Product figures.

wage tribunals and in larger awards than would otherwise have been the case. The critical point, however, is that such union activities have been primarily directed to bringing *political* pressure on the government and bear little or no relation to private joint negotiation or collective bargaining, the end for which the trade union movement has been so extensively nurtured.

In the organized segment of the private sector, however, collective bargaining has contributed to the maintenance of the real wage, the variable margin above the government rate described earlier. Despite the fact that collective bargaining and written agreements were very rare before 1962, a few firms, already paying premium wages, conceded wage increases equivalent to the rise in the cost-of-living as a necessary measure to keep their unions alive and in good health (a union which does not win wage increases soon loses membership support). The outstanding example of this pattern is the Nigerian Tobacco Company. A few other very large firms, also concerned with their public image, have tended to follow suit, even though collective bargaining and a viable union were frequently absent.[1] The United

[1] To a much greater extent than for most other employers, the non-routine, often arduous and judgment-demanding activity of certain phases of their operations induce the oil exploration companies to pay premium wages to attract the best quality labour, quite apart from considerations of their public image.

Africa Company and its union have negotiated collective agreements regularly since 1959, a unique instance of labour-management relations approximating the specifications of the Anglo-Saxon model. As a result of what happens in these companies, a certain sympathetic pressure comes to bear on other European firms to follow the wage-leaders.

The extent to which the large firms will accede to or resist pressure to increase wages depends upon a number of factors: the effect on sales of a cost-induced price hike, the share of wages in total cost, and the ease of introducing more mechanized labour-saving production processes. Given the monopolistic markets and satisficing entrepreneurial behaviour described in chapter 4, we can add the existence of an element of rent in profits (hence the ability to absorb the increase without a price rise) to the preceding three Marshallian factors. It is precisely because the European firms, relative to their Nigerian and Levantine counterparts, are capital-intensive (i.e. a low ratio of wages to total cost) and operate in oligopolistic markets that they can afford to pay higher wages.

Firms engaged in export production – groundnut crushing, tin mining and smelting, rubber processing, timber, etc. – face a highly elastic demand for their product and hence resist wage increases, which could only come out of profits. On the other extreme, firms producing for the highly income-elastic urban consumer market – cigarettes, beer, processed foods, cosmetics, etc. – can raise their price (often improving the profit margin as well as covering the added cost) because the adverse effect of a higher price is soon offset by the growth of the market, in the short run a function of higher urban wage incomes which the firms in question usually help to 'lever' by their own speedy granting of the demanded wage increase.[1]

In sum, there is little doubt that trade unions have raised wages in the organized labour market appreciably higher than they otherwise would have been. However this has not been achieved by private around-the-table bargaining between representatives of employers and employees as premised in the British system of voluntary collective bargaining; rather it has been achieved by bringing political pressure to bear on the government, which in turn has established independent wage tribunals. Private collective bargaining of sorts has operated, however, to maintain a modest differential between the government rate and that of foreign firms, approximately equivalent to the rise in the cost-of-living.

[1] This point is not a result of *ex-post* theorizing, but was frankly stated by respondents in two separate companies as a consideration in their deliberations whether or not to grant a particular wage claim.

III

The measurable economic results of a particular system of industrial relations, while of vital significance, do not provide a complete picture of the system's performance. In particular, such an assessment fails to disclose important qualitative human inter-actions of the system and its harmony or lack thereof with the country's overall socio-political structure. The following analysis of central trade union organization, individual house unions, trade union leadership, union members, and employer behaviour is aimed at achieving this more complete assessment of the system's performance.

HISTORY OF CENTRAL TRADE UNION ORGANIZATION

The same conditions which spurred the rapid growth in trade unions after 1940 – the colonial government's cultivation of the British trade union model and the war-time erosion of real wages (the cost-of-living index rose from 100 in 1939 to 151 in 1942) – fostered the emergence of a central co-ordinating organization in November 1942.[1] Forming around a 1940 federation of twelve government workers' unions, the African Civil Service Technical Workers Union (dominated by the Railway and Ports workers), the Trade Union Congress of Nigeria (TUCN) held its first conference in August 1943.[2] From the beginning the TUCN pursued the activities of conventional business unionism as well as those of a more radical character. By means of monthly consultative meetings with the Department of Labour, the Congress enjoyed productive and harmonious relations with the government. It assisted its member unions in the settlement of disputes, and it launched an ambitious programme of trade union education in co-operation with the Department of Labour. At the same time, the

[1] The sources for the following discussion of Nigeria's central trade union organization are Yesufu, *An Introduction to Industrial Relations in Nigeria*, pp. 33–47, 92–4; J. S. Coleman, *Nigeria: Background to Nationalism*, Berkeley 1958, pp. 255–9, 303–7, 463; Ministry of Labour *Quarterly Review*, March 1960; and R. L. Sklar, *Nigerian Political Parties*, Princeton 1963, pp. 75–84, 495–6.

[2] The evolution of the TUCN was described in more detail by its first President, T. A. Bankole, in November 1942: 'Following a rush for trade union registrations the number of registered unions connected with government departments subsequently grew so rapidly as to necessitate the formation in 1940 of the African Civil Servants Technical Workers Union – a combination whose main functions are to regulate and control the activities of its member unions. However, the formation in rapid succession of unions other than those connected with government departments which ensued during the C.O.L.A. agitation of 1941–2 made obvious the insufficiency of the ACSTWU as the sole negotiating combination, and led ultimately to the formation – sometime last year, primarily at the instance of that combination itself – of the Trade Union Congress of Nigeria.' (Cited by Yesufu, *An Introduction to Industrial Relations in Nigeria*, p. 43.)

Congress supported the establishment of a Labour party; it called for the nationalization of all privately owned utilities and exploitative industries (timber and tin mining); and it established contacts with the (later Communist) World Federation of Trade Unions (WFTU). 'Prior to the general strike of 1945, however, the leadership of the congress was very moderate, a fact which ultimately led to its repudiation by the workers.'[1]

Between government cost-of-living awards in 1942 and 1945 the cost-of-living index rose from 151 to 176. Whereas the allowances of European civil servants were revised upwards, no such revisions were made for Africans. This combination of wage erosion and racial discrimination led the African Civil Servants Technical Workers Union to give the government an ultimatum that unless the Union's demand, set forth eleven months earlier, for a substantial increase in wages of all African government employees was met in one month, the ACSTWU would call a general strike.

The proposed strike was supported by the TUCN until a few days before the deadline when it was persuaded, by the Acting Governor's response that such a strike was illegal under the wartime emergency regulations, to revoke the strike order. Nevertheless, seventeen unions, consisting of about 30,000 workers, went on strike for thirty-seven days. 'It was not the number of strikers that made the work stoppage significant, but the fact that most of them were performing services indispensable to economic and administrative life of the country; they were railway workers, postal and telegraph employees, and technical workers in the government departments. Although in many places the workers went back to their jobs after a few days, the strike was not terminated until the government had given assurances that there would be no victimization and that an impartial commission of inquiry would look into their grievances.'[2]

Between 1945 and 1963 central trade union organization made no positive contribution to the development of a viable industrial relations system; on the contrary, it impeded development by diverting energy from the fundamental task of building sound unions and, by virtue of fissure at the national level, set in motion yet another divisive force to weaken the already fragile house unions.

In 1946 the Congress was torn by the radicals' recriminations against the way in which the moderates had handled the general strike. In 1947 the ACSTWU was challenged by a rival federation which claimed to represent the government technical workers unions; personal rivalry for leadership in the TUC continued. In 1948, with the emergence of

[1] Coleman, *Nigeria: Background to Nationalism*, p. 257.

[2] *Ibid.* p. 257.

Yoruba nationalism and the founding of the *Egbe Omo Oduduwa*, an open split occurred when a majority of the Congress representatives voted to disaffiliate from the country's major political party, the Ibo-led NCNC. This caused the leftist politial-activists, headed by M. A. O. Imoudu and Nduka Eze,[1] to set up a rival Committee of Trade Unionists, which became known the following year as the Nigerian National Federation of Labour. The NNFL's aims were 'to impart political knowledge to the workers', 'to press for the socialization of important industries with a view to realizing a socialist government', and 'to work for the triumphant emergence of a World Parliament of the working class'.[2]

Spurred on by the wave of emotional solidarity that followed the Enugu shootings in 1949 and assisted by the good offices of the Department of Labour, the two organizations agreed in March 1950 to a reconciliation and the formation of a new body, the Nigerian Labour Congress. However when it became known that the militant Nduka Eze was to be the General Secretary and that the Congress would participate in politics, the TUC and the successor federation to the ACSTWU (now outside the TUC) refused to transfer their assets to the NLC. With funds from Eze's own UAC house union and others from Communist organizations abroad, the NLC established a daily newspaper, *Labour Champion*, won four seats in the Lagos election and then, in December, called a disastrously unsuccessful general strike of mercantile workers which wrecked both the NLC and the UAC union. 'By the end of 1950 the majority of registered trade unions including most of the largest were outside any of the central trade union organizations.'[3]

Save for the revolutionary aspect of Nduka Eze's 'positive action', which was more or less precluded after 1950 by the course of the country's political development – centring around well organized, well led, broadly based competing political parties – the 1948–50 pattern

[1] Michael Artokhaimien Ominius Imoudu became President of the Railways Workers Union in 1940; one of the leaders in the successful 1941–2 agitation for a cost-of-living allowance, he was deported from Lagos to his home village in Benin Province by the colonial government as a potential threat to the public safety under the Emergency Defence Regulations. He was released in time to play an important role in the general strike of 1945. Mr. Imoudu has been a leading figure in the radical labour group throughout the entire period 1940–65.

Nduka Eze, a mission-educated western Ibo, started work as a clerk in the United Africa Company. In 1946 he joined the quasi-revolutionary Zikist Movement (outlawed in 1950) and began to organize UAC's first union. By 1949 he was the Acting President of the Zikist Movement and the General Secretary of the second largest union in Nigeria. 'His object since 1946 had been to link the labour movement to the Zikist Movement for revolutionary action' (Sklar, *Nigerian Political Parties*, p. 76). After the failure of his revolutionary schemes in December 1950 and 1951, Eze entered the business world.

[2] Ministry of Labour, *Quarterly Review*, March 1960, p. 40.

[3] *Ibid.*

was repeated with depressing regularity until September 1963. New all-embracing central labour organizations were established in 1953, 1959 and 1962; each time in less than a year these organizations split into warring factions with one or more competing congresses soon emerging.[1] The issues – whether or not to participate directly in politics and whether to affiliate with the pro-West ICFTU or the Communist WFTU – remained constant as did the personalities. (The radicals were pro-WFTU and advocated direct political participation; the moderates were pro-ICFTU and advocated no direct connection with any political party.) Lack of interest in the health of constituent unions, self-seeking rivalry for leadership and a desire for a personal share in the ICFTU or WFTU money kept the cycle in motion.[2]

By 1963 there were five central labour organizations – the moderate group having split into three factions and the radicals into two; in addition, two political parties were launched by trade union leaders in that year.[3] The Joint Action Committee (JAC), the supra-congress coordinating body which managed the 1963–4 general strike, fissured in December 1964, producing the rival Supreme Council of Nigerian Trade Unions (representing two of the moderate confederations) in January 1965.

The general strike of 1963–4, coordinated by the JAC, represents the only successful industrial action of the central labour organizations

[1] The names, dates and principal officers of these organizations are as follows: (reconciliation mergers marked with *)

*All Nigeria Trade Union Federation (1953): Michael Imoudu, Gogo Nzeribe, S. U. Bassey, N. A. Cole, L. L. Borha
A Committee of Trade Unionists (1955) leading to
National Council of Trade Unions, Nigeria (1957): N. A. Cole, H. P. Adebola, L. L. Borha
*Trades Union Congress of Nigeria (1959): Michael Imoudu, L. L. Borha, S. T. Ese
Nigeria Trades Union Congress (1960): Michael Imoudu, W. Goodluck, S. U. Bassey, Ibrahim Nock
*United Labour Congress (1962): L. L. Borha, Michael Imoudu, H. P. Adebola, N. A. Cole
Independent United Labour Congress (1962): Michael Imoudu, S. U. Bassey, W. Goodluck
Northern Federation of Labour (1962): Ibrahim Nock
Labour Unity Front (1963): Gogo Nzeribe
Joint Commercial and Industrial Workers Council (1963): O. Durosomo
Nigerian Workers Council (1963): N. Chukwwra, E. Okongwu

[2] Yesufu has described the situation in even stronger terms: 'As things are the T.U.C. in Nigeria has become divided into two factions, each of which is in fact a puppet of one or more foreign organizations, and run almost completely with money from foreign sources: the Ghana T.U.C. and the W.F.T.U. support one section while the I.C.F.T.U. supports the other.' Yesufu, *op. cit.* p. 155.

[3] The Labour Party lead by Michael Imoudu and Tunji Otegbeye's Socialist Workers and Farmers Party. Although Dr. Otegbeye was not a trade unionist, his party was closely related to the IULC.

other than the 1945 strike.[1] After the unsuccessful austerity campaign of 1961 to reduce the salaries and allowances of ministers, parliamentarians and senior civil servants, public resentment against those in positions of power and privilege was on the rise. As 1 October 1963 approached, the day Nigeria was to be proclaimed a Republic, a rumour spread among junior government employees that a bonus of one month's pay would be given to all employees to celebrate. When Sir Abubakar summarily rejected these rumours, talk of boycotting the celebrations spread quickly; from this the idea of a strike to embarrass the government developed.

It was at this point that the trade union leaders entered and took command of the protest movement. Forming themselves into a Joint Action Committee, the leaders of the five central labour organizations and major national unions widened the original claim into a demand for a commission to review the entire wage and salary structure. Threatened thus, the government modified its position and agreed early in the last week of the month to pay an advance of one month's pay. This, however, did not satisfy the JAC: led by the railway, dock and municipal workers unions, a general strike for a full wage review was called on midnight of 27 September. Although the work stoppage was only effective in the communications sector, the government was sufficiently concerned with its international image on such an auspicious occasion to concede to the JAC's demand the night of 30 September, a few hours before the Republic was to be proclaimed.

The original JAC demand for a wage and salary revision was for a review of the entire wage and salary structure, anticipating downward adjustments for the highest paid salary-earners as well as upward adjustments for the lowest paid-wage-earners. The government, however, succeeded in confining the inquiry's terms of reference to junior employees. In organized labour's portrayal of the penury and inequity of the wage earner's situation there was no reference to the incomes of the vast majority of the country's labour force in agriculture and the small scale industry and service sector. That the unions' grievance was *not* fundamentally about low wages but rather one of relative deprivation was made clear by S. U. Bassey, a JAC co-chairman:

> We don't attempt to justify the unions' position in economic terms or to say just where the Government is going to find the money. That is their job. All we can see is that they are spending plenty on themselves. It's time we got our fair share.[2]

[1] This history of the general strike is based on the following issues of *West Africa*: 5 October, 16 November 1963; 6, 13, 20 June, 4 July, 15, 22, 29 August, 3, 17 October 1964, and 15 May 1965. See also Nigeria Employers Consultative Association, *NECA News*, published monthly.

[2] *West Africa*, 16 November 1963.

An independent six-man commission headed by Chief Justice Adeyinka Morgan of the Western Nigeria High Court began its hearings in November. On 30 April 1964 the commission submitted its report and recommendations to the Federal Government. The government neither published the report as it had earlier announced that it would, nor issued a White Paper setting forth the official position. After a month of inept stalling on the part of the government (approximately twenty of the thirty-six Ministers were abroad in Europe or America) a second general strike was called on 31 May. On 3 June a White Paper was published granting approximately half the increase recommended in the Morgan report. These proposals were rejected by the JAC; the strike continued. On 6 June the Prime Minister interrupted his holiday in the northern region to return to Lagos to call a cabinet meeting. On 8 June negotiations between the JAC and the government broke down completely and the government issued an ultimatum that unless the workers returned to their jobs in forty-eight hours they would be dismissed and would lose their accrued privileges when they applied for re-appointment. The following day thirty of the major firms, in response to pressure from the government, issued seventy-two-hour ultimatums. On the same day the Northern Federation of Labour and the Northern Civil Services Union ordered their members back to work after the Northern Premier had agreed to no victimization, strike pay and negotiation on the basis of the Morgan recommendations rather than the White Paper.[1]

On 10 June the Federal Government's ultimatum ended with only a few government employees back at work in Lagos. The ultimatum of the foreign firms was more successful, with about half the workers returning on the 12th. (Nigerian and Levantine employers were for the most part unaffected by the strike.) On 13 June the contending parties came to an agreement and the strike was called off. The agreement provided that the government withdraw the dismissal notices and give full pay for the period of the strike and that wage negotiations would be pursued by a tripartite body consisting of the JAC, the governments of Nigeria and the private employers' association. Although resurgent internal rivalry weakened the JAC's bargaining strength,[2] the pressure of nearing December elections induced the contending regional governments to improve their offers beyond the terms which the JAC accepted on 27 June.

[1] The Northern Federation of Labour was bitterly attacked in the south for 'selling out'. Evidence supporting the contention that NFL's General Secretary was influenced by considerations of personal gain is examined in *West Africa*, 3 October 1964.

[2] It was after alleged by one of the J.A.C. co-chairmen, H. P. Adebola, that during this time Michael Imouchu paid a nocturnal visit to the Prime Minister requesting the post of Federal Labour Adviser. (*NECA News*, March 1965.)

The terms that were made public on 1 July, known as the Okotie-Eboh settlement,[1] raised minimum wages by 29 % in Lagos, 27 % in the west, 47 % in the east, and 22 % in the north. In addition, these increases were to be retroactive to 1 January, permanent collective bargaining and minimum wage fixing machinery were to be established, the daily wage system (which does not provide for job security) was to be abolished for employees of more than five years, and government action was pledged in the fields of workers' housing, municipal transport fares and rent and price controls. The vote-buying element of these concessions was highlighted when the northern Premier announced a further wage hike (averaging about 10 %) in September '...in appreciation of the good leadership and maturity shown by the labour leaders in bringing to an end the last nation-wide strike. We hope they will appreciate this gesture and reciprocate accordingly'.[2]

The effective life of the JAC was ended in January 1965 after an unsuccessful political strike demanding nullification of the 29 December Federal elections. The strike had been called by the radical faction (Messrs. Goodluck, Nzeribe, Imoudu, Otegbeye and their respective organizations) without the consent of the moderates. Immediately after the strike the moderates (Messrs. Adebola, Borha, Chukwura and their respective organizations) resigned and set up a new body, the Supreme Council of Nigerian Trade Unions. The trade union movement thus reverted to its pre-1963 condition of internal wrangling and impotence. Not only did organized labour lose its influence over wage and industrial relations policy, but because the feuding parties could not agree on common representatives, progress in implementing the gains of the 1964 strike, particularly the establishment of permanent industry-wide collective bargaining machinery, was seriously impeded.

THE PRIMARY UNION

Of more fundamental importance than central trade union organization to the long term viability of a system based on voluntary collective bargaining is the health of the individual union and the nature of its

[1] Chief Okotie-Eboh, Minister of Finance, later insisted that the terms of this settlement were binding on all private employers of ten or more regardless of existing collective agreements. The Minister himself, however, did not pay the increase and in at least one of his industrial enterprises (a shoe factory) notified his workers that their employment would be terminated should they form themselves into a union. (*West Africa*, 22 August 1964.)

[2] Nigeria Employers Consultative Association, *NECA News*, September 1964. The 1 July settlement provided for four wage zones in the north ranging from 4*s*. to 5*s*. 4*d*. per day. The September increase consolidated these into two zones of 5*s*. and 5*s*. 6*d*. A similar political wage determination was carried out in 1954 just prior to regional elections by the western region government when the regional government wage was raised to 5*s*. while the comparable Federal rate in the west was 4*s*. 1*d*.

relationship with the employer. One approach to this subject is to review the experience of the older and more important unions. Scattered data are available in four such cases – the railways, the Enugu colliery, the Nigerian Tobacco Company and the United Africa Company.

The Railway Mechanics Union broke away from the Association of Nigerian Civil Servants in 1921.[1] The union's first recorded strike in 1925 – probably the country's largest and most successful strike prior to 1945 – resulted in a 50 % wage increase. From the early 1930s onward the railways have been organized labour's major source of militant political unionism. 'The officers of the railway unions were as often men prominent in Nigerian politics as railway servants from station, shed or shop; and as proof of their zeal on the ordinary workman's behalf, they eagerly exploited every opportunity and every grievance, real or imaginary, which came to their notice whether in the railway service or out of it.'[2] After independence, when the nationalist protest against the European colonialist was transformed into a socialist protest against the new Nigerian oligarchy, the railway unions played as large a role in leading the general strike of 1964 as they had in 1945. In Messrs. Imoudu, Borha and Adebola, railway union officers have been a dominant force in directing the country's central labour organizations.

An abundance of aggressive, ambitious leaders has had its drawbacks. Union fragmentation began in the late 1930s; by 1965 the management was dealing with thirteen separate unions. Nor have militant leaders made good negotiators: in the four comparatively peaceful years prior to the Apapa retrenchment riots of December 1959, seventeen disputes went to conciliation or arbitration. Despite the availability of elaborate negotiating and consultative machinery (the railways had the country's first Whitley council in 1945)[3] and despite the training in industrial relations that upwards of fifty union officers have received in England at the railways' expense, in virtually every major dispute union leaders have preferred to ignore the negotiating procedures to whose careful working out they have been party and instead have relied upon statements to the press, ultimatums, go-slow strikes and mass demonstrations.

[1] Sources for the following sketch of industrial relations on the railways are Nigerian Railway Department (Corporation after 1954) *Annual Reports*; Gilbert Walker, *Traffic and Transport in Nigeria*, H.M.S.O., London 1959, pp. 76–9; Nigerian Railway Corporation, 'Industrial Relations in the Nigerian Railway Corporation', cyclostyled, Lagos 1960; and the Corporation's files on labour relations, kindly made available to the writer in October 1964.

[2] Gilbert Walker, *op. cit.* p. 77.

[3] A Whitley council is the term by which negotiating and collective bargaining machinery is known in the public sector.

The history of industrial relations at the Enugu colliery is similar to the railways in that it has a long record of labour-management dissension and infrequent use of extensive negotiating machinery (a Whitley council was established in 1949).[1] From 1937, the year of the first strike, to 1965 there has been one or more strike or go-slow every year, save during the period 1954–6. Although multi-unions have not developed as in the railways, intra-union warfare has been the rule rather than the exception; as a consequence outside parties such as local tribal chiefs, the Enugu Council of Labour and officers from the Ministry of Labour have had to intervene periodically in order to re-establish communications between workers and management.

While both the railways and the colliery were committed as government-operated bodies to support their trade unions regardless of the latter's behaviour, few private firms prior to 1963–4 were willing to continue to recognize unions which conducted themselves contrary to the mutually agreed upon procedures or otherwise abrogated agreements. House unions began to be formed in various establishments of the United Africa Company in 1945; in 1947 the secretary of one of these unions, the energetic Nduka Eze, succeeded in combining them into the Amalgamated Union of UAC African Workers.[2] In 1948 Eze made his first claim, which was rejected by the company. The union then called upon the Ministry of Labour for a conciliator; after persuading Eze to formulate his case more specifically, the conciliator obtained a settlement on all but two points.

In December 1949, five months later, Eze made a second claim covering the two outstanding points and five new issues. In April while conciliation was in process Eze put forward six new issues to be added to the agenda; the company refused, whereupon Eze called a well organized strike demanding arbitration. 'The company agreed to the inclusion of the six extra points but not before there had been considerable violence by way of damage to property, kidnappings and assault upon workers not sympathetically inclined towards the strike.'[3] In August an 'illegal' two-day strike occurred as an outgrowth both of the heated proceedings of the arbitration tribunal and of a vitriolic newspaper campaign by Eze against the company and its personnel manager. In November the award of arbitration was published:

[1] The history of industrial relations at the Enugu colliery has been extensively documented in the Ministry of Labour's *Annual Reports* and *Quarterly Reviews*. In particular, see 'Industrial Relations in the Enugu Colliery 1915–60', *Quarterly Review*, September 1960 and March 1961.

[2] In addition to a rather erratic coverage in the Ministry of Labour's *Annual Reports* and *Quarterly Reviews*, the prime source for the 1945–50 period is: Award of Arbitrator (V. R. Bairamian) United Africa Company versus Amalgamated Union of UAC African Workers, *Nigeria Gazette*, 20 November 1950; for the later period, interviews with the U.A.C. Personnel Department, London, 1965.

[3] Ministry of Labour, *Annual Report* 1950–1, p. 33.

although it condemned the aggressive and irresponsible behaviour of Mr. Eze and dismissed the majority of the union's claims, it did award a 12½% cost-of-living wage increase. Eze rejected the award on the grounds that the wage increase was not back-dated to the first of the year. Taking the occasion to initiate his long-planned 'positive action', Eze, acting as general secretary of the Mercantile Workers Union and the Nigerian Labour Congress, called a nation-wide general strike against all foreign firms. The strike was violent, short and destructive of all the unions involved.

Between 1951 and 1955, UAC and its associated companies were without unions and it was not until 1959 that a viable company-wide union re-emerged. To fill the vacuum in labour-management communications the company established joint consultation committees. In theory the functions of the latter were to explain management's policies to the workers and to discuss matters of productivity; in fact these committees also provided a safety valve for labour grievances and informed management of any developing problems in the field of labour relations.

In 1955 a UAC house union was recognized in Lagos; in 1957 a well-led branch union emerged in Jos, and its secretary, F. N. Kanu, requested and was granted permission to form an amalgamated company union. From 1959 to 1964 the UAC and Associated Companies African Workers Union negotiated with the company eight national agreements and, after UAC's 1962 decentralization, fifty-five individual company agreements. In addition there were thirty-two meetings of a redundancy board, a body consisting of management and union representatives, to deal with the contraction of the company's labour force in 1962–3. Although the period witnessed several work stoppages, for the most part industrial relations were conducted through the established negotiating and grievance machinery; contact between the parties was continuous, grievances were quickly dealt with, and a wide range of matters were settled to the satisfaction of both parties. The successful participation of the company unions in these negotiations was largely attributable to the skill and leadership of Mr. Kanu.

The Nigerian Tobacco Company recognized its company union in 1945.[1] From that year onwards the company and its union met twice a year on a regular basis; the first signed agreement between the parties took place in 1953 in respect to lay-off procedures. In 1957 a joint industrial council was established, providing for comprehensive agreements covering wages and conditions of service, which were to be renegotiated every two years.

[1] The source for this narrative (although not, of course, the interpretation) is the companies' own files on the subject, kindly made available to the writer in October 1964.

The sequence of union leadership at the tobacco company has been the reverse of UAC's: the first union secretary, Mr. Falade, like Mr. Kanu, had both the temperament and ability to prepare and argue a case, to bargain and compromise and, in general, to perform all the functions of a labour representative and negotiator which are a prerequisite for the successful operation of the Anglo-Saxon model. Since the talented Mr. Falade left the union to take up a junior managerial position with Shell-B.P. in 1954, the union has been represented by a series of aggressive 'outside' professional secretaries or less hostile but untalented company employees, neither of which type has proved adequate to the job.

The fact that the Nigerian Tobacco Company has the longest record of continuous collective bargaining in Nigeria can only be attributed to the determination of the management, pursuant to its policy to be Nigeria's most progressive employer, to keep its union in existence and functioning at all times. Not only has the company been second to none regarding the level of its wages, but it has granted many other concessions which were far ahead of their time – such as subsidized meals, full medical care, free transport to and from work, and special leave allowances. Perhaps more important, the company has continued to deal with their union during intervals (e.g 1956) when union representatives were advancing irresponsible claims, making slanderous accusations against the company in the press, calling precipitous walk-outs and had lost the support of their membership, the TUC and the Ministry of Labour. To have publicly discredited the union officials, which is what virtually all other employers have done under similar circumstances, would have meant at least the temporary disappearance of the union.

Many of the characteristics of industrial relations in the four cases just described would apply to a 'representative' trade union situation in Nigeria. The major differences would be that in the typical case the labour force would be considerably smaller and management would be a good deal less charitably disposed toward dealing with a union.[1] In this typical case there would be a dormant house union, with no written agreement and no regular contact with management (there might or might not be a joint consultative committee, but this would be completely independent of the union). A major claim or grievance would arise; mobilized by individuals from the artisan and craftsman ranks,

[1] The basis for the following characterization of a representative trade union-management pattern are the narratives contained under the headings 'Industrial Relations' and 'Trade Unions' in the Ministry of Labour's *Annual Reports* and *Quarterly Review*, and the writer's own collection of case histories taken by interview in the autumn of 1964 ('Establishment Interviews in Nigeria and Ghana, I.L.O. Industrial Relations Survey', typescript, Geneva 1965, pp. 1–158).

members begin paying their union dues and the services of a professional trade union secretary are recruited. After a few preliminaries (perhaps including a few statements to the local press) the professional secretary confronts the management and threatens strike action if the claim is not conceded. If in the end, perhaps after a short strike, the claim is not granted the services of the secretary are dispensed with; equally, if successful, the absence of any energizing discontent is soon reflected in a falling off of dues and the exit of the professional secretary for want of remuneration – unless, of course, he can manage to generate a new dispute.

TRADE UNION LEADERSHIP

The prevalence of the foregoing pattern has meant that the 'strong man' type unionist has tended to survive. One common trait in this type of personality would appear to be his mode of discourse with management; passages like the following can be found in a high proportion of the Ministry of Labour's *Annual Reports* over the last twenty years:

The projection of personal antagonism between union officials and members of management into the sphere of industrial relations was, as in the past, an unfortunate cause of trade disputes in the country. The inability on the part of some trade union leaders to distinguish between personalities and principles invariably found expression in union-backed demands for the removal of senior management officials on grounds such as 'intimidation, oppression and subversive activities against the union."[1]

The alternative to the professional unionist is a company employee. However, company employees, as illustrated in the case of the Nigerian Tobacco Company, usually lack the personality and talent and are fearful lest they lose their job or damage their promotion prospects. The Ministry of Labour has stated the conundrum well:

. . . the management of a few establishments will not treat with officials who are not members or ex-members of their staff. On the side of the Union . . . it is argued that the professional Secretary owes his existence largely to the fact that in the past attempts by employers to curb Union activity have taken the form of discharging the leaders or promoting them out of the Union sphere. It is also argued that he provides the necessary degree of literacy and, in the absence of other adequate methods of communication, is free to make personal contact with remote branches to obtain support and explain issues. From the management side it is argued that a salaried official recruited from the clerical rather than the industrial class has little knowledge of and less interest in the working of the concern in which the men he represents are employed; that he must, to retain his job, demonstrate his power, create

[1] Ministry of Labour, *Annual Report*, 1957–8, paragraph 100.

grievances and refuse compromise; and that meetings between management and workers become the occasion not for a calm and logical examination of problems, but for a display of intransigence if not of outright rudery towards the management designed, above all, to impress the membership that the Secretary is the right 'strong man' for the job.[1]

Other faults widespread among individual company union leaders are failure to comply with legal minima for the administration of union affairs, the mis-management and peculation of union funds and 'a prevalent tendency to repudiate collective agreements and arbitration awards'.[2] In the larger unions, particularly in the public sector, leadership tends to fissure into rival factions: northern versus southern, Ibo versus non-Ibo, a mirror of the central trade union organization rifts, or simply unrelinquishing emeritus officers versus newly elected officers.

A reasonably dedicated trade union leadership, with a certain administrative competence and with an ability to negotiate, bargain and compromise within an accepted set of ground rules, is a rather obvious *sine qua non* for the operation of a system of industrial relations designed after the Anglo-Saxon prototype. Individuals possessing these qualifications have been in the trade union movement: former Premier Obafemi Awolowo, Ayo Ogunsheye, one director and upwards of ten managers in the United Africa Company, the managing director of the Nigerian Railway Corporation, a number of permanent secretaries, most of the senior officials in the Ministry of Labour, and so on. The relevant fact is that all these men left the labour movement, and after a fairly short stay. It was for this reason that the Ministry of Labour and the Railway Corporation discontinued their trade union scholarship schemes in 1953 and 1955 – returning unionists invariably used their new educational qualification to secure a better appointment outside the trade union movement.[3] Capable and/or educationally qualified individuals have always had opportunities of career advancement outside of the movement, and they have taken these opportunities. It is no mere coincidence that all the major figures who have remained in the Nigerian labour movement – Messrs. Borha, Imoudu, Nzeribe, Goodluck, Bassey, Kanu, Adebola – have failed to complete their secondary education. In short, the cause of organized labour has not commanded any appreciable loyalty, even from its own leaders.

TRADE UNION MEMBERSHIP

A glimpse at the rank and file union membership helps to illuminate the attitudes of their leaders:

[1] Ministry of Labour, *Annual Report*, 1956–7, paragraph 73. [2] Yesufu, *op. cit.* pp. 88–91.

[3] For example, of the six trade union officials who received U.K. scholarships in 1950, three joined the civil service, two obtained jobs in industry and one stayed in the U.K. to study law. Department of Labour, *Annual Report* 1952–3, paragraph 111.

> The interest of members in their trade unions remains largely intermittent, rising most whenever there are prospects of immediate material gain; otherwise real interest has been lacking. Monthly dues have been allowed to fall in arrears; attendance at union meetings has fallen off, and the machinery of union government has often been virtually surrendered into the hands of a few union officials.[1]

Even during 1964, the year of organized labour's greatest exertions, the Ministry of Labour reported, 'Attendance at ordinary union meetings continued to be poor and the state of general apathy continued'.[2] The explanation, or at least a substantial part of it, for the worker's general disinterest in his union is admirably stated by Yesufu:

> The worker's tribal organization, or 'improvement' union in the town provides benefits in desperate cases, financially assists those who want to get married, pays the burial expenses of a deceased parent, makes a present on the occasion of the birth of a new babe, honours the worker elevated to a chieftaincy, and repatriates the destitute. Some tribal organizations award scholarships to the young educated worker or to the children of others. It is this that explains the seeming paradox that whereas the worker will not regularly subscribe to the funds of a trade union (apparently because he is too poor) he does pay regular subscriptions to the funds of his tribal 'union'; and the contributions are usually higher than those required by the trade union.
>
> Thus the trade union is caught in a vicious circle: it is deprived of funds because the services which it ought to render are provided by non-industrial organizations supported by the workers, and it cannot provide rival services because it has not funds. The sociological factors are equally impressive. In the tribal 'union' for example, the worker can speak and be spoken to in a language he understands well, against a background of customs and traditions which he comprehends. Those with whom he has to deal give him that due personal respect to which the African attaches so much importance. In one word, the worker feels that in the gathering of his tribal organization, he truly 'belongs'. In the trade union meeting on the other hand, matters are often discussed against an industrial and economic background which the worker hardly understands; the secretary of the trade union may be of a different tribe; and if in addition, he belongs to a rival political party, all the seeds of failure have been sown.[3]

THE EMPLOYERS

Up to this point little explicit has been said about management attitudes toward industrial relations. In the early years there was some reluctance for small employers to recognize their unions. And as already noted, many firms whose initial experience with a militant

[1] Ministry of Labour, *Annual Report*, 1958–9, paragraph 77.

[2] *Quarterly Review*, June 1964.

[3] *Daily Times* (Lagos) 14 April 1958, cited by Sklar, *Nigerian Political Parties*, p. 496.

professional unionist had been an unhappy one, as for instance the United Africa Company and Nigerian Breweries, were unwilling, until about 1960, to recognize and deal with a union unless its secretary was an employee of the company. While the small firms prior to 1962 seldom encouraged collective bargaining as such, most large firms – who find the process of negotiation and collective bargaining the easiest and most efficient way to deal with the complexities of their labour relations – were more than willing to negotiate and sign agreements with those union leaders willing to negotiate and bargain; it is also true that the firms have usually offered these same capable leaders jobs on the management side. On the other hand, management reaction to the 'strong man' trade union official has almost been universally hostile and any opportunity to undermine the official, including fostering dissension and rivalry within the union, has usually been exploited.

Since its inception in 1957, the Nigeria Employers Consultative Association (NECA) had advocated collective bargaining in place of the prevalent unilateral fixing of wages by employers.[1] Beyond its attachment to collective bargaining for its own desirability, the NECA executive continually pointed out to its members that only through the implementation of collective bargaining could the private sector free itself from being tied to the government wage awards. Virtually compulsory, large wage increases, backdated as much as nine months, are a very cumbersome and costly arrangement (although it saves on wage costs during the intervals) for commercial enterprises, which are unable to raise their prices retroactively. In 1962 the membership of NECA launched a major effort to establish industry-wide collective bargaining; to this end various trade groups were set up for the purpose of agreeing on common bargaining procedures, job classification, etc. However, by the end of 1965, despite the Federal Government's parallel action to make national joint industrial councils virtually compulsory, no industry-wide agreements had been negotiated, save for the renewal of two pre-existing agreements in the construction and tin-mining industries. The explanation for this failure was the inability to bring together representatives on the labour side.

In the absence of an effective channel of communications with their workers through the unions, all the larger firms have established some

[1] NECA's position before the Morgan Commission in December 1963 was as follows: 'Pending the successful complete development of a voluntary system of collective bargaining, the Association is satisfied that the State has sufficient legal powers and the necessary machinery to protect industries which have yet to be brought into the orbit of the voluntary system. The Association believes that with mutual co-operation between Government, employers and workers these problems can be overcome within the framework of the present system, and that a new system is unnecessary.' *NECA News*, January 1964.

form of joint consultation, as described earlier with reference to the United Africa Company. In practice, many of the issues theoretically reserved for negotiation with the union are discussed in joint consultation – thus inadvertently further weakening the prospects of unions fulfilling their intended roles.[1]

The actions of the government, particularly the British colonial government, as an employer have been a significant cause of the miscarriage of the Anglo-Saxon model in Nigeria. In failing to fix the wages of its own employees by negotiation with employee representatives the government has *de facto* precluded the operations of the voluntary system for half of organized labour. And indirectly, by the quantitative and normative power of its example, the actions of government have done much to undermine the potential for collective bargaining in the private sector.

At least three ways in which the government has adversely influenced collective bargaining in the private sector may be identified. First, the fact of public awards and their obligatory nature for private employers has had the effect of over-riding and nullifying all existing collective agreements. Second, retroactive awards have tended to break the nexus between wage determination and economic principles, thus setting up false expectations about the kind of wage claim that might be legitimately advanced against management in the bargaining context. Third, by paying their employees for the period in which they were on strike, the government has removed for the workers the gravity of taking such action, which can only have the consequence of encouraging labour demands, the short-cutting of negotiating procedures and frequent recourse to the strike.

This brings us to the critical question of why collective bargaining did not succeed in the public sector. An investigation of the subject turns up many already familiar ingredients, plus a few new ones peculiar to public bureaucracies.[2] The first Whitley council for the civil service collapsed in November 1949 after less than one year of operation. A dispute concerning the wage differential between clerical and technical grades was taken to arbitration. When the employees' representatives declined to accept the arbitrator's award, the official side refused to continue negotiations. An attempt to reconstitute the

[1] In a survey of twenty-one firms in 1963, it was found that in six companies where the unions were defunct or 'in fragments' joint consultative committees had taken over the unions' functions outright and that in fourteen of the remaining fifteen companies, matters theoretically reserved for union negotiation were also discussed in the joint consultative committees. Nigeria Employers Consultative Association, *Survey on Joint Consultation*, mimeograph, Lagos, August 1963.

[2] Drawn from the author's 'Establishment Interviews in Nigerian and Ghana, ILO Industrial Relations Survey', pp. 4–7.

council in the following year foundered for lack of consensus on the employees' side as to which of the contending union officials should represent them. For a brief spell from late 1952 until regionalization in 1954 a three-tiered system of councils functioned without major mishap; however, considerable jurisdictional red-tape was encountered as to what matters were negotiable.

In 1954, with the constitutional changes and the creation of four distinct governments, the entire Whitley council structure had to be reformed. In the north and west, trade union organization among the employees was so weak that it was never possible to bring the councils into operation. In the east, the Chief Secretary of the regional government, sharing an antipathy to unions and protracted negotiations found among certain private employers, effectively limited the proceedings of the Whitley councils by an artful administration of trade union scholarships. The docile and cooperative Whitley council labour representative was recommended, after a suitable term, for one of the British or American trade union scholarships, the satisfactory completion of which would qualify the recipient for promotion into the executive scale (and out of the trade union). More aggressive labour representatives, on the other hand, were treated quite differently.

The Federal Whitley councils in Lagos fared little better, as evidenced by the establishment of the Gorsuch Commission in 1954, the Mbanefo Commission in 1959 and the Morgan Commission in 1964. Leadership rivalry and poor case presentation on the employees' side was balanced by officials who were reluctant to spend the interminable hours required by these negotiations. Meetings tended to be desultory and infrequent. In general, the will to make the negotiating machinery work was not present in any marked degree on either side. As an example of the government's attitude, the Trades Union Congress requested in 1959 that the matter of wage revision be handled, not by a commission, but through existing collective bargaining machinery. 'But in spite of the TUC request and in spite of its adherence to the principles of collective bargaining, the Federal Government expressed a preference for a Commission instead, and proceeded to appoint one...'[1]

IV

A review of the literature on trade unionism in other underdeveloped countries reveals that Nigeria's experience is by no means unique; in fact, it conforms to a very common pattern.[2] The constituent elements

[1] Yesufu, *An Introduction to Industrial Relations in Nigeria*, p. 59.

[2] Walter Galenson, ed., *Labor and Economic Development*, New York 1959; Galenson, ed., *Labor in Developing Economies*, Berkeley 1962; Saad Ed Din Fawzi, *The Labour Movement in the*

of this pattern include a preponderance of many small weak unions, apathetic non-dues paying membership, vociferous but inept outside union leadership dealing with foreign employers, mal-administration and theft of union funds, a primary focus on wage claims, inability to sustain strikes, and realized gains won by politically-interested government intervention.

The absence of the necessary conditions for a viable system of voluntary collective bargaining has been noted by all investigators. The prescriptions offered are, virtually without exception, to strengthen voluntary labour-management negotiations: by promoting joint consultation, works committees, conciliation procedures and the like; by outlawing certain types of anti-union employer practices; and by training union leaders and developing membership interest and participation.[1] The possibility of abandoning the model of voluntary collective bargaining as inappropriate and unworkable is never seriously considered. Yesufu's position is typical:

> The great necessity in Nigerian industry today, therefore, is not to sweep away the principles of industrial democracy, but for both sides of industry to realize the magnitude of what is at stake, and to heed the exhortation that they must learn to develop the necessary patterns of living together. Essentially this is a matter of employers reorientating their whole attitude towards labour and the trade unions, and for the latter to develop strong, more inclusive, and responsible organizations. It is believed that these can be achieved partly through sustained education on all sides, and partly through experience. We have nevertheless suggested some amendments to existing legislation or administrative machinery; but these have been few, and intended, not to replace existing policy, but to make it more effective. If previous attempts to improve industrial relations in Nigeria through the educative process have not shown all the results that might have been expected, it is not because such efforts have been misdirected; it merely emphasizes the magnitude of the work to be done.[2]

AN INTERPRETATION

Is traditional economic unionism, based on voluntary collective bargaining, a potentially viable socio-economic institution for present day underdeveloped countries? To answer this question we must first

Sudan 1946–1955, London 1957; William H. Knowles, *Trade Union Development and Industrial Relations in the British West Indies*, Berkeley 1959; James L. Payne, *Labor and Politics in Peru*, New Haven 1965; M. E. Galvin, *Unionism in Latin America*, 1962, and W. H. Friedland, *Unions and Industrial Relations in Underdeveloped Countries*, 1963, Bulletins 46 and 47, School of Industrial and Labour Relations, Cornell.

[1] Fawzi, *op. cit.* chapter XII; Yesufu, *op. cit.* chapter IX; Galenson, *Labor and Economic Development*, Introduction and *Labour in Developing Economies*, Introduction; Arnold Zack, *Labor Training in Developing Countries: A Study in Responsible Democracy*, New York, 1964.

[2] Yesufu, *op. cit.* p. 176.

identify the needs to which the development of unions was the natural response, and, second, assess the relationship between the functions fulfilled by unions and their capacity to engage in collective bargaining.

Against a background of pervasive insecurity the first union function to emerge historically was the provision out of union funds of 'friendly benefits' – mutual insurance for sickness, unemployment, old age and death.[1] A second purpose of labour combination has been to win economic concessions from the employer (covering remuneration, hours, conditions of work and fringe benefits); such economic concessions included the prevention of wage-cuts or other forms of 'exploitation'. The latter – specifically the protection of the journeymen's real wage in the face of new forms of organization and intensifying competition in the product market – was one of the strongest forces behind the emergence of unions in the early stages of industrialization in Europe and America. Finally, and related to the foregoing, in the psychological-social realm, unions have endeavoured to restrict management's prerogatives in all matters affecting labour (promotion, discipline, working rules, redundancy, etc.), thereby limiting as far as possible the subordination of the worker which is inherent in the employer-employee relationship.

How compelling have been these three needs, which have traditionally given rise to trade unions, in under-developed countries since World War II ?

As we have earlier implied, rather than being an exploited group, organized labour is already a highly privileged minority. Whether initiated by modernizing nationalists or the departing colonial benefactor, the full range of welfare measures contained in the ILO conventions (e.g. minimum factory conditions, workmen's compensation, a limited working week, paid holidays, old age and medical insurance, etc.) have now been implemented in the unionized sectors of nearly all the countries of Latin America, Africa, Asia and the Middle East. These measures, in conjunction with traditional arrangements based on the extended family, have *pari pasu* obviated the need for trade union friendly benefits. Likewise on the wages side, the labourer's earnings considerably exceed his opportunity income outside the organized employment market – in short he is enjoying a higher standard of living than he has ever before known.

The problems and tensions arising out of the adaptation to the industrial way of life in the less developed areas have proved to be

[1] Henry Pelling, *A History of British Trade Unionism*, London 1963; A. Flanders and H. Clegg, eds., *The System of Industrial Relations in Great Britain*, Oxford 1954; Neil W. Chamberlain, *Collective Bargaining*, 2nd ed., New York 1965; Mark Perlman, 'Labour Movement Theories: Past, Present and Future', *Industrial and Labor Relations Review*, Ithaca, N.Y., April 1960.

far less significant than nineteenth-century history or twentieth-century sociological theorizing would indicate.[1] Indeed it is difficult to find instances of *industrial* unrest in backward economies. There is much *labour* unrest but it has little to do with the absolute wage or conditions of work; rather it is, as in Nigeria, an expression of relative deprivation by the 'haves' *vis-à-vis* the even smaller minority of the 'have-mores'. As for the 'rigours' of factory discipline, these have proved far more congenial than the back-breaking work in primitive agriculture. The relative unimportance of adaptation problems has also been noted.[2] Messrs. Kerr, Dunlop, Harbison, and Myers come to this conclusion:

> The major point we 'unlearned' had been one of our central themes at the outset. Protest was not such a dominant aspect of industrialization, and did not have such an effect on the course of society as we once thought.
> ... In the mid-twentieth century, workers do not destroy machines. The protest of today is more in favour of industrialization than against it.
> ... The potential benefits to the individual worker everywhere appear to transcend the negative consequences of industrialization. This is not a moral judgment, but a description of the dominance of the demands for modern goods: clothing, transport, movies, education, health and so on.[3]

The absence of an environment and a set of felt-needs similar to those which produced the Anglo-Saxon model has far-reaching implications for its institutional transfer. The sustained loyalty and discipline required of union members, which was built up in the earlier era only after long years of struggling for recognition, can not be generated when the antecedent goals pursued by the trade union lose their primacy. And without such loyalty and discipline, unions cannot achieve the maturity and stability that is needed to successfully negotiate and uphold voluntary agreements on a regular and uninterrupted basis.[4] In short, the development sequence – the learning process – required to make collective bargaining viable as a technique for determining wages is denied to present day underdeveloped countries.[5]

[1] For example, see the very elegant sociological analysis of the problems of commitment by Moore and Feldman; their theoretical contribution is followed by empirical studies (papers by Gregory, Morris, Knowles) which conclude that problems of labour commitment are relatively insignificant. W. E. Moore and A. S. Feldman, eds., *Labor Commitment and Social Change in Developing Areas*, New York 1960.

[2] Galenson, *Labor and Economic Development*, p. 3.

[3] C. Kerr, J. Dunlop, F. Harbison and C. Myers, *Industrialism and Industrial Man*, London 1962, pp. 6, 7, 195.

[4] While the original functions of trade unions in advanced countries may have atrophied, the skills and traditions 'learned' in the earlier period have carried forward to provide the basis for the mature Anglo-Saxon model.

[5] There is another more general point to be made about the possibility of an effective institutional transfer. Allan Flanders in his essay 'Collective Bargaining' emphasizes the unique evolutionary process which has produced the well-adapted British system of collective

Under existing circumstances in underdeveloped countries, the trade union ceases to serve any 'essential' need and thus elicits no sustained loyalty from either its leaders or its membership. Instead, labour organization becomes a political instrumentality for channelling the protest of privileged wage-earners against the distribution of the national wealth between themselves and those above them at the apex of the distributional pyramid. An evaluation of the political desirability of this outcome – weighing the costs of disruption against the benefits of pluralism – is outside the realm of the economist; but it is important to recognize that the unions' political power is an unintended result of purely economic policies. Could not labour's political representation be better achieved through political parties?

The economic consequences of the politicized Anglo-Saxon model stem from organized labour's political power to raise wages in the government and foreign private sector higher than they would be in the absence of such power. First, the higher wage level has raised the cost of production in these sectors and, by causing a diversion of potential investment resources to consumption, may have slowed the rate of economic growth. Given the government's budgetary constraint, a higher wage has meant less public employment. Of far greater significance, a rising W_0 has widened the income gap between the agricultural and the urban sector and has thereby aggravated the rural exodus and urban unemployment (with all of its political ramifications). Finally, and not least of all, in relation to the pre-existing non-unionized situation the politicized Anglo-Saxon model has resulted in worsened, rather than improved, industrial relations.

V

Most, if not all, of the political leverage of the Nigerian trade union movement could be neutralized by two simple measures. The first would be to remove government wage determination (and indirectly that for the private sector as well) from the domain of tribunals by tying it to the consumer price index with automatic semi-annual adjustments. For the private employers this would do away with the problems of discontinuous jumps in labour costs and retroactive payment. The second measure would be to pass a law making it illegal for any Nigerian to accept money or gifts of any kind from foreign labour organizations (e.g. AFL-CIO, WFTU). The first measure precludes the immediate political objective of central trade union organization,

bargaining: 'But the fact that it has been fostered and formed by the pressure of circumstances, not in accordance with any theory, explains why the practice is now so deeply rooted, why the tender plant of a century ago has become so robust.' Flanders and Clegg, *Industrial Relations in Great Britain*, p. 315.

while the second cuts off its *de facto* means of sustenance. With the wage issue taken care of, house unions, in addition to handling grievances, would be free to negotiate with their employers on other conditions of service.

At a more general level Nigeria has now reached a point where her policy-makers must transform a heretofore unpremeditated incomes policy, implied in an assorted collection of taxes and expenditure programmes, into a carefully thought out policy which has as its goals economic efficiency and growth, political stability and social justice. The two major areas in need of remedial action are the rural-urban incomes imbalance and the urban salary structure.

Considering first rural-urban imbalance, we can identify five policy variables. The first is *per capita* earnings in agriculture, W_A, which is influenced by government programmes to increase physical productivity and by Marketing Board price policies. In connection with producer price policies we would stress the importance of viewing the economy as an interdependent whole rather than taking a 'balanced budget' stance *vis-à-vis* the Marketing Boards in isolation. Specifically, in terms of intersectoral balance and technical progress in agriculture we would argue that the marginal product of (say) £10m. of the multiplying oil revenues spent in raising producer prices *above* world prices is likely to be greater than in its best alternative use.[1] Such subsidies would (*a*) stimulate total output, capital formation, technological advance, etc., in the agricultural sector, (*b*) increase real farm income, and (*c*) reduce real urban incomes as a result of rising food prices (as farmers shifted out of food toward the now remunerative Marketing Board exports).

The second variable affecting the rural-urban imbalance is, of course, W_O. While it is seldom possible to reduce money wages, real wages can be reduced by manipulating the price level. Hence policies to inflate agricultural income should be launched if possible *before* tying W_O to the cost-of-living index.

The third variable, closely connected to W_O, is the towns' unemployment supportive capacity. Measures to reduce this capacity are various taxes which have only second-order effects on output incentives: urban poll taxes, expanded and increased urban property taxation, and a reformed progressive personal income tax. One other possibility is a *per capita* 'unemployment tax' which could be levied on heads of households for every unemployed male dependent age 15–40 who is not attending school or in some other way incapacitated.

The fourth factor affecting the rural-urban imbalance is the

[1] The possibility of using Marketing Boards as an instrument of negative taxation was suggested to the writer by Harley Hinrichs.

comparatively greater government-financed amenities in the towns, i.e. the implicit wage supplement. There is much that government can do to shift its utility-diffusing expenditures from the major towns to rural areas and smaller country towns – in the way of schools, medical facilities, sports stadia and the like.

The final factor noted in section II as influencing city migration is the country dweller's perceived probability of obtaining employment in the urban high wage sector. This is simply a matter of publicizing via newspapers and radio the lack of job openings and the extent of urban unemployment and its cruel hardships; this should be coupled with positive publicity about vocational possibilities in agriculture.

With this very substantial arsenal of policy instruments at their disposal, Nigerian policy makers have both the power and the situational flexibility with which to remedy the rural-urban imbalance.

The second major problem in the area of incomes policy is an inflated salary structure, which has its origin in government pay scales. The major economic consequences of a salary structure extended beyond the requirements of incentive are to reduce employment, output and growth,[1] and to induce a misallocation of educational resources. The political and social consequences, however, are far more important: arbitrary and wide differentials in income which find no justification in either scarcity or productive contribution are a major cause of political tension in general and the prime dynamic in trade union intransigence and aggression in particular. Considerations of social justice are no less compelling.

Table 77. *Government salary structure, 1965*

Educational attainment	Years of school	Entering salary (£ p.a.)	Normal ceiling (£ p.a.)	Highest post (£ p.a.)
Primary School Certificate	6	129	246	—
Section IV Certificate	10	168	397	—
WASC/GCE	11	198	828	—
HSC/GCE, A	13	336	1,890	—
B.A./B.Sc.	16	648	1,890	3,900
Honours B.A./B.Sc.	16	720	1,890	3,900

SOURCE: T. Elwood and R. R. Olisa, *Report of the Grading Team on the Grading of Posts in the Public Services of the Federation of Nigeria*, Ministry of Information, Lagos 1966, p. 20 and appendix IV.

As seen in table 77, the entering civil service salary for all without a Bachelor's degree is very compressed, although 5th and 6th formers have very much higher promotion ceilings. Bachelor degree holders, on

[1] We assume here that the marginal propensity of salary-earners to abstain from current consumption, apart from investment in urban real estate and education, is not great.

the other hand, start out at a salary double that enjoyed by those with three years less education: these scales hark back to pre-1960 scarcity conditions and the colonial principle of European-African pay parity, and can no longer be justified. Entry salaries of £500, ceilings of £1,200 and highest post of £2,000 represent the order of magnitude that should be considered for university graduates. And, as recommended by both the Morgan and Elwood commissions, the entire system of housing and car allowances should be abolished.

A far more drastic reduction in salary and allowances is required for Ministers (e.g. £8,625 in 1965),[1] junior ministers, public corporation officers and members of parliament. As a socially and politically disequilibrating factor, the unconscionable differentials enjoyed by this group are of greater importance than those in the civil service.

[1] *West Africa*, 10 April 1965.

Part 5

CHAPTER 10

INDIGENOUS ENTERPRISE

The last subject to be scrutinized is the development of the indigenous or small-scale industrial sector. Various aspects of this sector have been described in previous chapters. In chapter 1 it was estimated that about 100,000 persons were engaged in some form of urban small-scale manufacturing. It was noted that such production manifests wide diversity in the level of technology employed, utilization of capital equipment and factor proportions; on the demand side there is a parallel stratification of raw material inputs, product quality and sub-markets being served. Finally there is a corresponding variegation in entrepreneurial organization and labour employment.

In previous chapters considerable evidence was presented with regard to labour performance and organizational efficiency in the larger Nigerian firms. Workers are generally low-paid relative to those in the organized sector and unions are rare; technical skills are, for the most part, very limited. Managerial organization and supervision, as exemplified in the Pioneer oil mills and rubber crêping firms, are usually deficient.

In approaching the indigenous industrial sector, what are the questions that should be posed, what is the nature of our interest here? The conventional focus has been to concentrate on the scale of production, assessing the contribution of indigenous enterprise to economic development through an analysis of the potentialities of small-scale industry.

The benefits of small-scale indigenous industry, and the case for programmes to stimulate its development, are typically stated as follows.[1] The promotion of this form of industry lessens the need for foreign enclave-type enterprise. In contrast to concentration in a few cities with its implications of urban unemployment and political unrest, small-scale industry can be geographically decentralized, creating many 'islands of development'. Small firms provide a training ground or stepping-stone to larger scale enterprises. Small industry taps latent savings and skills that could not otherwise be mobilized. Because small-scale production entails labour-intensive technologies, for a given amount of capital (the scarce factor) both employment and output will

[1] See the writings of H. G. Aubrey, Bert Hoselitz and Eugene Staley. The presentation here draws on an excellent 'conventional' exposition by H. W. Singer, 'Small-scale Industry in African Economic Development' in E. A. G. Robinson, ed., *Economic Development for Africa South of the Sahara*, New York 1964, pp. 638–48.

be larger under a régime of small industry than under alternative forms of organization.

Several of these propositions do not stand up to the empirical test. To the extent large-scale production is financed by foreign investment, it represents a windfall gain in employment and output – in terms of the allocation of domestic capital the opportunity cost is zero. We saw in chapter 1 that the bulk of small industry is congregated in the major urban areas: they represent satellite activities with only limited possibilities for geographic decentralization. Backward in technology and managerial performance, small-scale industries rarely constitute 'islands of development' or an effective training school for larger industry. Much of small industry toward the lower end of the scale is characterized by atomistic competition, product dilution and zero profits; these characteristics combine to produce something akin to a low-level equilibrium trap.[1]

What then is the proper development perspective on the small-scale industrial sector? As a quasi-sponge for urban unemployment and a provider of inexpensive consumer goods with little or no import content, this sector serves important pressure-releasing, welfare-augmenting functions. Its more positive role in contributing to long run industrial growth is to produce an increasing number of firms that grow up and out of the small-scale sector. The emergence of wholly modern, medium-scale Nigerian industry is likely to be a prerequisite for any enduring industrialization. As we shall see subsequently, the problems encountered in attempting to develop the most promising firms are ultimately related to questions of entrepreneurship.

It is fortunate, if the foregoing analysis is correct, that most development programmes aimed at indigenous enterprise have been of a selective nature, directed to the 'high potential' firms. In following sections of this chapter we shall review the history of the four most important government assistance programmes: the textile development scheme of 1946–56, the Yaba industrial estate, the Federal Loans Board, and the lending activities of the regional Development Corporations.[2] The concluding section will deal specifically with observed patterns of entrepreneurial behaviour and their implications for the long run development of Nigerian industry.

[1] For a discussion of the full range of problems encountered by small industry and policy prescriptions, see the author's *The Development of small Industry in Eastern Nigeria*.

[2] Sayre P. Schatz is currently working on a study of government assistance programmes to Nigerian industry which will provide a more extensive treatment of the textile and regional loan schemes than the presentation given here. Professor Schatz also conducted a study of the Federal Loans Board at about the same time the author was carrying out the investigation reported in this chapter; the former's monograph (see Bibliography) appeared after the present study was written, and since differences are a matter of emphasis and interpretation, the original draft has not been altered.

I

The textile development scheme was launched in 1946 as part of the Ten-Year Plan. A project of the Department of Commerce and Industries, this scheme represents the largest single technical assistance effort undertaken by the government to foster the development of a Nigerian industry.

The initial project, budgeted at £380,000, involved the establishment of eight (later reduced to seven) textile centres; each centre was placed under the supervision of a resident European specialist whose duties were to investigate local methods, evolve and demonstrate improved techniques and, in general, to aid Nigerian weavers in solving whatever problems they might have.[1] The scheme developed with great promise. Despite early misgivings about peasant conservatism, the response of traditional frame-loom weavers was very positive. The innovations were accepted and training eagerly sought as it was quickly perceived that the new methods were more productive and would yield higher earnings. Developments were equally encouraging on the technical side. Simple inexpensive implements were successfully introduced; these included a miniature cotton gin, a hand-carding machine, a broad loom, and a spinning wheel – all made from local materials and capable of being constructed by the village carpenter. Fast, bright dyestuffs were developed from native plants and the indigo hydrosulphite vat dyeing method was widely adopted.

In 1949 the textile development scheme was broadened to include power-looms. This apparently evolved out of assistance given to three small power-loom operators in Lagos[2] and the decision to grant large loans for the establishment of two sixty-loom weaving factories. Government enthusiasm waxed; the growth of an extensive indigenous mechanized textile industry was foreseen. Accordingly, a Textile Research and Advisory Centre was set up in 1950 to undertake research on locally produced cloth and to advise entrepreneurs on types of equipment, overseas suppliers, plant design and layout, and other technological problems. A Mechanical Training Centre (three were initially planned) was also established; utilizing expatriate instructors and extensive textile machinery, the Centre was to provide a seven year (later reduced to five and then four year) course for training skilled textile mill supervisors ('overlookers').

[1] The following history of the textile scheme is drawn from the annual reports of the Department of Commerce and Industries. For developments after 1955 the narrative is based upon the annual reports of the regional ministries and the author's own field research during 1959–62 and 1964.

[2] Nubi Textiles (1 loom), Fast-Colour Textile Works (2 looms) and Ogunbiyi Textile Mills (4 looms).

At the mid-point of the Ten-Year Plan, 1950–1, an evaluation of the hand-loom programme was carried out. The findings were unexpected. It was discovered that upon returning to their home areas 'even the fully trained weaver almost invariably relapses into slovenly and inefficient ways and perhaps fails altogether'.[1] Consequently the emphasis was shifted from training to supervision – supervision of 'professional' weavers (operating commercially on a full-time basis) to be located as near as possible to the centres. The Ministry soon realized that not only were there difficulties on the production side, but in organization, purchasing and marketing there were even more extensive problems. It was found that 'the manual operation of a loom can be taught within a short time, but the management experience necessary to run even the smallest unit takes far longer to acquire'.[2]

Viable commercial enterprises did not develop. In the north the sponsorship of weaving units was to a large degree taken over by the Native Authorities. In the west most professional weavers joined one of several large co-operative societies; the latter received 'soft' loans from the regional Development Board and sold their cloth to public agencies at prices higher than those prevailing in the market place. Aided by government loans and periodic rural industry grants a few private concerns were formed in the east. Several of these were still limping along in 1964, providing a modest subsistence for the entrepreneur and training for his numerous apprentices.

In October 1954 the administration of the textile scheme was transferred to the regional governments. The principal effect of regionalization was to reduce the number of trained specialists engaged in field work. Most of the expatriates who stayed on after the change-over were drawn into administrative duties in the newly created ministries in Ibadan, Enugu and Kaduna. The Textile Research and Advisory Centre and the Mechanical Training Centre, still under Federal auspices, were closed down in March 1957. In the case of the latter, the first set of seven graduates had not been able to find employment, or at least on acceptable terms, with any of the then ailing power-loom operators.[3]

The history of Nigeria's first two textile mills is of interest not only from the point of view of the development of the industry, but equally as it illustrates the not untypical performance of Nigerian entrepreneurs in establishing pioneer industrial concerns, even when, as in this case, very considerable finance and technical supervision is provided by the government.

[1] *Annual Report of the Department of Commerce and Industries, 1950–1*, p. 14.

[2] *Annual Report of the Department of Commerce and Industries, 1951–2*, p. 20.

[3] The majority of these graduates were eventually employed as Assistant Textile Officers in the regional ministries.

In early 1949 J. F. Kamson & Company was granted a loan of £30,000 by the Colony Development Board for the purpose of establishing a weaving factory for the manufacture of grey baft, khaki drills and bleached shirting. In addition the Department of Commerce and Industries agreed to provide the technical management. In the same year some sixty power-looms, yarn preparation machinery and finishing equipment, all second-hand, were purchased in Lancashire through the Department of Commerce and Industries.[1] Two years later, in March 1951, thirty-six of the sixty looms came into production. After the first month the efficiency of machine operation was 70 %; the product was competitive in price and deemed superior in quality to much of the imported sheeting.[2] This promising start was cut short, however, by the withdrawal of the government textile officers upon an altercation with the proprietor over marketing strategy.

In addition to losing his technical managers, Mr. Kamson was caught in a market situation, brought about by the war in Korea, where the price of imported yarn was rising faster than the price of competing imported cloth. Rather than wait for this temporary situation to pass as advised by the Department of Commerce and Industries and the Loans Board, Kamson decided to buy spinning equipment which would allow him to convert Nigerian cotton lint into yarn. As the Loans Board observed Kamson's course of action extended an already weak position into an area of maximum uncertainty:[3]

> It was uncertain whether the machines would in fact spin Nigerian lint, and again whether Nigerian lint would produce an adequate range of yarn counts without a mixture with other lints; if it proves deficient in strength, the establishment of an indigenous spinning industry will be a difficult problem until greater skills are available locally. The Board therefore was naturally reluctant to consider Messrs. Kamson's application for a further loan of £20,000 for the purchase of spinning machinery. It may be that the firm will ultimately succeed in its fresh enterprise, but confidence in a management which has signally failed to make a success of an organization soundly established will be hard to find when the inadvisable complication of new techniques has been introduced.

In 1953–4 when the Loans Board decided to foreclose on the loan and sell the securities, the spinning equipment was not yet in operation.[4] In the same year weaving operations, still using imported yarns, also ceased.[5] In September 1955 upon the payment of £30,000 to the Loans Board, the mill was taken over by the Nigerian Spinning

[1] *Annual Report of the Department of Commerce and Industries, 1949–50*, p. 16.
[2] *Annual Report of the Department of Commerce and Industries, 1950–1*, p. 15.
[3] *Annual Report of the Colony Development Board, 1951–2*, p. 5.
[4] *Annual Report of the Colony Development Board, 1953–4*, p. 4.
[5] *Annual Report of the Federal Ministry of Commerce and Industry, 1955–6*, p. 24.

Company, a Nigerian partnership formed by Dr. A. Maja and Chief T. Doherty. The latter were financed by the National Bank, of which they were officers.

Once again the government textile officers assumed the technical management of the mill leaving labour relations, general administration and sales to the company.[1] Upon taking over the mill, the textile officers reported that 'none of the equipment was in working order; indeed, the machinery was in need of such complete over-haul as to amount to a virtual rebuilding'.[2] It was possible to recommission only half of the looms. Another thirty looms were ordered but an unspecified number of these were badly damaged in shipping; there were also difficulties in securing spare parts.[3] 'In accordance with the decision taken in 1957–8' the Ministry of Commerce and Industry's second stewardship came to an end in July 1958.[4]

During this second period of government tutelage the Ministry's annual reports emphasize improvements in quality, cost reduction and increases in output; 'future viability will largely depend upon how much money is forthcoming for improvements and additions to the equipment and buildings'.[5] In curious juxtaposition to these favourable and expansionist remarks, the Ministry also reports that stocks began to accumulate and that in the second year production had to be cut back – and this was during a period when only half of the looms were in working order. The blame is laid at the door of the proprietors who 'did little to push sales'.[6] Yet, as the latter were traders of proven ability and the textile market was large and expanding, it is difficult to avoid the conclusion that in failing to produce the quality of cloth the market required, the Ministry shared the responsibility for the venture's lack of success. Inadequate sensitivity to the many aspects of the market situation is a characteristic often found in public enterprise.

The other two weaving concerns in Lagos, operating on a much smaller scale, fared no better and indeed worse than the Mushin mill. Ogunbiyi Textile Mills was originally founded in the early 1940s. In 1948 the Nigeria Local Development Board granted the firm a loan of £1,500 to purchase several power-looms and other equipment; a further loan of £1,000 to cover an adequate stock of yarn was given the following year. The son of the proprietor was selected as one of the trainees for the Mechanical Training Centre. Despite considerable help from the government textile officers the firm went into liquidation, the

[1] *Annual Report of the Federal Ministry of Commerce and Industry, 1956–7*, p. 23.
[2] *Annual Report of the Federal Ministry of Commerce and Industry, 1955–6*, p. 25.
[3] *Annual Report of the Federal Ministry of Commerce and Industry, 1957–8*, p. 27.
[4] *Annual Report of the Federal Ministry of Commerce and Industry, 1958–9*, p. 26. [5] *Ibid.*
[6] *Annual Report of the Federal Ministry of Commerce and Industry, 1957–8*, p. 31.

loans defaulting: 'It was badly managed, having the outlook of a petty trader, kept no proper accounts, and failed to devise a long term programme.'[1]

The story of the second concern, Fast-Colour Textile Works, is best told in the words of the Colony Development Board.

> A loan of £1,920 had been made in July 1948. Unfortunately the firm had already installed machinery, including looms of a type that the Department of Commerce and Industries would not have recommended the company to buy, and it had placed a large order for yarn that on delivery proved to be warp yarn and unsuitable for the purpose for which it was intended. It had therefore by its commitments in both plant and yarn seriously jeopardised from the outset the possibility of efficient production. It defaulted on its first repayment of the loan, and shortly afterwards applied for a further loan of £30,000. An offer of £750 was refused, and the advice of the Textile Officers of Commerce and Industries was ignored. The Board came to the reluctant conclusion that legal proceedings should be instituted for the recovery of the loan. Judgement for a sum equal to the first and second instalments of the loan was given in February, and a Writ of Attachment and Sale was obtained. The defendants filed a Notice of Appeal and also sued the Board for £10,000 damages for breach of contract, alleging that the firm's acceptance of an offer by the Department of Commerce and Industries to take over and manage the factory had been ignored by the Department and the Board.[2]

The early history of the Kano Citizens Trading Company parallels that of J. F. Kamson & Company. A group of politically influential Hausa traders were given a loan of £35,000 by the Northern Region Development Board in 1949.[3] Again, used Lancashire equipment was ordered by the Department of Commerce and Industries, who also undertook management of the operations. Initial hurdles included the necessity to install a generator because the public authority could not supply sufficient current; an undisclosed number of machines were seriously damaged in transit. A second loan of £30,000 for 'working capital' was granted in 1950–1. Production, with less than half the looms in operation, began in November 1951. Both productivity and quality were low: 'The training of Hausa weavers is taking longer than expected and their speed of operation when trained is disappointing . . . under present conditions there is no comparison (with imports) either in quality or costs.'[4] A sales problem developed almost immediately.

Gradually, however, the mill's performance improved. Yet no repayments of principal or interest were forthcoming. In 1953–4 a Board of

[1] *Annual Report of the Colony Development Board, 1951–2*, p. 4. [2] *Ibid.*

[3] The following narrative is drawn from the annual reports of the Ministry of Commerce and Industry and the Northern Region Development Board.

[4] *Annual Report of the Department of Commerce and Industries, 1951–2*, p. 21.

Management was created; the board included representatives of the Ministry of Commerce and Industry and the Northern Region Development Board. Five years later (and still no repayments) the Board took over the assets as well as all phases of the management of the company. From 1958 onwards the mill showed a 'profit', rising from £15,000 to £30,000; this was, however, exclusive of interest charges, debt repayment and the cost of two expatriate managers.

Ever-increasing tariff protection and the Approved Manufacturers Scheme (i.e. government patronage) launched in the mid-fifties contributed to the viability of these two mills. In 1964 the Nigerian Spinning Company was operating at less than 50 % efficiency, but even at 300,000 yards a year the venture was turning a modest profit.[1] In the same year Kano Citizens Trading Company, still under European management and selling primarily to a captive government market, produced 2m. yards. Nevertheless, considering the time and resources expended on these two projects, the results have been rather disappointing.

II

The first industrial estates were opened in 1956.[2] The vast majority of these industrial parks, about two score in 1966, consist of undeveloped factory sites, feeder roads and utility connections. The advantages of long-term leasing within an estate as against individual acquisition of factory sites include the avoidance of land speculation 'hold-ups' and problems of securing legal title, economies of scale in utility installation, and rational location in terms of urban planning (e.g. effluent disposal, smoke dissipation, landscaping, parking, etc.). It is upon such estates that most foreign and government-operated industry is to be found.

In contrast to such industrial tracts, the Yaba industrial estate provides factory buildings, limited technical assistance (accounting aid and machine workshop facilities), and the full range of amenities (toilets, showers, canteen, garage, etc.)[3] Designed as an asssistance measure to indigenous enterprise, its purpose was 'to fill in the need for modern factory buildings for small-scale Nigerian industrialists. This need arises because every available space on the island of Lagos which can be used for industries is already over-crowded and the high cost of land and building inhibits the small industrialist from expanding his

[1] The information in this and the following sentence was obtained by interview with the respective factory managers in October 1964.

[2] For a description of Nigeria's industrial estates, the facilities they offer and rental costs, see 'Industrial Estates', *Nigerian Trade Journal*, July/September 1965, pp. 118–24.

[3] The sources for the following study of the Yaba estate are the author's interviewing on the estate in 1962 and 1964; 'Industrial Estate at Yaba', *Nigerian Trade Journal*, pp. 133–6 October/December 1958; and Sayre P. Schatz, 'Aiding Nigerian Business: The Yaba Industrial Estate', *Nigerian Journal of Economic and Social Studies*, July 1964, pp. 199–217.

existing premises.'[1] In addition to alleviating the capital requirement for budding small-scale industry, the estate was to function as an assistance-supplying nursery which its developing tenants would outgrow, to be replaced by new 'seedling' firms.[2]

The idea for such an estate was developed by the Department of Commerce and Industries in 1951; the IBRD mission gave its full support for the scheme in 1953.[3] An irregularly shaped 2¾ acre plot of Crown land was obtained in Yaba, just outside of Lagos; construction was undertaken by Nigerian building contractors under the supervision of the Federal Department of Public Works. Capable of housing thirty tenants in workshop units measuring 30 to 40 feet, the estate cost about £80,000 when it was completed in 1958.[4] The administrative and custodial needs of the estate are provided by permanently assigned personnel from the Ministry of Commerce and Industry at no cost to the tenants.

In addition to the availability of machine shop services to manufacture spare parts and technical advice from the resident industrial officer, tenants receive a rent subsidy for the first five years of occupancy. A 40 % discount on the 'full economic cost' rent is given in the first two years, and 14 % for the second three. Actually, as Sayre Schatz has pointed out, a number of important costs were not included in the full rent charge, with the result that even it carries a substantial subsidy.[5]

It was over the question of rent that difficulties with the operation of the estate were first brought to the surface. From the beginning there had been a problem with rent arrears. In mid-1961 the first jump in rent came into effect for early tenants. The latter refused to pay the increment (despite their earlier contractual agreement to do so) and began paying their rent, not to the estate, but into the Tenants' Association bank account pending the outcome of their dispute with the Ministry of Commerce and Industry.

In making their case against the increase in rent, the tenants advanced the following arguments, not all of which were strictly relevant to the rent issue.[6] First, their earnings were insufficient to pay the higher rent.

[1] 'Industrial Estate at Yaba', *Nigerian Trade Journal*, p. 133.

[2] *Ibid.* p. 134.

[3] International Bank for Reconstruction and Development, *The Economic Development of Nigeria*, p. 232.

[4] Schatz, *op. cit.* p. 203.

[5] *Ibid.* p. 204. The rent calculation did not allow for any ground rent on the Crown land, nor for an interest charge on the £80,000. Also it was assumed that the estate would be fully occupied and that all rents would be collected; amortization was set at thirty years although there was some question that twenty years might have been a more realistic estimate.

[6] The author at the time working on a report concerning the development of Nigerian industry was asked by the Ministry of Commerce and Industry to make an independent evaluation of the situation. See Peter Kilby, 'Measures to Promote the Development of Indigenous Industry – A Report to the Federal Ministry of Commerce and Industry', U.S. Agency for International Development, mimeograph, May 1962, pp. 8–11.

Second, the services of the engineering workshop were (*a*) over-priced and (*b*) not generally needed by the tenants. Third, the estate was unfavourably located with respect to marketing. Fourth, there was very little useful technical assistance actually given by the Ministry of Commerce and Industry.

Events (an adverse court decision in 1963 and capitulation by the tenants) proved the first argument false, while Schatz's investigations discredited the fourth.[1] Nevertheless it is true that as of 1964 there had been only two instances of successful 'development' – an electric equipment repair firm and a producer of inner-spring mattresses. Part of the explanation for this modest record is to be found in the type of industries the estate has housed; the figures in parentheses in the listings below indicate the number of firms.[2]

1959	1964
Electrical equipment repairs	Tarpaulin edging
Coffee grinding	Tyre retreading
Mattresses	Mattresses
Furniture	Furniture making (3)
Wood carving	Wood carving
Instrument repairs	Sanitary napkins
Vulcanizing	Lapel buttons
Printing	Printing (5)
Sound recording	Cosmetics
Tailoring	Clothing (4)
Singlets	Singlets
Sign writing	Sign writing (2)
Auto body repair and painting	Auto body repair and painting
Shoe repair	Shoe repair and manufacture
Ornamental ironwork	Teaching aids
Typewriter repairs	Typewriter repairs
Hair dressing and cosmetics	Electrical installation

The estate population has grown from seventeen tenants employing about 310 workers in 1959 to twenty-eight tenants employing 470 workers in 1964. Firm size in 1964 ranged from four to fifty-five employees. However, from the development-nursery perspective the most noteworthy point is the relatively high proportion of non-industrial tenants, even in 1964. Service, repair, simple assembly and craft activities are not the kind of activities the estate was designed to cater for. Only ten of the tenants in 1964 were employing fixed power equipment

[1] Schatz, *op. cit.* pp. 209–11.

[2] Data for 1964 collected by the writer. Data for 1959 from *Annual Report of the Ministry of Commerce and Industry, 1959–60*, para. 82.

for which the flooring has been especially constructed. An even fewer number had need of or patronized the engineering workshop.

Given the foregoing facts one is driven to the conclusion that the estate tenants were attracted not by the unique development assistance features at Yaba, but rather by the subsidized rent. This in turn suggests something about the effective demand for a 'fully packaged industrial estate' by those firms who are in a position to make use of its special features. Schatz's narrative confirms these conclusions.

> ... the Estate has been kept full only by relaxing the initial entrance requirements. The Ministry became less selective regarding the type of tenants they would accept, admitting many firms that originally would have been excluded as non-industrial. The Ministry has stimulated demand by giving concessions to potential new tenants. A new tenant, for example, may be given up to three months before rent payments start for moving in his equipment and getting the unit ready for operations. The already mentioned fact that the government is a 'soft-hearted landlord', as one of the tenants put it, and rent payments can be deferred for many months has also helped to keep the Estate occupied. Some tenants have entered the Estate on a 'heads I win, tails you lose', basis: if their businesses turn out to be profitable they ultimately pay their rent; if they are unprofitable, they simply leave the Estate, leaving their rent unpaid. (The government has been singularly unsuccessful in collecting rental debts from erstwhile tenants). An expatriate firm which had been operating in the Estate almost since its inception was still there on a month-to-month basis at the time of the writer's visit to September 1961 [still there in 1964]; this implies that no acceptable Nigerian firms had been anxiously awaiting entry into the Industrial Estate. Somewhat meagre demand for units is also suggested by the fact that the Industrial Officers not infrequently attempted to persuade businessmen to move to the Industrial Estate. A good many of the applicants to the Federal Loans Board, for example, especially during 1958 and 1959, were advised to do this.
>
> Despite concessions to tenants and other efforts to keep the estate full, there was a large turnover of tenants. During the Estate's first 35 months of operation, there were approximately 60 tenants, two-thirds of whom had vacated.[1]

The primary lesson to be drawn from the history of the Yaba estate is that the provision of inexpensive accommodation for small-scale industry should be kept quite separate from the nursery function of providing development assistance. Combining the two, as was done at Yaba, is both expensive and highly inefficient. Unfortunately, despite knowledge of the Yaba estate's performance, the Eastern Nigeria Ministry of Commerce is building another such estate in Enugu.[2]

[1] Schatz, *op. cit.* p. 212.

[2] 'Industrial Estates', *Nigerian Trade Journal, July/September* 1965, p. 122.

The optimum solution to 'the high cost of industrial land' is to set aside a tract of undeveloped crown land located near a major transport artery and, if possible, in the vicinity of a market. After stipulating minimum size and construction standards, plot sub-divisions, sanitation requirements and the like, plots would be leased directly to industrialists who would be free to develop their own structure in conformity to their individual needs and at a substantially lower cost than would be possible for public authorities. A variation of this scheme has proved most successful in Eastern Nigeria.[1] Such provision of land to small-scale industry should involve no subsidization to the tenants. The economies of agglomeration (which would be passed on in lower rent) should result in a slight lowering of the tenants' production costs; this is likely, however, to have little if any impact on the quality of entrepreneurial performance or the development of the individual firm. Only measures which effectively promote this latter objective can qualify for government subsidization.[2]

The development assistance, nursery function of a Yaba-type estate does qualify for subsidization in so far as the tenant firms are capable of utilizing the estate's facilities. The qualifications for tenancy should be twofold: a clear potential for further entrepreneurial development on the part of the proprietor, and the enterprise should in some sense represent a pioneer venture for the entrepreneur. Old small industrialists have remained small industrialists because, by and large, they lacked the requisite entrepreneurial potential. Thus we want a 'new' small industrialist, who appears to have the potential to grow out of small industry and who, as proof of such potential, is pioneering either a new industry or a larger scale of operation in his previous line of production.

Aside from the advantage of technical assistance, renting a pre-constructed factory premise, as opposed to acquiring land and commissioning a building, reduces both the risk of failure and the capital investment put at stake – a considerable virtue for high-risk pioneer ventures. Particularly appropriate candidates from this point of view are the recipients of sizeable government development loans. And it is to the subject of government lending programmes that we now turn.

III

In terms of financial resources, by far the most important development assistance to indigenous industry has been the provision of loan capital.

[1] Known as 'layouts', workshop space in these plots rent for about one-fifth the 'full cost economic rent' at Yaba. *The Development of Small Industry in Eastern Nigeria*, pp. 10–11.

[2] The appropriate analogy here is temporary tariff protection for a promising infant industry as against permanent tariff subsidization for the infant industry which lacks the necessary potential comparative advantage.

Between 1950 and 1965 over £4m. was loaned to Nigerian entrepreneurs by governmental agencies. This lending has been on a long term basis for the purpose of the borrowers acquiring additional productive capacity – an activity which private banking has found too risky to engage in.

The major portion of this section will deal with the Federal Loans Board, the most successful of the lending agencies and perhaps the most successful of all the development programmes directed at indigenous industrial enterprise. The more extensive but less efficiently administered activities of regional lending agencies will be briefly surveyed and compared with the performance of the Federal Loans Board.

HISTORICAL BACKGROUND

Nigeria's first public lending agency was the Nigeria Local Development Board set up in 1946. As implied by its name the Development Board was given wide jurisdiction '... making grants and loans to Native Administrations, Co-operative Societies and such other public bodies as may be approved by the Governor-in-Council for prescribed development purposes.'[1] In 1949 this single Board was dissolved, its functions passing to the newly formed Northern, Eastern and Western Regional Development Boards and the Colony Development Board. The latter was responsible for Lagos and the adjacent Colony Province.

Although the ordinance establishing the Colony Development Board enumerated, *inter alia*, experimental undertakings and welfare projects as proper fields of endeavour, the new Board determined to follow the comparatively cautious policy laid down by its predecessor of confining itself to industrial and agricultural loans for commercially viable projects.[2] Commitments inherited from the original Board consisted of six such loans, totalling £34,000.

The Colony Development Board was in operation for seven years, 1949 to 1956. The Board received a single grant from the Federal Government of £84,000 at its commencement. Of this amount £74,000 had been committed by May 1956 in some thirty-three loans, ranging in duration from two to ten years at 2 to 5 % interest. Agricultural loans, of which there were ten, were discontinued in June of 1954 '... because farmers are rarely able to offer proper security and because not a single agricultural loan made by the Board has been a success'.[3] Industrial loans including the six taken over from the Nigeria

[1] *Annual Report of the Nigeria Local Development Board, 1947*, p. 1. Unless otherwise indicated the source material for the following historical summary is drawn from the annual reports of the Nigeria Local Development Board and its successor agencies.

[2] *Annual Report of the Colony Development Board, 1951–2*, p. 1.

[3] *Annual Report of the Colony Development Board, 1954–5*, p. 1.

Local Development Board, were made to private ventures engaged in baking (£8,000), saw milling (£4,800), and the manufacture of ceramics (£37,000), textiles (£35,000) and furniture (£6,500). The two largest single loans were £37,000 for ceramics and £30,000 for textiles; in the main, however, the loans were of modest size – all but four were for less than £4,000.

In May 1956 the Colony Development Board was dissolved. Its commitments in the Colony Province were taken over by the Western Region Finance Corporation while its outstanding loans in the federal territory were passed on to the new Federal Loans Board. The purpose of the Federal Loans Board was 'to promote *industrial* development in and around Lagos and in respect of projects of a major nature to promote industrial development throughout the Federation'.[1] The ordinance provided that all loans exceeding £3,000 would require the approval of the Minister of Commerce and Industry and the approval of the Governor-in-Council for those over £30,000. Although the Federal Loans Board was intended to serve Lagos primarily, applications for loans of £30,000 or more from the regions would be considered. All loans were subject to a maximum limit of £50,000. The Board's liquid assets included a £150,000 Federal Government grant and £18,820 inherited from its predecessor. A second grant of £150,000 was made to the board in 1959 and a third of £139,000 in 1960.

As a result of a genuine feeling on the part of government leaders, especially the Minister of Commerce and Industry, that the Federal Loans Board should play a greater role in the industrial development of the regions, reinforced by pressure from the constituencies to step up the pace of loaning activity, the ordinance was amended in December 1958, increasing the size of loans which could be granted without the approval of the Minister from £3,000 to £5,000 and lowering the limit on loans to the regions from £30,000 to £10,000. In December 1961 the Board's terms of reference were further broadened. First, the minimum size requirement for loan applications from the regions was abolished completely. Second, by altering the phrase 'industrial development' to 'economic development' the door was opened once again not only to farmers but, of much greater quantitative significance, to building contractors, transport operators and the vast financially undernourished community of Nigerian wholesale and retail merchants.[2] In this respect the Federal Loans Board has become even more far ranging than the original Nigerian Local Development Board.

[1] *First Annual Report of the Federal Loans Board, 1956–7*, p. 1. Italics added.

[2] Pressure for government-sponsored financial assistance to the trading community had been building up since the late 1940s. The Advisory Committee on Aids to African Businessmen recommended in 1958 that separate lending institutions, capitalized at several million pounds, be established for this purpose; however the historical experience of such schemes in

PERFORMANCE OF THE FEDERAL LOANS BOARD[1]

The Federal Loans Board has been considerably more active than its predecessors. By July 1962, from over 600 applications fifty-four loans had been granted for a total of £344,776. The latter figure compares with £74,000 disbursed over an equal number of years by the Colony Development Board. Disbursements for the Federal Loans Board's first six years of operation are given below.[2]

	Paid-out (£)		Paid-out (£)
1956–7	28,500	1959–60	71,450
1957–8	42,240	1960–1	70,457
1958–9	42,000	1961–2	90,129

The major recipient industries were printing, sawmilling, baking, fishing, gramophone recording, hotels, furniture, Pioneer oil mills, rivercraft, and cinema.

The table shows an ever increasing rate of lending over the years. To a certain extent this is a result of improvements in the methods of communicating to potential applicants the exact purpose of the Board, projects likely to be accepted and the information required in an application. More basically, the growing volume of loans reflects a growth in the number and quality of Nigerian entrepreneurs and a corresponding increase in their 'absorptive capacity'. These two points can be illustrated by statements from some of the earlier annual reports of the Colony Development Board.

> The outstanding feature revealed by the investigation of loan proposals is the extremely poor knowledge of business affairs and methods displayed by almost all the applicants and despite the fact that in almost every case the Board's Secretary interviewed the applicant before the submission of a formal application, only two applications were received in a form which made it possible to prepare them for submission to the Board without the most extensive and laborious revision, occasioning lengthy correspondence and many subsequent interviews.
>
> The experience of the Board has indicated the falsity of the view strongly held in some quarters that there exists in this area a substantial number of persons possessing every qualification for establishing businesses which would contribute to the betterment of the country, but lacking only the necessary

Ghana and other countries, plus a shortage of funds, had led to the decision to open another 'window' in the Federal Loans Board as a token measure. An additional £500,000 was set aside for the Board in the 1962–8 Development Plan.

[1] The following evaluation of the Federal Loans Board's performance covers the period 1956–62. The author, assisted by Sylvester Obi, spent approximately one month working with the files of the Board in April–May 1962. A number of the recipients were also interviewed at their establishments.

[2] *Annual Report of the Federal Loans Board, 1961–2*, p. 1.

capital. On the contrary, it has become increasingly apparent that, in the Colony at all events, the majority of the Africans who possess the qualifications required for the efficient conduct of a commercial enterprise have already succeeded by their own unaided efforts, and that the number of those whose activities have been handicapped solely by the lack of capital is infinitesimal. (1949–50, p. 8.)

Apart from the vexatious problem of adequate security, the fundamental difficulty was to find a borrower who had the serious intention of applying a loan to the purpose for which it was made; in the majority of cases the intention was to secure as large a sum as possible and then use it for trading, in many other cases for the pursuit of some private ambition of no interest to the purposes of the Board. The Board had also to remember that its borrowers seldom recognize any obligation to observe the terms of the formal agreement and to make the refunds punctually. (1952–3, p. 4.)

The intention of many if not most of the applicants still was to secure a large loan for an imaginary project attractive to the Board, and then use it for trade, the settlement of private debts or a lucrative bus or transport enterprise. (1953–4, pp. 4–5.)

After 1954 there is no further mention of insufficient absorptive capacity or misdirection of loan funds. As already noted the increased

Table 78. *Loan recovery performance of the Colony Development Board and the Federal Loans Board*[a]

	Principal and interest outstanding (£)	Arrears (£)	Loans outstanding	Loans in arrears
1953	77,187	13,498	26	13
1956	68,812	16,792	32	16
1959	119,284	6,173	36	11
1962	301,256	26,536	59	27

[a] The figures are exclusive of any provisions for loss and include the commitments of predecessor agencies. The sharp reduction in arrears from 1956 to 1959 resulted from the division of the assets and liabilities of the Colony Development Board between the Western Region Finance Corporation, which acquired the lion's share located in the Colony Province, and the Federal Loans Board which received the minority inheritance in Lagos proper.

SOURCES: *Annual Report of the Colony Development Board*, 1952–3 to 1955–6; *Annual Report of the Federal Loans Board*, 1958–9 to 1961–2.

tempo of lending is concrete proof to the contrary: during the seven years of its operations the Colony Development Board lent at an average annual rate of £10,600; the corresponding figure for the Federal Loans Board in its first six years was £57,000. Do such statistics necessarily indicate a rise in productive investments by the Board, or do they simply reflect a political decision to disburse more public funds? The financial accounts of the Colony Development Board and the

Federal Loans Board show clearly that there has been no relaxation of standards; indeed, the performance of the Federal Loans Board in recovering its loans has been more satisfactory than that of its predecessor.

The record of the Federal Loans Board is revealed even more remarkable in light of endeavours to confine its lending activities as far as possible to new and relatively undeveloped industries. At its first meeting the Colony Development Board laid down a policy of refusing applications for the building contracting, baking, tailoring, printing, soap making, road transport, and granting loans only in exceptional cases for water transport, electrical workshops, laundries and dry cleaning. Singlet manufacture and sawmilling in the Lagos area were added to the list in 1957. In a few cases, notably transport and contracting, the exclusion was made because hire purchase arrangements or contractors' advances were also available to the applicants. Usually however the decision was taken on the grounds that the industry was already 'adequately developed'. Avoiding the issue of whether or not the Board is a good judge of when an industry is adequately provided for, adherence to such a policy simultaneously restricted the area and increased the risk of its lending activities. A second policy of lending only to established ventures with a record of profits[1] lessened the risk factor but further contracted the potential sphere of operations. In practice exceptions are made to both of these principles when the applicant shows unusual ability in his proposed venture; for example three bakers and a tailor, all trained abroad, were given loans before they had achieved viable enterprises.

The foregoing analysis should not be interpreted as suggesting that the Federal Loans Board has been an unqualified success. The fact that well over 90 % of all loans are recovered is in part attributable to the sale or threatened sale of assets securing the loans of projects which have failed. Many other firms have managed to make their repayments without achieving any lasting success, either in the way of profits or further expansion; in some cases the loan-financed equipment itself soon falls out of use from lack of maintenance. But the record of the Federal Loans Board does refute the frequent criticism that government-sponsored lending agencies cannot be run on economic principles but rather will always be used to reward the political supporters of the government party, that very little of the funds loaned are ever recovered and that, in general, such bodies contribute little or nothing to economic development.

[1] 'Loans are normally granted by the Federal Loans Board only to industrial enterprises which have a sound past record of profitability. Only in exceptional cases will advances be made to new ventures.' (From the application form.)

THE DETERMINANTS OF PERFORMANCE

Having examined the over-all record of the Federal Loans Board it is now necessary to go a step further and enquire into the factors which have shaped this performance – investigation procedures, selection criteria and loan administration.

The loan application begins with a written request to the Secretary of the Board for an application form. This form, seven foolscap pages in length, provides for a detailed description of the applicant's existing enterprise, including a statement of sales and profits, the purpose for which the loan is requested, and the proposed use of the funds as between buildings, equipment and working capital. A second section, first by order of sequence, covers the applicant's past financial history, a certified balance sheet and a description of all his assets – real estate, bank accounts and other business interests. As soon as the form has been satisfactorily completed (often requiring considerable time and correspondence) a technical investigation is undertaken by the Senior Industrial Officer of the Ministry of Commerce and Industry and at least one other officer of the Ministry. These investigators interview the entrepreneur, go over the firm's accounts, and make an examination of the intended site, any contractors' estimates and the suitability of proposed machinery; the Ministry also makes any additional outside enquries (e.g. to machinery suppliers or previous creditors) which are deemed necessary.[1] On the basis of this investigation the viability of the project is analysed with particular reference to past management performance of the applicant, technical considerations and the market situation. The analysis, along with the Principal Industrial Officer's recommendation, is then presented to the Members of the Board.

The final decision to approve, reject or refer loan applications lies with some ten to fifteen (the number varies) Members of the Board. Appointed by the Minister of Commerce and Industry, Board Members, following the tradition laid down by the Nigeria Local Development Board, are drawn from the Lagos business community, the Lagos Town Council, the upper legislative houses in the three Regions (i.e. Chiefs, Obas and Emirs) and the Ministry of Commerce and Industry. The Board is convened six times a year. With very few exceptions the Board has always followed the recommendation of the Principal Industrial Officer, although the Board sometimes alters the actual amount of the loan.[2] Whatever extra-economic considerations are

[1] Any attempt to corruptly influence Ministry Officers or members of the Board is punishable by two years imprisonment.

[2] The writer knows of only two cases, both involving saw-milling, where a negative recommendation, on the grounds of no business records and the availability of hire-purchase arrangements, was ignored. In both cases the loans proved successful. In another instance the Board twice refused to approve a recommended loan for a particular Lagos bakery.

brought to bear are done so at an earlier stage, prior to the Principal Industrial Officer's recommendation.

Before an approved loan can be paid out the securities (nearly always real estate) must be screened for encumbrances. This is carried out by the Chairman of the Board. Nominally the Board requires that the assets offered have a current market value three times that of the loan;[1] in practice coverage of about 150 % is acceptable. The margin is necessary because buyers, sometimes owing to collusion but more often simply acting on a long established tradition, are seldom willing to offer the government a price comparable to what they would pay a private party. About 10 % of approved loans are lost for want of adequate security. For loans of under £500 the Board will accept a mortgage on the property of a guarantor. In the history of the three Boards only one unsecured 'character' loan has been granted, and this for £140 in 1958.

Once the securities have been dealt with the loan is ready to be disbursed. Only the working capital component is paid in cash to the entrepreneur. For the erection or alteration of buildings remuneration is made directly to the contractor; a similar procedure is followed with respect to the purchase of machinery. Experience has taught the Board how to further refine these prudential arrangements. Because it has discovered that the contractor and the loan recipient might covertly agree to split the difference between the stipulated cost supported by the Board and the actual cost of a somewhat inferior structure, the practice was changed whereby the contractor is paid for each stage of the work as it is completed and inspected. And as a result of one loan recipient persuading an overseas equipment supplier that the Board's cheque represented a down payment for a number of items, the procedure was tightened up so that payment is made only upon the delivery of the pre-specified equipment. As additional security, a bill of sale on all movable equipment is executed in favour of the Board for the duration of the loan. Repayment of the principal and interest in quarterly instalments commences one year from the date of the first disbursement.

Such are the mechanics of project investigation, the selection process and loan administration. How do these procedures work out in practice? What in fact distinguishes rejected applications from those that are approved? What effect does the way in which the Board administers its loans have upon the performance of the assisted enterprises? And finally among the latter, are there any recurring characteristics which distinguish the successes from the failures?

What distinguishes the nine unsuccessful applications from the one

[1] *Guide to all Applicants for Loans from the Federal Loans Board*, p. 2.

that is approved? The most frequent cause for rejection, often combined with other factors, is a manifest lack of business organization and managerial competence. This critical insufficiency reveals itself in the mal-administration of existing operations, in embarrassingly crude or faulty proposals and in an inability to provide any comprehensible business records. Four other fairly common reasons for rejection may also be identified. The proposed venture may lie outside the broad limits of the applicant's experience. Many applications are *ultra vires*, requesting finance for such activities as property development, trading or farming which are outside the ordinance's terms of reference. The securities offered may be obviously inadequate or, conversely, the entrepreneur may have adequate resources of his own for undertaking the scheme. Finally, the industry in question may be judged overcrowded, characterized by excessive competition and unneedful of further development assistance.

And what of successful applications? Paralleling causes for rejection, the surest way for an aspirant to secure a loan is to show marked administrative or managerial capabilities. Likewise, candidates who possess unquestioned technical competence, typically having completed a recognized training course abroad, are seldom turned down. Even when on other grounds the proposal would normally have been rejected – an industry which is overcrowded or not quite within the Board's terms of reference as, for example, catering – concrete evidence of true managerial or technical competence is nearly always sufficient to evoke a favourable decision from the Board.

For a minority of the loans granted, certainly no more than a quarter, other considerations not directly related to the applicant's competence have been decisive. Such considerations may be a particularly favourable demand situation for the industry and area in question, the desirability of pioneering a certain new industry, the felt-need for greater equity in the geographic apportionment of loans or, finally, political influence.

Loans for the establishment of hotels in the regions are the outstanding examples of a purely demand criterion. The textile and ceramics loans made in the late 1940s appear to have been granted primarily out of a desire to pioneer important industries, with insufficient attention given to the technical and organizational complications involved. The pressure for greater equality in the regional apportionment is a natural desire although, of course, imprudent; that this factor was becoming of increasing importance in 1962 (especially in the case of northern applicants) derived from (*i*) the policy emphasis on making the Federal Loans Board a truly national institution and (*ii*) the fact that the political parties based in the two 'neglected' regions controlled the

Federal Government and hence, indirectly, appointment of the Board's members. Finally there is the possibility of direct political influence being exerted to grant a loan to a particular applicant. Given the number and composition of the members on the Board, the primary focus of such effort is the Minister of Commerce and through him the Principal Industrial Officer who makes the recommendation. The writer knows of only one case where such pressure was successfully applied.

On the other hand, political considerations may be of considerable importance in a negative sense. The heterogeneity of the Board members' interests, which promotes economically rational selection procedures as the only acceptable policy, stops short of variety in political affiliation or sympathy. Thus a well-known member of the opposition party would be unlikely to have his loan application approved. Owing to this and the additional fact that such a person receives favourably-biased treatment from the lending institution of his own region, no applications were in fact submitted by known supporters of the Opposition.

Next we move on to an examination of the ways in which loan administration impinge upon the operations of assisted enterprises. Two aspects of loan administration seem to be pertinent in this connection, timing and supervision. Dealing first with the temporal question, the very considerable amount of time (one-and-a-half to two years) that elapses between the date of the application and the actual paying out of the loan can add materially to the entrepreneur's problems. The extra risks so imposed are not difficult to identify: investment costs rise, the applicant's financial position changes, his resources become tied-up and, perhaps most important, the initial enthusiasm and momentum may be dissipated.

Many sources contribute to the long gestation of a loan commitment. Among those amenable to improvement, the chief factors are the entrepreneur's laxity in fully developing his project in the original application, the shortage of investigatory staff (there is usually a back-log of applications of about six months) and the time consumed in screening securities *after* the loan has been approved. While the first source of delay could be shortened by appropriate educational efforts, the latter two can only be overcome at the cost of employing additional trained personnel.[1]

The second way in which time considerations impinge upon the success of a loan is through the terms of repayment. Repayment begins

[1] If the loan commitment time is to be shortened by having securities screened concurrently with the investigation, the average cost per application will rise as a result of the ten-fold increase in security screening.

one year from the pay-out of the first instalment. Given the fact that construction of a building and the ordering of imported equipment is usually involved, it is not surprising that the majority of projects have not yet come into production when their first repayment falls due. Often the applicant will make this first payment with a portion of his working capital provision and for a few instalments thereafter fall into arrears – thus accounting for the proportion of loans in arrears at any one time. The entrepreneur is thus handicapped before he starts by insufficient working capital and the threat of foreclosure. In cases where other complications develop, repayment arrangements greatly increase the jeopardy of the already beleaguered entrepreneur. Repayment might begin eighteen months after production starts or three years from the date of disbursement, whichever is sooner: generous repayment terms rigorously enforced are more beneficial to all concerned than stringent terms that must be waived.

In the realm of loan supervision the contribution of the Federal Loans Board is a positive one. The pre-loan investigation almost always turns up some relevant facts or highlights some problem areas which the applicant has missed. The efforts of the Ministry of Commerce and Industry to insure that the proposed machinery is the most appropriate obtainable have averted serious error in many instances. The granting of a loan is conditional upon the maintenance of a comprehensive book-keeping system and periodic inspection by the lender. And, the necessity of meeting a repayment schedule, *ceteris paribus*, helps to impose much needed discipline. This is not to suggest that the supervisory content of loan administration is in any way adequate to the needs of loan recipients; nevertheless what superintendence is provided is worth a great deal.

The final question to be considered, although a very vital one, is in a strict sense only tangentially pertinent to the operations of a lending agency. In retrospect, what distinguishes those loan recipients who succeed from those who do not; or to put it in a more useful form, what appear to be the deficiencies, the causes for failure? In view of the number of loans issued since 1946, there are surprisingly few assisted ventures which have failed outright; although it must be admitted that a relatively high percentage of the more ambitious loans fall into this category. Three textile projects, a large ceramics factory and a colour printing venture failed primarily for want of sufficient technical knowledge. Three out of six producers of expensive furniture failed because the quality of their product was not up to that of their competititors; two shirt-makers closed down because they could not meet the price of imports. For two printing establishments, a soft drink bottler and a ferry service no one or two controlling deficiencies can be singled out.

Any enumeration of the sources of trouble must begin, once again, with that ubiquitous requisite, management. While every exigency that arises calls for the exercise of some specific skill – marketing, purchasing, technical know-how, accounting, etc. – the prior responsibility of anticipating probable difficulties and mobilizing the remedy rests with management. It is this lack of preparedness on all fronts and disinclination to immediate energetic action that is the most common deficiency of loan recipients. Of specific problem areas, imported machinery has provided the most frequent stumbling block. The hitch may come at one or more of the following five stages: ordering the right equipment, prompt safe delivery, installation, correct operation and maintenance. Working capital shortages frequently develop as a result of unforeseen delays. For the fully operational firm, problems of product quality and production control are the most common; the first is usually attributable to the level of technical skill while the second reflects a lack of organizational ability.

A second Federal development lending agency, the Revolving Loan Fund was established in 1959 with £200,000 contributed under the U.S. foreign aid programme. Also administered by the Ministry of Commerce and Industry, its purpose is to make loans of between £10,000 and £50,000 for industrial projects. As of February 1962 at the time of the first audit only three loans had been issued. Two loans of £39,000 and £20,000 were granted for the expansion of a tyre retreading plant and a nail factory; the third loan of £50,000 was supplementary to a £100,000 advance from the Northern Nigeria Development Corporation for the establishment of a large shoe factory. Despite expatriate managers in all three ventures, two of the projects were experiencing serious difficulties. Ominously, perhaps, the auditor concluded his report by recommending that the £10,000 minimum limit be abolished and that future emphasis should be on a large number of more modest undertakings.

REGIONAL LENDING SCHEMES

In addition to the Federal Loans Board and Revolving Loans Fund, each of the regions has its own development loans scheme. In terms of the volume of their operations the latter dwarf the two federal institutions: nearly £4m. have been issued from the regional agencies as against a little more than £0·5m. from the Federal Loans Board and Revolving Loans Fund. Without tracing their genealogies it will suffice to recount that these lending operations began with the partition of the Nigeria Local Development Board in 1949, that the existing institutions – the Western Region Finance Corporation, the Northern Nigeria Development

Corporation, the Eastern Nigeria Development Corporation – came into being in 1955–6. Subsequent discussion will deal primarily with the current institutions and only in regard to their activities in the industrial loans field. Agricultural loans and advances to local governments will not concern us, while direct investments by these agencies have been discussed elsewhere.

Of the three regional schemes that of the ENDC, with less than £200,000 issued as industrial loans, has been by far the smallest. The bulk of these loans, £161,000, were authorized in the Corporation's first year, 1956; these covered such fields as food processing,[1] handwoven textiles, bricks and tiles, river transport, baking, a Pioneer palm-oil mill (accounting for the largest single loan of £26,285), soap making, a mechanized laundry and two limeworks.[2] These loans were issued with little or no investigation, conditional only upon the provision of security or willing guarantors; political factors played a part in selection procedures. After 1958 it was decided to remove the development loans from the political arena and the administration of the scheme, with the primary emphasis on loan recovery, was turned over to an expatriate who operated it on lines very similar to those described for the Federal Loans Board. Although the recovery rate has been about 80 %, only a small share of the repayments has come from earnings of the loan-financed enterprises.[3]

By 31 March 1963 Northern Nigeria Development Corporation had authorized 5,285 loans for approximately £2m.[4] Numerically the bulk of these loans have been for food processing mills and sewing machines. Other areas include bus and lorry transport, small hotels, carpentry, automotive repair, baking and various trading activities. The duration of the loans have ranged from three to eight years. Project evaluation is minimal, the principal concern being with the security. In 1964, about one-half of the outstanding loans were in judgment-debtor status.[5] Although political influence of one kind or another is important for the approval of loans in excess of £5,000, for lesser amounts anyone with security or guarantors and not known to be hostile to the ruling party is eligible for a loan.

The lending activities of the Western Region Finance Corporation

[1] Loans for food processing (total £8,413) range from £150 to £400 for such items as corn mills, rice mills, ground nut decorticators, sugar crushers and cassava graters. Hereafter such loans will be described as being for 'food processing mills'.

[2] First and second *Annual Report of the Eastern Region Development Corporation, 1955–6* and *1956–7*, pp. 16 and 18 respectively.

[3] Interview with the expatriate Credits Manger, September 1964.

[4] The cumulative number of loans was 2,578 in March 1959; 1,840 and 867 new loans were issued during the following two years. In 1961–2 and 1962–3 no loans were made. *Annual Report of the Northern Nigeria Development Corporation*, various years.

[5] Interview with the Loans Manager, August 1964.

parallel those of its northern counterpart: the largest number of loans have been for food processing mills; all types of activities (except trading) have been assisted; and the volume of lending has been great. At 31 March 1961, the year prior to the western region crisis and the suspension of WRFC's activities, 538 loans (including 44 non-industrial advances) were outstanding for a total of over £1,400,000. Projects included stone crushing, saw mills, rubber crêping, brewing, metal working, motor repair, contractors' advances, rivercraft, bakeries, hotels, weaving, dry cleaning, laundering, food processing mills, and the manufacture of paint, soap, soft drinks, prepared food, shoes and musical instruments. With a few qualifications this record faithfully mirrors the expansive policies of the Corporation, conceiving its mission

> ... to help people to help themselves; to stimulate private enterprise thus removing poverty and unemployment and increasing the citizen's self-confidence in his own business ability by extending justifiable loan assistance to all without any consideration other than prudent business and economic considerations.[1]

Reviewing the operations of WRFC, the first observation to be made is the high percentage of applications that are approved; for instance, 290 out of 430 and 302 out of 451 applications were approved in 1959–60 and 1960–1 respectively. This yields a ratio of two out of every three in contrast to one in ten for the Federal Loans Board. To some extent this may be attributed to the lower risk of investments such as food processing mills which perhaps are not justly classified as development loans. Yet even if the latter are excluded the ratio of approvals is still one out of every two. This suggests *prima facie* that its standards for granting a loan have been considerably lower than those of the Federal Loans Board.

The writer's inspection of the technical investigation reports, which are carried out by the (largely untrained) Industrial Officers of the regional Ministry of Trade and Industry, revealed the complete absence of any systematic project analysis. Indeed the 'investigation' typically consisted of an off-hand appraisal of whether or not the applicant has sufficient technical knowledge in the field of his project and an estimate of the severity of competition. In most cases the investigator recommends rejection where the applicant has no experience; occasionally, however, it is stated that a technical manager can be employed and that the loan should be granted. But the most common cause for rejection is 'the incidence of competition' or market saturation. This concern with the market, along with an oblique criticism of the

[1] *Fifth Annual Report and Accounts of the WRFC, 1959–60*, p. 3.

quality of technical investigations, is expressed in the 1959–60 *Annual Report:*

The tendency on the part of the public appears to be to apply for a loan simply because another person has succeeded therein. Applicants hardly bother to make sufficient market research to find out whether the market would support existing and prospective participants... The above suggests that investigations now being carried out... deserve to be supplemented by more market information. The technical advice received from the Ministry has proved to be of great value and unless the Corporation itself is in a position to assure such technical advice it would be advisable to impress on the Regional Government that the quality of such technical advice must be high. This needs to be more so as the Corporation has no remedy in any case where a faulty recommendation is made in the first instance and a loss has to be sustained ultimately (p. 7).

The Corporation's own valuation officers assess the proffered securities concurrently with the technical enquiry. The final recommendation is made by the Senior Assistant Secretary who then submits the application to the politically appointed Board of Members. Since about 1958 the latter have included no civil servants, professional or 'non-committed' members of the business community; a similar situation obtains in the north and the east. That other than purely economic considerations play an important role in selection is well brought out by the following: of the fifty-nine approvals out of 119 applications (net of deferrals) for industrial loans other than food processing mills considered by the Board from March 1959 to October 1960, twelve loans were granted despite strong recommendations to reject and seventeen authorizations were for amounts in excess (sometimes many thousands of pounds in excess) of the pledged securities.

One noteworthy aspect of WRFC's loan administration has been in respect of food processing mills. Given the volume of demand for these mills the Corporation organized at the outset its own staff of mechanics, equipped with motor cycles, who install each machine and provide, at the borrower's expense, regular maintenance and repair service. The Corporation thus helps to insure the recovery of its own investment and at the same time adds to the life of the entrepreneur's and the community's real capital.

Between 1955 and 1962 WRFC lent out £1,735,486 (plus the value of 1961–2 repayments) of which over £400,000 had been recovered by 1962. At 31 March 1961 loan principal in arrears was £105,851 or 13 % of loans outstanding. Although the Corporation Chairman expressed the opinion that as much as £200,000 of the £1,400,000 outstanding might eventually prove unrecoverable,[1] a careful examination of past

[1] *Report of the Coker Commission of Inquiry into the Affairs of Certain Statutory Corporations in Western Nigeria*, vol. II, Federal Ministry of Information, Lagos 1962, p. 44.

experience shows that, in fact, the great majority of loans in judgment-debtor status are eventually repaid.

Our analysis of the regional agencies has focused on the mainstream of their development lending activities. In recent years all of these agencies have been involved in the now much publicized disbursement of large unsecured loans to politically influential persons. The Military Government in Kaduna has revealed that between April 1963 and December 1965 NNDC gave out £291,600 in eight development loans to various political figures, including the Premier; by and large the proceeds of these loans were diverted to personal consumption.[1] In each of the three regions unsecured loans ranging from £250,000 to £6·2m. have been granted to companies engaged in Lagos real estate speculation; in at least one case, the chairman of the Development Corporation was also chairman of the real estate concern.[2]

Such spectacular corruption is not, however, directly relevant to an assessment of how far the regional lending agencies have attained their objective of providing capital to indigenous industry; no worthwhile loan applications were sacrificed as a result of these abuses. Between the five federal and regional agencies, no viable project has gone wanting for capital.[3] The entrained technical assistance and organizational discipline enforced upon Federal Loans Board borrowers represents a windfall additional to the provision of capital. The fact that such lending activities have produced only a modest number of unambiguous 'development' successes merely reveals that lack of capital is not a major 'missing component' for Nigerian industrial development.

IV

As we have seen, all the major government programmes to develop indigenous industry have achieved disappointingly modest results. In contrast to the FIIR's performance in the field of applied research or government investments in turnkey factories, the major responsibility

[1] Northern Nigeria, *A White Paper on the Military Government Policy for the Reorganization of the Northern Nigeria Development Corporation*, Kaduna 1966, pp. 2-3, 36-40.

[2] This case was the African Real Estate and Investment Company which received £1m. loan from ENDC. Helleiner, 'The Eastern Nigeria Development Corporation: A Study in Sources and Uses of Public Funds, 1949-62', *Nigerian Journal of Economic and Social Studies*, March 1964, p. 117. In Northern Nigeria, as reported in the White Paper cited in footnote I, pp. 9-10, £500,000 was lent to Mepco Properties and A.B. Properties by NNDC. The Coker Commission, vol. 1, pp. 41-73, disclosed that the National Investment and Properties Company received £6.2m. in unsecured loans from the Western Nigeria Board.

[3] Subject, as any loan scheme must be, to the applicant's ability to offer collateral security. Although there is no necessary correlation between a young man's entrepreneurial talents and command over real property, in many instances family, relatives or friends have been persuaded to offer their property in security for a loan to a promising project. Nevertheless, it is true that the security requirement is an important constraint.

for a lack-lustre record in this instance can not be attributed to badly conceived policies or delinquent administration. While the former may have played a part in the failure of the textile scheme and the latter may have been manifest in the regional loan agencies, the weight of the evidence points to lack of absorptive capacity on the part of the aid recipients as the principal bottleneck. The problem of inadequate absorptive capacity can be restated as the problem of deficient entrepreneurial capabilities.[1]

Various fragments of evidence on management practice have come to light in our review of government assistance programmes. The picture of Nigerian business performance suggested from these sources is corroborated by a considerable number of industry studies.[2] Systematic efficiency measurements have been made in the rubber crêping, baking and sawmilling industries; extensive descriptive data have been collected on business performance in the manufacture of furniture and clothing, printing, transport and banking. The findings in each case have been very nearly identical.

In the baking industry the author documented the loss of three quarters of potential profits to raw material wastage, damaging of bread during baking and extensive employee pilferage.[3] Lawrence Okigbo found that 52 % of Nigeria's sawmills were operating at less than 50 % efficiency during the hours in which they were operating; and Harris and Rowe report '... most Nigerian sawmills are producing only 10 to 20 per cent of the lumber that the installed machines are capable of producing'.[4] A similar magnitude of under-utilization was found in Firms IV and V (the private Nigerian firms) in the rubber crêping industry, as reported in chapter 7.

The factors which lay behind such poor performance are, on the

[1] The remainder of this chapter focuses only on those attributes of Nigerian industrialists which are judged to be limitational factors. For a more complete discussion covering such subjects as the nature of entrepreneurial motivation, the influence of the extended family, reinvestment of profits, ethnic distribution of entrepreneurial propensities, etc., see chapter 8 in the author's *African Enterprise: The Nigerian Bread Industry*. The findings of the baking industry study have since been duplicated for other industries by Mary Rowe, John Harris and Wayne Nafziger in the works cited in the following footnote.

[2] W. T. Newlyn and D. C. Rowan, *Money and Banking in British Colonial Africa*, Oxford 1954, pp. 97 ff.; E. K. Hawkins, *Road Transport in Nigeria*, London 1958, chapter 4; Peter Kilby, *The Development of Small Industry in Eastern Nigeria* and *African Enterprise: The Nigerian Bread Industry*, chapters 5 and 8; Lawrence Okigbo, *Sawmill Industry in Nigeria*, Federal Department of Forest Research, Ibadan 1964; J. R. Harris and M. P. Rowe, 'Entrepreneurial Patterns in the Nigerian Sawmilling Industry', *Nigerian Journal of Economic and Social Studies*, March 1966; J. R. Harris, 'Factors Affecting the Supply of Industrial Entrepreneurship in Nigeria', mimeograph, December 1966; E. W. Nafziger, 'Nigerian Entrepreneurship: A Study of Indigenous Businessmen in the Footwear Industry', unpublished Ph.D. dissertation, University of Illinois, 1967.

[3] Kilby, *African Enterprise: The Nigerian Bread Industry*, pp. 57–67.

[4] Both citations from Harris and Rowe, *loc. cit.* p. 78.

production side, failure to regularly maintain equipment, inadequate co-ordination of raw material purchases with product orders, and the absence of conscientious supervision in the work place. Profits are further reduced through extensive pilfering and embezzlement of funds by the senior clerical staff.[1]

To conclude our description of entrepreneurial performance let us quote the findings of the 1965 Harris and Rowe survey of 268 of the largest indigenous industrial firms, presumably representing the cream of Nigeria's entrepreneurs.

> Generally, the level of efficiency within the firms was very low. Substantial increases in output could be achieved without additional investment. Closer supervision, better organization, improved layout, and quality control are desperately needed on the production side. Low levels of capacity utilization are largely a result of management deficiencies.
>
> The general standard of financial management is also very low. Although 249 of the firms had some kind of accounting systems, they were not systematically used as management tools. The larger firms had annual statements prepared by outside auditors for the purposes of establishing tax liability (thus avoiding arbitrary assessment), but for the most part these documents were lying on the shelf gathering dust. Surprisingly, records of asset values were more available than records of output and sales . . .
>
> This widespread lack of financial control was reflected in the fact that barely more than half of the entrepreneurs had an adequate understanding of depreciation, and only one-half of them could make a reasonable estimate of the minimum production per day needed to break even. Only 31 of them had any organized system of cost accounting, and separation of business and personal accounts was rare.
>
> Most of the firms were one-man operations. When the business expands beyond the point that the owner can control everything himself, serious problems are encountered. The ability to delegate responsibility and authority, while still keeping control, is generally lacking. Admittedly, it is difficult to find capable subordinates and managers in Nigeria, but little has been done by these entrepreneurs to train and develop such personnel. Several cases were encountered of successful small firms foundering badly after major expansion. Experience of the entrepreneurs with hired expatriate managers has been largely unhappy.[2]

[1] See particularly Newlyn and Rowan, *op. cit.* p. 98; Hawkins, *op. cit.* p. 52; Kilby, *African Enterprise: The Nigerian Bread Industry*, chapter 5.

[2] J. R. Harris, *op. cit.* pp. 40–2. With regard to the last point, the author's investigations uncovered a similar near-universal lack of success with expatriate managers. The problems most frequently encountered among the European recruits are related to their integrity, competence or sobriety; experienced men of the requisite qualities are seldom willing to accept non-tenured contract employment under largely unknown conditions in an African country. On the employer's side there are failures of communication and of fully understanding and accepting the exceedingly high salary and maintenance cost of an able expatriate. There is also, though it is difficult to specify, a 'two cultures' problem. On the other hand, the few *partnerships* involving an expatriate (on the technical side) and a Nigerian (sales, public relations) have worked very well.

What are the attitudes and behavioural characteristics of the entrepreneurs which are responsible for such business performance? With few exceptions, Nigerian industrialists are unwilling to provide continuous surveillance of their business operations, in terms of both physical supervision in the factory shop and in utilizing the principal instrument of management control, written records. This disposition is combined with a general lack of interest in production efficiency and in possibilities for improving product quality. Nigerian entrepreneurs are generally slow to move when their operations hit a snag. They show little propensity to undertake innovations.[1]

The better educated entrepreneurs and those from a trading background have a high propensity to launch a second or third business venture, a dispersion of effort which frequently entails a high cost in lost efficiency.[2] Finally, Nigerian businessmen are typically unaware that their managerial performance is in any way wanting; they impute full responsibility for their difficulties to external factors over which they have no control, and they see their principal problem as lack of capital.[3]

Other factors contributing to poor performance which are beyond the direct control of the entrepreneur, are related to questions of delegation and joint-enterprise. Delegation of authority requires that the subordinate accept responsibility, carry out supervisory functions and respect his employer's property rights; with very few exceptions, the author's interview respondents (including fifteen of the country's most successful businessmen interviewed in 1964) stated that their continuing inability to locate such individuals constituted their greatest management handicap. Similarly the author and Sayre Schatz have presented evidence to show that a significant number of joint-enterprises have failed to develop because of financial dishonesty, or the fear of it, between partners – a result of the absence of an accepted code of business ethics.[4]

[1] 'Out of the 268 entrepreneurs in this sample, only fifty-two could be considered as having innovated, and this is using a very loose definition of innovation. Four opened up a new market for a good, two introduced the use of a new material, twelve introduced new production processes, twenty-five introduced new products, and five pioneered new business methods. All of the innovations represented adaptation of products or processes to Nigeria which were already in use in industrialized countries', J. R. Harris, *op. cit.* p. 27.

[2] Out of the sample of 269, 133 had interests in additional businesses. Dispersion of effort is least pronounced among craftsmen-entrepreneurs, and most pronounced among those from a trading background and among the better educated. *Ibid.* p. 42 and Kilby, *African Enterprise: The Nigerian Bread Industry*, pp. 97–8.

[3] Cited in all the studies. See particularly Schatz, 'Aiding Nigerian Business: The Yaba Industrial Estate', *Nigerian Journal of Economic and Social Studies*, July 1964, p. 210, and his 'Economic Attitudes of Nigerian Businessmen' *Nigerian Journal of Economic and Social Studies*, November 1962, p. 266.

[4] Schatz, 'Economic Attitudes of Nigerian Businessmen', *Nigerian Journal of Economic and Social Studies*, November 1962, pp. 262–3; Kilby, *The Development of Small Industry in Eastern Nigeria*, p. 13.

Before we draw any conclusions from the foregoing evaluation, it is useful to look at the education and occupational backgrounds of the entrepreneurs. Table 79 presents such data collected from 298 firms

Table 79. *Entrepreneurs' education and occupational background by size of firm*

	Size of firm[a]				
Education (no. of firms)	Small (225)	Medium (34)	Large (20)	Very large (19)	H & R sample (268)[b]
None	18	18	20	5	13
Partial primary	29	9	10	5	13
Full primary	39	50	40	42	35
Partial secondary	3	12	5	5	24
Full secondary	8	5	5	11	8
Post secondary	3	6	20	32	7
	100	100	100	100	100
Occupational background					(54)[c]
Farmer	6	—	—	—	—
Trader	9	32	30	21	22
Craftsmen[d]	74	59	50	52	45
Clerical-admin.	2	9	5	11	
Teaching	3	—	5	11	33 (Clerical-admin., Teaching, Professional)
Professional	1	—	5	5	
Domestic	5	—	5	—	—
	100	100	100	100	100
Occupational sector					
Government[e]	10	9	15	26	15
Foreign firms	17	6	10	32	85 (Foreign firms, Indigenous)
Indigenous	73	85	75	42	
	100	100	100	100	100

[a] Size of firm measured by investment in tools, equipment and fixtures at original cost (excludes investment in land and building). Small: under £1,000; medium: £1,000–£2,000; large: £2,001–£5,000; very large: over £5,000.

[b] Stratification of educational data by size of firm not shown for the Harris and Rowe sample. The sample includes 123 firms employing less than 20 and 22 firms employing over 100.

[c] Occupational data shown by size of firm; these 54 firms employed more than 50.

[d] Includes a small number of building contractors and transporters.

[e] Includes teaching for all but the last category.

SOURCES: Interviews taken by the writer 1960–2, assisted by Sylvester Obi for Lagos firms; J. R. Harris, 'Factors Affecting the Supply of Industrial Entrepreneurship in Nigeria', mimeograph, December 1966, tables 16 and 17.

throughout the country in 1960–2 by the writer and from 268 firms interviewed by Harris and Rowe in 1965. The latter focused on the larger firms (median firm assets, £10,000); their sample overlaps with and extends beyond the medium, large and very large categories used by the writer.

Looking at occupational background first, two-thirds of the entrepreneurs come from trading or craft production. This pattern conforms to findings in other developing economies.[1] Clerical, teaching and professional backgrounds are found in the medium and larger firms, but their proportion is small. As would be expected, individuals coming from the modern sector tend to be more successful than those coming from the indigenous sector.

The most interesting fact revealed in table 79 is the weak correlation between education and entrepreneurial success. Within the writer's fourfold stratification the expected positive association between size of firm and education is seen only in the post-secondary and less-than-primary categories. Similarly Harris reports an unexpectedly low correlation (Gamma = 0·161) within their sample.[2]

We have concentrated up to now on the deficiencies of entrepreneurial performance. It was noted in connection with the Federal Loans Board that there appears to have been a definite improvement in the quality of entrepreneurship since the early 1950s. With regard to the activity that economists tend to see as the central role of the entrepreneur, perceiving and responding to economic opportunities, all observers agree that Nigerian businessmen excel in this area. Indeed it is their extreme sensitivity to market signals and their willingness to enter industries (technical knowledge and capital requirements permitting) that have produced intense competition, excess capacity and low profits in many lines of production[3] – circumstances which make further expansion for any individual entrepreneur very difficult, save where the latter achieves a quantum jump in the quality of his product or the efficiency of his production process. The situation is thus one of a large group of entrepreneurs with a comparatively small number of industries in which they are capable of operating; the solution to both atomistic competition and movement into a broader range of industry is to increase the managerial and technological capabilities of the entrepreneurial group.

In interpreting the limited development of Nigeria industrial firms, Sayre Schatz takes a rather extreme position, contending that the

[1] See John J. Carrol, *The Filipino Manufacturing Entrepreneur: Agent and Product of Change*, Ithaca, N.Y. 1965; James J. Barna, *Industrial Entrepreneurship in Madras State*, New York 1960; Alec Alexander, *Greek Industrialists*, Athens 1965; Fritz Redlich, 'Entrepreneurship in the Early Stages of Industrialization', *Weltwirtschaftliches Archiv*, Band 75, Heft 1, 1955.

[2] J. R. Harris, *op. cit.* p. 24. The correlation between education and an index of profitability and growth of assets was even weaker (Gamma = 0·154).

[3] Marketing problems and inadequate demand are frequently cited as impediments to the development of indigenous firms in Nigeria and elsewhere. Actually what is being observed in most cases are simply the results of a perfectly competitive market structure.

principal bottlenecks are not endogenous to the firm but rather arise from external sources – unavailability of suitable machinery and maintenance services, of skilled labour, of adequate markets, of loan capital, etc. – which are inherent in the economic environment.[1] Although John Harris recognizes the poor managerial and technological performance of Nigerian entrepreneurs, he interprets these impediments as temporary bottlenecks which will soon be ameliorated with experience and the availability of more trained personnel.[2]

Our evaluation of the observed data is that the roots of entrepreneurial deficiencies that have been described may run deeper than the mere lack of experience and training. The underlying attitudes and dispositions of entrepreneurs enumerated earlier would seem to a considerable degree to be independent of the level of education or training. We saw in table 64 that education has a very modest influence on improving entrepreneurial performance. And without an acceleration in the rate of change in underlying entrepreneurial attitudes the availability of trained personnel will have little impact on business performance in the near future. Again, the problems of business ethics and delegation of managerial authority are unlikely to disappear quickly. The latter, intimately connected with deficient supervisory capabilities, discussed in chapters 7 and 8, is rooted in the same socio-cultural context as are the entrepreneurial shortcomings.

In brief, what is being suggested here is that the development of certain requisite entrepreneurial characteristics, relating to performance in the organizational and technological spheres, is being impeded by traditional socio-cultural factors common to all of Nigeria's ethnic groups.[3] The personality characteristics which these socio-cultural factors tend to produce are manifest in the realm of economic activities not only among entrepreneurs, but among supervisors, civil servants, Nigerian managers in the public sector, etc.

If this hypothesis is correct, it implies that formal training and experience will not in themselves enable Nigerian entrepreneurs to substantially displace over the next few decades foreign enterprise which now dominates medium and large-scale industry.

Several features of traditional society which have tended to impede the effective functioning of Nigerians in technological and organizational roles may be mentioned. The technology of traditional subsistence agriculture was both simple and static; with every contingency anticipated

[1] Stated in all his writings, but see particularly his 'Economic Environment and West African Enterprise', *The Economic Bulletin* (*Ghana*), December 1963.

[2] J. R. Harris, *op. cit.* pp. 42, 44, 47, 50.

[3] Of course these traditional factors are gradually being eroded or transformed, but the process is a slow one.

in accumulated customary practices, technical talents were seldom called upon. Concomitantly a division of labour extending no further than age and sex required only a minimum of organization and supervision. While Yoruba and Ibo patterns of status mobility based on achieved wealth provide a strong incentive to establish a business enterprise as a means of obtaining high social status,[1] once established there are no antecedent roles conferring respect for efficient managerial performance. On the contrary, because conspicuous leisure is the principal manifestation of superior status, the carrying out of supervisory functions (concern with the task performance of subordinates) represents a socially degrading activity.[2]

Because of the universality of organizational requirements in modern economic activities, the overcoming of entrepreneurial deficiencies is likely to occur as a part of a general transformation of traditional social structure which sees changes in the efficiency of human performance in a wide range of productive roles. While economic forces will play an important part in this process, developments in political institutions and ideology, in bureacratic administration, in education, and in technology will in aggregate probably exert a greater influence. This is but an important instance of the homely truism that economic development involves far more than mere economic change.

[1] For a lucid exposition of Yoruba, Ibo and Hausa social structures and their relation to achievement motivation, see Robert A. LeVine, *Dreams and Deeds: Achievement Motivation in Nigeria*, Chicago 1966, chapters 2 and 3.

[2] For a fuller appreciation of the importance of leisure status norms, see *ibid.* pp. 3–7.

Part 6

CHAPTER II

CONCLUSION: A STRATEGY FOR INDUSTRIALIZATION

In the preceding chapters we have reviewed the historical development of those sectors and areas of activity which are most closely related to the development of industry. In brief, we have considered the principal characteristics of industrial production under the rubrics of import substitution, export and domestic processing, and indigenous enterprise; we have analysed entrepreneurial and labour inputs; and we have described the pertinent public institutions, government programmes and policies. In each chapter an attempt has been made to isolate the critical determinants of performance for the sector under study; policy criticisms have been made during the course of the analysis, while policy prescriptions typically conclude each chapter. In this final chapter we shall draw on our findings from the prospective of an overall development strategy. Here the focus will be on the costs and returns of alternative ways of deploying resources between industrial and non-industrial production and between different uses within the industrial sector.

I

Virtually all students of the subject are agreed that a certain amount of industrialization is likely to be a necessary condition for successful economic development. A preponderant specialization in primary production on the part of an underdeveloped country, as dictated by existing comparative advantage, faces the serious drawbacks, when viewed over time, of a low income elasticity of demand for primary products,[1] possible disruptive instability in export earnings and, most important, limited transmission of technological and organizational stimuli to other sections of the economy.[2]

[1] The fact that the commodity terms of trade for primary products in aggregate have failed to experience any secular deterioration does not invalidate (*a*) the operation of Engles' law, (*b*) the growth of synthetic substitutes, (*c*) the raw material-savings bias of technical progress, and (*d*) the growing proportion of national income going to services. Rather the observed secular constancy reflects the failure of primary producers to expand output at a rate equal to the growth of the advanced industrial economies. Successful programmes of primary export expansion, if undertaken by all underdeveloped countries, would result in the prophesied deterioration and, depending upon changes in productivity, possibly a deterioration in the factoral terms of trade as well.

[2] The proposition that primary production has a limited 'carry-over' and does little to improve the quality of the indigenous factors of production is based upon the assumption that the economic organization and technology involved in such agricultural pursuits (in so far as it involves domestic factors) is of the same rudimentary character as that which obtains in the economy at large. Such crops as flue-cured tobacco would represent exceptional cases.

There are four possible bases for industrialization:

1. Export of simple manufactured goods to advanced economies.
2. Industrial processing of primary exports.
3. Production for a regional common market.
4. Import replacement (present and prospective) and increased processing of domestically consumed goods.[1]

Protectionist policies in the advanced economies severely restrict the opportunities for both manufactured goods and valorization of exports.[2] Moreover, with regard to the export of manufactured goods, a few of the more advanced developing countries (e.g. Japan, Hong Kong), whose comparative natural resource endowment is less favourable to primary production, appear to have a substantial cost advantage. The valorization of exports is also limited by the volume of exports and the extent of possible processing – the multiplicity of end-uses necessitates that advanced stages of processing be carried out in close proximity to the final market. With regard to regional common markets, both past experience and continuing trends of political stress between (and within) developing countries render meaningful customs unions an unobtainable ideal, at least for some time. Hence, although these possibilities should be pursued with all vigour, the great majority of underdeveloped countries will have to place major emphasis upon import replacement.

TWO IMPORT SUBSTITUTION STRATEGIES

Fortunately the two major strategies of industrialization are both centred around import substitution. The first strategy is that most commonly identified with Ragnar Nurkse's theory of balanced growth.[3] This theory starts from the proposition that domestic markets are frequently too small to support that size industrial plant which will achieve full economies of scale. However,

> The difficulty caused by the small size of market relates to individual investment incentives in any single line of production taken by itself. At least in

[1] The possibilities for home production of goods not previously traded, increasing the degree of industrial processing of domestically consumed goods, and substitution for handicraft and cottage production are likely to be rather modest in aggregate. Production of the first two types is clearly desirable, while the last type may or may not be, depending upon circumstances. For purposes of manageability we will omit further discussion of these non-importable domestically consumed goods.

[2] See chapter 5, and H. G. Johnson, *Economic Policies Towards Less Developed Countries*, London 1967, chapter III.

[3] R. Nurkse, *Problems of Capital Formation in Underdeveloped Countries*, Oxford 1953. An earlier statement of balanced growth appeared in P. N. Rosenstein-Rodan's 'Problems of Industrialization of Eastern and South-Eastern Europe', *Economic Journal*, June–September 1943. The conceptual ancestry of both balanced growth and the Fleming-Hirschman theory, discussed subsequently, can be traced to Allyn Young, 'Increasing Returns and Economic Progress', *Economic Journal*, December 1928.

principle, the difficulty vanishes in the case of a more or less synchronized application of capital to a wide range of different industries. Here is an escape from the dead-lock; here the result is an over-all enlargement of the market. People working with more and better tools in a number of complementary projects become each others' customers. This basic complementarity stems, in the last analysis, from the diversity of human wants. The case for balanced growth rests on the need for a 'balanced diet'.[1]

Each of a wide range of projects, by contributing to an enlargement of the total size of the market, can be said to create external economies to the individual firm. Indeed, it may be that the most important external economies leading to the phenomenon of increasing returns in the course of economic development are those that take the form of increases in the size of the market . . .[2]

While the validity of 'horizontal' external economies on the demand side has continued to be recognized, debate during the decade following 1953 uncovered a wide assortment of difficulties with the balanced growth strategy of industrialization.[3] Basically, Nurkse's theory rests upon the assumption of a close economy and unemployed resources. And since capital, entrepreneurship and all varieties of skilled labour are in scarce supply, they can only be employed in new industry by bidding up their prices and attracting them away from their current productive uses. Thus there is no guarantee that increased factor costs will not swamp economies of scale or that national output will be increased. As to the magnitude of the demand effect, the larger part of the newly created income will not in fact be spent upon the products of decreasing-cost domestic industries, but rather will go to the purchase of food and imports – goods which in aggregate are likely to be characterized by increasing per unit resource inputs.[4]

The second major strategy of industrialization, itself an outgrowth of the debate over balanced growth, shifts the focus from horizontal external economies on the demand side to vertical external economies on the supply side. This approach was first developed by Marcus Fleming.[5] Just as market prices understate the true social profitability of a particular investment because they fail to account for the entrained outward shift in demand schedules for the products of other industries (hence raising their profitability), on the supply side they fail to reflect the economies of scale that may be realized by those producers selling

[1] Nurkse, *op. cit.* p. 11.

[2] *Ibid.* p. 14.

[3] In order to maintain a clear focus on the issue of industrialization *per se*, here and in what follows the constellation of problems associated with the required complementary development of the agricultural sector are ignored.

[4] Other 'leakages' of potential purchasing power are personal savings and taxation.

[5] J. Marcus Fleming, 'External Economies and the Doctrine of Balanced Growth', *Economic Journal*, June 1955.

inputs to the new industry. Reduced cost of inputs will tend to lead to further (albeit diminishing) rounds of expansion in the consumer industries, and so on. Fleming contended that such a strategy, based upon a moderate number of vertically linked industries, would create concentrated external economies of a greater magnitude than those obtainable under a balanced growth strategy, while the attendant external diseconomies would be smaller.

Albert Hirschman's theory of 'unbalanced growth' is similar to Fleming's formulation, but it places major emphasis on the disequilibrium path of the growth process and the need to induce investment decisions.

> ... our aim must be to keep alive rather than to eliminate the disequilibria of which profits and losses are the symptoms in a competitive economy. If the economy is to be kept moving ahead, the task of development policy is to maintain tensions, disproportions, and disequilibria.[1]

> The way in which investment leads to other investment through complementarities and external economies is an invaluable aid to development that must be consciously utilized in the course of the development process. It puts special pressure behind a whole group of investment decisions and augments thereby that scarce and non-economizable resource of underdeveloped countries, the ability to make new investment decisions.[2]

Investment in an industry which requires a high proportion of intermediate product inputs (strong backward linkages) induces investment in the supplying industries, e.g. beer brewing leading to the production of glass bottles. Similarly, although less forcefully, investment in an industry producing another industry's raw material (forward linkage) encourages the establishment of the second industry, e.g. aluminium sheeting leading to the manufacture of household utensils.

A CRITIQUE

Several observations can be made about the effective strength of Professor Hirschman's investment-inducing mechanisms. Forward linkages based on excess supply are economically productive only when the domestic product is cheaper than the previously available import – a rare occurrence.[3] In like manner, a substantial excess of domestic cost over the duty-free price in the backward-linked industry creates pecuniary external diseconomies for the originating industry, reducing profitability and the size of its market. The evidence from other countries as well as Nigeria is that in many cases an additional tariff-subsidized

[1] A. O. Hirschman, *The Strategy of Economic Growth*, New Haven 1958, p. 66. [2] *Ibid.* p. 73.

[3] We assume that new industries are permitted to import input requirements duty-free. Whether or not this is always so, it is the c.i.f. import price that must be used to determine whether a given linkage has augmented or reduced the country's aggregate real output.

price hike is required for the survival of the originating industry. The realization of backward linkages is in fact typically resisted by existing producers who fear, quite rightly, not only higher costs but poorer quality inputs and irregular supply. Examples of such resistance in the Nigerian case were the bakers' opposition to flour milling, the brewers' opposition to the production of glass bottles, and the textile printers' unwillingness to use domestically produced grey cloth. On the other hand, linkages which naturally tended to be undertaken by existing firms were of a horizontal conglomerate nature aimed primarily at exploiting their established marketing network, e.g. cigarette manufacturers into biscuits, confectioners into candles.

The aforementioned impediments to the achievement of backward and forward linkages (plus a number of others) did not escape Professor Hirschman.[1] These impediments are overcome in his strategy through inflation and import restrictions induced by balance-of-payments crises – the necessary profit-creating disturbances which activate the specified inter-industry linkages.[2] The critical difficulty here is that the required import restrictions invariably provide excessive protection, and protection which is not differentiated with respect to comparative advantage. Consequent pyramiding of high-cost manufacture through successive stages of production, shifting up supply schedules and – given less than perfectly price-inelastic demand functions – dwindling markets quickly choke off industrial expansion. In the extreme, and not infrequent case, import replacement results in a price increase which exceeds domestic factor earnings, e.g. clinker grinding, textile printing. Moreover, the deleterious effects are not limited to the industrial sector: increased prices of manufactured goods and imports purchased by the agricultural sector turn the terms of trade against the latter, particularly with respect to export production, where no partially compensating price rise can be expected with an inward shift in supply. Not only are real farm income and demand for domestic manufactures diminished, but export earnings – critical for financing the heavy foreign exchange component of industrial inputs – will tend to be depressed.

In addition to a common neglect of the cost factor,[3] both the balanced and unbalanced strategies of industrialization are founded upon the premise that substantial pecuniary external economies exist and that these economies will not be realized through the normal operation of the market mechanism. The basis of all pecuniary external economies

[1] Hirschman, *op. cit.* chapters 6 and 7, especially pp. 99, 100, 111, 118, 125.

[2] *Ibid.* chapter 9.

[3] While Fleming does consider changes in factor costs he does not consider the far more essential question of comparative cost.

is that producers whose demand is increased as a consequence of an investment elsewhere in the economy are operating below their optimum capacity; expanded production is thus accompanied by reduced costs.

Three questions are relevant in appraising the external economy argument. First, what is the quantitative significance of potential economies of scale? Second, is it true that unaided entrepreneurial decisions will fail to bring about these economies? And third, how important is the size of the market as a general impediment to the establishment of industry?

How important are potential economies of scale? They are likely to be most important for a few transport-intensive goods (primarily cement) and non-traded commodities (primarily electricity). For goods whose production is characterized by lumpy investment (e.g. railway and harbour facilities) added demand may create either economies or diseconomies depending upon the relation of existing output to the point of minimum cost production. For import-competing industries receiving only moderate protection, substantial economies from expanding plant production are unlikely to be available: if there were important economies of scale previously unattainable the industry would not have been established.[1] On the other hand, offset against whatever economies of scale other producers may realize are higher prices for scarce factors and increased costs to the public authorities in providing education, housing, welfare services, etc. (the implicit wage supplement) for the additional labourers and their dependents who are attracted into the city as a result of the new employment opportunities.

The importance of external benefits is further reduced when consideration is given to the capacity of the entrepreneur to appropriate the economies that accrue to other firms as a result of his investment. As Tibor Scitovsky has pointed out, the source of pecuniary external economies is incomplete information:

> The proper co-ordination of investment decision, therefore, would require a signalling device to transmit information about present plans and future conditions as they are determined by present plans; and the price system fails to provide this. Hence the belief that there is need either for centralized investment planning or for some additional communications system to supplement the pricing system as a signalling device.[2]

In actuality, those entrepreneurs whose investments are of sufficient

[1] Public projects built ahead of demand would, of course, be an exception. For supporting evidence as to the relatively limited range over which significant economies of scale are available, see J. Bain, *Industrial Organization*, New York 1959, pp. 154 ff. and E. A. G. Robinson, *The Structure of Competitive Industry*, 4th ed., Chicago 1958, pp. 149 ff.

[2] T. Scitovsky, 'Two Concepts of External Economies', *The Journal of Political Economy*, 1954, reprinted in A. N. Agarwala and S. P. Singh, *The Economics of Underdevelopment*, London 1958, p. 306.

size to generate external economies do not rely on existing prices as their guide to decision-making. Their initial field investigation and consultations with government agencies and the major firms acquaints them with the circumstances of their prospective suppliers and customers, as well as imminent changes in the economy (e.g. plans for a hydroelectric dam). Profitability is then determined on the basis of negotiated, not current, input prices with due allowance for probable future changes in sales or cost conditions. Hence, while the comparative smallness of the under-developed economy – and consequent lumpiness of individual investments – may render price signalling less efficient in conveying 'correct' information than in a highly developed economy, the smallness makes it more nearly possible to obtain all the required information by other means.

Finally, assuming the absence of external economies, is the size of the market, in fact, a pervasive limitation to the establishment of industry? Certainly in the Nigerian case, where multi-plant industries have predominated, the answer is no. Given the comparative industrial self-sufficiency of each of Nigeria's regions, by extrapolation only a minority of underdeveloped countries are likely to be critically bound in the early stages of industrialization by inadequate markets.[1] Admittedly, as the smaller scale production possibilities are taken up, at some point the size of the domestic market becomes an important deterrent to further import replacement. However, as the country is likely to be at a greater comparative disadvantage in the precluded larger industries, and as existing import replacement is typically characterized by high cost and little net import substitution (foreign exchange savings), extending industrial production into still further import markets is not likely to be a desirable course of action.

A wiser policy would comprehend: (*a*) promoting the substitution of domestic for foreign factors of production in existing industries, e.g. technical, managerial and supervisory personnel, capital share holdings; (*b*) eliminating any rent in the return to capital by appropriate lowering of tariffs or increasing profit and excise taxation; and (*c*) pursuing other measures to increase productivity and to reduce cost. Cost reduction widens the markets for those industries that achieve it; their expanded output, conjoined with increasing agricultural production (particularly exports), progressively generates the growth in income which enlarges all markets.

[1] In a 51-country cross-sectional analysis relating output by industrial origin to levels of *per capita* income, it was found that even at the comparatively high level of £300 per person (e.g. ten times that of Nigeria) industries which have significant economies of scale and their smaller scale supplier industries account for only 40 % of manufacturing production. See H. B. Chenery, 'Patterns of Industrial Growth', *American Economic Review*, September 1960, vol. L, pp. 645–6.

AN ALTERNATIVE APPROACH TO IMPORT SUBSTITUTION

Granting the priority of the above three measures, the question nevertheless remains: what criteria should be used when selecting imports for domestic replacement? Since we have reason to doubt the empirical importance of an uncompensated bias in the factor markets with regard to actual prices and true social opportunity costs (see chapter 2), on the one hand, and the existence of pervasive external economies on the other, we may salvage a slightly qualified comparative cost principle as our guide. The comparative cost principle tells us to choose that product whose potential domestic unit cost is lowest relative to the duty free import price. The 'comparative advantage' of an import replacing industry will vary with the proportionate size of (*a*) the cost of ocean freight in the c.i.f. import price, and (*b*) the input requirement in the production process of factors in abundant supply, e.g. domestic raw materials and unskilled labour; it will vary inversely with the proportionate size of (*c*) input requirements of factors in scarce supply, e.g. technical skills, organization, capital, imported materials and (*d*) economies of scale.

A hypothetical ranking of all possible import substitutions on the basis of relative competitiveness is shown in the top panel of figure 6.[1] Employing a comparative statics approach, the lower panel shows post-infant industry costs adjusted for Pareto optimality conditions. Cost estimates in the lower panel differ from initial market costs owing to the achievement of internal economies and the receipt of subsidies equal in value to the net non-reciprocal external benefits created by the industry.

Production of commodity *C* represents the least harmful import replacement; assuming the opportunity for investment elsewhere in the economy yielding any positive rate of return, the production of *C* diminishes the national output. Import substitution will add to real income when the domestic cost of production is brought below the c.i.f. value. The latter may happen in one of two ways: increased factor productivity (reduced unit costs) or lower factor prices stemming from declining terms of trade for those goods whose production is an alternative, e.g. primary exports, food. Even when this occurs, however, investment in the most competitive import-replacing industry represents an optimal strategy only if it is the most profitable of all possible investment opportunities in the economy.

[1] The technique of presentation in figure 6 follows George B. Baldwin, 'What Price Domestic Industry?', *Finance and Development*, vol. III, March 1966, p. 27. We have assumed an equilibrium exchange rate; if such is not the case, 'true' c.i.f. values are calculated using an appropriate shadow exchange rate – shifting the 100 % line upwards (if overvalued) or downward (if undervalued). We have assumed a single *ad valorem* tariff rate of 50 %.

What determines the size of the adjustments made to initial market costs when calculating the industry's long-run social cost? First, there are the internal economies discussed in chapter 2 – improved efficiency as a result of learning on the part of operatives and management, reduction in the number of foreign supervisors, and a lower cost of capital after the period of prime risk. Of conventional external economies, we are willing to subsidize a producer for the transferable skills he

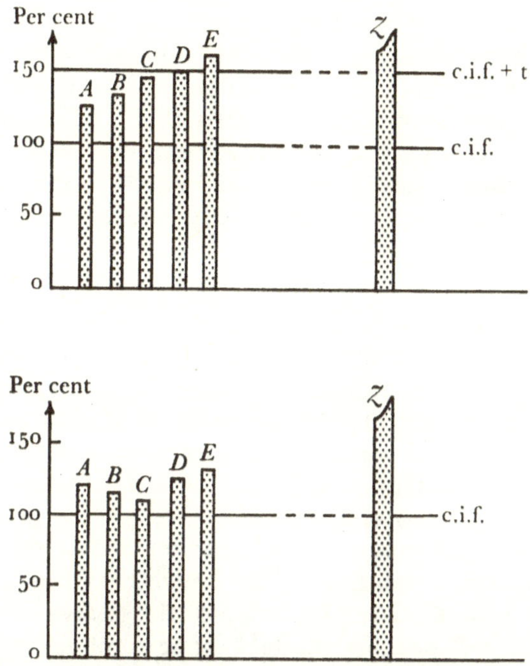

FIG. 6. Domestic production cost as a per cent of c.i.f. import cost.

imparts to workers who leave the industry and for such cost reduction in electricity generation permitted by his additional demand which has not already been passed on in the negotiated rates. Third, long-run social costs should be reduced by an amount equal to the estimated increase in factor productivity which results from the transference of technology and organization to other industries. The cigarette industry's conscious transferal of skills and organization to Nigerian tobacco farmers is a case in point. Probably such subsidy-qualifying transferals have been most prominent in the agricultural export industries: certain marketing techniques, cultivation practices, tools, insecticides, etc., required for export crops have been adopted for use in domestic food production. Policies for maximizing this 'technical carry-over' are discussed in the following section.

We have so far omitted one frequently claimed justification for subsidizing new industry – the stimulation of investment in vertically linked industries. This argument is valid when the induced investment does not itself require protection, i.e. domestic production is cheaper than duty-free importation. If such an instance should occur, on *a priori* grounds we would expect the initial project to be enlarged to include the more profitable manufacturing process, thereby increasing the entrepreneur's rate of return. Empirically no non-integrated, unprotected linkage has occurred in Nigeria; nor does the writer know of such instances in other developing countries.[1] On the other hand, unprotected linkages to the service sector do occur – and to the extent that induced output and income is generated that would not have arisen elsewhere in the economy if the import-substitution investment had been foregone, then a subsidy is justified equal to that portion of the generated income taken to represent the 'producers' surplus'.

II

In our discussion of industrialization strategy we have been considering how to select the most beneficial areas for new investment. We now turn to the more limited, although not entirely independent problem of choosing the particular technique of production once an industry has been selected. The most complete theoretical statement of the subject has been given by Amartya Sen.[2]

The basic assumptions of the choice of technique analysis are that the existence of single homogeneous product and factor markets, and considerable technical substitutability between labour and capital in the production process. The conclusion of the analysis is that over the appropriate range of possible capital-labour combinations, for a given investment expenditure choice of a labour-intensive production technique will maximize net output and employment while the capital-intensive alternative will give capital a larger share of its smaller output. On the assumption that all profits are reinvested and all wages spent on consumption, if profits under the capital-intensive method are absolutely greater, then choice of the less productive capital-intensive technique will result in a larger capital stock and higher consumption at some future time.[3]

[1] Such unprotected linkages have occurred in export industries in Nigeria – groundnut crushing and various inputs into the petroleum extraction industry. Professor Hirschman has suggested to the writer (who remains sceptical) that the fact that certain industries obtained 'normal' protection does not mean they could not have been set up without it.

[2] A. K. Sen, *Choice of Techniques*, 2nd ed., Oxford 1962.

[3] The choice between a given increment of consumption now or more consumption later is resolved by applying an appropriate social time preference discount to compute the present value of the alternative techniques.

Our study of instances of choice of technique in Nigeria suggests that a number of the conventional assumptions may be questioned. The first, and perhaps most fundamental, is the postulate of a single homogenous product market. As described in chapter 2, the majority of consumer product markets are in actuality highly segmented. Goods produced by small scale labour-intensive techniques are of a very much lower quality, both in finish and in their raw material make-up, and they sell at substantially lower prices. Within individual submarkets there are only slight variations in production techniques.

The 'choice' of technique is thus, in most cases, derived from consumer choice, the latter in turn a function of income. As income rises and the value placed on quality increase (e.g. the consumer progressing from tyre-sandals to plastic sandals to factory-made leather sandals), the share of inferior labour-intensive goods falls. Nor is this pattern limited to Nigeria; even in the most celebrated case, Indian textiles, planners have recently realized that the choice of technique is essentially a choice of product.[1]

Despite the fact that in most instances the possibilities for varying factor proportions are rather narrow, being confined to a single technology, there are instances where choice between widely differing techniques is feasible. The processing of palm fruit provides an example. What are the general characteristics of this particular case which permitted a true choice of technology? It is possible to discern five defining attributes.

1. The physical properties of palm oil are such that the organization and skill required of the small-scale producer in order to attain the threshold of product quality are relatively simple.
2. A similar permissive factor is the absence of extensive capital or organizational requirements in the marketing of final output or raw materials acquisition.
3. A substantial weight loss in production endows disbursed processors with important transport savings.
4. Small-scale operation with negligible fixed overheads permits costless shut-down – an important factor in industries characterized by variation in cost or revenue conditions (e.g. seasonality of demand or raw material supply).
5. The supply price of labour to producers in the semi-modern or unorganized sector is very much lower than that which faces their larger scale competitors.

[1] Raj Krishna, remarks at a Stanford University seminar on 'Industrialization and Agricultural Development', 26 February 1966. See also Jagdish Bhagwati, *The Economics of Underdeveloped Countries*, London 1966, p. 191. The writer has examined the situation in Pakistan in 'Investment Criteria, Productivity and Economic Development: Reinterpretation', *Quarterly Journal of Economics*, vol. LXXVIII, August 1964, pp. 488–95.

When these five factors are present and where the superiority of the advanced technology in converting inputs into outputs is not of an overwhelming nature, a simple labour-using technology constitutes a competitive or superior alternative to modern capital-using producing techniques.

Several of the preceding points can be further amplified with the aid of a conventional diagram. In figure 7 capital and labour inputs are represented on the vertical and horizontal axis respectively; the isoproduct lines convex to the origin show the various combinations of capital and labour that can be used to produce a given volume of output.[1] Panel A contains an analysis of potentially coexisting modern and

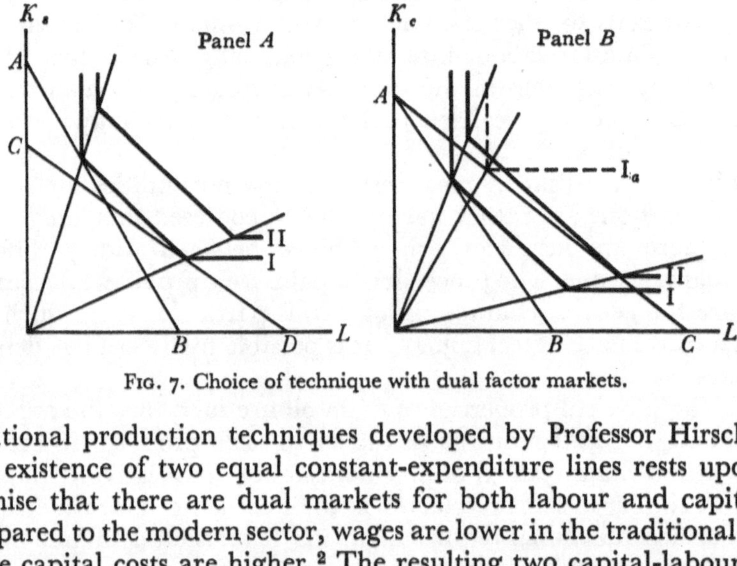

FIG. 7. Choice of technique with dual factor markets.

traditional production techniques developed by Professor Hirschman. The existence of two equal constant-expenditure lines rests upon the premise that there are dual markets for both labour and capital: as compared to the modern sector, wages are lower in the traditional sector while capital costs are higher.[2] The resulting two capital-labour price ratios are reflected in the differing slopes and intercept points of *AB* and *CD*.

In panel *B* is it postulated that only the labour market is segmented; the cost of capital is assumed identical to both sectors. This condition is approximated where the small-scale sector has access to government development loans (on which the interest cost is about 20 % less than the most favourable commercial rate), where there is a well organized

[1] These isoproduct curves are constructed from observed input coefficients as distinct from hypothetical production possibilities based on engineering data.

[2] 'While labor is cheaper in the underdeveloped sector of the economy, capital is typically more expensive, also for a variety of reasons: access to the banks is difficult and interest charges are higher; machinery, equipment and tools are bought at retail rather than imported directly from the foreign manufacturer at important savings, etc.' A. O. Hirschman, *The Strategy of Economic Development*, New Haven 1962, p. 127.

market for the capital equipment being acquired and in so far as building construction is concerned (which is more expensive in the modern sector). In most of the Nigerian cases examined the assumptions of panel *B* were the relevant ones.

In panel *B* the capital input is measured not in terms of the total capital stock (K_s) as in panel *A*, but rather in terms of capital service (K_c), made up of capital consumption, an allowance for obsolescence and interest; the advantage of K_c is that it converts capital into a flow input consistent with labour, and that it is empirically and conceptually much simpler to deal with.[1] At existing producers prices the same cost expenditure yielded a higher output from the traditional method. Moreover it can be seen that the lower wage advantage possessed by the small-scale sector may permit a technically inferior production method to be economically competitive: a hypothetical third technique associated with the dotted isoproduct line I_a requires both more labour and more capital than the modern technique (shown immediately below and to the left) to produce an equal output ($I = I_a$), and yet it is economically competitive with the latter. A not insignificant proportion of Nigeria's small urban industry probably falls into this category.

The desirability of choosing the least-cost technique should not be allowed to obscure the fact that economic efficiency combined with low productivity means poverty. When we turn from a static view, our central objective, particularly with regard to the indigenous sector, is to pursue those policies which will shift the isoproduct curves inwards, i.e. to increase the efficiency with which inputs are converted into outputs. The sources of simultaneous increase in the productivity of labour, capital and intermediate inputs are the introduction of superior technology and the taking up of organizational slack within any given technology.

The introduction of more advanced technology into indigenous production involves the effective absorption of new technological knowledge by members of the local population. For the most part such learning occurs in institutions of technical education and on-the-job in the expatriate-operated firms. To date in Nigeria the latter has been of much greater importance than the former; however as the complexity

[1] Given that the capital equipment employed in different technologies will not be of identical durability, to make K_s comparable as between techniques it is necessary that the isoproduct lines represent the present value of the capital equipment's lifetime output and that labour represent the aggregate input of labour time required over the life of the investment. When using K_c the true K/L ratio can be calculated from any time-dimension of output (e.g. hourly, daily, annual) without worrying about durability, future prices and discount rates. The one implicit assumption in the K_c approach is that the investment is permanent, i.e. the initial capital equipment will be replaced.

of the technology to be transferred grows, so does the importance of a prior formal education on the part of the carrier (see chapter 8). The technology-diffusing potential of foreign enterprise varies inversely with its scale and the complexity of the techniques it employs.[1] The large, capital-intensive soap factory, brewery, flour mill, etc., have had no visible 'carry-over' in Nigeria – they have remained technological enclaves. On the other hand, small, modestly financed, individual or family-owned concerns (predominantly Levantine) employing the most rudimentary and unadorned production processes have spawned hundreds of Nigerian firms in soap-making, metal-working, sawmilling, rubber crêping, baking, umbrella assembly, singlet manufacture and construction. The reason for this is simply that learning is a continuous process, comparable to an individual climbing a ladder in the sense that if too many rungs are missing, if the technological gap is too great, upward progress ceases.

Turning to the second source of productivity increase, organizational slack or technical inefficiency, as we have more frequently described it, is a pervasive feature of the Nigerian economy as documented in the preceding chapters. In the case of the firm, improving technical efficiency encompasses nothing more esoteric than (*i*) increasing through repair and maintenance and 'flow management' the proportion of available hours that capital equipment and labour force are in effective use, (*ii*) accelerating the rate of production per effective hour by conventional industrial engineering techniques, (*iii*) eliminating loss of product from theft and raw material wastage, and (*iv*) raising revenue-product by improving quality. We shall return to this subject later in the chapter.

It was stated earlier that in the majority of cases the possibilities for varying factor proportions are rather narrow and confined to a single technology. There are two principal ways that labour may be substituted for capital within a given technique. The first is to substitute labour and superintendence for capital equipment; the second is to employ used machinery.

Substituting men for equipment is extensively practised in Nigeria by the Levantine business community. The two most efficient producers of the five rubber crêping firms discussed in chapter 7 are cases in point. While the labour-capital ratio is more or less fixed for the central mechanical or chemical process, Levantine entrepreneurs invariably opt

[1] For a very suggestive discussion on this subject, centred on the complexity and quantum of the technological transplant, in relation to the success of international corporations in transferring effective technical knowledge to subsidiary plants in developing countries, see Jack Baranson, 'Transfer of Technical Knowledge by International Corporations to Developing Economies', *American Economic Review*, vol. LVI, May 1966, pp. 259–67.

for manpower over machine-power in the setting-up sequence, materials handling and packing operations; similarly they almost always operate two shifts.[1] This labour-using bias flows from the Levantines' limited financial resources relative to other firms operating on a comparable scale, and the availability of members of the extended family at moderate cost to maintain and supervise a work discipline which is not equalled by producers of any other nationality.[2] In terms of factor-intensities, these practices lower both K_s/L and K_c/L.

The employment of used machinery is the second method for lowering the capital-labour ratio, a method which is attracting increasing attention from international development agencies.[3] In Nigeria the practice of installing second-hand equipment has been most prevalent in the textile industry. Primarily aimed at minimizing the initial capital put at risk, this method has had the effect in the textile case of maximizing employment and output for a given capital expenditure. On the other hand, because of the shorter life and lower rate of output of used equipment, K_c/L is not lowered either to the extent of K_s/L or in sufficient degree to offset its higher labour costs. Thus unit cost is higher with used equipment and the rate of return is lower. This outcome conforms to Sen's model described earlier. Note however that used equipment with its higher unit cost is only feasible in a non-competitive market: removal or decreasing utilization of the protective tariff on textiles, as a result of expanding domestic supply, means that only the more capital-intensive low-cost producers will survive.[4]

Whether the preceding statements about used capital equipment are valid in other industries can only be determined by examining the character of technical improvements embodied in new machinery and supply and demand conditions in the used equipment market. In the case of the metal working industry, the evidence suggests that older machine tools are both capital-saving and cost-minimizing in a low-wage economy.[5] While it is not possible to generalize whether a higher or lower level of operative skills is required by old machinery, three categorical points can be made:

[1] The possibility of varying factor-intensities in this way has been recognized by Hirschman, *op. cit.* pp. 151–2.

[2] Unlike all other expatriates who live in residential estates, Levantine industrialists build their homes within a few hundred feet of the factory. It is primarily because they cannot command supervisory services of so intense and comprehensive a character that European and American corporate investors substitute automated processes for superintendence where possible.

[3] *Report of Expert Group on Second-Hand Equipment for Developing Countries*, United Nations, New York 1966, and the citations therein.

[4] More generally, given unsegmented factor markets and a competitive product market, there is no choice of technique.

[5] *Report of Expert Group on Second-Hand Equipment for Developing Countries*, passim.

1. Older equipment needs more maintenance attention, but of a lower skill level than new machinery.
2. New equipment is more demanding with regard to the quality of its complementary inputs, e.g. uniformity of raw material, regulated temperature and humidity, speed of operation.
3. Spare parts for old machinery are more difficult, and hence more costly to obtain.[1]

Probably the most critical requirement for effective use of second-hand equipment is an intimate knowledge of the production process and of the relative capabilities, limitations and servicing inputs of the possible varieties of new and used equipment. Save in industries consisting of a single, relatively simple manufacturing process, the amount of technical knowledge and commercial experience needed is likely to be found only in large, long-established firms. In the Nigerian textile industry this is well illustrated by the performance of Indian Head Mills, on the one hand, and the two Nigerian ventures and Nortex, on the other. Yet, if the analysis of chapters 3 and 4 is correct, the considerations leading a large foreign firm to favour installation of used as against new equipment would probably also induce demands for other terms which may render the project of questionable value. This implies that a policy of encouraging the use of second-hand equipment should be approached with extreme caution.

In addition to the above, there is a wider question as to the relevance of choice of technique considerations wherever foreign investment is involved. There is no investment opportunity sacrificed in the underdeveloped country as a result of a larger rather than a smaller capital commitment by a private external source. The appropriate policy goal is thus not to maximize output or reinvestment for a *given* expenditure, but rather to maximize the amount of foreign investment consistent with minimum social costs. As a qualification, it should be stated that a possible future cost in terms of reduced foreign exchange availability arises where payments abroad for capital services exceed net import replacement.

The last aspect of the conventional choice of technique analysis we want to scrutinize is the assumption that of the income generated by a particular investment, a substantially larger share of profits is likely to be reinvested than of wages. Although correct in its narrow formulation, the situation appears quite differently in its institutional setting, at least in Nigeria.

Particular techniques for producing a given product (or differentiated products) are typically associated with specific categories of investors: indigenous entrepreneurs, foreign firms and public enterprise.

[1] *Ibid.* chapters 3 and 4.

The production techniques employed by the first are labour-intensive (L/K_s), while those of the latter two are capital-intensive. After a certain point, foreign investors have a very high propensity to remit their profits to the home country.[1] On the other hand, as we have seen, public enterprises, owing to political pressures and bad management, seldom make the reinvestible profits they are technically capable of. The share of income reinvested from private Nigerian establishments may be small; however the opening up of technically-feasible investment opportunities induces a shift in average saving propensities, financing a rapid expansion in output up to the point of sharply diminishing profitability. The bulk of the small industry sector attests to this elasticity of saving in response to profitable commercial opportunities.

It would seem that the most important lesson to be drawn from our discussion of the various aspects of the choice of technique issue is that, given the elasticity of capital availability, cost-minimization should take primacy over all other criteria.

III

Harking back to the Introduction, it was stated that economic growth could be envisaged as being dependent upon three factors: the size of the investible surplus, the allocational efficiency of resource use, and the efficiency (technological and organizational) of converting resource inputs into commodity outputs. Our analysis of Nigeria's experience suggests that of the three determinants, improvement in the last category offers the greatest potential gain for accelerating growth. Stated another way, the bottleneck exerting the primary drag on economic progress is organizational inefficiency. In the realm of import substitution this inefficiency is reflected in domestic cost schedules whose height above the world supply curves exceed combined transport costs and infant industry considerations. Given the price distortions, rigidities and vested interests associated with a highly protected industry, it is much wiser – as well as less sacrificing of national income – to up-grade factor efficiencies *prior* to the initiation of import replacement, rather than trusting it can be achieved afterwards.[2]

What policies are available for raising the efficiency of factor combination? The traditional remedy is to increase competitive pressures. This approach is clearly desirable for expatriate-operated industry

[1] The government's share in profits, via corporate taxation, is an important qualification.

[2] Friedrich List, perhaps the most famous of all protectionists, stated clearly that tariff-induced import replacement was only justifiable when the country had obtained a political, social and technological level comparable to the most advanced industrial nations. *The National System of Political Economy*, London 1928, p. 247.

which has the managerial and technical capability of responding. In industries where new firms are still starting up, healthy price competition is more likely to occur if the firms are of differing nationality – gentlemanly collusion is more difficult to achieve. For an established industry increased competition via a lowering of the tariff eliminates any economic rent as well as spurring cost-reducing innovation. The application of industrial engineering techniques, probably the most important tool for raising physical productivity, should be encouraged by subsidizing the provision of industrial engineering services, withdrawing tax reliefs for producers who fail to operate their equipment above some per cent of its rated capacity, and other similar measures.

When we turn to indigenous enterprise, the educational system, government departments and the public corporations the remedy of increased competition is of little use owing to either inapplicability or incapacity to respond. Following our analysis of the previous section, the encouragement of smaller scale, labour-using foreign investment (probably Levantine) will maximize the technological and managerial carry-over from the foreign sector. The prime policy objective for Nigerian enterprise and public corporations should be improving the quality of the managerial input; performance changes are required with respect to the utilization of written records as a control technique, the maintenance of supervision, and concern with the production process, product quality and technological betterment. In addition to what has already been suggested, specific measures to help bring about the desired performance changes encompass adjustments in technical education curricula, the establishment of technical assistance extension services to existing producers,[1] and promoting sub-contracting arrangements with expatriate firms analogous to the Nigerian Tobacco Company's relationship with tobacco growers. But because learning is imbedded in the total socialization process, as we have argued in chapter 10, full realization of the desired performance in carrying out managerial roles is likely to depend upon an elevation in the status rewards accorded such roles, which implies certain changes in social values and child-rearing.

The task of public bureaucracies is more complex than that of market-directed producers because they must not only produce a particular service but they have to decide exactly what that service should be. They thus face problems not only of administrative efficiency but of policy formulation as well: educational content, skill levels, graduate output mix, a strategy of applied industrial research, criteria for

[1] A well-designed scheme providing three-week courses for small firm entrepreneur-managers, as well as technical extension services, was launched at Owerri in the eastern region in 1962–3 as a joint AID-Eastern Nigerian Government project.

selecting individual research projects, types of aid to indigenous business men, devising an industrial relations policy, etc. Our review of the operations of government agencies in these areas suggests that the quality of policy formulation has been more important than administrative inefficiency in limiting the aggregate value of services rendered.

Beyond mis-allocation and inefficiency which spring from political considerations, the policy-making process is typically wanting in one or more of three respects. A minimum of systematic information about the subject may not be obtained, reliance being placed on limited facts and intuitive judgment, e.g. the alleged shortage of technician skills, development corporations' projects, assistance schemes to Nigerian entrepreneurs. Second, the full range of a particular policy's economic and social consequences may not be rigorously worked out, e.g. cassava processing, palm oil producer prices, wage policy, Third, a full scale programme may be mounted in uncharted areas where the inherent uncertainties of the situation call for a pilot venture and critical evaluation of its feed-back, e.g. educational curriculum reform, agricultural processing industries based on commercially untried crops.

Promulgation of basic procedural guidelines for policy-making would probably contribute to improvement. More important is the recruitment of personnel. The major change required is a shift in emphasis from quantity of staffed positions to quality of performance. Where there are insufficient Nigerians with the called for abilities, much can be done to augment the number of high-quality foreign specialists with the ministries in data-collecting and advisory capacities. The use of extended-tour contracts, combined with the recruitment services and salary supplements which UNESCO, AID and the Ford Foundation are willing to provide, should go a long way in upgrading the quality of policy formulation.

These, then are the policies designed to increase the technical efficiency of factor combination. Augmenting the conventional drive to maximize profits, measures fostering internal and external competition will work to create the *incentive* to raise productive efficiency, while another set of policies – the widespread application of industrial engineering, the encouragement of high 'carry-over' small-scale labour-using foreign investment, the development of indigenous managerial resources, rationalization in the public sector – are directed at building up the *capacity* to respond to these incentives. In so far as these policies achieve their objectives, a decrease in unit resource input requirements will accelerate the growth of national product through its joint impact upon output and reinvestible surpluses. Stated another way, given that changes in the efficiency of factor combinations have their effect upon average rather than marginal productivities, there is good reason to believe that a shift in emphasis in the development effort from maximizing public investment and the savings ratio to improving organizational efficiency will yield a higher rate of economic growth in the short-run, and create necessary conditions for the absorption of new technology over the long run.

APPENDICES

APPENDIX A

Federal wage rates: general labour

	Lagos		
	s. d.		*s. d.*
1939	1 0	1946	2 7
1940	1 0	1947	2 7
1941	1 1 (1*s.* 3*d.*)	1948	2 7
1942	1 9	1949	2 7
1943	2 0	1950	2 8
1944	2 0	1951	3 0
1945	2 2 (2*s.* 5*d.*)	1952	3 4

					Minimum Federal rates in the regions		
	Lagos	Ibadan	Kaduna	Enugu	West	East	North
	s. d.	*s. d.*	*s. d.*	*s. d.*	*s. d.*	*s. d.*	*s. d.*
1953	3 5	2 7	2 5	2 7	2 7	2 3	1 10
1954	4 8	4 1	3 6	3 6	3 2	3 2	2 4
1955	4 8	4 1	3 6	3 6	3 2	3 2	2 4
1956	4 8	4 1	3 6	3 6	3 2	3 2	2 4
1957	4 8	4 1	3 8	3 6	3 2	3 2	2 4
1958	4 8	4 1	3 8	3 6	3 2	3 2	2 4
1959	5 10	4 11	4 3	4 3	3 10	3 10	3 0
1960	5 10	4 11	4 3	4 3	3 10	3 10	3 0
1961	5 10	4 11	4 3	4 3	3 10	3 10	3 0
1962	5 10	4 11	4 3	4 3	3 10	3 10	3 0
1963	5 10	4 11	4 3	4 3	3 10	3 10	3 0
1964	7 8	6 3	5 4	6 3	6 3	6 3	4 0
1965	7 8	6 3	5 4	6 3	6 3	6 3	4 0
1966	7 8	6 3	5 4	6 3	6 3	6 3	4 0

SOURCES: Department of Labour, *Annual Reports*, 1942–53; Federal Ministry of Labour, 'An Outline of the Development of Wages and Wage Structures in Nigeria', mimeograph, February 1966.

APPENDIX A (Cont.)

Consumer Price Index

	Lagos		Ibadan		Kaduna		Enugu		Port Harcourt and Aba	
	Food	All items	Food	All items	Food	All items	Food	All items	Food	All items
1939		100								
1940		...								
1941		...								
1942		151								
1943		167								
1944		163								
1945		176								
1946		226								
1953	100	100	100	100			100	100		
1954	109	105	109	...			118	...		
1955	116	108	113	108			105	105		
1956	124	117	125	114			112	112		
1957	127	119	126	117	100	100	115	112	100	100
1958	124	119	112	110	105	103	113	115	...	...
1959	130	124	113	112	108	109	116	119	...	...
1960	136	132	118	117	101	108	112	119	...	...
1961	148	140	131	127	111	115	120	122	128	122
1962	158	145	143	137	120	122	152	149	116	121
1963	148	145	125	128	111	119	131	143	106	116
1964	150	149	123	127	107	118	135	147	111	118
1965	155	154	131	131	113	122	138	148	...	...
1966	178	168	158	146	133	131	172	166	...	...

SOURCE: Department of Labour, *Annual Reports*, for 1939–46 data. Federal Office of Statistics, *Digest of Statistics*, various issues.

APPENDIX A (Cont.)

Summary Consumer Price Indices, 1948-65

	Western Region (1948 = 100)	Eastern Region (1948 = 100)	Northern Region (1948 = 100)
1948	100·0	100·0	100·0
1949	101·5	106·7	103·5
1950	98·6	108·5	99·9
1951	129·8	133·5	138·6
1952	125·7	137·2	124·8
1953	112·5	135·5	110·7
1954	118·2	151·8	99·5
1955	121·5	142·3	98·6
1956	128·3	151·8	104·0
1957	131·7	151·8	104·2
1958	123·8	155·9	107·3
1959	126·1	161·2	113·6
1960	131·7	161·2	112·5
1961	143·0	165·4	119·8
1962	154·3	202·0	127·1
1963	144·0	193·8	124·0
1964	142·9	199·2	123·0
1965	147·3	200·5	149·1

SOURCE: G. K. Helleiner, *Peasant Agriculture, Government and Economic Growth in Nigeria* Statistical Appendix.

Western Region:

1947–8 to 1952–3 inclusive: Annual averages of United Africa Company (UAC) index of wholesale prices of imported goods at Lagos using the 1948 average (not August 1948, as does the original index) as base. (The index for calendar years was used in conjunction with the latter of the two years stated in the crop years, e.g. 1948 with crop year 1947–8.)

1953–4 to 1961–2 inclusive: Federal Office of Statistics Consumer Price Index for Ibadan (calendar years corresponding to crop years as before). This was linked to the index for the earlier period.

Northern Region:

1947–8 to 1956–7 inclusive: Annual averages of UAC index of wholesale prices of imported goods (Kano), using the 1948 average as base. (Calendar years corresponding to crop years as before.)

1957–8 to 1961–2 inclusive: Federal Office of Statistics Consumer Price Index for Kaduna. This was linked to the index for the earlier period.

Eastern Region:

1948–1952 inclusive: Annual averages of the UAC index of wholesale prices of imported goods (Port Harcourt) using the 1948 average as base.

1953–1962 inclusive: Federal Office of Statistics Consumer Price Index for Enugu. This was linked to the index for the earlier period.

All Regions:

1963–5 inclusive: Federal Office of Statistics Indices for Ibadan, Kaduna, and Enugu. These were rebased so that 1953 = 112·5, 1957 = 104·2, and 1953 = 135·5, respectively.

APPENDIX B

Purchases of palm products by Regional Marketing Boards in Nigeria, 1955–1965

(tons)

A. Palm oil by region or type of holding

Year	East	West	North	Smallholder	Plantation	Total
1955	165,169	22,174	3,280	184,691	5,932	190,623
1956	161,876	18,934	3,521	177,967	6,364	184,331
1957	153,651	15,527	1,934	165,788	5,324	171,112
1958	167,052	15,398	1,905	177,611	6,744	184,355
1959	170,067	18,818	1,358	182,865	7,378	190,243
1960	170,003	19,129	973	183,078	7,027	190,105
1961	160,693	12,370	370	164,635	8,798	173,433
1962	120,884	7,661	—	120,600	7,900	128,545
1963	139,412	9,619	—	139,700	9,400	149,031
1964	138,900	9,000	—	138,700	9,200	147,900
1965	153,600	10,600	—	153,500	10,700	164,200

B. Smallholder palm oil by region and grade

	East			West			North		
Year	Special grade	Grade I	Grades II–III	Special grade	Grade I	Grades II–III	Special grade	Grade I	Grades II–III
1955	128,485	33,207	622	340	7,289	11,468	511	2,769	—
1956	128,162	30,310	162	413	5,774	9,625	619	2,902	—
1957	117,133	34,129	91	384	5,283	6,834	483	1,451	—
1958	137,109	26,549	121	358	5,446	6,121	186	1,719	—
1959	135,286	30,463	941	808	7,668	6,341	208	1,150	—
1960	132,952	33,492	460	939	8,528	5,734	381	592	—
1961	127,703	28,144	183	1,312	3,844	3,079	361	9	—
1962	99,100	17,100	300	1,200	900	1,900	—	—	—
1963	114,700	19,100	400	1,800	1,600	2,100	—	—	—
1964	109,000	24,200	200	2,400	1,500	1,400	—	—	—
1965	112,400	34,800	200	2,800	2,100	1,400	—	—	—

C. Palm kernels by region

Year	East	West	North	Total
1955	194,904	204,280	14,467	413,651
1956	211,202	231,612	14,219	457,033
1957	201,611	191,954	13,013	406,578
1958	211,024	225,990	18,331	455,345
1959	211,558	197,574	18,731	427,863
1960	208,173	196,680	18,364	423,217
1961	208,483	200,940	20,806	430,229
1962	168,953	173,878	19,318	362,149
1963	197,048	197,695	18,317	413,060
1964	203,000	184,000	15,000	401,000
1965	221,000	203,000	25,000	449,000

SOURCE: Commonwealth Economic Committee, *Tropical Products Quarterly*, various issues.

APPENDIX C

1960–1962 Entrepreneurial survey data, 298 firms

Industry	Total	Number of firms[a] Small	Medium	Large	Very large
Baking	44	26	6	5	7
Tailoring	15	14	1	—	—
Auto repair	31	30	1	—	—
Printing	27	12	4	5	6
Furniture	50	46	2	1	1
Engineering	4	1	2	—	1
Shoe-making	18	15	2	1	—
Weld/W. iron	18	15	1	2	—
Dry cleaning	2	1	—	—	1
Upholstery	2	1	—	1	—
Soft drinks	3	1	2	—	—
Singlet	6	—	5	1	—
Cosmetics	1	1	—	—	—
Clothing	5	3	—	2	—
Photography	3	2	1	—	—
Tinkering	11	11	—	—	—
Saw milling	7	2	1	1	3
Soap	2	—	2	—	—
Plastic bag	4	4	—	—	—
Rice milling	5	3	2	—	—
Other[b]	40	37	2	1	—

[a] Size of firm measured by investment in tools, equipment and fixtures at original cost (excludes investment in land and building). Small: under £1,000; Medium: £1,000–£2,000; Large: £2,001–£5,000; Very large: over £5,000.

[b] 'Other' includes shoe repair, rubber stamp making, corn milling, mattress making, auto painting, bus-body building and leather goods (purses and bags).

APPENDIX D

THE POLITICAL CLASS AND ECONOMIC GROWTH[1]

by JAMES O'CONNELL

Department of Political Science, University of Ibadan

Politics developed in Nigeria within a three-dimensional historical context: the evolution of the traditional communities, the framework and policies of the colonial authorities, and the nationalist awakening and anti-colonial agitation of the members of the formally educated intelligentsia. If these three factors are distinct, they are not separate. They can be studied only in their inter-locking development.

The colonial structure was oriented initially almost exclusively to maintaining law and order. Since its taxes were geared to this kind of rule, a British officer assisted by a few Nigerian auxiliaries looked after a huge population and an enormous slice of territory. Though the colonial régime did in its later stages take on social welfare responsibilities, especially in education and health, it remained dominantly a night watchman operation.[2] Its power to crush those who opposed it impressed the Nigerian peoples generally and the nationalist leaders particularly. This impression led them to magnify the power of government – a power that was already linked in their minds with transforming modernization in society. It led them to over-estimate what political control might achieve. It was only when they had held power themselves for some time that the Nigerian political class began to appreciate how scarce were the resources that a government in a poor country could mobilize, and how few in numbers and how thinly spread through the country was the administrative service that had once looked so all-pervasive. But before they had made those shattering discoveries, Nigerian politicians had over-committed their resources and personnel. They had also opened Pandora's box of aspirations with welfare schemes that whetted peoples' hopes at least as much as they fulfilled their expectations.

[1] Reprinted with slight abridgements from *Nigerian Journal of Economic and Social Studies*, vol. 8, March 1966. With permission of the author.

[2] To get a good account of earlier British colonial administration in Nigeria and to catch some of the flavour of the period one might consult M. Perham, *Native Administration in Nigeria*, London 1937 and A. N. Cook, *British Enterprise in Nigeria*, Philadelphia 1943. Cook's book contains an excellent bibliography. In a letter to his wife, Frederick Lugard described quite graphically and succinctly the tasks that he found waiting for him when he arrived to take up his work as Governor in 1912. See M. Perham, *Lugard: The Years of Authority*, London 1960, pp. 392–3. The exception to a law and order operation by the British in Nigeria was their notable contribution to the development of communications.

Up to the time that Nigerian politicians were on the verge of taking over the country – the effective date of their coming into power was 1951 under the Macpherson Constitution, less than ten years before independence – they and with them the educated élite of the country were largely excluded from all central and regional decision-making. For that reason they were inevitably impeded in thinking in terms larger than the local communities from which they came.[1] They also tended to identify themselves with their communities; and in those communities their presence, though usually episodic, was often effective. Here lie some of the roots of the communalism that has dogged Nigerian politics ever since the end of World War II. Yet decision-making in local communities hardly ever went beyond schools, health facilities and water supplies. These matters concerned social welfare rather than formed part of the direct growth-producing sectors of the economy. For long years communalism and social welfare went hand in hand. The British colonial officers hardly thought in radically different terms. When Margery Perham, a scholar closely aligned with the attitudes of the more intelligent officers, set out in 1936 to envisage the political future of Nigeria, she elaborated the ideal of a federation of local government units.[2] In some ways her ideal came far too close for comfort to being realized in the 1950s. Several thousand communities in search of a nation-state produce a fragmenting effect that dissipates political and economic energies.

With some hindsight British West African decolonization policy is highly praised. But the Richard Constitution which the London government in collaboration with its colonial officials got ready between 1944 and 1946 was illiberal towards the nationalist leaders both in its conception and in its implementation. This constitutional approach prolonged agitational politics in Nigeria. Such politics offered peculiar opportunities to flamboyant types of leaders whose talents more easily set in motion loosely led popular movements than organized and structured

[1] 'Their [i.e. traditional communities] members, yesterday active, independent, and self-reliant, have passed under the control of foreigners, remote in culture from themselves, and suffer to-day a sense of bewilderment and inferiority that diminished their full human stature... [But] their institutions, even if weakened, persist, and their members remain united by their culture, their language which is part of their culture, and their common associations and territory. A wider sense of civic obligation does not conveniently spring into being to fit the new political and economic boundaries, and it is the main belief underlying indirect rule that this sense can best be developed through a gradual extension of existing social conceptions.' M. Perham, *Native Administration*, p. 354.

[2] '... the ideal development would be a gradual increase in the responsibilities of the Native Administrations which should at a later stage be encouraged, though not pressed, to federate. This federation would probably have to be very loose and mainly financial in its early stages and would be likely to occur first between the more homogeneous groups.' M. Perham, *Native Administration*, pp. 356–7. It might be remembered that this view was being stated less than ten years before the Richards Constitution was begun to be prepared.

parties.[1] Many well-known politicians came to the fore during this period. Power politics followed very quickly in the whole country on the heels of agitational politics. But the abrupt transition to power politics combined with the continuing strength of communal loyalties, the competition for posts and wealth among members of the Southern intelligentsia, the intact structures of the Hausa-Fulani and Kanuri traditional hierarchies sent the politicians to organize support along communal lines. National issues were not thought through, and could not in any case be easily translated into terms that the opinion leaders in the local communities could understand. The one issue that remained an exception was education. Against the rear-guard action of the British officers who had shifted their defence of colonial rule from the 'white man's burden' to their possession of manpower skills[2] the nationalist leaders carried on campaigns to have the educational system be more widely spread and carried to higher levels. The demonstration effect of the economic opportunities and the benefits of those who had received education harnessed the energies of the communities to the urgings of the nationalists. Nigerian nationalism took on its social welfare character dominantly through education. Nigerian nationalism also – like most of the nationalisms of the period – was socialist almost from the beginning. We shall return to this last point.

The Nigerian political class consisted of four main groups.[3] There were the first-on-the-scene nationalist leaders – Nnamdi Azikiwe and Obafemi Awolowo were the most famous of these. To them should be added the leaders from the North who stepped into the power vacuum created there when the British withdrawal was effectively announced – Ahmadu Bello and Abubakar Tafawa Balewa were foremost among these. The second were the professional and business men who joined early on with the first group – Festus Okotie-Eboh, Michael Okpara and S. O. Sonibare belonged to this group. Once elections got under way most communities wanted their own sons to represent them. Those who came into politics that way might best be called 'communal champions'. They formed the third group. They were the vast majority of the elected parliamentary representatives. Some of them – Shiaka Momodu and Omo-Osagie in the Mid-West are examples – were able to play a

[1] On the prolonging of agitational politics, see J. S. Coleman's description of the reaction of the political intelligentsia to the Richards Constitution, *Nigeria: Background to Nationalism*, Berkeley and Los Angeles 1958, pp. 275–95.

[2] This theme – not in a bad or dishonest sense – runs through the *Memorandum on Educational Policy in Nigeria*, Lagos 1947: Sessional Paper 20, 1947.

[3] On this particular approach to Nigerian political leadership, see J. O'Connell: 'Political Parties' in Blitz (ed.), *The Politics and Administration of Nigerian Government*, London 1965, pp. 161–4. Compare the remarks in R. S. Sklar, and C. S. Whitaker, Jr. 'Nigeria', in J. S. Coleman and C. G. Rosberg (eds.), *Political Parties and National Integration in Tropical Africa*, Berkeley and Los Angeles 1964, pp. 612–19.

considerable role in regional politics. Finally, there was a large class of political activists made up of the 'opinion leaders' in the various communities. These were the new men – teachers, clerks, traders and others – who possessed enough education to lead villages, wards, and towns through the hazards of social change. In the Hausa-Fulani North they were the members of the native authorities. But the role of the new men must never be dissociated from that of the elders of the communities, with whom they must work if they are to have effective influence.

The top leadership was made up mainly of the first two groups. Nigeria enjoyed a permanancy in its top leadership between 1951 and 1966 that even the Tory leadership in Britain did not enjoy during the same period. One important reason for that was that the early nationalist personalities and the professional and business men who joined them closed ranks against would-be entrants into the upper ranks of the political class through a judicious use of power and patronage. They showed in the process that they possessed greater ability than the challengers. Most of the latter came from among the communal champions whose vision and range were considerably limited. And those who challenged on ideological grounds never had a chance in the existing state of politics. The parties organized by these men were primarily 'parties of communal integration'.[1] They mobilized the various communities politically and they gave them a sense of being represented where decisions on the control of power and the share-out of well-being were made. There was however, evidence of a growing solidarity of interests, especially economic, between the top members of the political class that reached beyond the interests of the communities they claimed to represent.

Anti-colonial nationalism in Nigeria proclaimed itself socialist. Embedded in that attitude was a populist outlook that spurred the leaders to identify themselves with the masses of the people and to claim to represent their interests over against the foreign rulers. But other factors also underlay their socialism. These politicians had experienced big business only in the shape of foreign enterprise which, they were convinced, had for long years made exorbitant profits. Such businesses also in the shape of the banks were considered to have discriminated against indigenous businessmen. The period itself was one in which the success of the Russian planning had become widely known, and in which for those in a British sphere of influence the most

[1] On the classification of Nigerian parties, see O'Connell, *loc. cit.* pp. 165–6. The classification used in the text is a modification of that used by Sigmund Neumann in his chapter, 'Towards a Comparative Study of Political Parties', *Modern Political Parties*, Chicago 1956. The best study of Nigerian political parties is that by R. S. Sklar, *Nigerian Political Parties*, Princeton, N.J. 1963. Though his focus is different from Sklar's there are important contributions in K. W. J. Post's study, *The Nigerian Federal Election of 1959*, London 1963.

powerful ideological example was the exhilarating experience of the 1945–51 Labour government. Most of the Nigerian political ideas emanated from salaried people, teachers and other professional persons who had built-in anti-chrematistic biases. And not least among the factors favouring socialist attitudes was that government – and socialism in its essence is a combination of the advocacy of governmental initiative and the desire for social equality – was the one powerful society-changing organizational device that the nationalist leaders knew.

But there were certain features of political behaviour that at the moment of the take-over of power at the regional level began to suggest that no purely socialist system would operate under the Nigerian political class. From the start, the new holders of power assumed most friendly relations with the business community. Expatriate firms found that politicians placed radicalism in wresting power from the colonial officials rather than in tampering with the only economic system that they had experience of. The politicians were further softened by the ease with which expatriate firms were willing to pay for protection in money and kind. Some politicians were also businessmen themselves and the parties had received support from the businessmen of their own communities. Hence, a co-operation that would soon degenerate into collusion grew up between the politicians and the indigenous businessmen. A study of the banking system, the development corporations and the loans boards – not to mention the number of inefficient and mismanaged schools that were being run by politicians and their friends – makes clear how much the new political and commercial élites shared governmental resources between them in a spoils system.[1] Not the least interesting form of economic speculation that the politicians and their friends became involved in was speculation in land which is one of the surest means of growing rich in a developing economy when persons have political power and know-how.[2] Finally, the politicians who went on talking about socialism seemed to be little sensitive to the differences in the standard of living between themselves and the people they

[1] C. V. Brown: *Government and Banking in Western Nigeria*, Ibadan 1964; M.S. Baratz, 'Public Investment in Private Enterprise: A Western Nigeria Case Study', *Nigerian Journal of Economic and Social Studies*, vol. 6, March 1964; *Report of the Coker Commission of Inquiry into the Affairs of Certain Statutory Corporations in Western Nigeria*, 4 vols., Lagos 1962; G. K. Helleiner, *Peusant Agriculture, Government, and Economic Growth in Nigeria*, Homewood, Illinois 1966, chapter 10; *Report of inquiry into the rise in Fees charged by Public Secondary Grammar Schools and Teacher Training Colleges in Western Nigeria*, Ibadan 1963.

[2] One minister who had leased land from the government sub-leased the same plot to a government agency at a vastly greater rent. Over a relatively short period he would have made a profit of £40,000. One part of his defence was to argue that this sum was 'chicken-feed'. The Prime Minister, Sir Abubakar, did not ask him to resign. The inaction contrasts strongly with Dr. Kenneth Kaunda's insistence that two ministers, associated with a firm that had received a governmental loan, should resign. See *Nigerian Opinion*, 1, 3 March 1965, pp. 1–2.

represented. Not only did those differences exist but they were heightened by conspicuous consumption of a lavish kind: not one but several large houses, a Mercedes, elaborate dress styles, lavish entertainment, foreign travel, foreign education of children, and the upkeep of numerous retainers as well as the fairly indiscriminate handing out of largesse (gifts, scholarships and contributions to communal charities). In the beginning people were glad to see Nigerians acquire goods and perquisites that had once belonged almost exclusively to foreigners, and communities basked in the vicarious glory of the brick-and-mortar monuments that were erected in their midst by sons of the soil. But the political class took little notice of changes in public attitudes as pride in Nigerian achievement gave way to resentment and to questions about how certain forms of wealth had been built up. Those questions became sharper as cheap colonial rule was replaced by rising levels of taxation and as aspirations created by education and increasing urbanization remained relatively unfulfilled for many individuals. One last kind of conspicuous consumption consisted not of personal but of public spending by politicians: television stations, sports stadia, and luxury hotels bore little relation to the masses of the people or to economic growth.[1]

Since much Nigerian economic growth depends on the public sector it is important to examine the relations between the political decision-makers and their public servants.[2] Again the historical evolution was influential in shaping attitudes. The British civil servants in Nigeria, more desirous of protecting their own interests and more conscious of the defects of the nationalist politicians than was the government in London, fought a rear-guard action, if not against independence, at least against what they considered its excessively fast onset. The conflict over the integration of ministries and departments was a salient episode in the re-adjusting of the roles of politician and administrator. Especially in the Southern regions the difficulties of such readjustments generated a lack of trust between the politicians and administrators. That lack of trust, added to the heady wine of new power, left the politicians less willing than they might have been to accept the technical advice of the bureaucrats. When the Nigerian administrators succeeded the British, they stepped into this situation.

With this bureaucratic heritage went another set of factors. The

[1] On this issue see J. O'Connell, 'Some Social and Political Reflections on the Plan', *Nigerian Journal of Economic and Social Studies*, vol. 4, 2 July 1962, pp. 144–6.

[2] There is little enough that is valuable written on public administration and economic development: See J. La Palombara, *Bureaucracy and Political Development*, Princeton, N.J. 1963; K. M. Panikkar, *The Afro-Asian States and their Problems*, London 1959, pp. 31–43; W. J. Siffin (ed.), *Towards the Comparative Study of Public Administration*, Bloomington, Ind. 1957.

reserves built up during the Second World War and the prices boom of the Korean period made a great deal of public capital readily available. Since the education system had not yet begun to turn out candidates for employment on an alarming scale, the politicians easily cherished the illusion that there was plenty of time and money available – and, in fact, there was enough money available for the few limited projects (outside the education schemes) that the governments had thought up. In this way the politicians remained for vital years insulated from the urgency of economic development. The bureaucrats themselves who had inherited many British colonial attitudes as well as similar conditions and salaries possessed little enough sense of the urgency of economic development. Again, those political leaders whose support rested on ethnic and communal support felt little incentive – even if they had the knowledge or capacity – to galvanize their bureaucrats into action. Even in areas like customs and immigration where economic growth, efficiency and integrity are linked and where the political visibility of inefficiency and corruption is high little political determination was shown in improving the implementation of policies.

One last point is worth making. The politicians took little detailed interest in the day-to-day running of their departments. That lack of interest together with the frequent absence of politicians on tour offered fascinating opportunities to bureaucrats to amass power.[1] By and large they did not do this. Partly they feared to offer the faintest evidence to the politicians that they were competing with them for power – and partly, as has been said already, they felt under no great obligation to press on with development in a way that outdistanced considerably political effort and morality.

At this stage we can try to analyse more directly the socio-psychological attitudes of the politicians, so as to underpin better the descriptions that have been given in this paper and the analyses that have been made. Basically the failure of the politicians to contribute substantially to economic growth derived from a lack of developed modern attitudes. In other words, they were deficient in analytico-causal, historical and inventive attitudes; they tended too often to defend themselves against the risk of social change by financial corruption; and they excessively ignored national considerations for the sake of their own communities. Each one of these factors merits an expanded analysis.

(*i*) The politicians were much more deeply traditionalist than the more formally educated bureaucrats.[2] They often possessed the exqui-

[1] The *raison d'être* behind a great part of the touring was that expense accounts were so lavishly designed that they were an important source of revenue.

[2] L. Pye has some fascinating remarks on the social identities of Burman politicians and administrators, *Politics, Personality, and Nation Building*, New Haven 1962, pp. 211–66.

site sensitivity of members of small communities to personal relations. But they came from communities that had had little need to quantify resources in detailed and extensive ways in relation to income and expenditure. Unfortunately this lack of a tradition of quantitative analysis left them impervious to projections that covered financial estimates for a period of years. They could see little enough connection between the award of contracts – when their interests and the interests of their friends were involved – and the equipment, business structure and integrity of the contractors. They were careless in working out the connections between government investments and the returns on the money invested. Little accustomed to the exigencies of mathematical time they were unresponsive to the pressing need for feasibility studies and the strategically timed award of contracts: economic decisions waited indefinitely on cabinet meetings; and cabinets were most unwilling to delegate financial decisions where their members might be able to get a cut. They thought that censuses could be manipulated as political weapons and they had no conception of a census as a tool of economic development. They paid small heed to the proper and relative autonomy of public corporations, and saw no incompatibility between using these organizations as instruments of patronage and personal gain and using them as instruments of public investment. In short, there was missing an understanding of the structured relations between resources, expenditure, timing and allocating.

(*ii*) The essence of living in society is trust. Trust is based on the capacity to predict the behaviour of other persons. But in a rapidly changing society the level of predictability in social behaviour falls.[1] The hazards of the struggle for power reduce still further the levels of predictability available to politicians, so they resort to various devices to protect themselves against the hazards of change. An obvious recourse is to build up financial wealth with which to regulate and render predictable the actions of those with whom they have to deal. There is no honest way of accumulating the wealth that the Nigerian politicians considered that they needed to make safe, or to advance, their interests. This situation was made worse by the absence of regular sources of party funds (such as can be tapped in the developed countries) – devious ways had to be found for raising money for elections and general organizational needs.[2] Inevitably a portion of the funds raised for the party stayed in a minister's pocket – after all, he knew that there was no more deserving member of the party than himself. Great harm

[1] Much the same reasons explain the ubiquity of corruption in public life in Britain during the eighteenth century and in the United States during the nineteenth.

[2] On Party Finance, see the relevant sections in the works of Post and Sklar; also *Nigerian Opinion*, 1, 3 March 1965, p. 2.

was done by these blatant forms of fund-raising to the possibilities of national mobilization. Those whose own financial integrity was suspect among practically all sectors of society were in no position to ask for sacrifices and to insist on honesty. Tasks like public capital accumulation and rationally conceived imports policies became much more difficult than they might otherwise have been.

(*iii*) Politicians not only drew their political support from, but formulated their social identity in terms of, their communities of origin. They wanted to surround themselves with men from these communities whom they believed that they could trust. They wanted to divert – and often succeeded in doing so – projects to their areas of origin, irrespective of the national or regional economic considerations. They wished to secure immediate returns in gratitude and esteem, so they thought in terms of social welfare rather than growth producing projects; they preferred prestige projects like hospitals, secondary schools and rest houses to sophisticated and worthwhile but less tangible projects like public health campaigns and agricultural extension schemes. One of the most ironic illustrations of political communalism was seen in the siting of the national secondary schools that were intended to foster political integration. The three ministers who decided their location came from Sokoto, Warri and Afikpo: the schools were allocated to Sokoto, Warri and Afikpo. An unfortunate consequence of communalism was that the distrust of communities for one another was deepened. National planning was difficult in that kind of atmosphere.

The observations that have so far been made do not present the most flattering description of the political class. Yet it would be a mistake and unfair to underestimate the positive contribution that they made.[1] This contribution looms much larger when we move away from directly economic affairs[2] to more general sectors of social development. Their contributions to the latter sectors can be looked at in reference to national unity, the civil service, education, and the role of social welfare in awakening the rural communities. Each one merits a short analysis:

(*i*) Nigeria had much to gain – economically, psychologically and

[1] The most sympathetic account of the Nigerian politicians is to be found in Sklar, *Nigerian Political Parties*. It was written at a moment when it still could seem to make sense to consider them the heroes of the nationalist revolt. This seems the place to say that we are not now short of studies of the nationalist movements and the struggle for power that took place during the period of terminal colonialism. What are needed at this stage are studies of the uses of power in the new states. For generally unsympathetic but well-informed views on African politicians, see R. Dumont, *L'Afrique noire est mal partie*, Paris, 1962 and D. H. Hapgood, *Africa: From Today to Tomorrow*, New York 1965.

[2] The impression of political stability and the dominantly pro-Western policies of the Nigerian Federal Government were quite probably factors in the decision of Western oil companies to go ahead with exploiting Nigerian oil. In a world where new sources of oil are not immediately necessary there was a political element in the companies' decision.

politically – from remaining one country. Its political leaders not only enabled the country to stay as one unit but with the exception of some elements in the Northern Region consistently accepted a national ideology. There were several moments in the 1950s when other leaders might have yielded to the temptations of dismemberment. Again in the censuses and election issues of the 1960s the option of secession, though it was considered, was rejected. The continuing consensus on political integration was underlined by the facility with which a slightly changed formula for the allocation of revenue between the centre and the regions was agreed on towards the end of 1965. But two words of caution are needed. The first is that a sharing of economic interests by Cabinet members of the federal coalition parties was a factor favouring unity – but this factor had side effects inimical to economic growth. The second is that until recently the social pressures on the regional governments (and the latter governments in practice dictated the policy of the Federal Government on internal affairs) had not been effectively felt. The situation however was changing rapidly. Eastern reaction to Northern obstructionism on the steel mill would, for example, have inevitably grown increasingly bitter and would have compounded explosively with the struggle for political power.

(*ii*) For all the indifference with which they treated the advice of their bureacrats, the politicians left the structures of the civil service intact. They did not interfere with appointments and promotions to the extent of badly damaging the morale of the services. The exception to this was the attempt to increase the proportion of Northerners in the federal public service. Because, however, this proportion was so small, a good case in social equality could be made out for the policy. Since a great part of public expenditure continues relatively unchanged from year to year, and since it needs more the continuing assent of ministers than their active intervention, the civil servants were able to oversee and safeguard entire sections of public spending.

(*iii*) Bent on fostering manpower skills to legitimize their take-over from the British, to promote economic growth and to underpin the sense of national and human dignity, this first generation of politicians concentrated resources on education much more than their counterparts have done in the vast majority of developing countries.[1] Given not only the limitations of the administrative structures, the weakness of development economics during the early 1950s and the lack of available projects, to have spent money on education – for all the problems of recurrent expenditure and social frustrations – was an act of vision that is likely to provide the social context for economic development and

[1] Nationalist intentions are very well set out in a pioneering set of proposals, *Proposals for an Education Policy for the Western Region, Nigeria*, Ibadan 1952 (Ministry of Education).

provide political pressures for many years ahead. All these factors serve to impede a classical Latin American situation of apathy in Nigeria.

(*iv*) Social welfare projects (in spite of the malutilization of funds in particular instances and the relatively unhealthy ratio of spending on the welfare and growth sectors of the economy) tied in with the championing of community identity and interests, have fostered aspirations in the rural areas and helped modernizing attitudes to develop among vast sections of the population. Further means of harnessing communal energies to economic growth still need to be worked out. But it has been important, indeed indispensible, to mobilize socially the traditional communities. An element of communal championing is important in Nigerian political leadership.[1]

To finish this paper there is something to be gained from attempting a tentative forecast on the basis of the analysis that has been made.[2] This is only another way of trying to distinguish the significant factors in the present politico-social situation, to suggest the relations that exist between them, to say how these relations might evolve, and what new factors might emerge to be added to those that are already operating.

In the early growth stages of the now developed countries the pattern has been that a small oligarchy – capitalist in the U.S., Western Europe and Japan, managerial in the USSR – provided the leadership and top organizational structures. The present qualitative spread of education in Nigeria through graduates and school certificate holders is almost certainly the only way in which in a society like the Nigerian a conception of economic development and the motivation to achieve it might be supplied. Undoubtedly the expensive over-spending in producing certain skills is going to be accompanied by the underproduction of other skills, particularly intermediate skills. But a new qualitative element is being introduced into society.

This qualitative element is likely to have two relatively immediate effects. The first is that graduates are on the point of being obliged to disperse to the secondary schools that are dotted around the countryside. A new educated presence is bound to raise the standard of political sophistication in the communities. For the first time the old-style communal champions (rough, unscrupulous, yet with a popular touch) are going to be effectively challenged. The second is that there is going to be unemployment of persons with either higher education or secondary education. Such unemployment is going to compound with the unemployment of primary school-leavers. To understate the matter:

[1] See Post, *op. cit.* pp. 376–436.

[2] Those paragraphs of this paper up to this point were originally written in the present tense. The paragraphs that follow have been left as they were. The paper was read to the Nigerian Economic Society on the morning of the 15 January 1966 – a time from which future historians may care to date the demise of the first Nigerian Republic.

a lot more social pressure is going to be exerted on the political leaders. But this pressure is not going to be exerted uniformly in all parts of the country. We cannot ignore the implications of this latter situation.

The southern regions are more economically developed than the North. They are growing faster than the North in absolute if not in relative terms. But there are approximately ten times more children in primary schools in the southern regions than in the North, eight times more secondary pupils, and perhaps twenty times more university students. These people in the pipeline have to be considered in relation to the more than ninety per cent southern personnel in the federal civil service, the southern predominance in the police and in the officer-corps of the army.[1] Efforts being made to redress these unbalances are meeting not only the vested interests of entrenched personnel with their promotion prospects but the entry into the labour market of the southerners in training. The revolution of rising frustrations that is already simmering amidst the slower-than-hoped-for economic growth of the independence era is also being aggravated by the smaller share of southern political control and the erosion of constitutionalism through two abortive censuses and two mismanaged elections.

What kind of forecast does one dare to make. Broadly speaking, a telescoped Latin American process may be anticipated. In other words, it is difficult not to foresee a period of political instability in which the army may intervene. During this period the civil servants are likely to take over much more of the decision-making in economic growth than has hitherto been the case. This may remove some of the old arbitrariness but it is likely to lead to economic faltering from bureaucratic stagnation. Impatience with this stagnation however is likely to lead to leadership that will pressure the bureaucrats to move a good deal more efficiently and rapidly than those people tend naturally to move. The period may for several reasons be painful. But it may enable the country to work at an abiding political settlement which may serve to balance the different areas of the country in an effort of social equity, to co-ordinate the roles of the towns and the countryside, to plan the size and proportions of manpower skills, to face up to the relation between growth and employment, and to overcome the arbitrariness of corruption so as to come close to a situation of predictable social integrity.

[1] For the ethnic composition of the police, see P. V. White, 'The Police Force in Nigeria', *Nigerian Opinion*, 1, 7 July 1965, pp. 7–8; for the army in 1962, see W. Gutteridge, *Armed Forces in New States*, London 1962, pp. 36–7.

BIBLIOGRAPHY

I. Official Sources

A. Recurrent departmental reports

Central Bank of Nigeria, *Economic and Financial Review*, vols. 1–3, Federal Ministry of Information, Lagos 1963–5.
Eastern Nigeria Development Corporation, *Annual Report, 1954–63*, Eastern Region Development Corporation, Enugu.
Eastern Nigeria Ministry of Agriculture, *Annual Reports, 1954–64*, Federal Government Printer, Enugu.
Eastern Nigeria Marketing Board, *Annual Reports, 1954–63*, Eastern Nigeria Marketing Board, Port Harcourt.
Federal Minister of Finance, *Annual Budget Speech, 1957–65*, Federal Ministry of Information, Lagos.
Federal Ministry of Commerce and Industry, *Handbook of Commerce and Industry in Nigeria*, 5th ed., Federal Ministry of Commerce and Industry, Lagos 1962.
Federal Ministry of Commerce and Industries, *Industrial Directory*, a list of major manufacturing plants in Nigeria, Federal Ministry of Information, Lagos 1964.
Federal Ministry of Education, *Annual Digest of Educational Statistics, 1957–63*, Federal Ministry of Information, Lagos.
——, *Statistics of Education in Nigeria, 1957–64*, Federal Ministry of Information, Lagos 1965.
Federal Ministry of Labour, *Quarterly Review, 1942–64*, Federal Government Printer, Lagos.
Federal Office of Statistics, *Digest of Statistics* (renamed *Economic Indicators* in 1965), quarterly, Federal Government Printer, Lagos 1948–67.
——, *Annual Abstract of Statistics*, Federal Government Printer, Lagos 1960–4.
——, *Trade Report*, annually, Federal Government Printer, Lagos 1941–61.
——, *Trade Summary*, monthly, Federal Government Printer, Lagos 1960–7.
West African Institute of Oil-Palm Research, *Annual Reports, 1959–60, 1960–1, 1961–2*, W.A.I.F.O.R., Benin.
Annual Report of the Colony Development Board, 1949–50 to *1955–6*, Federal Government Printer, Lagos.
Annual Report of the Federal Loans Board, 1956–7 to *1961–2*.
Annual Report of the Federal Ministry of Commerce and Industry, 1946–7 to *1964–5*, Federal Government Printer, Lagos.
Annual Report of the Nigeria Local Development Board, 1946–7 to *1948–9*.
Annual Report of the Northern Nigeria Development Corporation, 1955–6 to *1962–3*.
Annual Report of the Western Region Finance Corporation, 1955–6 to *1960–1*.

B. Non-recurrent governmental reports

Department of Education, *Memorandum on Educational Policy in Nigeria*, Federal Government Printer, Lagos 1947.
——, *Ten-Year Education Plan*, Sessional Paper No. 6 of 1944, Federal Government Printer, Lagos 1949.
Department of Statistics, *Population Census of the Eastern Region of Nigeria, 1953*, Bulletin nos. 1–7, Federal Government Printer, Lagos 1955.

——, *Population Census of the Northern Region of Nigeria, 1952*, Bulletin nos. 1–13, Federal Government Printer, Lagos 1956.

——, *Population Census of the Western Region of Nigeria, 1952*, Bulletin nos. 1–9, Federal Government Printer, Lagos 1956.

Eastern Nigeria Ministry of Agriculture, 'Notes on Eastern Nigeria Oil Palm Grove Rehabilitation Scheme', mimeograph, Enugu 1961.

Eastern Nigeria Ministry of Economic Planning, *First Progress Report, Eastern Nigeria Development Plan, 1962–8*, Federal Government Printer, Enugu, 1964.

Eastern Nigeria Ministry of Education, *Education Handbook*, Federal Government Printer, Enugu 1964.

Federal Ministry of Commerce and Industry, *Industrial Labour: An Introductory Guide for Prospective Investors*, Federal Ministry of Information, Lagos 1963.

Federal Ministry of Labour, 'Employment Market Information. First Basic Report. (The Situation at the end of March 1961)', mimeograph, Lagos 1961.

——, 'Employment Market Information. Report on Employment situation as of 30th April, 1962', mimeograph, Lagos 1963.

Federal Office of Statistics, *Industrial Survey of Nigeria 1963*, Federal Office of Statistics, Lagos 1966.

——, *Lagos Housing Enquiry*, Federal Government Printer, Lagos 1961.

——, 'Lagos Pilot Survey of Small-Scale Industry', mimeograph, Lagos 1966.

——, 'Productive Activities of Households', mimeograph, 1966.

——, *Report on Labour Migration, Sokoto Province*, Federal Government Printer, Lagos 1955.

National Manpower Board, *Nigeria's High-level Manpower 1963–70*, Manpower Study No. 2, National Manpower Board, Lagos 1964.

——, '1966 Survey of Education and Training Content of Occupations', mimeograph, Lagos 1967.

Northern Nigeria Ministry of Trade and Industry and Sir Alexander Gibb and Partners, *The Industrial Potential of Northern Nigeria*, Ministry of Trade and Industry, Kaduna 1963.

Eastern Nigeria Development Plan, Official Document No. 8 of 1962, Federal Government Printer, Enugu 1962.

Report of the Federal Advisory Committee on Technical Education and Industrial Training, Federal Government Printer, Lagos 1959.

Statement of Policy proposed by the Federal Government on the Report by a Committee appointed to advise on the Stimulation of Industrial Development by affording Relief from Import Duties and Protection to Nigerian Industry, Sessional Paper No. 10 of 1956.

Statement on Industrial Policy, Sessional Paper No. 6 of 1964.

The Role of the Federal Government in Promoting Industrial Development in Nigeria, Sessional Paper No. 3 of 1958.

C. REPORTS COMMISSIONED BY THE NIGERIAN GOVERNMENTS

Arthur D. Little, Inc., *The Economics of a Cocoa Processing Plant for Nigeria*, Arthur D. Little, Inc., Cambridge 1962.

——, *Recommended Action to Improve Nigeria's Trade Position*, A report to the Federal Ministry of Commerce and Industry, Arthur D. Little, Cambridge 1962.

Ashby, E. *et al.*, *Investment in Education*, Report of the Commission on Post-School Certificate and Higher Education in Nigeria, Federal Ministry of Education, Lagos 1960.

Banjo, S. A. *et al.*, *Report of the Commission Appointed to Review the Educational System of Western Nigeria*, Federal Government Printer, Ibadan 1961.

Caunce, F. and Cottier, W. L., 'Report on the Development of Technical and Commercial Education, 1961–76', mimeograph, 1961.

Coker, G. B. A. *et al.*, *Report of Coker Commission of Inquiry into the affairs of Certain Statutory Corporations in Western Nigeria, 1962*, Federal Ministry of Information, Lagos 1963.

Dike, K. O. *et al.*, *Report on the Review of the Educational System in Eastern Nigeria*, Federal Government Printer, Enugu 1962.

Elias, T. O. *et al.*, *Report of Elias Commission of Inquiry into the Administration, Economics and Industrial Relations of the Nigerian Railway Corporation*, Federal Government Printer, Lagos 1960.

Elwood, T. and Olisa, R. R., *Report of the Grading Team on the Grading of Posts in the Public Services of the Federation of Nigeria*, Federal Ministry of Information, Lagos 1966.

Gailer, J. W., 'A National Plan for the Development of Technical Education in the Federal Republic of Nigeria', mimeograph, Federal Ministry of Education, Lagos 1964.

Gardner, J. C., *Oilseed Processing in Nigeria*, A Report to the Government of Nigeria and the Nigerian Groundnut Marketing Board, London 1952.

Goldway, Michael, *Report on Vocational Education in Eastern Nigeria*, Federal Government Printer, Enugu 1962.

Gorsuch, L. H. *et al.*, *Report of the Commission on the Public Services of the Governments in the Federation of Nigeria, 1954–5*, Federal Government of Nigeria, Lagos 1955.

International Bank for Reconstruction and Development, *The Economic Development of Nigeria*, Federal Government Printer, Lagos 1954.

(Jackson, E. F. and) Okigbo, P. N. C., *Nigerian National Accounts 1950–7*, Federal Ministry of Economic Development, Enugu 1962.

Mbanefo, L. N., *et al.*, *Review of Salaries and Wages*, Federal Government Printer, Lagos 1959.

Miller, W. L., 'The Economics of Field Operations of the Stork Hand Hydraulic Oil Palm Press: Report to the Government of Eastern Nigeria', mimeograph, Economic Development Institute, 31 July 1964.

Morgan, A. *et al.*, *Report of the Commission on the Review of Wages, Salary and Conditions of Service of the Junior Employees of the Governments of the Federation and in Private Establishments, 1963–4*, Federal Ministry of Information, Lagos 1964.

Okigbo, L., *Sawmill Industry in Nigeria*, Federal Department of Forest Research, Ibadan 1964.

Robinson, H. *et al.*, *The Economic co-ordination of Transport Development in Nigeria*, A Report prepared by the Stanford Research Institute for the Joint Planning Committee, National Economic Council, Federation of Nigeria, Stanford Research Institute, Menlo Park, 1961.

Straker, A. P., 'Survey of Technical Manpower Requirements', mimeograph, August 1959.

D. REPORTS COMMISSIONED BY OTHER GOVERNMENTS

Kilby, Peter, 'Measures to Promote the Development of Indigenous Industry – A Report to the Federal Ministry of Commerce and Industry', U.S. Agency for International Development, mimeograph, May 1962.

——, *The Development of Small Industry in Eastern Nigeria*, U.S. Agency for International Development, Lagos 1962.

Prest, A. R. and Stewart, I. G., *The National Income of Nigeria, 1950–1* (Colonial Research Study No. 11), H.M.S.O., London 1953.

Stewart, I. G. *et al.*, *Nigeria: Determinants of Projected Level of Demand, Supply and Imports of Farm Products in 1965 and 1975*. A Report for the Economic Research Service, ERS – Foreign – 32. U.S. Department of Agriculture, Washington D.C., 1962.

Report of the Commission on Higher Education in West Africa, H.M.S.O., London 1945.

Report of the Mission Appointed to Enquire into the Production and Transport of Vegetable Oils and Oil Seeds Produced in the West African Colonies, H.M.S.O., London 1947.

Report of the Visitation: Nigerian College of Arts, Science and Technology, H.M.S.O., London, March/April 1958.

West Africa Palm Oil and Palm Kernels: Report of a Committee appointed by the Secretary of State for the Colonies, September 1923, to consider the best means of securing improved and increased production, Colonial Office Report No. 10, H.M.S.O., London 1925.

II. Private Sources

A. Annual company reports, 1955–65

Alcan of Nigeria Ltd.

Dunlop (Nigeria) Ltd.

John Holt and Company Ltd.

Nigeria Cement Company Ltd.

Nigerian Sugar Company Ltd.

Nigerian Tobacco Company Ltd.

Paterson Zochonis Ltd.

United Africa Company Ltd.

B. Other

Federation of British Industries, *Nigeria: An Industrial Reconnaissance*, London 1961.

Griffith, P. and Watt, J., *Report on a Visit to Nigeria and The Gold Coast, 1955*, Federation of British Industries, London 1955.

Nigerian Employers Consultative Association, *N.E.C.A. News*, monthly 1957–66.

——, *Wage and Salary Survey, 1965*, Lagos 1965.

Nigerian Tobacco Company, Tobacco in Nigeria, Lagos 1960.

Scheuer Textile Consultants Inc., *Feasibility Report on Integrated Textile Mill in the Eastern Region of the Federation of Nigeria*, Rockefeller Bros. Fund, New York 1961.

III. Secondary Material Related to Nigeria

A. Articles

Ajayi, J. F. A., 'Henry Venn and the Policy of Development', *Journal of the Historical Society of Nigeria*, vol. 1, December 1959.

——, 'The Development of Secondary Grammar School Education in Nigeria', *Journal of the Historical Society of Nigeria*, vol. v, December 1963.

Are, L., 'An Assessment of Some Plantation Problems in Western Nigeria', *Tropical Agriculture*, January 1964.

——, 'Palm Plantations in Eastern Nigeria., *E.N.D.C. Oils*, Enugu 1964, pp. 13–17.

Armstrong, R. G., 'Some Technical Gaps in the Nigerian School Curricula', *Proceedings of the West African Institute of Social and Economic Research*, mimeograph, Ibadan 1953.

Behrend, H., 'Voluntary Absence from Work', *International Labour Review*, vol. LXXIX, February 1959, pp. 109–40.

Boston, J., 'The Igala Oil-Palm Industry', *Nigerian Institute for Social and Economic Research Proceedings*, 1962.

Callaway, Archibald, 'Nigeria's Indigenous Education: the Apprentice System', *University of Ife Journal of African Studies*, vol. I, July 1964, pp. 1–18.

Coppock, J. T., 'Tobacco Growing in Nigeria', *Erkunde*, Band XIX, 1965, Bonn, pp. 207–306.

De Briey, P., 'The Productivity of African Labour', *International Labour Review*, vol. LXXII, August–September 1955, pp. 119–37.

Gray, J. E., Faulkner, O. T., Lewin, C. S. and Barnes, A. C., 'Native Methods of Preparing Palm Oil', Parts I, II, III, *Annual Bulletin of the Department of Agriculture Nigeria*, Federal Government Printer, Lagos 1922, 1923, 1924.

Hartley, C. W. A., 'Advances in Oil-Palm Research in Nigeria in the last Twenty-Five Years', *The Empire Journal of Experimental Agriculture*, vol. XXVI, April 1958, pp. 136–51.

Helleiner, G. K., 'The Fiscal Role of the Marketing Boards in Nigerian Economic Development, 1947–61', *Economic Journal*, vol. LXXIV, September 1964, pp. 582–610.

International Labour Organization, 'The Influence of International Labour Conventions on Nigerian Labour Legislation', *International Labour Review*, July 1960.

Kilby, Peter, 'African Labour Productivity Reconsidered', *The Economic Journal*, vol. LXXI, June 1961, pp. 273–91.

Mackintosh, J. P., 'Politics in Nigeria: the Action Group Crisis of 1962', *Political Studies*, vol. 11, June 1963, pp. 125–55.

Manlove, D., 'Palm Oil in Nigeria', *Journal of Tropical Agriculture*, July 1931.

May, R. S., 'Direct Overseas Investment in Nigeria 1953–63', *The Scottish Journal of Political Economy*, vol. XII, November 1965, pp. 253–66.

Mbanefo, T. C., 'Pioneer Oil Mills in the Extraction of Palm Oil', *E.N.D.C. Oils*, 1964, pp. 8–12.

Nwanze, S. C., 'The Economics of the Pioneer Oil Mill', *Journal of the West African Institute for Oil Palm Research*, vol. II, April 1961, pp. 231–56.

Pearson, S., 'The Political Economics of Nigerian short-term Borrowing', in J. D. Montgomery and A. Smithies, eds., *Public Policy*, vol. XV, Graduate School of Public Administration, Harvard University, Cambridge, Mass. 1966, pp. 337–60.

Prothero, R. M., 'Migratory Labour from Northwestern Nigeria', *Africa*, vol. XXVII, July 1957, pp. 351–61.

Richardson, J. E., 'Technical Education in Nigeria', *Journal of the Royal Society of Arts*, March 1957, pp. 316–28.

Schatz, S. P., 'Economic Environment and West African Enterprise', *The Economic Bulletin (Ghana)*, December 1963.

Scott, Richenda, 'Production for Trade', *The Native Economies of Nigeria*, Part II, Margery Perham, ed., Faber & Faber, London 1946.

Singer, H. W., 'Small-Scale Industry in African Economic Development', *Economic Development for Africa South of the Sahara*, E. A. G. Robinson, ed., St. Martin's Press, New York 1964.

Smith, M. G., 'Exchange and Marketing Among the Hausa', *Markets in Africa*, P. Bohannan and G. Dalton, eds., Northwestern University Press, Evanston 1962.

Stolper, W. F., 'Politics and Economics in Economic Development', *Rivista Di Politica Economica*, vol. LIII, June 1963, pp. 3–28.

Winder, R. B., 'The Lebanese in West Africa', *Comparative Studies in Society and History*, vol. IV, April 1962, pp. 296–333.

Nigerian Trade Journal, Published Quarterly by the Ministry of Commerce and Industry,

'Industrial Estate at Yaba', October/December 1958, pp. 133–6.

'Electricity Supply in Nigeria', July/September 1965, pp. 112–17.

'Industrial Estates', July/September 1965, pp. 118–24.

The Nigerian Journal of Economic and Social Studies, 1958–, The Nigerian Economic Society, Ibadan, three times a year. Articles cited:

Baratz, M. S., 'Public Investment in Private Enterprise: a Western Nigeria Case Study', March 1964, pp. 60–71.

Bispham, W. M. L., 'The Concept and Measurement of Labour Commitment and its Relevance to Nigerian Development', March 1964, pp. 51–9.

Bryce, M. D., 'Creating a Practical Industrial Development Programme', November 1962, pp. 233–46.

Charle, E. G. Jr., 'An Appraisal of British Imperial Policy with Respect to the Extraction of Mineral Resources in Nigeria', March 1964.

Eke, I. I. U., 'Population of Nigeria: 1952–1965', July 1966, pp. 289–310.

——, 'The Nigerian National Accounts – A Critical Appraisal', November 1966, pp. 333–60.

Hakam, A. N., 'The Motivation to Invest and the Locational Pattern of Foreign Private Industrial Investments in Nigeria', March 1966, pp. 51–66.

Harris, J. R. and Rowe, M. P., 'Entrepreneurial Patterns in the Nigerian Sawmilling Industry', March 1966, pp. 71–96.

Helleiner, G. K., 'A Wide Ranging Development Institution: The Northern Nigeria Development Corporation, 1949–62', July 1964, pp. 239–47.

——, 'The Eastern Nigeria Development Corporation: A Study in the Sources and Uses of Public Development Funds, 1949–1962', March 1964, pp. 98–123.

O'Connell, J. C., 'The Political Class and Economic Growth', March 1966, pp. 129–40.

Schatz, S. P. and Edokpayi, S. O., 'Economic Attitudes of Nigerian Businessmen', November 1962, pp. 257–68.

Schatz, S. P. 'Aiding Nigerian Business: The Yaba Industrial Estate', July 1964, pp. 199–218.

Teriba, O., 'Development Strategy, Investment Decision and Expenditure Patterns of a Public Development Institution: The Case of WNDC 1949–1962', July 1966, pp. 235–58.

Ugoh, S. U., 'The Nigerian Cement Company', March 1964, pp. 72–91.

——, 'The Nigerian Cement Industry', March 1966, p. 109.

Williams, S., 'Start-up of a Textile Industry', November 1962, pp. 247–56.

Yesufu, T. M., 'The Nigerian Manpower Problem: A Preliminary Assessment', November 1962, pp. 207–27.

B. BOOKS

Bauer, P. T., *West African Trade: A Study of Competition, Oligopoly and Monopoly in a Changing Economy*, Cambridge University Press 1954.

Bohannan, P., *Tiv Farm and Settlement*, H.M.S.O., London 1954.

Coleman, J. S., *Nigeria: Background to Nationalism*, University of California Press, Berkeley 1958.

Hancock, W. K., *Survey of British Commonwealth Affairs*, vol. II, Royal Institute of International Affairs, Oxford University Press, London 1942.

Hawkins, E. K., *Road Transport in Nigeria: A Study of African Enterprise*, Oxford University Press, London 1958.

Helleiner, G. K., *Peasant Agriculture, Government and Economic Growth in Nigeria*, Richard Irwin, Homewood, Illinois, 1966.

John Holt and Co., *Merchant Adventure*, Published privately about 1950.

Kilby, Peter, *African Enterprise: The Nigerian Bread Industry*, Stanford University, The Hoover Institution on War, Revolution and Peace, Stanford 1965.

Leubuscher, C., *The Processing of Colonial Raw Materials – a Study in Location*, Colonial Office, London 1951.

——, *The West African Shipping Trade*, A. W. Sythoff, Leyden 1963.

LeVine, Robert A., *Dreams and Deeds: Achievement Motivation in Nigeria*, University of Chicago Press, Chicago 1966.

Martin, Anne, *The Oil Palm Economy of the Ibibio Farmer*, Ibadan University Press, Ibadan 1956.

McPhee, A., *The Economic Revolution in British West Africa*, Routledge & Sons, Aberdeen 1926.

Newlyn, W. T. and Rowan, D. C., *Money and Banking in British Colonial Africa*, Oxford University, Clarendon Press, London 1954.

Okigbo, P. N. C., *Nigerian Public Finance*, Northwestern University Press, Evanston 1965.

Pedler, F. J., *Economic Geography of West Africa*, Longmans, Greene & Co., London 1955.

Perham, Margery, ed., *Economics of a Tropical Dependency*, Faber & Faber, London 1948; vol. I, *The Native Economies of Nigeria*, and vol. II, *Mining, Commerce and Finance in Nigeria*.

——, *Native Administration in Nigeria*, Oxford University Press, London 1937.

Schatz, S. P., *Development Bank Lending in Nigeria: The Federal Loans Board*, Oxford University Press, Ibadan 1964.

Sklar, R. L., *Nigerian Political Parties, Power in an Emergent African Nation*, Princeton University Press, Princeton 1963.

Sokolski, A., *The Establishment of Manufacturing in Nigeria*, Frederick A. Praeger, New York 1965.

Walker, G., *Traffic and Transport in Nigeria: The Example of the Underdeveloped Tropical Territory*, Colonial Research Studies No. 27. H.M.S.O., London 1959.

Wells, F. A. and Warmington, W. A., *Studies in Industrialization: Nigeria and the Cameroons*, the Nigerian Institute of Social and Economic Research, Oxford University Press, London 1962.

Wilson, C., *The History of Unilever, a Study in Economic Growth and Social Change*, Cassell and Company Ltd., London 1954.

Yesufu, T. M., *An Introduction to Industrial Relations in Nigeria*, Oxford University Press, London 1962.

C. MIMEOGRAPHED MATERIAL

Akinrele, I. A. *et al.*, 'Gari Pilot Plant (1 Ton a Day): Results of 3 Month Trial Run', FIIR Research Report No. 13, Lagos, May 1962.

——, 'The Manufacture of Gari from Cassava', FIIR Research Report No. 12, Lagos, May 1962.

Banks, L., *et al.*, 'Estimates for a Factory Producing 10 Tons a Day of Gari', FIIR Technical Memorandum No. 14, Lagos, July 1962.

Carter, N. G., 'An Input-Output Analysis of the Nigerian Economy 1959–60', M.I.T. Working Paper, 1963.

Eicher, C. K. and Miller, W. L., 'Observations on Smallholder Palm Production in Eastern Nigeria', Economic Development Institute, Enugu, December 1963.

Gugler, J., 'Life in a Dual System', *East African Institute of Social Research Conference Papers*, January 1965.

Harris, J. R., 'Factors Affecting the Supply of Industrial Entrepreneurship in Nigeria', December 1966.

Hinrichs, Harley H., 'Mobilizing Government Revenues for Development in Nigeria', January 1966.

Host, M. and Topse, H., 'Memorandum Concerning Applied Research in Nigeria', Ford Foundation, 1963.

Kilby, Peter, 'Establishment Interviews in Nigeria and Ghana, I.L.O. Industrial Relations Survey', typescript, Geneva 1965.

MacFarlane, D. L. and Aworen, M., 'Investment in Oil Palm Plantation Operations in Nigeria: An Economic Appraisal', Economic Development Institute, Enugu, 1964.

Miller, W. L., 'An Economic Analysis of Oil Palm Fruit Processing in Eastern Nigeria', unpublished Ph.D. Dissertation, Michigan State University 1965.

——, 'The Economics of Field Operations of the Stork Hand Hydraulic Oil Palm Press', Economic Development Institute, 1964.

Northern Nigeria Marketing Board, 'Scheme for Sale of 1963/1964 Crop Groundnuts for Local Processing', Memorandum No. 6364/LPG/1.

Oloko, Olatunde, 'A Study of Socio-Economic Factors Affecting Agricultural Productivity in Annang Province, Eastern Nigeria', Nigerian Institute of Social and Economic Research, 1963.

Seibel, H. D., 'Industrial Labour in Nigeria', 1963.

Skapski, A. S. *et al.*, 'Report of the Comparative Technical Education Seminar Abroad', Lagos, June 1966.

——, 'The Development of Technical Education and its Relation to the Educational System in Western Nigeria', Lagos, May 1962.

Takes, C. P., 'Socio-Economic Factors Affecting Agricultural Productivity in Some Villages of Oshun Division, Western Region', Nigerian Institute of Social and Economic Research, 1963.

D. PERIODICALS

United Africa Company, *Statistical and Economic Review*, 1948–63.

Daily Times, 1959–64, Lagos.

Inter-African Labour Institute Bulletin, 1957–64, Bamako.

Nigerian Journal of Economic and Social Studies, 1959–66, Published by the Nigerian Economic Society.

West Africa, weekly, 1960–7.

INDEX

For EU product safety concerns, contact us at Calle de José Abascal, 56–1°, 28003 Madrid, Spain or eugpsr@cambridge.org.

www.ingramcontent.com/pod-product-compliance
Lightning Source LLC
LaVergne TN
LVHW090301210926
848480LV00001B/90